THE ARTILLERYMEN

OF

HISTORIC

FORT MONROE, VIRGINIA

Phyllis T. McClellan

HERITAGE BOOKS
2016

HERITAGE BOOKS

AN IMPRINT OF HERITAGE BOOKS, INC.

Books, CDs, and more—Worldwide

For our listing of thousands of titles see our website
at
www.HeritageBooks.com

Published 2016 by
HERITAGE BOOKS, INC.
Publishing Division
5810 Ruatan Street
Berwyn Heights, Md. 20740

International Standard Book Numbers
Paperbound: 978-1-55613-529-3
Clothbound: 978-0-7884-5980-1

"What's past is prologue; learn from the past."

Pennsylvania Avenue entrance, National Archives
Wm Shakespeare, "The Tempest."

HOW TO USE THIS BOOK

The first part of this book takes the reader on short walking tour of historic Fort Monroe, beginning at the Casemate Museum on the southwest side of the fort and proceeding towards the east gate. From there, one leaves the walls of the fort, crosses the moat, and turns right on Fenwick Road. Following Fenwick Road until it passes the post office, one turns right on Ingalls Road and proceeds towards the main entrance to the fort. Many points of interest, both past and present, are highlighted on the tour.

Two maps are included in the front of the book, and may be removed for easy reference while reading. One is a hand-drawn map; the other is the modern post map, used by permission. This official map may be used by the reader to find the sites visited on the tour. Many of the buildings mentioned in the text are listed with the numbers assigned to them by the post, and may be easily found on the map. However, some sites featured on the tour do not have a number; these are labeled on the map for the reader's convenience.

The sketch below may be compared to the official map in order to orient oneself with the direction of the tour.

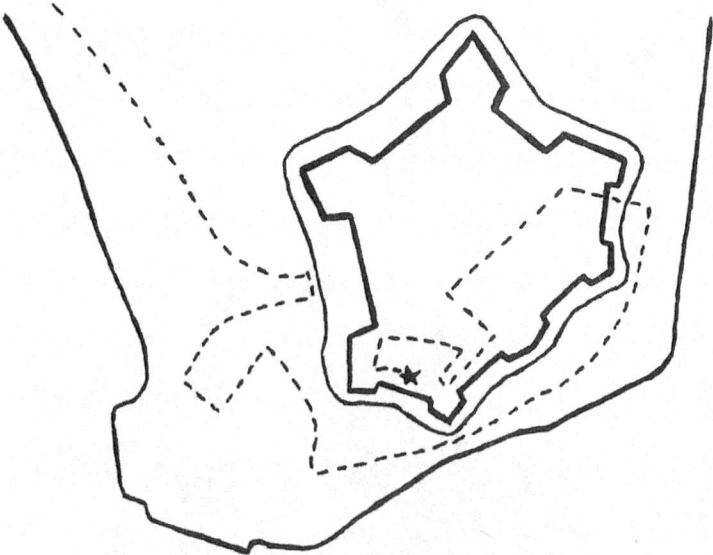

TABLE OF CONTENTS

vation of the name of the area, Old Point Comfort). Construction started in 1819 using slave labor, then military prisoners, and finally paid labor. The fort was completed by 1834 and named for the fifth US President, James Monroe.

A report in an 1837 *Army Navy Chronicle* described the "Old Point":

This is a spot celebrated as a bathing place, but still more for its extensive fortifications. Fortress Monroe is an immense work, enclosing some sixty acres of land, and presenting a circle of wall more than a mile in extent. It is built of stone, all brought from a distance; is laid out on the principles of modern science; and is said to be larger than any fortification in Europe which does not enclose a town or city. It is surrounded by a wide and deep fosse [ditch], filled at all times with water. It will mount about 400 guns. In the area are officers' houses, long ranges of barracks, store houses, etc, and in one quarter extensive workshops belonging to the Ordnance Department. The works are finished, we believe, except the parapet, but only a small number of cannon are mounted. In time of war, not less than eight thousand men will be required to garrison it.

We saw no soldiers, the garrison being at present in Florida. About 500 recruits were collected there, and great exertions were used to bring them into a state of discipline as speedily as possible. They were rough materials, however, more than half foreigners, and we could scarcely credit the assurances of officers that, in three or four months, the erect port, measured tread, and martial bearing of the soldier could be, by the most indefatigable drilling, induced upon such men. So long as voluntary enlistment is relied upon, and the demand for labor continues, our army can never be supplied with materials of better description.

In digging the foundations of the fort, we learn that remains of a brick fortification were discovered, entirely submerged by the sand. It was a regular work, according to the old system. The date of its erection was, it is presumed, long anterior to the revolution, possibly in the early days of the colony. We are told, however, that no allusion to any such fort is found in our early histories, or in the public archives....New theories are rife in these days, and among these, is that of the uselessness of fortifications. But we are not afraid that the progress of this heresy will prevent the completion and equipment of these magnificent works, which will give security to the James River, our largest Naval Depot, and the finest roadstead in the world.

We cannot say much for the attractions of Old Point as a bathing place. The accommodations are only tolerable. The absence of trees, and the glare of the sun upon the sand and the water, render the heat very oppressive, in spite of the sea breeze. We suspect that...there will be few visitors.

The deed drafted in 1821 ceding the land on this sandspit to the US Government was not recorded by the Commonwealth of Virginia until 1838. The deed states the property will revert to the State of Virginia if not utilized for national security purposes.

Since 1819, Fort Monroe has witnessed, as well as made, history. There were times when the Army was low in strength and the barracks were nearly empty, and other times when it bustled with patriotic fervor and a full house carried out wartime missions. It was such a formidable bastion that it was never attacked, nor did it ever fire a shot in anger. It was here that the oldest branch service college was established in 1824 for instruction of members of the Corps of Artillery. In 1907 when the Corps split into Field and Coast Artillery, it became the home of the Coast Artillery (CA) for the next 40 years. When an Army bride naively asked: "What is the CA?" back came this terse answer: "Madame, the Coast Artillery is the 'Lord's Anointed'."

At the close of WWII it was evident that although masonry forts afforded protection from direct naval gunfire, they were highly vulnerable to destruction by aerial bombing. Therefore, shortly after WWII it was decided to abolish the Coast Artillery as a separate branch of service. Its guns were dismantled and scrapped, its submarine mines turned over to the Navy, and its military reservations used for other purposes. The next command to occupy Fort Monroe was the Army Ground Forces in 1946, then the Continental Army Command in 1955, followed by the Army Training and Doctrine Command in 1973. Since the office buildings and quarters have been renovated and well-maintained, the facilities capably serve a high headquarters command independent of a troop complement.

Quarters at Fort Monroe were always woefully inadequate. From the time of the establishment of the Artillery School for Instruction in 1824, the Commandant, Brevet Brigadier General J R Fenwick begged for housing:

This garrison should contain ample quarters, or at least commutation [this was not remedied until 1870] for officers

3

without quarters. It is practically impossible for a married officer to be assigned to a post where he cannot board out without pecuniary ruin, or where he is allowed only a half-room. It is disagreeable for families to live or board in taverns.

From 1834 through the Civil War, no new permanent quarters were built, but during the isolationist period just prior to World War II, the Artillery Corps became the darling of the services and received the most attention and support. Reestablishment of the School of Artillery in 1867 authorized construction of several handsome frame houses, but the biggest building boom followed the split of the Corps of Artillery in 1907, when Fort Monroe became the home of the Coast Artillery.

Observing these handsome, historic homes, one cannot help but wonder: Who were the people who lived and served here? What were their lives like? What did they contribute to history? Voices from retired rolls answer some of these questions as they recall a lovely, albeit faded, picture of the past. One Army wife stated that her grandmother told her that her idea of heaven was to be nineteen years old again and to live at Fort Monroe for eternity.

SELF-GUIDED TOUR OF FORT MONROE

Casemate Museum

To take an easy mile and a half self-guided walking tour around this gem of a fort, start at the Casemate Museum. The establishment of this museum can be credited to the personal enthusiasm and private zeal of a local Hampton physician, Dr Chester Bradley. In 1950 he was authorized to use casemate rooms for storage of the memorabilia he had collected in research of his hobby: the preservation of the history of Fort Monroe. These were the same rooms where young Lieutenant Jefferson Davis delivered Indian Chief Black Hawk for confinement, and where years later, the Confederate President Jefferson Davis was himself confined.

Through the turn of the century, casemates on this front were used as two-room sets of quarters for officers. The gunner's room, facing the interior of the fort, was used as a sitting room. There were no doors, so openings leading to the sleeping room overlooking the moat were covered with drapes. Photos show the arched opening to the next set of casemate rooms also covered with drapes, but it is presumed that these connecting openings were boarded up to afford privacy.

Retired Brigadier General F S Strong, Jr wrote that:

My father was stationed at Fort Monroe as a Second Lieu-tenant after graduating from West Point in 1880. In those days, the Hygeia Hotel was quite a popular vacation spot for visitors from New York and other northern cities. It was under these circumstances that my father met a pretty 20-year old girl from Brooklyn. They were married in 1883 and assigned a casemate as quarters. This was a unique experi-ence for a young lady brought up in the city where there were modern conveniences. My mother recalled that visitors

5

Colonel Joseph Roberts, staff, and families, 1864.

constantly asked in which casemate the President had been kept--they referred, of course, to Jeff Davis.

Postern Gate

Close by the entrance door to the Museum, beyond the cistern, is a casemate leading to the postern gate. A postern is a small passageway under the rampart for the use of foot traffic. An entry from a Quartermaster Report states that the stables had been located in the postern bastion from 1844 to 1874, but that "lumber arrived [on 10-22-1874] to build the Postern Bridge." Families quartered in the inner fort had strongly objected to the location of the stable for over thirty years. Finally the animals were moved to the present location of Moat Walk.

This is a good area to explain the terms pertaining to the construction of a fort. The moat is retained by stone facings called scarps. Against the fortress scarp, vaulted rooms called casemates are constructed to house guns which can be fired through embrasures (openings in the scarp). Earth is mounded above the casemates to form the rampart, or wall of the fort. The top of the rampart is leveled for additional gun emplacements. This area is called the terreplein (from the French "terre"--earth, and "plein"--field). The parapet is on the forward face of the rampart which is raised several more feet to form a protective face for the gunners. This casemate room affords a view of the interior and exterior angling of the embrasures (windows) which allows weapons to swivel on an iron rail to cover different fields of fire.

Fort Monroe is the only active military installation surrounded by a water-filled moat. Its width varies from 60 to 150 feet, and the average depth of eight feet fluctuates with the tide since it is maintained with a saltwater inlet and outlet. It is crossed by three gates, or sallyports (from the French "salle," room, and "porte," doorway; also, troops were said to sally forth to face the enemy). Each entrance originally had a drawbridge operated by a hand windlass. Later, tracks were laid for a horse-drawn railway used primarily for movement of supplies and personnel. At the west, or Main Gate, are confinement cells and rooms for the guard detachment.

18 Bernard [named for General Simon Bernard, aide-de-camp to Napoleon]

Backtrack by the cistern and note the white frame house on the left built in 1880 at a cost of $5,000. During a recent

7

renovation, an inspector crawled up into the attic. In a gloomy recess beneath the eaves, he saw a dingy box the size and shape of a coffin. He fearfully lifted the lid expecting to encounter a skeleton, only to deduce that the lead box must have been used as a reservoir for rainwater. In this house the widow Berry operated an officer and family mess during WWI. Here also, a door opens itself at random, and a rocking chair rocks when so inclined, according to *The Ghosts of Fort Monroe* by Polanski and Drum.

A small area on the rampart above this set of quarters was commandeered for use as a pet cemetery. Former residents used to inquire if "Fido's grave marker was still standing." During depression days in the 1930s, a utility engineer was reprimanded for expending time maintaining the pet cemetery. His defense was that the rampart had to be mowed, whether or not there were pet graves beneath the high grass.

The Tuileries, 37 and 41 Bernard

Facing the Casemate Museum are two three-story structures known as the Tuileries, possibly so-called because the French designer of the fort, and the French engineer, Colonel Gratiot, felt that the arcaded effect created by the pillars resembled the Paris residence of the Bourbon Kings. An 1824 sketch shows the two Tuileries were to be joined by a central building with graceful staircases fanning out to each wing. These are the second-oldest surviving buildings, probably ready for occupancy about 1823, designed to provide two-room suites for eight bachelor officers on each of the second and third floors. Because the interior of the fort is about sea level, the lower floor was too damp for habitation, and here were located the cistern, storage rooms, and perhaps even shelters for animals, as was common in Europe. Bathroom facilities were earth-filled closets beneath the flagstaff bastion. In the early years, if husbands were away on detached duty (such as fighting the Indians), families could remain in the quarters, but they were not allowed to draw a fuel ration.

An historical marker points out the building in which Lieutenant Robert E Lee lived from 1831 to 1834. Mrs Lee did not care for the climate nor the hours her husband worked, and therefore spent much time in the comfort of her family's home in Alexandria, Virginia.

The units were designed without kitchens since the occupants would have taken two meals a day, at 9:00 AM and 3:00 PM, at a central mess or at one of the civilian hotels nearby. Even after kitchens were added in later years, WWI brides reported that they couldn't manage the monstrous old Army ranges and preferred to eat at the Sherwood Inn. As late as 1925, families recalled that they cooked in the linen closet and did dishes in the bathtub. Wives complained that whereas cannon balls were painted regularly, the quarters never were, and they had to scrub the walls constantly to remove grime caused by the shallow coke-burning fireplaces.

51-53 Bernard

One reference states that this house was constructed in 1875 as a double set of quarters for captains. A plan in the National Archives calls for a house to be built on this site for the use of Reverend M L Chevers who served as the Protestant chaplain from 1828 to 1867, but no proof was found that he occupied the quarters.

Throughout the years the house has been much abused. It was converted to a four-family dwelling, turned into bachelor officers' quarters during WWI, and then reverted into a duplex. Lieutenant P B Taliaferro brought his bride to these quarters in 1918. She recalled that there was a horse-drawn omnibus with a colored driver that took the ladies into the village of Phoebus to shop, and on occasion, even went so far as Hampton. Lieutenant C M Mendenhall, Jr lived here [1926 to 1930] and looked across at the casemates where his father was born in 1859.

Although a kitchen had been added by 1930, there was no back door, so Lieutenant and Mrs L T Vicker's ice was delivered through a window. During a blackout in WWII, the wife of Post Surgeon Heinitsh panicked when the air raid sirens sounded and hid in a closet beneath the stairs, only to find there was no doorknob on the inside. She remained there until her husband got off duty many hours later. Mrs F J French recalled that General and Mrs Tracy came to pay a visit and admired the marble fireplace mantel, and jokingly threatened to have it moved to their own quarters.

This house has a playful ghost who nudges people, moves things about, stands before the fireplace, and is said to have been photographed showing only a "white mist." Five gas street lamps along this front of the fort are symbolic of the original lighting.

Casemate Officers' Club

Proceeding toward the Flagstaff Bastion, the sidewalk to the right of the ramp led to the front door of the Casemate Officers'

Club, located here from 1871 to 1959. It consisted of casemated rooms which were lovely to decorate as the Twelve Days of Christmas. A glass-enclosed porch for dining and dancing extended out over the moat. Brass cannon were mounted upright against the granite interior wall. Access to the club from the oceanfront was provided by a small boat affectionately known as the *Maid of the Moat*. A hand-pulley arrangement allowed passengers to convey themselves across the moat. The return trip was somewhat more precarious, and there are many tales of midnight swims. The boat was replaced with a footbridge, long since dismantled.

When the price of meals was raised in the civilian hotels, a mess was established in the club. It is said that the club was the site of a continuous poker game from the Civil War to WWI [when ladies were first allowed to attend] monitored by the club mascot, the Oozlefinch. The creation of this mythical bird is credited to Captain H M Merriam, an Artillery School instructor. While shopping in Hampton, Mrs E R Tilton, wife of the Constructing Quartermaster, found a toy resembling his description, and gave it to the Club. Since the bird kept disappearing, it was finally placed in a glass case behind the bar where it remained for 40 years, guarded by Keeney, the Club Steward.

Reportedly, the Oozlefinch faintly resembled a duck, with an ostrich-like neck which was topped by a flat head with bulbous, unlidded eyes. Having no eyelids made him ever vigilant, but also forced him to fly backwards. However, he didn't care where he was going, he only wanted to know where he'd been. His feathers had been blown away by a muzzleblast, and one leg was shorter than the other from running around the parapet. The mascot disappeared when the Field Artillery moved to California in 1945. It is reported to have been reincarnated at a Texas Army Post where it carries a missile under its wing.

Lovely memories abound about the Casemate Club, where ivy from the rampart crept through the mortar into the casemate rooms; where water stood knee-deep during the hurricane of 1933; where Father Time was carried out on horseback and Baby New Year was delivered in Lieutenant Van Buskirk's small car; and where officers and ladies were smoked out of a Friday night happy

The *Maid of the Moat*, the small ferry used to cross to the casemate club, circa 1915.

hour due to an officer's son having stuffed his leather jacket in the rampart chimney. (Unfortunately, the son's name was in the jacket and he remembers the severe reprimand his father, Captain E "Reb" Barber, gave him.) The high cost of maintaining the damp, dark rooms forced the closure of the Club, whose activities were thereafter assumed by the Beach Club--called by all who knew the charming casemate club, "a hot dog stand."

Flagstaff Bastion

From the Flagstaff Bastion where retreat is held each evening, there is an excellent view of the Chesapeake Bay, Thimble Shoals Lighthouse, Hampton Roads channel and harbor, Fort Wool, Willoughby Spit, Ocean View Beach, the US Navy Base and the Naval Air Station.

This commanding viewpoint has witnessed the symbolic firing of gun salutes, a custom which evolved from armed warriors rendering their weapons harmless to prove their visit was peaceful. Starting about 1810, an honor salute fired the same number of rounds as there were states in the Union. Early warship salutes would fire seven rounds and land batteries would reply with three times that number since their supplies were greater and closer at hand. Now when gun salutes are given for American or foreign dignitaries, the number of cannon fired is in accordance with the position held (i.e., from 15- to 21-gun salutes).

An event which occurred on 13 November 1833 may have been viewed from this bastion. The Commanding Officer was asked to report to the Secretary of War about this "singular mete-oric appearance," and to obtain statements from observers. The *Alexandria Gazette* reported that,

from day-break until broad day-light, [there was a] continu-ous display of brilliant meteors or shooting stars...they moved from the zenith in all directions....During this phe-nomenon the appearance of the heavens was most sublime. It seemed as if showers of fire were descending; again large flashes would shoot athwart the sky rendering every object around visible. A meteor of about six inches exploded with considerable noise. Some formed long trains of fire which remained in the sky for several seconds. [Halley's Comet did not appear until 1835.]

From the Flagstaff Bastion, one can see Fort Wool. Lieutenant Robert E Lee was assigned the frustrating task of forming a gun emplacement at this spot, needed because coastal guns could not bridge the distance across Hampton Roads. As granite was barged to the shoal and walls raised several feet, the island would sink again due to settling or slippage down an inclined plane. By 1837, after 60,000 tons of granite had been deposited, the island held. It was not completed by the outbreak of the Civil War, but renewed effort allowed its use before the war ended. Work was discontinued until the Spanish-American War in 1898 when Fort Wool was again manned. It was garrisoned during WWI and a submarine net was spread between the island and the fort. There were only caretakers there until it was manned again in WWII. In 1967 Fort Wool was turned back to the state of Virginia.

Seven miles up the harbor to the west is where the clash of the famous ironclads, the *Monitor* and *Merrimac*, took place in March 1862. Another historic event which took place on 21 February 1922 could have been observed from the Flagstaff Bastion:

The hydrogen-filled dirigible, the *Roma*, left its hanger at Langley Field and floated into the sky above Hampton and Newport News. This complicated, massive airship was an unique Italian import for the US Army Air Service....As it sailed toward Norfolk with a crew of 45 aboard, it developed trouble as it hovered over the Norfolk Army Quartermaster Depot. The craft's nose pitched forward and partially collapsed....Sparks ignited the hydrogen and gasoline tanks turning the Roma into a roaring inferno. A crumpled steel skeleton containing 34 bodies was all that remained....Eleven crew members managed to survive the disaster by jumping clear of the craft as it neared the ground. Captain W J Reed, designated as the pilot, was one of the survivors. He concluded his career as a Brigadier General in the Army Air Force and served as president of Sears Roebuck Company in Mexico. He died in St Thomas, the Virgin Islands, in 1963. [By David Ennis, "*Roma* Made '22 History," *Times Herald*, 21 February 1976.]

About three miles to the left of the Flagstaff Bastion, the USS *Missouri* ran aground in 1956. When it began to appear that it might not be salvageable, the Commanding Officer of Fort Monroe sent word to the ship's captain that he would be glad to accept the ship as an annex to the Officers' Beach Club. There is no record of a reply. There is still an area of deep water in the fishing grounds known as the Missouri Trench.

Casemate Fronts 2 and 3

The casemates presently housing the Chapel Center were the sites of the mess and quarters for noncommissioned officers and their families, as were the casemates beyond the ramp leading to Jefferson Davis Memorial Park. Early photos show wooden porches extending in front, and lines of Army uniforms hanging out to dry between the porch uprights. One Post Commander tried to limit the times of day when laundry could be hung out, but found it an order impossible to enforce. The rooms to the right of the ramp were for the post bakery and the sutler's store.

The Seminole campaigns of the late 1830's emptied the post, which then fell into serious disrepair. The *Army Navy Chronicle* of 21 September 1837 reported that of the 1,400 troops destined for Florida under the command of Brigadier General A Eustis; all were recruits with the exception of ten experienced officers. The article continued:

War has means of destruction more formidable than the cannon and the sword....Very few ever feel the stroke of an enemy; the rest languish in tents and ships amidst damps and putrefication, pale, spiritless, and helpless, gasping and groaning, unpitied by men made obdurate by long continuance of hopeless misery, the waste of life, and the inroads from such causes in Florida.

There was a system of rotating artillery units along the entire eastern seaboard from Maine to Florida. This caused financial hardship and distress for military men with families. Military ships could not take families, who were left behind as paupers in the parishes. Transfers made by sea were expensive, and the mortality rate was high for troops unaccustomed to the southern sun and exposure to malaria spread by the ever-present mosquitos and flies. Units of the 2nd and 3rd Artillery sent to Florida to enforce migration of the Seminoles west of the Mississippi were decimated in an engagement on 28 December 1835, called Dade's Massacre, where 107 officers and enlisted men were killed.

The Indian and Mexican Wars had occupied the artillery, but by 1856 troops were once more available for duty at Fort Monroe to reorganize the Artillery School, and in December 1857

14

the school reopened under the command of Lieutenant Colonel H Brown. It lasted four years until the outbreak of the Civil War. Colonel Brown was much interested in the fort and set out 500 trees, half inside the fort and the rest along the waterfront and both sides of the causeway to Mill Creek. Social activities of this period were steamboat excursions from Norfolk, Richmond, Washington and Baltimore; exchanged amenities with crews of foreign war vessels anchored in Hampton Roads during hurricane season; parties, receptions, calls, afternoon concerts by the band, and evening parades. Post regulations for this period give some idea of daily life:

♦ Dogs are limited to one per company.
♦ Poultry will not be allowed to roam free.
♦ Liquor sold by the sutler must be consumed on the spot.
♦ Vendors may not shout out their wares.
♦ Scraping of the moat for fish or oysters is prohibited.
♦ Dirt or filth shall not be thrown into the moat.
♦ The market house shall be open from sunrise until 11:00 AM.
♦ No sea bathing except after sunset and before 6:00 AM, and then not in sight of dwellings; negroes not allowed any time.
♦ Cattle are not permitted to graze on the ramparts.

The fort played an important role during the Civil War, although no battles ever took place closer than Big Bethel, twelve miles north. By the end of 1861 there were 1,500 troops at Fort Monroe, 4,000 at Camp Butler, and 5,000 at Camp Hamilton which had been established across Mill Creek and 200 men on Fort Wool. In addition, there were about 20,000 "contraband negroes" (escaped slaves) in the area, large numbers of whom were destitute. Many had performed capably as laborers for the government, even though they had not been paid for at least 12, in some cases up to 20, months. They were sheltered, clothed and fed, and only a few were sick or feeble.

President Lincoln, who had refused General McClellan's request to use General Wool's force of 10,000 men at Fort Monroe, visited in May 1862 to discuss military plans. Dilapidated barracks were replaced in 1863 with seven batten-and-board buildings with shingle roofs, each capable of housing 700 men. The Quartermaster had run up a bill of $404,000 expanding the fort, and requested 20,000 more board feet of lumber to furnish 40 to 60 coffins per day.

Some of the first black troops formed as the First Regiment of Cavalry, Colored, were sent to Fort Monroe; the 2nd US Colored

Cavalry and the 2nd Colored Artillery were formed at Fort Monroe. A post order stated that colored troops would be treated with the greatest respect by all guards belonging to the command and have the same rights and privileges as white soldiers, and warned that violators would be punished. However, when discussion of prisoner exchange came up, a November 1863 message from Secretary of War Stanton to Major General Butler at Fort Monroe read:

...It is known that the Rebels will exchange man-for-man, and officer-for-officer except for blacks, and officers in command of black troops--these they absolutely refuse to exchange....This is the point on which the matter hangs. This is an abandonment of colored troops and their officers to their fate, and would be a shameful dishonor of the government [not] to protect them.

At the close of the war, the post took part in the exchange of prisoners, return of deserters, and transport of convalescents. Major Franz Von Schilling of the 3d Pennsylvania Artillery was ordered to command a boat to New Orleans to return officers and soldiers of Lee's Army to their homes, but there were still hundreds of prisoners without money or means of reaching their homes. Trains and transports had to be scrounged.

After the Civil War, the shrunken Army was completely reorganized. The post had to be cleared of shacks and temporary wartime construction that had accommodated more than 100,000 troops passing through. Although the wooden barracks showed wear, it would be some time before they could be replaced. Not until 1867 were funds obtained to reopen the Artillery School for the third time. Instruction was occasionally interrupted due to troops being ordered to quell labor riots, respond to Klu Klux Klan activity, or to serve election duty.

The Chapel of the Centurion

Beginning in 1827, religious instruction at Fort Monroe was provided on alternate Sundays by Chaplain Mark L Chevers. In 1838, Chevers moved on post and continued to serve as Chaplain until 1867, when he was replaced by Chaplain Osgood Herrick. A Sunday School was established in 1831 and children were encouraged to attend but required to be clean and decently clothed.

The chapel is the direct result of a violent explosion which destroyed the Fort Monroe Arsenal on 22 June 1855. While two

enlisted men were mixing gunpowder to make fireworks to cele-
brate the arrival of dignitaries, an explosion occurred, killing Artificer Francis McKnight, and so badly burning Artificer Henry Shef-
fis that he later died. Although he suffered painful burns, the life
of their commander, Lieutenant Julian McAllister, was spared.
Attributing his escape to divine intervention, he vowed to build a
chapel. The McAllister Tiffany stained glass window in the Chapel
bears this quotation from the book of Luke: "For he loveth our
nation and he hath built us a synagogue."

The frame of the Chapel, designed by Richard Upjohn, was
raised in September 1857. A memo signed by Colonel Brown
emphasized that the chapel was private property, but under the
control of the commanding officer, and that it would be removed if
exigencies of service demanded, and would not be used for military
purposes except in great emergency--which would probably never
arise. It was agreed that the chapel would serve all denomina-
tions, and that military personnel would have the right to worship
there at all times; however, it was erected, consecrated, furnished,
and maintained by Episcopalians. At various times, it has been
painted red, green, and is now white.

On 14 July 1876, Chaplain Herrick reported that nineteen
windows of the chapel were destroyed by a premature gun explosion. He requested $200 to repair them. The Chapel presently
contains thirty stained-glass memorial windows, some of them
from Tiffany studios. The altar windows were commissioned and
given by the Easterbrook family in memory of their father, who
served as Chief of Chaplains from 1923 until 1926. Other memorial windows of note include those of Generals W B Barry, Edward
DeRussy, Justin Dimick, Emory Upton, and Captain Albion Howe.

In June 1880, a Moller organ was donated to the Chapel by
the Ladies Union Mission Society of Albany, NY.

In 1933, the garrison at Fort Monroe consisted of 1,700
Coast Artillery Harbor Defense and Coast Artillery School troops.
In one of his frequent efforts to get the men to come to church, the
Post Chaplain visited the first sergeants of the fort. Sergeant
Austin told him point blank that if he ever set foot inside a church
it would burn down.

Shortly thereafter, Sergeant Austin died of a heart attack
and his funeral was set to take place in the chapel. Midway
through the service a cry of "Fire!" was heard. In the chapel nave
above the sanctuary arch, fire had broken through the ceiling and
was burning strongly, right over poor Austin. The casket was
carried to the front porch of the quarters immediately opposite the
front door of the chapel and placed on the porch, as were the

historical flags. The fire was soon under control, and fortunately no stained glass windows were damaged. When order was restored, the band marched Sergeant Austin's caisson to the cemetery with due ceremony. A respected old NCO literally left this world in a blaze of glory.

The cause of the fire was laid to workmen who had been scraping old paint off the eaves. However, Colonel Wertenbaker's daughter admitted that her dogs were fighting with those of Colonel Glassburn and caused a workman with a blowtorch to set the church afire.

The church underwent a major restoration in 1968 and was raised two feet to allow installation of air-conditioning. The iron bars below the ceiling are to reinforce the upright walls. During the 1970s, the needlepoint cushions in the altar area were worked by ladies of the post with an original acorn and leaf design created by the mother of General C L Bolte.

101 Bernard

The first occupant of this 1911 house in front of the Chapel was Major Andrew Hero, whose nearby neighbor was Captain Coward. Hero retired as a Major General, but Coward's fate is unknown. In 1947 the John Eisenhower-Barbara Thompson wedding in the Casemate Chapel was filmed from an upstairs window of this house, and golf champion Lawson Little was born here.

In 1974 an enlisted aide was asked to spend the night alone in the house to safeguard household goods delivered that day. About 2:00 AM the military police found the aide huddled on the screened porch moaning: "I'm on fire!" A thorough hospital examination found no cause to explain his eerie experience. Could Sergeant Austin's ghost have reappeared and frightened him?

Ruckman Road Quarters

This street was named for General John Ruckman, who is acknowledged as the organizer of the first *Journal of the US Artillery* in 1895. The frame quarters on this crossroad bisecting the inner fort were constructed for Artillery School students in the 1880s.

In the 1930s, the Reb Barbers lived in the half of the house next to the Chapel. The house may not look much like JFK stadium in Philadelphia, but during their tour it served as such on the day of the Army-Navy game. All the furniture was removed from the living room and temporary bleachers were erected. A football field was diagrammed on the floor, and the windows thrown wide open to receive the full blast of the November weather. The radio broadcast blared forth while the Army rooters and their Navy guests followed each play of the game as they ate hot dogs and drank warming libations.

Next door, 32 Ruckman, is a single house built for Captains in 1880 at a cost of $5,500. It was struck by lightning in 1975, and the estimate for repair was more than the old house seemed worth. Its fate still undetermined, it is now used as an annex and office area for the Casemate Museum.

The Ghosts of Fort Monroe records that a malicious poltergeist with no apparent appreciation of beauty nor respect for private property inhabits this house and breaks things. Also, a red-uniformed visitor simply appears and disappears at will.

The last two houses on this street (24-26 and 28-30 Ruckman) have the same floorplan as a duplicate set which stood on the corner and was consumed by fire in 1945--the only set of quarters lost by fire. In this area the thin notes of a fife have been heard, shadows reportedly pass the windows, and unseen things brush against one.

A wife who lived here in 1913 recalled that there were fears about war breaking out in Europe, yet it seemed so vague and far away that they went along enjoying lobsters from Maine served at the Chamberlin Hotel, and keeping a continual bridge game in session while their husbands studied.

Parade Ground

Glancing across the Parade Ground, shaded by the largest stand of live oak trees this far north in the United States, and guarded by an imposing 15-inch cannon, one sees the barracks on the left, which were built in 1902 on the site of the old hospital to house two companies of artillery. The next small brick building is the Post Library, and behind it, in Bastion Seven where Carroll Hall originally stood, a new main guardhouse was erected in 1900. Later, this building housed the Army Band.

Although not authorized by Congress, Fort Monroe always had a band--with Army permission. Band members could only hold the rank of private and receive private's pay. A report in 1888 said that "Private M____ is totally worthless as a trumpeter. He cannot blow First Call, or any other Call, and he cannot be taught anything." Band members' meager livelihood was subsidized from sutler's profits and assessments against private citizens conduct-

Part of the 3rd Pennsylvania Heavy Artillery Regiment, 1864.

ing business on government property. For many years there were no private or commercial bands in the Tidewater area and the Fort Monroe band was often hired for private functions and hotel dances. The entire unit was always called upon to perform at official ceremonies in the Nation's capital, especially inaugural parades. Records in the National Archives frequently mention stray band members who did not make it back to Fort Monroe after the inaugural, and the various methods used to reunite them with their duty stations.

The wartime wooden barracks eventually rotted and in 1879 were replaced by the present building to house six companies of artillery and the accompanying band. Originally, it was two stories high, but the center was raised to full three-story height following the turn of the century. Single women who followed garrisons to act as laundresses were housed behind the barracks. Three of these poor creatures were caught bringing whiskey onto the post for the soldiers. According to Colonel V M Kimm, they were court martialed, sentenced to have their heads shaved and covered with a pig's bladder, and to be drummed off the fort to the tune of the "Whore's March."

The original sand and dirt parade ground was practically unusable because of the clouds of dust raised by marching soldiers. Water was too scarce and precious to wet it down, so it was covered with a layer of crushed oyster shells. This surface formed a disagreeable mulch in the winter, and in dry weather it cut army boots to shreds. The final solution was to cover it with four inches of clay obtained from nearby Strawberry Banks, dug and transported by soldiers of the garrison. The clay was a sodden mess when storms inundated the sea level area with salt water.

Colonel Milo G Cary mentioned that when he served at Fort Monroe during 1923 and 1924, special reviews were held inside the fort in which the Post Commander and members of his staff were mounted, as was Lieutenant Colonel Jones, Commander of Harbor Defenses and his staff. Chaplain Smith was the only officer who owned his own horse; the others rode government mounts.

Retired Brigadier General T M Osborne wrote that he,

thoroughly enjoyed the year 1923-24 at Fort Monroe except for the horseback riding which I detested. I had chosen the Coast Artillery thinking that was one place where I wouldn't have to ride a horse. Lo and behold! Upon reporting in, it was once more "slow trot, feet out of the stirrups," and of all things, the instructor, Major Spiller, was a NAVAL ACADEMY GRADUATE!

During a mounted review in the 1930s, an Adjutant who could not control his government mount found himself heading for the East Sallyport and the stables. He had presence of mind enough to call back, "Parade--Rest," before he disappeared from sight. Another officer, unceremoniously dumped from his horse, continued the review on foot. Instead of being reprimanded, he was commended for a perfect display of "Dismounted Drill."

The hurricane of 1933 caused the entire post to be under three to five feet of salt water, killing many of the trees and shrubs. Mrs M D Meyers recalled that during the hurricane her husband was at Fort Monroe with the Reserves, staying in an old WWI frame barrack. When he awakened the morning after the storm he found that the building had moved, and his window no longer faced the bay. From this disaster, new buildings and reclamation projects were provided from relief funds and National Recovery Act sources.

The Ordnance House, 121-129 Bernard

The date of construction of this white brick duplex set of quarters is in question. Major Arthur's history of Fort Monroe states the house was built in 1819 for the constructing engineers, but there is no supporting proof. Also, it is sometimes referred to in error as the Robert E Lee house, but he is known to have lived in the Tuileries.

An Ordnance map of 1839 shows a building of this same configuration in this location. This date coincides with the date of the General Order establishing an arsenal at Fort Monroe and may indicate when Ordnance funds were granted, to include construction of this set of quarters. Records of occupants indicate the house was assigned to Ordnance officers through 1883. It is probably the fourth oldest house on the post.

A letter dated June 1876 complained that during parades and ceremonies, seats in front of this house should be reserved for officers and their ladies, and that enlisted men should be restricted to the opposite side of the parade ground. The author found it intolerable to lead his lady among such crude ruffians and feared an encounter in upholding her honor.

Lieutenant Rose, who lived here from 1912 to 1914, is recalled as having complete disregard for uniform regulations. He would stroll across the parade ground on his way to work in a blue blouse and khaki trousers, or some other nonregulation attire. He was thought to have been color blind, but it may be that he just didn't give a hoot.

Captain and Mrs H P Detwiler were assigned these quarters in 1930, and when told the building was 100 years old, they immediately thought: "That means 100 years of dirt to clean out of the cracks." Mrs. Detwiler continued:

It did have cracks, and I never got them all cleaned. My husband was among the group who remained in rank for 17 years without promotion, but all of our associates were in the same position, so it didn't matter. However, an Army wife learns to make a home wherever she is, with or without money. We made nice furniture from the good wood used in the heavy packing crates used for shipping household goods, and made curtains from the muslin used to wrap furniture. It was a good life.

A Christmas card sent out by Captain and Mrs R E McGarraugh (who lived here from 1933 to 1938) read in part:

Through the aged hand-rolled panes of our front windows, we see the same parade ground where Lafayette reviewed our early army. On this same soil marched Edgar Allen Poe as a young Sergeant Major. Here, too, the broken and defeated Jefferson Davis took his daily walk as a prisoner. Our south windows frame the part of Hampton Roads where the Merrimac and Monitor contested, and the era of metal-clad warships was begun. Shading our immediate yard stand moss-grown live oaks and boxwoods--deep-rooted in virgin swamp. Over this land, Sir John Smith and Chief Powhatan passed a peace-pipe in 1610. Reminiscent of the day when a barred gate meant safety, we are surrounded by grim walls and a moat. And providentially, above these ivy-clad walls waves the same proud flag as in their beginning over a century ago.

The daughter of Colonel A M Wilson, Jr (who lived here in 1936 and 1937) wrote:

I remember well being stationed at Fort Monroe during some of the most memorable years of my young life. I attended the post school, belonged to Girl Scouts, rode horseback every week with Major Trigg in classes and horse shows, attended Sunday School at the YMCA with Major H R Jackson as Superintendent, took piano lessons from Mrs E C Englehart, went to dancing school held upstairs at the Coast Artillery School building, rode bicycle, walked and roller-skated on every road, sidewalk and seawall, climbed the ramparts, had beach hikes and cookouts, rode the ferry to Willoughby Spit, had Scout Camp at Fort Story, spent summer days at the "new" beach club, and later attended dances at the Chamberlin Hotel, Casemate Officers' Club and Beach Club. These were the most full and happy years in my memory.

Slave Quarters, 125 Bernard

Behind the Ordnance house is a small house referred to as the annex, or slave quarters. Early maps show several small buildings in this area, but none appeared to be of a permanent nature. The National Archives contains an 1886 plan labeled "servant's quarters." By 1887 the area was shown as being connected to the large duplex by a long double hall with numerous room arrangements.

Polanski and Drum wrote that:

The slave quarters is a cozy house with thick walls, and, on the upper floor, wide, planked, wooden floors. Originally on the second floor there were two long rooms to house the servants for the officers' quarters in front facing the parade ground. The only access was the outside stairs on the porch. The inner stairs are a recent addition when the rooms were renovated in 1947 for living quarters.

The lower rooms were originally separated by a cobblestone passageway to the main houses in front. On the street side there was a barn door, and horses were ridden through the passageway up to the back doors of the main houses. The present kitchen and storeroom are the same as in the original building.

No record was found of these quarters being assigned to junior officers until the 1930s. The H W Cochrans who lived in the east side of the Ordnance House in 1932 had this building assigned to them, and stated that the upper floor had been converted into an apartment and was unoccupied. The first recorded occupant was First Lieutenant L A Zimmer in 1934.

Colonel J B Morgan states he occupied the upper floor of this house from 1939 to 1940 as a First Lieutenant, but in December 1941 his family was moved to a room with a bath in the Chamberlin Hotel.

Trophy Park, circa 1905.

Colonel N B Wilson moved into 125 Bernard Road in March 1947, stating that he was the first occupant after the war, during which time the house had served as bachelor officers' quarters. The inside stairway had been removed but he replaced it, and there was a row of four toilets in the hall between the kitchen and dining room. Having to pass through this area to serve dinner guests made entertaining unusual. He also redid the entire interior with paint furnished by the Quartermaster.

The Ghosts of Fort Monroe tells of a mouse who invaded the kitchen, and a cat being placed there overnight to perform her duty. The next morning the cat was found outside, meowing to get in. Other strange activities were documented such as furniture and bric-a-brac being moved and clocks being dismantled until an irate Colonel's wife told the "being" to "get out and stay out."

Quarters #126, 127, and 128 (107-109, 145-47, and 163-65 Bernard)

These three brick double sets of quarters for captains were completed in 1909 at a cost of $27,000 each. Former residents recall the parade ground surrounded by captured cannons and pyramids of cannon balls and being called Trophy Park.

Quarters #3 (167-169 Bernard)

This fine brick dwelling was built in 1875, and then converted into two sets of officer's quarters in 1910 at a cost of $7,067.

Captain Percy Smith who lived in the set of quarters nearest the barracks applied for a compassionate change of quarters because his children were adopting bad language due to the close association with the soldiers. The Billeting Office replied that he could move from the west side to the east side of the house, which, of course, would not have solved his problem.

Lieutenants W H Dunham and D B Latimer shared the duplex when a fire broke out in the attic in December 1933. They were off participating in a fox hunt; when they came home they found that the 51st Coast Artillery personnel had removed all of their possessions in about ten minutes. The fire had started from sparks from the A Battery chimney which blew into the attic window, but the old beams were so thick that they did not have to be replaced when the attic was repaired.

Before moving on toward the East Sallyport, note the largest live oak at Fort Monroe which has a circumference of 20 feet two inches. Steel cables strengthen its mammoth limbs. Take the sidewalk to the front of the white brick mansion nestled on the curve of Bernard Road.

Quarters #1 (151 Bernard)

As the first permanent set of officers' quarters constructed at Fort Monroe in 1819, this house derives its significance from its age, its role as the meeting site for national strategy and defense planning, its fine architectural design, and for famous people who lived here or visited here. The construction engineer, Major C Gratiot, was the first occupant. Sometimes it is erronously called the DeRussy house, but that noted military engineer lived in quarters outside the fort which no longer exist.

An 1824 report describes Quarters #1 as a brick building, with three floors, each floor having two rooms measuring 17' x 19', with a passage through the center. Attached are two brick wings, two floors high measuring 17' x 25'. A frame building 50' x 20' was used as a stable and carriage house and had a room for the hostler. There was also a smokehouse, greenhouse and other necessary buildings--the whole surrounded by a neat enclosure.

In 1832 the house was transferred by the Engineers to the Commanding Officer of the fort, Colonel A Eustis. He wrote to the Quatermaster General that the house needed paint and wallpaper, and requested $400 to replace the laundry, bakery, and woodshed which had burned. He also asked for $998 to build a piazza on the front of the quarters, and requested that the two wings be raised another story, stating that the two chambers in the body of the house were almost useless without private stairs and dressing rooms.

During the Civil War, private individuals in the surrounding communities requested permission to store valuable paintings and furnishings in the house under protective custody. An 1880 inventory indicated that some of these personal possessions were not reclaimed, and some items may still remain.

General G W Getty and family lived here from 1877 to 1883. In a privately printed booklet by his granddaughter, Mrs. A H Armstrong, there are stories of visits from Presidents Hayes, Garfield, and Arthur and their wives. Quarters #1 housed many dignitaries, as well as visitors from foreign countries, i.e., the Marquis de Lafayette, Secretaries Chase and Stanton, and Generals Grant, McClellan, and Sherman.

In 1881, David Kalakaua, King of the Sandwich Islands (Hawaii) became the first monarch to take a trip around the world.

He visited the heads of state in Japan, China, Siam, India, Italy, Portugal, and England. Upon his arrival in Washington, DC, his party sailed to Fort Monroe to visit the Hampton Normal and Agricultural School. Although General Getty was willing to entertain the King, he could not bring himself to permit his wife and daughters to sit at the table with with a man of color, so they had to be content with peeking over the stair rail in hopes of catching a glimpse of the king in his royal feathered cloak.

Another story told of King Kalakaua's visit was that before departing from San Francisco, he was lured into a poker game in the Palace Hotel by some wily card sharks. The pot had grown quite large when Kalakaua drew a hand containing four kings. As might be expected, one of the professional gamblers turned up with four aces. Kalakaua took a look and raked in the pot. The gambler protested: "When did four kings ever beat four aces?" "Ah," replied Kalakaua, "but there are five kings here."

In 1888, Colonel Tidball wrote to the Quartermaster General that the house was dilapidated beyond repair for officers' quarters, and the next occupant, Colonel Frank, complained that the 8" rifle was positioned too close to his quarters, and that unless all the windows were open, the concussion from the discharge broke their delicate china and glassware.

By 1906 the house was divided into two sets of quarters for junior officers and bachelors, and remained as such until 1942. Residents during this period recall a beautiful semi-circular living room facing the parade ground, and a fan-shaped stairway with a recessed dome containing 13 gold stars (for the original states) on a blue background.

All of the shallow fireplaces burned coke and the floors were inlaid wood. Sliding doors could combine the two apartments into one big house for entertaining. There was rumored to be a sealed tunnel which ran under the moat to the ocean, built for contraband slaves seeking asylum.

Lieutenant L T Vickers and wife lived in half of the house during the depression. They told of enduring a fifteen percent pay cut, and once going three months without a paycheck. The Old Point Bank in Hampton extended them credit knowing that they would receive repayment of every penny.

Colonel J S Davis' father lived there as a Second Lieutenant and recounted that he was assigned half of the house because the heat did not work well. He said he used a roller skate key to bleed the radiators, and after that the heat worked perfectly. As a result, the quarters were upgraded and given to a Captain.

When Colonel R F Moore lived in half the house from 1937 to 1938 as a First Lieutenant, it was known as The Lincoln House:

Our part of the house included the sun parlor, the long hall to the kitchen and a bedroom that had a window that opened onto the front porch. A sealed door prevented access to the main entrance hall, but we could open the communicating parlor doors to give parties with our neighbors, First Lieutenant and Mrs R L Williams.

After 1942, major renovations restored the house to a single family dwelling for senior officers.

The Ghosts of Fort Monroe documents different reports of ethereal apparitions said to inhabit this house, such as Abraham Lincoln standing by the fireplace in a dressing gown; an Indian chief tentatively identified as Chief Black Hawk; and other playful spirits who cause rustles, laughter, strew rose petals, etc.

Major General and Mrs B E Huffman occupied the quarters from 1974 to 1975. They told an overnight guest that there was no need to set an alarm because the General would awaken him. Before daylight, General Huffman heard whistling and water running in the bathroom and assumed his guest had risen early and was shaving. He got out of bed to check, but there was no one in the bathroom, and his guest was in bed sleeping soundly.

Water Battery

Passing through the East Sallyport, note that there are no gun embrasures on the scarp facing the ocean. This is because a Water Battery once housed the weapons which faced the sea. This was a beautifully arcaded rampart which ran along the front edge of the moat. Postern gates and bridges crossed the moat to the water battery. Remnants of the masonry can be seen on the left edge of the moat. It was ordered torn down--the stone to be used to construct a seawall--and new beach defenses built nearby.

To the north are the Wherry Housing family quarters, built to replace substandard barracks apartments. The project was interspersed around the coastal gun installations. There is little of historical interest in this area, but a drive along the waterfront will lead to the present Officers' Beach Club.

WATER BATTERY

CHESAPEAKE BAY
FROM RAMPARTS – LOOKING EAST.

RAMPARTS.

Fort Monroe water battery and ramparts, circa 1895.

Officers' Beach Club

The first Beach Club was built while General S D Embick was in command from 1930 to 1932. It was constructed entirely by troop labor using available Club funds assisted by the Post Quartermaster. It was made of stone and brick set on concrete foundations, with walls of pine logs cut by "pioneer" troops in training at the nearby Fort Eustis military reservation. It withstood the 1933 hurricane, but the logs began to rot.

A new Beach Club was completed in 1936 which retained the foundations, stone, and brick, and added a large fireplace, an outside dance floor, and a saltwater pool. It was a long, rustic structure with a large main room, a stage, tall French doors, and outside sheathing simulating logs.

In 1938, Captain N A Congdon, a student attending the Advanced Course, was assigned to oversee the grading operation of the landfill behind the Beach Club seawall. He was authorized to use one of Captain J H Featherstone's tractors for this operation, and believing in going first class, used one of the specially painted inspection-type tractors rather than a working vehicle. [Featherstone had two sets of everything, the old one for daily use and a new one for inspection only.] Congdon succeeded in sinking the borrowed tractor in the muck and was only saved from an abysmal fate by the intercession of their superior officer, Major L W Goeppert.

This Club was destroyed in June 1944 by a fire apparently caused by a cigarette carelessly thrown into a wastebasket. That summer it was replaced by a circus tent and the present Club was started that fall. Funds were limited and it took scrounging from many sources to get it built of brick, on the original foundations with the old fireplace intact. It remained as the Beach Club until 1961, when General Bruce Clark decided to abandon the Casemate Club altogether and make the Beach Club the main Club.

Continental Club

Bordering the bay and facing the East Sallyport is a frame building housing the Noncommissioned Officers' Club. The fort had suffered much damage during the hurricane of 1933, and this club was constructed in 1934 during a massive building program to stimulate the economy and offset the depression. In earlier times, an enlisted men's bathhouse stood on this site, and later a West Point Cadet Camp was located here which provided summer training for future artillerymen.

31

An officer stationed at Fort Monroe in 1916 told of the blitz courses given to turn out officers. A Drill Sergeant would explain the troop commands, and then let the novice officer attempt to conduct the drill. One of the officer trainees found he had the troops marching directly toward the moat. Unable to remember the proper command he yelled: "Oh, my gawd, STOP!" It was obvious he was not leadership material.

Fenwick Road

Turn right on Fenwick Road, named for Brigadier General J R Fenwick, the first Commandant of the Artillery School for Instruction in 1824. Batteries Parrot and Irwin were built at the turn of the century and adapted during WWII with coastal guns to protect the mouth of Hampton Roads harbor. Early photographs show a railway running the length of Fenwick Road to carry ammunition to the detached batteries. At Battery Irwin there are two 3" rapid-fire artillery pieces which fulfill the stipulation made in March 1821 that the Federal Government could use the land ceded by the Commonwealth of Virginia for as long as Fort Monroe served to protect the State.

Engineer Lane

The two buildings on this short street were designed by Major J E Keeler in 1910 as quarters and an office for the Resident Engineer. The construction engineer activity moved to Norfolk in 1935 and these buildings were taken over for post housing. Starting in 1946, they were reserved for senior officers.

Public Health House, 71 Fenwick

The white frame house on the right of the lighthouse belonged to the Public Health Service, and only became available for Army use when the wharf by the Chamberlin Hotel was demolished in 1961. A medical doctor was always in residence to perform quarantine inspection for the boats and ferries that docked at Old Point Comfort. The Hampton-Norfolk tunnel put the ferry boats out of business. The Chesapeake Bay steamers were no longer hauling payloads to Cape Charles, Norfolk, Baltimore or Washington, and with no ships stopping at Old Point Comfort, the Public Health Service no longer needed to maintain a quarantine station.

Lighthouse

The Old Point Comfort Lighthouse was built in 1802 and is the oldest structure on the post. Major Arthur's book states that it was an outgrowth of the light exhibited at night by the caretaker assigned to guard the ruins of Fort George which was swept away by hurricane in 1749. To combat boredom in his lonely occupation, he posted a light at night for the benefit of passing ships.

An 1837 Law of the US, #40, appropriated $6,000 to move the lighthouse on Old Point Comfort inside the fort. The Chief of Engineers replied that to move the lighthouse to a position in bastions #4 and #5, it would be necessary to remove the stables by Quarters One. The subject was never mentioned again.

By 1884 the Chief of Engineers informed the Commanding Officer of the Coast Artillery School that there was no copy of a deed of conveyance for the lighthouse reservation, nor did any description set the metes and bounds of the property. The conveyance of 250 acres at Old Point Comfort dated 1 March 1882 states the land is "adjunct to and part surrounds a tract of two acres heretofore granted by the Commonwealth to the US."

Another letter dated 22 January 1886 stated that the original marker for lighthouse property had been lost, that a new map of Fort Monroe was being prepared and a decision would be made as to the starting point of lighthouse property. By June, two stones were sent by Bayline steamer to mark the two corners of the Old Point Comfort lighthouse reservation.

Lighthouse Keeper's House, 67 Fenwick

This Queen Anne-style frame house was constructed about 1870 for the keeper of the lighthouse, and remained as such until 1973 when the Army acquired the property from the Coast Guard. The Coast Guardsmen who lived here manned a radio-radar net with ships at sea.

Engineer Wharf

Note the historical marker at the wharf. Although the pier no longer serves a military purpose, it is a great place for local residents to fish and net crabs.

The Gold Coast

Proceeding west, the homes from here to the Post Office were labeled the Gold Coast because of the preponderance of brass (senior officers) who lived in the fine houses in this area. When built, these quarters were intended to accommodate senior officers of the newly designated Coast Artillery. Subsequent headquarters stationed at Fort Monroe were composed of more one- to four-star general officers than the Gold Coast could accommodate, thus many houses inside and without the fort were designated as general officer quarters.

The Flat-tops, 51 and 53 Fenwick

These two handsome colonial style quarters were completed in 1910 at a cost of $13,500. They are built without basements, and early photographs show a waist-deep drainage ditch around each house, with entrance to the front porch over a wooden foot-bridge. They were highly subject to flooding during high tides or hurricanes before the seawall was built.

These houses were ordinarily reserved for the School Commandant and the Post Executive Officer. Retired Lieutenant General H C Connelly wrote:

I was ordered to Fort Monroe in 1930 and quartered in one of the flat-tops. On the second-story sunporch supported by the large white pillars we assembled on hot summer evenings in porch chairs and swings to capture the gracious easterly sea breeze. The house was roomy and comfortable as were all Coast Artillery quarters when Arthur Murray was Chief of the Corps. He was a cunning fox with many abilities blended into good balance. He had a natural bent for architecture and design.

When the Quartermaster General turned down his plan for these colonial quarters pointing out that as designed the roofs would blanket the view of the range-finders in the ramparts, he promptly and skillfully lopped off the tops of the houses without sacrificing space, convenience, or arrangement of rooms. He wanted these houses on the waterfront, and did not propose to let range-towers or blueprints alter his decision.

A succession of general officers have lived at 51 Fenwick. Just after WWII when General and Mrs C L Bolte lived here, while the general was away a burglar entered the house and was apprehended by their dog. The robber shot and killed the dog, at which point Mrs Bolte bravely grabbed her husband's service pistol and returned fire, causing the burglar to flee.

The parking lot beyond the flat-tops served the guests of the Casemate Officers' Club. The gateway is now overgrown with honeysuckle and vines, but can be seen in the far left corner. The sealed up doorway in the scarp can be noted just opposite the gate.

Until 1900, the area between this parking lot and the Post Office was considered to be outside the fort. Prior to the Civil War, rude shelters occupied this area to accommodate engineer activities, civilian enterprises, and living quarters. These temporary buildings were gradually razed as the second Hygeia Hotel and bathing beach expanded. Having been evicted in 1863 from the original site (where the YMCA now stands by the West Sallyport), the second hotel started as a small dining salon that gradually expanded into a huge Victorian frame structure, offering luxury accommodations for guests who arrived by rail or steamer.

Since large sums of money had been approved for expansion of Fort Monroe, it was necessary to clear the waterfront. The hotel was notified to vacate the property. By 1902, all traces of the grande dame of Hampton Roads had disappeared. [See Appendix VI, Hygeia Hotel.]

57-63 Fenwick

This four-unit brick apartment building is the same design as the student quarters near the main entrance to the post--all having been built in the 1930s as part of the Works Project Administration (WPA) following the 1933 hurricane. These apartments often were reserved for aides of general officers quartered on the Gold Coast facing Hampton Roads harbor.

First Lieutenant H Whipple (West Point class of 1936) who lived here as an aide in 1941 found himself a full Colonel in General Douglas MacArthur's South Pacific Command assigned to draw up plans for the Japanese surrender ceremony aboard the USS Missouri on 2 September 1945. Every senior officer of every nation clamored to be present. Just before the ceremony began, ranking personages were still milling around the deck. General "Vinegar Joe" Stilwell came to Colonel Whipple's assistance: "Look son, if you're having trouble lining up these people, just tell me where to stand, and tell everyone else to fall in beside me. They probably haven't obeyed that order for some time, but they will."

The Hygeia Hotel, circa 1880.

37, 42, 43 Fenwick

The two-story double brick duplex at 42-43 Fenwick was built in 1908 at a cost of $26,625 as quarters for captains, and the single house at 37 Fenwick was reserved for the Post Commander when Fort Monroe was the home of the Coast Artillery.

Commanding General's Quarters, 33 Fenwick

The architectural style of this house is Classic Revival, an adaptation of the classic Greek and Roman styles first popular in the United States from 1820 to 1850. This house was built in 1907 for about $25,000. The same floor plan was used to build quarters at Fort Totten, NY and Fort Francis B Warren, WY. Retired Major General J M Lentz recalls living in the Fort Warren quarters when he was a Lieutenant because the Post Commander didn't want to live in the big house he called a "Tabernacle."

Colonel Ira Haynes lived here from 1913 to 1916. He is said to have eaten a second lieutenant, raw, for breakfast each day. He was followed by William R Smith who was assigned here during prohibition. He was nicknamed "Sahara Bill" when he banished an officer to Panama because he had gone on a three-day toot. A plaque in the house listing former occupants reads like a Who's Who of the U.S. Army. The renowned DeRussy house once stood in the area of the rear rose garden. [See DeRussy House in Appendix VIII.]

29 Fenwick

The house next to the Post Office was built in 1908 at a cost of $13,775. Despite the antiquated heating and plumbing, and the lack of air-conditioning, the value of the house and lot would be hard to determine on today's market. In 1925, Colonel W S Abernethy requested the Post Engineer cut a doorway between the spacious master bedroom and the adjacent bath. The request was summarily denied because it would be unsanitary.

Continental Park and Bandstand

The waterfront homes frequently suffered from high tides and tropical storms. After the 1933 hurricane washed away the original bandstand, the present one replaced it. The Adjutant assigned the job to a new Second Lieutenant. He checked from time to time to see how it was coming along, but when the pillars were

Mrs. Rene DeRussy and family in their quarters, circa 1890.

erected, he became alarmed. To his eye they didn't look straight. In questioning the Lieutenant, the Adjutant found that he had no blueprint, and had never heard of a plumb bob. By pure luck the acoustics are quite good.

Post Office

For a long while there was confusion over the official name of this military installation. War Department orders of 1832 plainly stated that the post at Old Point Comfort was a Fort, not a Fortress. However in 1880 when the U.S. Postal Service decided to change the name of the post office from Old Point Comfort, they renamed it Fortress Monroe. This is a misnomer, for a fortress encircles a city, whereas a fort encloses a military garrison only. It took until 1941 to get the Postal Service to change the name.

The present Post Office was built in 1898. In the 1920s, the Post Office corner was the meeting place for Army wives awaiting the horse-drawn omnibus to take them for a morning of shopping in nearby Phoebus or Hampton. Postmaster John Kimberly occupied the apartment on the second floor for 16 years. His pretty daughters did not want for beaus, and his lack of privacy and large grocery bill reflected the number of suitors who remember calling on his daughters. It is not surprising that the girls all married Artillerymen.

After the Spanish-American War and reopening of the Artillery School there was a request for over $4,000,000 to update facilities. It was noted that the Post Office was out of line with all surrounding buildings as well as those to be constructed, and would mar the general appearance of the post where the most handsome buildings were to be located. Nothing was done about repositioning the Post Office, so Ingalls Road meanders around it and curves again around the Catholic Church.

Across the street, the building facing the Chamberlin Hotel was built in 1906 as headquarters for the Coast Artillery Board. It was the first building to have air-conditioning added.

Chamberlin Hotel

The present hotel replaces the original Chamberlin, which was built in 1896. The old hotel had been noted the world over as a health resort with gourmet cuisine: fresh Chesapeake Bay oysters, fish, and crabs prepared for discerning diners. Among the trendy health treatments available were hot sea tub baths, ionic medications, Aix and Vichy water systems, radium baths, Nau-

39

heim baths, electro-therapeutic treatments with Finsen rays, and drinking of Alkaline-saline spring water from a spring running beneath the sun porch. The Pompeiian pool had a 70 foot atrium; the palm garden, sun parlor, and pavilion over the bay promised restoration of health and well-being. During the winter the hotel attracted affluent easterners who arrived by yacht, steamer, or palatial railroad cars.

A Hack Stand provided a line of drays and carriages to meet the boats and trains. There were often disputes over the right to operate transportation facilities which had to be settled by the Post Commander. Fines were imposed, and court appeals were made for permission to resume business. Similar squabbles continued when motor cars replaced the horse-drawn vehicles.

The origin of the fire which destroyed the hotel in March 1920 was never discovered. Many service families who lived in post quarters at that time recalled the staggering spectacle of the blaze, and spoke of buying china, glassware, and other items from the Chamberlin fire sale.

Old Point Comfort was without a hotel for eight years until the present one opened in 1928. It was furnished with items taken from the impounded French luxury liner *Normandie*. It was originally called the Chamberlin-Vanderbilt and had white Christopher Wren towers atop the two elevator shafts. During WWII, the hotel was leased by the Government for quarters for Navy personnel and the towers were removed because they provided an excellent target from the sea. An Officers' Club occupied the top floor during the war years.

Relying heavily upon its curative health assets, the hotel had high hopes of becoming a resort similar to the famous spas in Europe. However, regarding the digestive merits of the mineral spring that supposedly ran beneath the hotel, retired Colonel C N Myers declared that after the hotel burned he arduously searched the area but found no evidence that the spring ever existed. Later he was told by one of his superiors that the water which bubbled from a fountain in the hotel lobby was a hoax--that he once helped the bartender mix it in a tank on the roof from plain tap water and club soda.

The ballroom was originally located in the first story wing which has been converted to an elegant dining room with an unmatched view of the ever-changing excitement of the harbor. The Chamberlin has never been owned by the government, but if it should become a military impediment, it could be ordered removed. [For more, see Appendix VII.]

First Chamberlin Hotel, circa 1910.

Ingalls Road

Turn north on Ingalls Road, named for an artillery officer whose monographs were used for instructional purposes until textbooks were printed for the Artillery School. The first building on the left is Murray Hall, named for Major General Arthur Murray, Chief of Coast Artillery (1906 to 1909) when the post was undergoing its major enlargement. Murray was an 1874 West Point graduate who attended the Artillery School as a First Lieutenant in 1880. In this building junior officers were taught the technicalities of their service and attended seminars for free discussion of national and international topics. Students were encouraged to submit military monographs, but warned to avoid arousing America's contiguous neighbors to speculate about US expansionist aims. The bricked-in windows above the wrought iron balcony were in the auditorium where tea dances were held on Wednesday and Friday afternoons, and gala hops were held on Saturday nights. The first floor awnings were regularly set ablaze by cigarette butts tossed over the balcony on dance nights.

Just behind this building is Callan Hall, named for the School Commandant from 1924 to 1927. Classes were conducted here for enlisted artillery specialists.

The building next to the Post Office was the former home of the Coast Artillery School Library. In petitioning Congress for funds to construct a fireproof library, it was pointed out in 1896 that Fort Monroe's 60,000 volumes constituted the most valuable collection of military books outside of the War Department Library. This building was completed in 1909 and continued in use until the arrival of the Continental Army Command in 1955, when more office space was needed. It was named for John Wisser, the first editor of the *Journal of the US Artillery*.

The pathway beside Wisser Hall leads to the Postern Gate and the inner fort. Free passage through posterns was strictly limited to persons on duty. Unauthorized trespassers were severely reprimanded. However, children who sneaked across this footbridge enroute to school recalled how fascinated they were to observe the sponges growing in the moat and the Portuguese Men-of-War which drifted through the sluice gates.

The area in front of the moat from here to the West Sally-port was the site of the first Hygeia Hotel, which the War Department allowed to be built by a civilian to house workmen constructing the fort. It continued in operation until the Civil War when it was ordered razed to prevent an influx of sightseers into the war zone. One wing was left to serve has a hospital, but was later torn down to permit the construction of permanent military quarters in this location. [See Appendix VI, Hygeia Hotel.]

The handsome brick home at 32 Ingalls was built for field grade officers (majors and above) from the same floor plan as the set of quarters in front of the Chapel of the Centurion. It sits on the site of the original Engineer's Office.

White Elephants

The frame duplexes at 34-36, 38-40, and 46-48 Ingalls are three of seven identical quarters built in 1891 at a cost of $8,530.36. They were dubbed "white elephants" because of their size and color. Some contain diamond mutinied casemate windows in the gables, but much of the gingerbread porch moldings is gone. The houses were modified in 1908 to include indoor plumbing, pantries, and electricity.

In 1912 when retired Major General S P Spalding was a young bachelor sharing the house at 36 Ingalls with a classmate,

[His] Company was the 69th, and the whole team was wiped out in a 12" gun blowback. R C Marshall, James Kirk and I had to reinforce the football team. There was real fighting spirit in company encounters. I...had to keep Corporal Brasham, a fellow halfback, from fist-fighting with a burly player on the champions' team. The games were held on the parade ground in front of the Casemate Officers' Club.

A W Ford, who lived at 36 Ingalls during 1916 and 1917 said:

My wife's ancestor was Captain Nicholas Martian (1591-1657). He was educated in England as an engineer of military fortifications and was put in charge in Virginia of the work of planning and building fortifications. One of the three places he selected for immediate fortification was Old Point Comfort, now Fort Monroe, Virginia.

During WWI individual rooms in these houses were assigned to bachelor officers. O A Axelson shared the house at 34-36 Ingalls with ten of his classmates while attending a course at the Artillery School in 1918. He took meals at Mrs Berry's Officers' Mess inside the fort or at the Sherwood Inn. He recalled that the Casemate Club did not serve meals nor liquor, but offered off-duty relaxation overseen by Keeney, the Club Steward.

43

From 1923 to 1925, student officers of the field grade course were generally housed in the Sherwood Inn, according to E C Bomars, who lived at 38 Ingalls. "Married student officers in the grades of Captain or Lieutenant were usually housed in much less desirable quarters in old temporary WWI barracks which had been converted into apartments of a sort."

The daughter of Captain B L Simpson, whose family lived at 46 Ingalls from 1944 to 1946, said: "While most of my father's service was with the mine planting batteries, in 1940 he designed and commanded (until December 1945) the Observation Station above old Club--a joint Army/Navy effort designated as the Harbor Defenses of Chesapeake Bay."

Commissary Officer's Quarters

The single frame house at 42 Ingalls is listed as having been built in 1880 for $5,500. However, an 1887 blueprint shows a house of this configuration in this spot which is labeled "Commissary." It is known that both the Commissary and Quartermaster officers were assured of "position" housing during this period. [The Quartermaster was housed near the Baltimore Wharf at the end of Ingalls.] The kitchen and bathroom were modified in 1908, and although lightning struck the house in 1927, only the wiring and moldings suffered loss. The shutters and most of the ginger-bread trim have been removed, and the house was re-sided with aluminum in 1960.

Lieutenant H J Hatch lived here in 1900 when his course of instruction started "Hatch-ing out incubates (Incs)" of the Coast Artillery School. Twenty-five years later, he had been promoted to Colonel and was entitled to be assigned the handsome brick home next to Wisser Hall. Many artillery officers served repeated tours at Fort Monroe having returned to take advanced courses, or to serve on the staff or faculty of the school.

"The Beehives"

Across the street at 35 and 41 Ingalls are two quadriplex family apartments built in 1910 at a cost of $25,606. When retired Colonel John DeCamp was a teenaged paperboy at Fort Monroe during the 1930s, he had a terrible time keeping track of customers in these buildings, especially after the annual "quarters drawing." This custom allowed senior officers to select the house they preferred to live in, even if it meant bumping out junior officers down the line to the rank of Second Lieutenant. This is one reason for the military expression "RHIP" (rank hath its privileges); another expression is "pulling rank".

When General Lyman Lemnitzer was an instructor at the school from 1936 to 1939, he became quite annoyed one day at the lack of attention his class was paying to his lecture. They were fascinated by something going on in one of the Beehives, and informed him that an apartment was on fire. Looking out of the window he exclaimed: "Good heavens! I live in that building!" A formal dismissal of class was unnecessary.

Quarters #123 (46-48 Ruckman)

This two-story brick duplex was erected in July 1909 as a double set of quarters for captains at a cost of $26,662.20. It stands on the site of the original Hygeia Hotel. When retired Major General G R Meyer lived in 4 Ruckman (as a Major) from 1923 to 1924, he recalled that the yard between his house and the Young Men's Christian Association (YMCA) building was used for ball practice.

A famous Army boxer named Speedie Lawrence used to come over and hit fly balls to us kids. While living there as a youngster, I don't know how many times we tried to locate the mouth of the secret tunnel going underneath the moat from Quarters One, but each attempt seemed to be blocked by darkness and spider webs.

Major H F Loomis was assigned this house from 1929 to 1932. Mrs Loomis had been one of the wives who helped the "Elephant Squad" learn to dance at West Point. J H Pitzer (a bachelor in Sherwood Inn in 1930) recalled the Loomises and said:

Since riding instruction followed dance class, we sometimes wore our white trousers over our breeches and leggins to save time. Mr Vizey, the Frenchman who taught dancing, blew his top when he discovered this. He insisted on the one-two-three-glide routine, and I saw graduates still dancing that dumb way years later. When General MacArthur let our group attend a dance at Fort Dix, I was "skinned" for dancing cheek to cheek....No hops were held in the Coast Artillery School auditorium while I was there in 1930--rather they were held either in the Chamberlin, or the wonderful old Casemate Officers' Club within the fort.

45

The Perry House

A small brick and frame building constructed in 1889 at a cost of $3,300 for occupancy by civilian employees of the Quartermaster Corps sits at the corner of Ingalls and Tidball Road. [This street was named for Colonel J C Tidball, Commandant of the Artillery School from 1883 to 1888.] The post electrician lived in one half of the house until 1974; the other half was usually reserved for the fire chief. The building was then converted into quarters for enlisted men visiting the post. Air-conditioning was installed in 1985 when further renovation took place.

At some point it was labeled the Perry House, presumably to register the historical fact that First Sergeant Edgar Allen Poe served at Fort Monroe in 1829 under the pseudonym of Perry. Poe quickly tired of the life of a noncommissioned officer, and his stepfather paid Sergeant "Bully" Graves $75 to finish out his enlistment. From Fort Monroe, Poe went to West Point to enroll in the Military Academy. Since he was a poorly disciplined student and found classes and homework equally boring he was dismissed within a few months. Long after, when he had become a noted writer, he returned to the peninsula to recite his lovely poem, "Annabelle Lee," before an admiring audience seated on a moonlit porch of the Chamberlin Hotel.

The Sherwood Inn

The Sherwood Inn stood on the site now called Sherwood Park. In 1843, the privilege of erecting a private dwelling was granted to Assistant Army Surgeon Robert Archer. In 1850, the house was purchased by the post quartermaster, Major J C Martin. It further passed through the ownership of A Mehaffee; G C Mellon, sutler; George Booker; and was eventually sold to Sarah F Eaton. By 1879 the cottage had grown to a fair-sized house, and Mrs Eaton was granted permission by the Secretary of War to enlarge the premises and to offer room and board to Army and Navy officers and their families. For a time the establishment was known as "The Little Hygeia" with a claim to being able to serve 175 persons. However, military families often referred to the boarding house as the "Shy-of-Food Inn."

A letter dated 6 August 1895 from George Booker, manager of the Sherwood Inn, indicated that Post Trader Baulch had complained to Colonel R T Frank that geese congregating at his house prevented him from sleeping after 3:00 AM. Booker responded as follows:

Sherwood Inn, circa 1910.

"Sir: Your communication informing me that complaint had been made to the commanding officer to the effect that my geese had proved a nuisance has just been received. Two months ago, when two sedate and well-behaved geese in good faith and decorous manner added seven goslins to the feathered stock of the Sherwood's reserve, I had but little thought that beyond the guests at my table they would ever receive attention, and I am very sorrowful that their geese-like dispositions have led to complaint. As I have regarded from time to time with pride of proprietorship the growth of the geese I have cherished the idea that they might serve as those of Rome, in some nobler purpose than padding pillows and furnishing food for an impecunious people. I know nothing of the attack upon my devoted flock; enough for me to know that it is a nuisance. I recall a charge upon a flock of geese that put them all to flight, save one sturdy gander, but in obedience to the tenor of your letter, I have deemed it best to slay my entire flock, and I take pleasure in assuring the Commanding Officer, that by this hour of high noon tomorrow that these presumptuous and perilous birds will be slain in cold blood and the sleepless nights of all our friends be fully avenged. With greatest respect, I have the honor to be,

Your Obedient servant,
Geo Booker

In December 1896, the top three stories of the Sherwood Inn burned. The building was modified and expanded over the years, but not without problems involving gambling, the serving of alcoholic beverages, inadequate sewage, and frequent fires. The government bought the premises in 1918 and operated it as quarters for officers and their families until 1932. It was razed when Randolph Hall was constructed (near the main gate) to accommodate bachelor officers.

St. Mary's Catholic Church

The cornerstone of the first St. Mary's, Star of the Sea, was laid on 9 August 1860 with the approval of the Secretary of War, with the stipulation that it was subject to removal if it offered impediment, and was only to be used as a place of worship. Prior to this first edifice, Father Thomas Hore, an Irish Jesuit, attended to the religious needs of the area from 1824 to 1834, followed by Father Walter Moriarity of Portsmouth, who served until 1844.

48

Reverend Matthew O'Keefe was the first pastor of the new church, and nursing of the ill was carried out by the Sisters of Charity and Mercy. Records state that this first church was painted "either red or black." Permission to build a frame house at 7 Frank Lane for the priest's residence was granted by the Virginia Legislature Act (1876) and by the Secretary of War in 1876. Permission was required because the chapel was owned by the church who provided priests.

The erection of the present church was started on 15 February 1903 on land deemed to be under the control of the commanding officer of Fort Monroe. The engineer department was requested to outline the metes and bounds. When the wooden spires on each corner tower became unsafe, they were removed in 1965.

Noncommissioned Officers' Quarters, Tidball Road

The first four sets of brick duplex quarters along Tidball, west of the Catholic Church, were built in 1906 at a cost of $6,019; the last three sets, facing west, were built for noncommissioned staff officers in 1909 at a cost of $7,193.85.

C S Hough (pronounced Huff) wrote that his father, Sergeant H P Hough, came to Fort Monroe as an army field clerk at the turn of the century, and that he had been born in a house at 3 Frank Lane, which no longer exists. His father went to France in WWI as private secretary to Chief of Staff General Peyton C March, stayed on with General Westervelt, and spent a total of 45 years in the Army. As a warrant officer, he was chief clerk and private secretary to General Short when Pearl Harbor was bombed in 1941. His son had this story to tell about General Matthew B Ridgway:

> When Matt was eight or nine years old, he used to like to beat up Sergeant Hough's son. When Matt's father heard of this, he told the Sergeant that if he ever caught Matt doing anything deserving of punishment, he should take care of it on the spot. Not long afterward, young Matt felt Sergeant Hough's belt on the seat of his pants. Matt was indelibly impressed, for when they met again in General Short's office during WWII, General Ridgway pointed his finger at Hough and said: "I remember you--you once gave me a heck of a whacking!"

49

Colonel W D Wooldridge wrote that was he born at 23 Hatch Street in 1925, and lived at 28 Tidball and 19 Murray Streets until 1942. He recalled

...the Post Commander riding around the fort on his horse followed by a red daschund; the old Liberty Theater near Reeder Circle; the elementary school near the Postern Gate; the demise of the riding rings due to construction of the present theater; fishing trips on the Mine Planter Schofield, etc. But, during my own career I never had the good fortune to be stationed at Fort Monroe.

Lieutenant Colonel W P Farley wrote that he lived at 24 Tidball Road, opposite the old Chesapeake & Ohio railroad station, during the depression years (1933 to 1935). He recalled observing the Civilian Conservation Corps boys detraining and marching to the hospital for physical exams, then being outfitted by the Quartermaster Corps with clothing and equipment. He stated they were able to process about 300 men per day.

YMCA

In 1889 the YMCA was granted six casemate rooms formerly assigned as officers' quarters. By 1903, electric lights had been installed in these rooms where night classes were given in writing, history, geography, algebra, spelling and grammar to an enrollment of 183 enlisted men. The present YMCA was built in 1903 with funds given by Helen Miller Gould in memory of her husband. It was suggested that the new building should include one billiard table and three pool tables inasmuch as the men "took kindly" to pool. It is unusual for a civilian establishment to be erected within a military post.

West Sallyport

The guard rooms and jail were located within the inner walls of this gateway. Escapes were rare, and sentences included: hard labor with a 32-pound ball and chain on one leg; an iron collar with five- to ten-pound weights; solitary confinement; a diet of bread and water for up to 40 days; sitting on a wooden horse under a gallows with a rope around the neck; being indelibly marked with india ink with a "D" for deserter, or with an "M" on a hip or arm for mutineer; or having the right side of the head shaved and the other side tarred and feathered.

There is some conjecture that a flagstaff might have been located at this main gate. A letter dated 11 May 1868 from the Post Surgeon to Major General W F Barry drew attention to a serious matter regarding the placement of the flagpole:

I have observed that the flagstaff is located immediately over one of the principal magazines of the fort. The Ordnance Department has affixed a lightning rod to the staff, thereby acknowledging the danger. Should the rod become in the slightest degree out of order, the danger would be greater than if it wasn't there, for the electric fluid would be attracted to it and carried by it to the parapet, and thence to the magazine. Should the magazine explode, this fort would be blown to atoms, and in all probability, the lives of all in it destroyed. Would it not be prudent to have the flagstaff moved to the bastion over the Sutler's Store?

In 1898, the Inspector General cited inadequate storage of ammunition in the Carroll Hall magazines and suggested that it be removed as worthless and a menace to the post. He stated that loaded shells, fixed ammunition, etc., left over from the "late Rebellion or previous wars," constituted a dangerous situation due to split barrels spilling powder all over the floor.

There were frequent requests to place memorial tablets in various places on the post. A standard reply was that a General Order dated 19 March 1890 stated that the only inscription or emblem proper to place over the main entrance to a work like Fort Monroe was "that which was descriptive of the character, object or purpose of the work," and that a more appropriate place for proposed memorial tablets would be the Chapel. However, in response to a letter to the War Department of 28 May 1890 requesting permission to place a bronze metal tablet in the masonry work of the main entrance of Fort Monroe, the adjutant general informed the commanding officer of Fort Monroe that: "Permission has been given for a tablet to be placed by the main gate to the fort to commemorate the service of the 3d Pennsylvania Heavy Artillery and 188th Pennsylvania Volunteers [during the Civil War]."

Carroll Hall, where ex-Confederate President Jefferson Davis was moved from the damp casemate rooms, stood in the bastion to the left of this sallyport. A ramp was built from his upper floor cellrooms to the rampart to permit him to exercise unobserved. The building was razed in 1902.

Moat Walk

The small double sets of quarters facing the moat at 5-7, 9-11, and 13-15 Moat Walk were completed in June, 1911 for noncommissioned officers. They were constructed from General Quartermaster Plan #85 at a cost of $6,663.69 and are described as a colonial revival style. The two-story brick building at 21 Moat Walk was built in 1900 as quarters for the Hospital Steward at a cost of $3,124. A kitchen was added in 1918.

Administration Building or Post Headquarters

At the West Sallyport, the administration building was constructed in 1894 at a cost of $10,833. Before laying the concrete floor, water and sewage pipes were installed to a cesspool outside the building, and sinks and closets were provided for. A basement was added in 1914 and the fireplaces and chimneys removed. At one time the wide breezeway entry and offices on either side were handsomely carpeted.

Engine House and Children's School

The site for an engine house with a schoolroom to be located on the second floor was approved in October 1886, and $5,000 was allotted for construction in December. Furniture for the schoolroom was ordered in May.

Regarding a children's school, in 1856 it was suggested that families send their youngsters to be instructed by the chaplain. In 1864, Private J H Stover was detailed to teach a post school located at "one end of the Officers' Billiard Room" in the casemates. The school was open five days a week, from 9:00 to 12:00 AM, and from 2:00 to 5:00 PM for children, and from retreat until tattoo for the soldiers. An October, 1878 report stated there were 123 children at Fort Monroe, 52 of whom were over the age of five.

There are 36 attending school: 26 go to the Catholic School at $1/month; five attend Miss Lindsay's school at $1.50/month; and five attend Mr. Hughes school at Mill Creek for $1/month. Three children, 7-9 years of age, already work.

In December 1878, the Adjutant General's Office declared that all children not working should attend school and, directed the commanding officer to establish a school for children of noncommissioned officers, but not to interfere with parochial or private schools.

Hospital Building, 23 Ingalls

The first hospital was located inside the fort and was described as a three-story brick building of 12 rooms with a slate roof, cistern, and pillared porches on the first and second floors. The present structure was constructed in 1898 for $22,695, and in 1912 an isolation building was placed between the hospital and the noncommissioned officers' quarters on Moat Walk. Wings were added and later replaced, and the building has undergone so many changes that it has lost all architectural integrity. The hospital was downgraded to a clinic in 1974 and surplus rooms were converted into offices.

A nurses' quarters for six females was constructed in 1921 at 7-9 Patch Road at a cost of $25,000. The building was converted into duplex quarters in 1950.

Brick double quarters on west side of Ingalls

On 8 May 1904, the Quartermaster General directed that three double sets of quarters be constructed on the ground north of the Catholic Chapel. Architect Paul Pelz is credited with designing the floor plans of these spacious houses which were completed in March 1906 at a cost of $35,153.48 each. As a child, General Matt Ridgway lived at 59 Ingalls.

Retired Brigadier General H F Nichols wrote that he remembered Major Fulton Quintus Cincinnatus Gardner (retired as a Major General) who lived at 63 Ingalls from 1925 to 1927, who had the left fender ripped off his Ford when he foolishly left it parked on the street on New Year's Eve.

Quarters at 67-69 Ingalls

These two-story brick quarters have the same floor plan as the units at 2-4 Ruckman, and were completed in 1909 for captains at a cost of $26,537.45. As a Major, R W Pearson (Dental Corps) lived in rented quarters in Hampton when the Hotel Chamberlin burned. He recalled that they

purchased a set of ironstone breakfast dishes at the fire sale, and from 1921 to 1924 we lived at 69 Ingalls where our premature twins were born. Our young sons still remember Old Black William who drove a cab slowly through the officers' quarters to pick up those who wished to go shopping.

Lieutenant Colonel G L Wertenbaker lived here from 1920 to 1921. He was ordered to Fort Monroe in 1924 to replace Major W S Bowen as director of the advanced course. Teetotaler Brigadier General "Sahara Bill" Smith was in command and prohibition was in effect. "Werty" was caught "under the influence" and was tried, fined, relieved, and ordered to Panama where he did a commendable job and walked the straight and narrow until his honorable retirement in 1932.

The Arsenal

The original arsenal was an accidental outgrowth from the establishment of the Artillery School in 1824. When Congress reduced the Army, the Ordnance Corps was abolished from 1821 to 1832, when it was reinstituted. During this period, ordnance officers and men were assigned to artillery units. By 1832 there were two officers and four enlisted men doing ordnance work at Fort Monroe. In 1833 the installation became an Ordnance Depot, and by 1836 it was termed an Arsenal, employing 39 workers.

The arsenal blew up on 22 June 1855 while explosives were being mixed to prepare fireworks. The present building was erected in 1860 and employed up to 500 men during the Civil War to manufacture rifled cannon. In June 1868, the Ordnance Department approved the use of part of the facility for a lab for the Artillery School, and the entire building was eventually turned over to the Artillery units by 1891. The arsenal was declared closed by 1901. In 1911 the building was used as a warehouse for quartermaster supplies until the Post Commissary was installed there in 1946. Later it served as the Quartermaster Sales Store, then as the Signal Field Maintenance Shop until 1973 when it was converted into office space.

Noncommissioned Officers' Quarters on Hatch Lane and Patch Road

The odd little one-story brick quarters at 17-19 and 21-23 Hatch were built in May 1908, for firemen of the Coast Artillery Corps at a cost of $4,780. The heating systems were added in 1946 and the kitchens and bathrooms modernized in 1966. The quarters on Patch were built in 1911 at a cost of $6,376.69.

73 Ingalls

Across from the arsenal is a two-story, single set of quarters built for a field grade officer in 1909 at a cost of $14,987.10. Until 1945, this house was almost exclusively assigned to an officer of the Medical Corps due to its proximity to the Post Hospital.

75 Ingalls

The actual date of construction of this fine set of officers' quarters is not certain. It is shown with the same small outbuildings on a June 1877 blueprint and is labeled "Ordnance Quarters." An 1885 Quartermaster report states that the building was "recently built." It could have been built by the Ordnance Department as quarters for the commanding officer of the Fort Monroe arsenal and turned over to the Artillery Corps when the arsenal was abandoned. The small two-story brick structure in the side yard was built about the same time. It is sometimes referred to as a garage, but may have been used as an office, or a carriage house and servant's quarters. The house was originally oriented toward the south, facing a road that ran to the Hampton wharf. Doors were placed on the east side to reorient the house toward Ingalls Road. Baths were added in 1900; the building was extensively remodeled in 1910-11; and the kitchen was updated in 1950.

Major L Babbitt, Ordnance, was the first recorded occupant from 1883 to 1887. Major R E Callan lived here from 1913 to 1916; an 1896 West Point graduate, he became Commandant of the Coast Artillery School and retired as a major general in 1936. Major Robert Arthur, the Coast Artillery School's librarian from 1924 to 1927, lived in this house while compiling data for *The Coast Artillery School, 1824-1927* (The Artillery School: 1928).

Colonel E A Coates, Jr (Medical Corps) lived here from 1931 to 1936:

We've many happy memories of Fort Monroe and the people we knew there. Less happy are the memories of the hurricane which flooded our yard, and at high tide, came within a quarter of an inch of entering our front door. Our car was in the shed beside the house, and the salt water came up to the seats. The only fortunate ones were those who drove their cars up the ramparts.

Armistead Hall, Visiting Officers' Quarters

An April 1875 drawing describes a concrete two-story bachelor officers' quarters to be built at 80-81 Ingalls with a piazza on the front, and 16 officers' rooms, each with a fireplace. In the attic there were to be four rooms, a bath, and a water closet. Servants were to be allowed to cook there--if done with care.

The present brick structure was built in 1897 from a Paul Pelz design at a cost of $14,963. The building remained a Bachelor Officers' Quarters (BOQ) until 1933. Kitchens were added in 1927 for eight two-room suites. The heating system was replaced in 1957, the fire escape added in 1970, and the structure was converted to four VIP suites in 1972. Brass plaques in these apartments commemorate the visit of Mamie Eisenhower; the residence of Major General Elizabeth Hoisington, when assigned these quarters as a Major; and the residence of Medal of Honor winner Major General Charlie Black from 1974 to 1976.

The Old Hundred Building on Ingalls

This building designed by Paul Pelz in 1903 and constructed in 1906 had 30 bachelor apartments, each consisting of a parlor, bedroom, and a bath. In 1925, the twenty apartments on the lower two floors were converted into ten larger apartments for married officers. In doing this, some parlors were turned into bedrooms, and some bedrooms were converted into dining rooms. Five two-story rear wings were added to provide kitchen facilities. The building was modernized in 1941 and rewired in 1958. Bathrooms were modernized in 1960 and the molded tin ceilings removed. In 1964, the building was converted to office space and in 1985 the structure was entirely gutted and redone as offices.

There are many stories told about this building by former occupants. Contrary to its name, the building was neither a hundred years old, nor had a hundred people living there at the same time. However, these brick walls witnessed many more than one hundred officers who arrived there as second lieutenants and rose to high rank before retirement. The roster of "Bars to Stars" is impressive. [See "Bars to Stars: General Officers" for a listing of men who attained the rank General.]

Retired Colonel J H Cochran said that his West Point class graduated the largest number of cadets up to that date:

Of those, 31 were assigned to the Coast Artillery, and 22 went to Fort Monroe as their first station. Five brought their brides and lived in the Tuileries. The rest lived in the Old Hundred Building.

Social calling was mandatory, and Sunday afternoons were devoted to this exercise in futility. This became particularly burdensome when the new school class came in November. So, Sunday afternoons, John Kahle and I would don blue dress uniforms and white gloves and fare forth, armed with a pocket full of calling cards. We would first find a married couple similarly engaged and use them as bird dogs. We followed them so long as they failed to gain admission anywhere, and left our cards behind theirs. However, as soon as they found someone at home, we cut off and found another pair of bird dogs. That way we made our Sunday afternoons quite profitable.

Lloyd Shepard said that when he and his wife occupied rooms in this building in 1926, they modified the unit by adding a folding shelf over the bathtub, and a two-burner hot plate over the commode, thus making a kitchen/bath unit. "Our other luxurious accommodations at this lovely old post were during the Field Officers' Course in 1929 when we lived in WWI barracks in The Fill, which had been converted into duplexes." [The Fill was land reclaimed from Mill Creek on the north side of the fort. Here, 250 barracks were built for the Training Center, which turned out 4,400 officers in 15 months. After the war, these cantonment buildings were used as quarters for captains and lieutenants attending the Coast Artillery School. Many retirees recalled this substandard housing where a Steinway grand piano might be overshadowed by a sawdust-filled ice box.]

Retired General R W Haines brought his bride to the Old Hundred Building in 1933, arriving a few days after a hurricane had devastated the shoreline of the post, and a few days before the arrival of a second but less severe hurricane. He was a lieutenant assigned as a battery officer in Battery F, 52nd Coast Artillery (Railway) which had two eight-foot railway guns as its primary armament.

Retired Colonel F E Day recalled Clem and Claud Gunn, identical twins who lived at Fort Monroe about 1937 or 1938. He remembered that the twins had a unique manner of dealing with the required social calls. Retired Colonel C O Gunn told the story this way:

My brother and I came to Fort Monroe to attend the Battery Officers' Course. Trying to get settled in the Old Hundred

57

Building, we took time out to get dressed and make our social call on Brigadier General J W Gulick [he later became Chief of Coast Artillery] and his wife. As we neared their quarters, Claud's wife noticed that he was wearing a red [sic] tie instead of a uniform tie. Since we were far from our quarters, and since we were identical twins, we decided that my wife and I would call, return to our car unseen, and I would take Claud's wife and return to the Commanding Officer's quarters to pay their call. This we did, without him or his wife knowing--we thought. Both were very cordial to me and each of my wives on both calls.

Retired Brigadier General Seth L Weld, Jr (son of a Mexican Border Service Medal of Honor winner) wrote:

When we lived in the Old Hundred in 1939, it had been converted into married quarters by cutting through the bathroom walls, leaving one bathroom, and converting the other into a pantry, and putting the kitchen in an added wooden structure on the back of the building. Each unit had a living room, dining room, and two bedrooms, but only on the first two floors. The two bachelor units on the third floor were handled differently. Each retained the living room and bath configuration, and was augmented by space on the fourth floor [attic] where a kitchen was installed along with another room which could be a bedroom or a dining room. Of course, access to the fourth floor was the public stairway in the center of each division of the building.

General H A Miley, Jr arrived at Fort Monroe in 1941 as a new Second Lieutenant with his bride of six weeks:

The Old Hundred Building was our first set of Army quarters, and we loved every minute of our life there. The quarters were unusual, even for those days. The sitting room and bedroom were on the fourth floor. To get from the third floor rooms we had to emerge into the common hall and climb the common stairwell which could be awkward. For reasons not quite clear to me now, every Saturday afternoon when the weather was good, I donned my blue uniform and walked with my wife and two beagles down to the ferry landing to buy the New York Times. Years later, another resident of the post at the time told me that this formation was a conversation piece among the garrison.

Haarlem, or the second half of the White Elephants

Colonel J H Cochran recalled that the double sets of frame quarters on Ingalls Road across from the Old Hundred Building were popularly known as Haarlem. The origin of the name is unknown; perhaps it was considered a "suburb" of Phoebus, and so given the name of New York's suburb of Haarlem. Fort Monroe Facilities Engineer records call these frame houses the rest of the White Elephants built in 1891. The original cost of each house was $9,503; they were modified with kitchens and bathrooms in 1908, and entered on permanent historical records in October 1939.

At 93 Ingalls, General Matthew B Ridgway was born in the south front second-story bedroom on 3 March 1895. [The Ridgway family also lived at 59 Ingalls 1906-1908, and at 37 Fenwick 1908-1909]. General Ridgway wrote that: "Of my years in Hampton High School, I have the happiest of memories. I could never then have dreamed of such an honor as to have a park named after me." [This park is located in Hampton, off Mercury Boulevard.]

Captain J P Wisser, for whom the Coast Artillery School Library was named, lived at 89 Ingalls from 1897 to 1902. A West Point graduate of 1874, and graduate of the Artillery School in 1878, he was editor of the *Journal for the US Artillery* from 1895 to 1901.

R D Brown, who lived at 87 Ingalls from 1920 to 1921 recalled:

> Since I had been overseas in WWI, I was assigned to Fort Monroe to teach Artillery Fire Problem Calculation and Military Law. Along with Major O L Spiller, I also taught equitation to junior officers. We were both US Naval Academy graduates--teaching equitation! It was a colorful sight to see the long line of riders pass along Ingalls every afternoon. The horse I rode was named "Pershing." Few officers liked that horse as he was rather wild. On one occasion he was sentenced to be shot, but I intervened.
>
> I returned for the Advanced Course in 1925 and lived in those awful quarters on "The Fill." Prior to reporting in, we had been in Paris for two years where I attended the *Ecole Superieur de Guerre*. We lived most comfortably there, for the rate of exchange was in our favor. To step down to converted barracks where our little quarters were heated by a small iron stove in the living room was truly a case of feast or famine.

During 1923 and 1924, Major Spiller, commander of the 61st Anti-Aircraft Artillery Regiment, lived at 91 Ingalls. Retired Colonel M G Cary recalled that during that time,

> Major Spiller received several remounts from a camp west of Washington DC, and he spent extra time training them. The riding stable was maintained at the Coast Artillery School with at least fifty or more horses. Riding classes were given to all students. However, when I returned in 1926, the horses were gone and the stables which had stood near the Chesapeake & Ohio railroad station were being torn down.

The fire department records report that a Studebaker sedan parked in front of 81-83 Ingalls on 1 January 1932 caught on fire, severely damaging the upholstery and rear seat cushions. The car bore New Jersey license plate M-25192, and a Fort Hancock post sticker #19. Was the owner a guest, or one of the residents at the time (Captain C Kerr or First Lieutenant R I Glasgow)?

As a captain living at 89 Ingalls from 1933 to 1936, H T Benz recalled that in 1934, many lieutenants had 16 years of service, for the "accelerated promotion with ten years-in-grade" did not become effective until the summer of 1935. This was the Depression era. No one was promoted, no increases in pay were given, and many times, no paychecks were issued. Even Eisenhower was a Captain for 17 years. If anyone was promoted with only ten years in grade, that was considered "accelerated".

As a Lieutenant, A R Thomas lived at 95 Ingalls Road during 1934 and 1935. He had these memories to share. He praised a lady named Alma who served as cook, amah, cleaning lady, and lavandera. He also remembered the time his oldest son, then three and one-half years old, started the car and drove off. Fortunately, his mother-in-law was in the car and averted a tragedy. He enjoyed weekend hops at the Casemate Club, as well as hunting for ducks and frogs at Big Bethel reservoir, for fox near the Mariner's Museum and Toana, for raccoon and turkey at old Fort Eustis, and for deer near Savage Station:

> I never got back to Fort Monroe while on active service. After I retired in 1942, I helped install the gun-data computers for the new 16-inch rifles at Fort Story. I wrote the technical manuals for that equipment while with Sperry Gyroscope. Everything was probably scrapped years ago.

Major H C Mabbott lived at 85 Ingalls from 1934 to 1936.
He is credited with the following poem written after WWII:

"Tay-time"
The General sat on the anxious seat
Watching his troops in the battle's heat
When a courier rode up in the shell-torn street
With a message grave that spelled defeat
Unless the reserves could stem the retreat.
The General studied his battle map,
He figured a plan to escape the trap
He jumped in his Jeep and buckled his strap,
But his batman placed a tray in his lap
And his Adjutant said, "I sye ol' chap,
You cawn't do it now--it's tay-time."

From her rural abode to the big city's grime,
The innocent girl was lured by the swine,
The villain had told her her form was divine,
He clothed her in furs and lingerie fine,
He showed her his etchings and plied her with wine.
She drank one too many, but she didn't know,
In the villain's embrace her resistance was low,
But she slapped him aside as she started to go,
And she said to the CAD, non-plussed by the blow,
"I won't be seduced for an hour or so,
You cawn't do it now--it's tay-time."

And soon we will come to the end of the War
When the culprits are caught and are free no more,
With Benito and Adolph behind a steel door,
And a mass execution as our last dirty chore.
"Death by the musket," the world will demand,
And Monty's picked troops, with rifle in hand,
Stand ready to shoot at the word of command,
When some noisy Cockney, sipping Lipton's best brand,
Will stop the whole show by a shout from the stand,
"You cawn't do it now--it's tay-time."

As a Captain, L W Bartlett lived at 93 Ingalls from 1938 to
1939. He recalled a fellow officer named George Ray Burgess who
married a wealthy girl. In 1930, they lived in a three-story mansion in Hampton and gave memorable parties. George Ray was

driven to class each day by a chauffeur. Despite having the best polo equipment available, he never became adept at the game, but he wore a long camel's hair polo coat which Colonel Bartlett envied and still remembered.

The Cavalry House

This 2-story brick building at 101-103 Ingalls was erected in 1909 for $22,942.55 as a double set of quarters for captains. It was called the Cavalry House since it was usually reserved for the equitation officer assigned to the Coast Artillery School.

The following extract is from *Chronicle of Aunt Lena*, by Brigadier General Frank S Clark, who lived in 103 Ingalls from 1919 to 1924:

As I look back over the years, I realize that Fort Monroe which we knew during 1919-1924 was the callingest garrison in which we ever served....The reasons for the diminution in calling are obvious. In those early days, very few officers owned automobiles, so there was less urge and opportunity to leave the post during free time. As garrisons became larger, the requirements for formal paying and repaying first calls became so onerous that the practice was quite generally adopted of holding a garrison reception, by which the obligations of first calls and their repayment was discharged....

I recall the Cape Henry seafood restaurant, O'Keefe's, which we reached by taking the ferry to Willoughby Spit, and a trolley on 16 miles to Cape Henry. The specialty was roasted Lynnhaven oysters, served on a slab of heavy plank at each place to hold hot oysters on the half-shell. The dinner plate held the hot soup plate--so hot that when melted butter was dropped in it the butter would sizzle. There was a covered dish of French fried potatoes, a bowl of melted butter, condiments, appetizers, and coffee. You received a complete new layout for each dozen oysters ordered. I once had four dozen! Such was youth!

In June 1920 I was demoted from LTC to my permanent grade of Captain, and in August promoted to permanent Major. I served as a Major for over 13 years before becoming a Lieutenant Colonel again.

Retired Colonel J R Bartlett described post life in the late 1920s:

Everyone who has spent any time in the service can tell many an amusing story, and a few fatal ones. Major H N Estes, the Cavalry Instructor for the Field Officers' Course, was a lifelong cavalryman, and very rightly had a very low opinion of the riding ability of Coast Artillery officers. [He lived at 103 Ingalls from 1927 to 1930.] I had grown up on a ranch in Kansas, so I rode horses before I was tall enough to mount without climbing on a wagon or fence. Knowing that, Major Estes assigned me the horse privately owned by the Chaplain. She was a nice, small mare, only green-broken. One day when Estes had us jumping she threw me. I had taken her toward a four-foot jump, and she started her jump one leap before I expected it. I was sitting flat and it hurt her. She whirled and knocked me off against the gate. I wore my arm in a cast for a while.

When Major Estes took off his headgear, he bore a striking resemblance to the infamous Italian dictator, so of course all the students called him Mussolini (but not to his face). The riding class left the corral in columns of two and went up the beach. After leaving the post, Estes would give the arm signal to gallop, and right away the whole class was in a dead run. One day, when the tide was out, there were many tidepools left on the beach. Estes came to a large pool cut quite deep by the tidal flow and he and his horse went end over end. He brushed himself off and said: "That's a good example of dismounting without a command."

A fire at 101 Ingalls in 1939 started on the second floor and burned into the attic. The fire was confined to two attic rooms, but spread under the tile roof and went over the firewall due to arched tile forming the passageway. The damage was recorded at $4,750. The post has an enviable fire-free record. Only one house was lost to fire, and only one warehouse fire caused assistance to be requested from nearby civilian fire stations. That could have been avoided had a railroad engineer not elected to move his engine, for reasons known only unto himself, thereby cutting the fire hoses strung across the track.

Another warehouse fire was reported as "being caused by children, locked in a room at one end of the building." There was no further explanation in the fire log entry.

K C Smith recalled that when the Fred Chamberlains lived in 103 Ingalls in 1940, Mrs Chamberlain asked the Post Engineer,

Walt Ellis, to cut an archway between some rooms. When he wouldn't, she took an axe and made the opening herself.

Student Quarters

Proceeding toward the main gate, the quadriplex quarters on the east side of Ingalls were built in 1934 (under Roosevelt's Works Project Administration) as quarters for students of the Coast Artillery School. The period from 1934 to 1941 was the only time that housing was considered to be adequate at Fort Monroe. At one time a railway gun was located in Reeder Circle which many Army children remember playing on. (It was melted down during WWII.) These four-unit apartments were quite adequate for junior officers attending the Artillery School. However, after WWII, when Fort Monroe began serving as a high headquarters, many senior officers eagerly sought the small apartments, since industry had expanded rapidly in the Tidewater area without a comparable increase in housing. Although these quarters are not old enough to be considered historical, their officer occupants are recorded. When housing needs permit, these units are now offered to senior noncommissioned officers.

Randolph Hall

When the Sherwood Inn was ordered demolished, authority was granted to build bachelor officers' quarters by the main entrance to the post. Located on the east side of Ingalls, Randolph Hall was completed early in the 1930's for a cost of $143,149.42. It was named in honor of Brigadier General W F Randolph, Chief of Artillery from 1903 to 1904. It continued in existence until converted to barracks in 1969. The porch was removed in 1971, the slate roof replaced in 1978, and air-conditioning was added in 1987.

* * * * * * * *

The walls of Fort Monroe's historic quarters have witnessed rich personal histories that echo laughter and tears, pride and disappointment, camaraderie and keen competition--preludes of individual destinies. Here, dedicated professionals have progressed from wide-eyed youths, to well-trained soldiers, to valiant commanders and heroes in the service of their country.

Further information about items of interest preserved in the National Archives, Washington, DC, follow as appendices.

APPENDIX I.   COST OF FORT MONROE BATTERIES

Nov 1901: Chief of Engineers to the Secretary of War: "The old Water Battery lying in front of masonry at Fort Monroe is now obsolete and forms no feature of modern defense. It must be removed to insure safety of the detachments in the new batteries to be erected upon the beach...the spalls thrown out by impact of a hostile shot passing over the new batteries would be certain to imperil the men at the guns...the stone could be used in the construction of seawalls between jetties #1 and #2...work will commence next March."

May 1903: Engineer Office to the Commanding Officer of Fort Monroe records the following information regarding the date and cost of erection of completed batteries at Fort Monroe.

8" BL Rifles, completed Nov 1898 for $3274.61.

Battery DeRussy, constructed from 1889 to 1901 for $142,348...deactivated in 1944 and its armament removed for scrap.

Battery Ruggles built 1897; cost $48,670.

Battery Anderson built 1897; cost $194,720.26.

Battery Gatewood built Sep 1898; cost $2,955.63.

Battery Church built 1901; cost $90,473.33.

Battery Eustis completed Jan 1901 for $80,766.67; guns mounted 1899; not turned over to the Artillery until 1900).

Redoubt A completed Mar 1897 for $175,347.50.

Mining casemate near main entrance to main work completed Oct 1901 for $29,456.15.

Mining casemate near Redoubt A completed Dec 1901 for $16,046.97

Battery CO's Station (Mortar) completed Oct 1901 for $5,852.26.

Fire CO's Station completed Feb 1898 for $1,788.64.

[The Fort Monroe Facilities Engineer states that Battery Irwin was built in 1903, and Battery Parrot in 1906; no costs are given.]

APPENDIX II. UTILITIES AND SANITATION

1849 to 1854: Casemate families are to clean out privys or they will be torn down and families turned out of quarters.

Jul 1856: All bathing in the sea is prohibited between 6:00 AM and 8:00 PM, and never within sight of dwellings; negroes at no time.

Oct 1861: If there are not enough prisoners to cut wood, the police detail shall help.

Feb 1862: The yards in the rear of the officers' quarters are filthy. All slops and ashes will be placed in barrels behind the quarters for the police cart to pick up. Empties may be obtained from the Commissary.

May 1862: All noncommissioned officers will march men to the bathing ground in front of the Water Batteries. Stragglers will be confined. Prisoners will be heavily guarded and will bathe only on Wednesdays and Saturdays.

1863: Fresh water in the gravel stratum was so diminished as to allow seepage. The Engineers went 930 feet seeking an artesian well; a water company plans to go 2,000 feet.

Aug 1865: Without authority, a cistern, built in accordance with a plan during General Wool's tenure, was constructed of old brick. It didn't cost much, and allowed the fire equipment to be washed.

Dec 1865: Colonel Burton to the Adjutant: "You are ordered to inspect buildings and areas needing cleanup and work. The obnoxious odours and vapors arising from filth, decaying wood, and piles of garbage indicates too clearly what may be expected later unless measures are taken promptly."

Feb 1873: Quartermaster General to Post QM: "Regarding your request to use kerosene oil for illuminating, provided it is used in the Cleveland Patent Safety Lamps, you are informed that experiments at Willets Point in the Hurricane Safety Lamp were not satisfactory. Authority has been given to experiment with the same oil in metal lamps without cotton filling but the report is not in."

May 1873: Commanding Officer General Barry to Major Craighill, QM: "You are authorized to build a brick cistern of 60,000 gallons."

Jun 1874: Post Engineer to Gen Barry: "There are three cisterns: One at Engineers office, one near the carpenter's shop, and one behind the Catholic Church. There are 60,000 gallons of particularly good water which is being drained from clean slate roofs. They are all full, and cannot accept further rainfall. It may be well to drain off some of the water."

Nov 1874: QM to Adj: The cost of emptying sinks and slops, and payments made by Company, civilian enterprises, and officers:

Co A	$8.85	Mr. Baulch	$3.00
Co B	$9.05	Browning	$.75
Co C	$10.80	Winnie	$1.00
Co K	$9.00	Dare	$1.00
Co I	$14.50	McGrew	$1.50
		Officers	$18.40

Total:	$60.20
4 months pay for night soil men:	$180.00

Sep 1878: The Secretary of War orders that "water closets in buildings are prohibited. They must be in a room detached from the body of the dwelling, and shut off by a closed door."

Sep 1880: QM to Adj: "As this post is dependent on rain for its water supply, I report the following cistern capacities:

2 cisterns, new barracks	252,000 gals
1st Front Casemate circular cistern	34,000 "
2nd Front Casemate circular cistern	34,000 "
3d Front Casemate circular cistern	34,000 "
Four Tuilerie cisterns	18,000 "
Carroll Hall cistern	19,700 "
Hospital cistern	7,800 "
Two cisterns Quarters #1	13,500 "
Chapel cistern	14,000 "
Condensed water cistern	47,000 "
One cistern at new Co Officers' Qtrs (Colonel Lodor, near Chapel)	28,000 "
One cistern at Photograph Room	6,500 "
Two cisterns at Ordnance storehouses, outside the fort, 52,000 gals each	104,000 "
Total cistern capacity	612,500 "

Mar 1883: Officers in casemates have either earth closets in each set for their families, or a small exposed building for bachelors despite the order of the Secretary of War prohibiting this practice.

Jan 1884: Approval is granted by the Adjutant General's Office for a new sewer system to be constructed.

Dec 1885: Post Surgeon, Joe Smith, to the Adj: "A six-month supply of medicines has been received with "the exception of 4 ounces of nutmeg." [Needed for eggnog?]

Jan 1886: Col Tidball to the US Engineer: "When there are heavy rains or irregular tides, water stands upon the parade ground to such an extent as to be highly injurious and inconvenient. This is due to water retained in the moat by the sluice gates which prevents drainage of the inside of the fort. Surplus water must be removed from the moat requiring about two hours daily. The NW sluice gate can be opened by means of a capstan and chain, the weight raised being 1,000 pounds. A horizontal windlass similar to that used on a ship to hoist the anchor is needed for each gate. A better arrangement would be to have the automatic gate attached to a frame sliding vertically, thus needing less power to raise it."

Jan 1886: All children on post shall be vaccinated.

Jun 1886: Six cases of malaria have occurred in two days.

Jun 1887: A tank is being built to test the proposal of flushing sewer pipes. Effort will be made to use iron pipes to replace the terra cotta pipes which have rough spots at the joinings causing choking substances to cling there.

Sep 1887: The QM was responsible for stores of cords of hard and soft wood and anthracite coal for heating; oats and hay forage for draught animals; and straw which was used both for animal bedding and to stuff mattresses of soldiers.

Oct 1887: Col Tidball to the AGO: "The Soldiers' Home in Hampton, and the hotels at Fort Monroe are to be lighted by electricity. Permission is requested to have estimates made for electrifying Fort Monroe."

Nov 1887: The analysis of the cistern water shows that it is unusually pure. There is an axiom that there is no better water than that from a slate roof, contained in masonry cisterns. The cisterns stand above ground so that no soaking can enter.

Nov 1887: Col Tidball to the AGO: "The sinks are quite recent (1880), and built of brick with brick floors laid on cement. They are impervious to drippings. The interior arrangements were put in after the introduction of the present water supply three years ago, and work satisfactorily. The drippings of urine complained about are the same as occur everywhere men urinate. It is kept swabbed up, and the little dribblings that go out the doors are so triffling as hardly to make an item for objections. There are objections to emptying the main sewer into the bay instead of Mill

Creek. It probably wouldn't even work, and if it did, the discharge would be on the beach in front of the fort to the great discomfort of anyone setting foot on the reservation. Discharge into Mill Creek is free from offense to anyone, owing to the low and flat condition of the site. The sewage problem here is not to be solved by a hasty glance over the premises."

Jun 1888: The Adj to Captain W P Rose: "The CO desires that you give your attention to the subject of electricity and make yourself familiar with it so as to be able to instruct in it. Your mechanical turn of mind will be of great advantage to you."

Jul 1888: Col Tidball to District of Columbia Engineers: "Water consumption at Fort Monroe is 25,000 gallons per day, for 692 persons, not counting any connected with the hotel nor [the] boarding house, 435 of whom live within the fort."

Aug 1888: Col Tidball to the Mayor of Norfolk: "In view of the yellow fever epidemic now prevailing in Florida, and the number of people fleeing from there, what precautions have you taken to prevent the disease entry into your city? I shall try to do the same for this side of the bay."

Aug 1888: Col Tidball to the AGO: "It is requested that the moat at Fort Monroe be cleaned. Nothing has been done in this regard for 30 years, resulting in deleterious gases and odors."

Dec 1888: Col Frank to the AGO: "Approval of 25 lamps for illumination of posterns, sallyports, passageways and exteriors of quarters and barracks is a very small number for a post of this extent, and at best can only imperfectly light it."

1888-89: An appropriation of $25,000 was made for a sewer system and placed in the hands of the Engineers. "The lowest bid exceeded the dollar amount provided. If a civilian sewer system is included with the problems of the fort, another $50,000 would be needed to be borne by the hotels and civilian users. How this plan purports to be mainly in the interest of hotel owners surpasses imagination!"

Apr 1889: Col Frank to the Corps of Engineers: "The late severe storm and high tide, beyond any on record, caused considerable damage, carrying away one of the sluice gates with much of the embankment. It also swept away the target range and damaged the Mill Creek Road and bridge. Repairs are urgently needed. As a result of the recent storm, the parade ground has been flooded for the past six weeks preventing parades and other military exercises."

Nov 1889: Adj to Company COs: "Fifty-seven percent of cases of sickness are venereal, and confined principally to young soldiers. It is believed that this disease is contracted through the inmates of vile dens in Chesapeake City and vicinity, to which it is the custom to go about on payday, where diseased women are sent from other places. Please advise your soldiers of the great danger they run from commerce with any of these people."

Feb 1890: The Hampton Electric Light and Power Company was granted a license to furnish electricity and power. Fort Monroe did not opt to use the service.

Feb 1890: Col Frank to AGO: "It is requested that the introduction of electric lights in such officers' quarters as may desire them be approved on condition that the wire be introduced at the expense and risk of the company, and fixtures not be subject to removal by the company nor the occupants."

Mar 1890: Pullman Palace Car Company requests ten to twenty buckets of water from Fort Monroe cisterns. They will pay for water and labor.

Apr 1890: The War Department approved the above request.

Apr 1890: Col R T Frank to the QM Gen: "The present sewer system is limited to the interior of the fort. This leaves all exterior property, where are now four sets of officers' quarters, quarters for some of the NCOs and married soldiers, civilian employees, Post Office, QM shops, warehouses, Arsenal, and an entire civil population unprovided with sewage.

"The fort sewer system consists of a main starting from the moat on one side, and running centrally through the fort and moat on the opposite side, and empties into Mill Creek, a shallow and almost enclosed arm of the sea. Laterals extend from the main sewer to different points of the interior. The system is operated by using sluice gates to maintain the water in the moat at a higher level during the falling of the tide than it is in Mill Creek, thus causing the water during this period to flow from the moat through the sewer into Mill Creek. During this time the laterals must be flushed by hand.

"When the tide rises, a reverse motion takes place, and the water backs up into the sewer and laterals and is prevented from flowing through the mouth of the sewer to carry contents of the sewer into the moat by a valve, which has to be operated by hand at this point. This flowing back into the sewer and laterals causes frequent stoppages, exceedingly difficult to remove. If the valve is not opened and closed at the proper time, disagreeable and harmful results follow. The most serious trouble rises during exceedingly high tides which occur several times a year, continuing for several days. Then the water backs up through the sewer and manholes onto the parade ground, flooding it and covering it with sewage which has to be policed when the water subsides. The discharge into Mill Creek is also very objectionable."

May 1890: Col Frank to the AGO: "Before 1860, the post was partially supplied by cisterns, and sometimes water was hauled from a private spring a mile away or purchased from waterboats coming from the upper James River. Cisterns were augmented by a condenser from about 1861 until 1875 during the warm and dry months. In 1871, the nine rainwater cisterns had a capacity of 180,000 gallons, and the steam condenser yielded 5,000 gallons daily when working 20 hours. 1874 was a dry year, and the post resorted to condensation. New cisterns were added with new barracks and quarters, the most important being those built in 1879 in [the] rear of the new barracks. They were connected by pumps with four galvanized iron tanks giving a capacity of 24,000 gallons.

"On introducing the sewage system in 1885, saltwater was supplied for flushing by pumping. At about the same time, the fresh water supply was increased by driven points put down about 50 feet on a reservation north of Mill Creek, whence it was pumped through a six-inch pipe to a wooden tank of 50,000 gallon capacity built over the ramparts. Thence it was had by six-inch mains to the post.

"In 1889, the supply from these points having decreased, additional ones were driven, and the old and damaged ones replaced. The supply then reached 80 gallons per minute. Not long after this, the water was found to be very hard and disagreeable to the taste. About the first of May 1890, such of the points as was found to draw brackish water were removed. The water is now satisfactory."

Sep 1890: The Post Adjutant sent letters to civilian enterprises at Fort Monroe suggesting they get together and plan a sewage system to be approved by the Secretary of War.

Dec 1891: The congressional appropriations for fortifications set aside $6,000 for a water well at Fort Monroe.

Sep 1892: Col Frank to AGO: "The Artillery School has moved to quarters heated by steam. The boilers are run by dynamos and will require 13 tons of coal per month."

Apr 1895: Col Frank to the AGO: "Proportionment of cost of new sewer: the Sherwood has requested to extend their building 40 feet southwesterly (40 x 80 feet) to add a bar, bowling alley, and billiard room. The Engineer has money in excess of the construction costs of a new sewer, and it can be returned pro rata as shown below:

%moiety cost of sewer

Hygeia	995	guests	44.3
Chamberlin	1,012	guests	45.2
Sherwood	133	guests	6.0
C&O RR	25	employees	1.1
Adams Express	8	persons	.4
Kimberly	15	persons	.7
Baulch	14	persons	.6
Watkins	20	persons	.9
Lighthouse	7	persons	.5
Capt Evans	4	persons	.2
Catholic Manse	3	persons	.1
Total	2,236	Total	100%"

Nov 1895: "Now that water has been introduced into servants' water closets, all of the old out-buildings shall be removed, specifically those behind the Tuileries and the building occupied by Captain Greenough and those vacated by Colonel Miller [Qtrs #93]."

Jan 1896: Col Frank to the AGO: "Mr Harper has just dug a water well for the Chamberlin starting with an eight-inch, then a six-inch, and lastly a four-inch pipe, and finding water at 945 feet. The water is salty and contains some sulphur, but is getting better.

"It is recommended that Mr Harper be hired to drill a water well at Fort Monroe using the $6,000 appropriation of 1891 for this purpose."

Jun 1896: Col Frank to the AGO: "The new sewer has been under construction since early April along every road and every yard. Trenches have been dug from four to twelve feet, and due to sand and tidewater, are supported by revetments. Water is pumped out on the ground or into the moat. No police is feasible under these conditions. Once the sewer was outside the fort, all was restored, and has been for some time."

Jan 1897: Col Frank to the AGO: "Cost of Electricity vs Oil:

	Electricity	Oil
Barracks, offices	.22 cents	.25 cents
Streets, posterns, covered ways	.33 cents	.15 cents
Exterior and interior	.26 cents	.21 cents

"Lighting of officers' quarters not being furnished by the government is not included above. Consideration should be given to the safety of electricity vs oil in regard to fire."

May 1897: The officers' bathhouse is without privacy, and the enlisted bathhouse has only saltwater.

Jun 1897: The Adjutant directs Captain J P Story to have electric lights removed which were installed in his quarters without approval.

Jul 1897: Col Frank to the AGO: "The wires of the Hampton Electric Company are already used at the post by the hotels, businesses, and the post chapel, and will soon light the streets exterior to the main work. To permit individual officers to install electricity in quarters would result in want of system and confusion with attendant dangers."

Nov 1900: Col Guenther to the AGO: "Preparation for electricity at this post is not yet completed, and but few of the public buildings are using electricity at present. Each set of officers' quarters and NCO quarters should have a meter."

Jul 1902: There is no objection to the request to demolish cisterns if they are properly filled in. No rubbish will be burned except at designated times and places.

Jan 1903: The civil assessment for repair, operation, and maintenance of sewer system has been reduced to one-third. The US Government will pay two-thirds of the cost.

Aug 1904: "The post is using distilled water for cooking and drinking. The garrison will be excused from calisthenics when the weather is too hot."

Nov 1905: The Inspector General reported that each time he inspected Fort Monroe he found 90 sources of poison-threatening typhoid: "[There are] twenty-one earth closets and 39 privies within the work, and 24 privies and six cesspools without the fort....The servant's closets are priveys built at the back of the houses which at certain times are flushed into the sewer. They cause a most offensive odor which pervades these quarters and are dangerously unsanitary. Besides they are too handy for outsiders. It is proposed to do away with these priveys and to put sanitary house closets in small rooms next to the laundry, and to provide them with ventilation."

APPENDIX III. TRANSPORTATION

According to data in the Casemate Museum, the Engineer Wharf on Fenwick was built about 1818. There is no consensus as to whether the rock-barge delivery for the construction of the fort came to this wharf, or to another dock at the entrance to Mill Creek. National Archives' records contain the following entries pertaining to transportation facilities at Fort Monroe:

Sep 1830: General Order #1, sent from Major General Macomb to Colonel Walbach, "ordered a bridge to be built by men stationed at Fort Monroe from Hampton to Old Point...under the supervision of the Engineers and Lieutenant Colonel Worth. Construction to begin immediately."

Jan 1868: "The road from the fort to Mill Creek Bridge (which is the one named in the Act of Cession by the State of Virginia to the US as reserved for free use of citizens of Virginia and the US) is in such bad condition as to be unsafe."

May 1868: Col Barry to the Adjutant General's Office: "It is suggested that a wharfage fee be charged for nonmilitary freight delivered at the Fort Monroe wharf, the cost of which would defray books for the Artillery School."

May 1868: AGO to Col Barry: "I endorse the idea of charging wharfage, but since the Baltimore Wharf was built by the Quartermaster, funds should go to them for maintenance."

Jun 1868: The AGO approves Major General Barry's request to have a barge constructed at the Norfolk Navy Yard.

Sep 1873: "The steamer *Lady of the Lake* struck its bow on the wharf opening it to the extent that it cannot be repaired with materials at this post."

Mar 1874: QM General to Commanding Officer, Fort Monroe: "The steam launch *Pulaski*, owned by the QM Department and built for use of the garrison...is now at Charleston, SC, laid up, there being no further use for her in the Military Division of the South. Her length is 50 feet, width 10 feet, with a capacity for carrying about 30 men, or towing barges loaded with supplies. Can such a launch be used at Fort Monroe, manned by officers and enlisted men of the post, with no expense to the QM."

Apr 1874: QM Gen to CO, Fort Monroe: "Your reply indicated that you could accept the launch *Pulaski*, and it shall be ordered to Fort Monroe as soon as the weather is suitable."

1875: Plans for a new wharf at Fort Monroe.

1881: Plans for rebuilding the wharf at Fort Monroe.

Jul 1884: An Act of Congress "permits the Chesapeake & Ohio (C&O) Railroad to extend its roadbed to a point on Hampton Roads, on lands of the United States at Fort Monroe, limited easement only, for the benefit of the military reservation. C&O President Ingalls and the Secretary of War agree to a crossing of the high road leading from the fort to Mill Creek Bridge, the railroad company to provide a bridge at the crossing, and the elevation and grading of the high road with suitable ingress and egress of small boats to the cove, with a terminus with three terminal trackways, not to exceed 60 feet in width, limited to passenger traffic only with supervision of the Post Commander."

Jul 1884: The AGO states that the QM is allowed sixteen horses and no more. Condemned animals should be returned for service, or sold at public auction.

Aug 1885: Iron pilings are approved for use on the new wharf.

Feb 1886: Col Tidball reports to the US House of Representatives the following data showing the amount of traffic upon the main wharf at Fort Monroe and across the Mill Creek bridge: "The [following] figures are for the last seven days of June 1885, an average week,...making the amounts 52 times these figures:

104 Steamers	64 Sail Vessels
60 Rowboats	805 Carts
62 Single Wagons	58 Double Wagons
165 Single Carriages	86 Double carriages
137 Other single vehicles	61 Other double vehicles

During the month of March, over Mill Creek Bridge:

7,672 Double Carriages	9,721 Single Carriages
607 Horsemen	28,086 Footmen."

May 1886: In addition to the main wharf, there is another at the lighthouse, and one for unloading coal.

Aug 1887: Col Tidball to the AGO regarding draught animals: "Replying to the letter directing sale of four of the 19 draught animals at this post, there are strong reasons for retaining the entire number. There are 35 officers on duty here which is more than any other place except Fort Leavenworth. This causes increased hauling of fuel and other supplies, plus increased police work. Throughout the year there is constant hauling of shot, shell, and other items of ordnance material since larger amounts are used here than at any other post, or indeed, at all other posts in the Army combined.

"The Arsenal uses much hauling. One mule is constantly employed from about the first of May until the middle of September on the lawn mower to keep the grass on the parade ground cut. Gravel and shells have to be brought from the beach to keep in repair an unusual stretch of road around the fort and Mill

Creek, and clay has to be brought from a long distance for this and other purposes. The pumping station beyond Mill Creek has to be supplied with fuel over three miles of road which is deep in mud most of the year, and therefore must be covered with shells.

"Two draught horses are needed for the steam fire apparatus, and heavy target material which must be hauled through deep sand. Siege and field guns and mortars have to be transported from the firing ground.

"Transport is based on the number of companies or batteries, and the number here is five. There is barely an adequate amount of transport for the exponent of work to be done."

Oct 1887: Col Tidball to the AGO: "The boat *General Wool* has not been overhauled since she was built in 1883. She can be spared now, and request the work be authorized."

Jan 1888: Col Tidball to the AGO: "Enclosed is a modification of the plans to permit parking for unloading wagons. During the trucking season, wagons extend in a queue for a quarter of a mile causing great delay in unloading. The road of the wharf is only 22 feet wide, and I propose to increase it to 35 feet. The triangle will give room for unloading and piling merchandise which should be done on the wharf. Loading delays cause steamers to occupy the wharf too long while others are waiting in the stream for their turn. If no more money can be allotted, I propose that instead of 140 feet at the loading area, it be made 120 feet which is sufficient for a steamer, and would lower construction cost."

Sep 1888: Col Tidball to the AGO: "The QM General suggests wharfage be charged to keep the wharf in repair. This was requested in 1872 but the Secretary of War did not approve. Will he now reverse his decision?"

Oct 1888: Adj to Groton Bridge Company: "Permission has been granted for your company to make a temporary building for wharf workmen, to be removed when the wharf is finished."

Nov 1888: Assistant QM Report of wharf activity for the month:

Landings

Steamer	AM	PM	Class	Vehicle Class	On/Off
Ariel	6	6	Passenger	1-Horse Wagon	551
Lady-Lake	14	10	Passenger	2-Horse Wagon	115
N. Hampton	25	24	Passenger	1 Carriage	27
Georgia	13	11	Passenger	2 Carriages	11
Luray	26	26	Passenger	Carts	409

Steamer	AM	PM	Class	Vehicle Class	On/Off
Old Pt Comfort	28	27	Passenger	Drays	58
Cape Charles	2	2	Passenger	Express Freight	89
Gaston	9	-	Freight		
Thomas Bain	1	1	Tug		
Excelsior	7	6	Passenger		
Virginia	12	11	Passenger		
Ajax	1	1	Tug		
Old Dominion	-	1	Passenger		
Atlas	-	2	Sailing Vessel		
Olive Branch	2	1	Tug		
Ocean King	1	-	Tug		
R T Wilson	1	-	Tug		
James Mosely	4	3	Passenger		
Jessamine	1	1	Lighthouse Tender		

Landings for the month: 286

Feb 1888: Col Tidball to Director, Levy Company, New Atlantic Hotel in Norfolk: "It is inadvisable to charter or loan our government tug for a trip to Norfolk on the 15th. It is impractical for officers to attend night performances in Norfolk without greatly interfering with important duties. Thank you for your offer of a private box, but it is impractical for me to attend."

Jan 1889: Col Frank to AGO: "I understand the parties who fell off the temporary wharf were safely landed from a boat. The wharf consists of a stem with a T-shaped head. There is a rail along the stem, but none along the head, nor can there be a rail there due to landing parties. The parties landed at night and were confused by the hotel lights and walked into the water."

Sep 1889: Col Frank to the AGO: "The Chesapeake and Ohio (C&O) Railroad was supposed to raise the grade of Mill Creek Road to pass under the railroad beneath it. If this is done, it would interrupt travel while the work is in progress. I propose a road of uniform width of 42 feet, with a low rate of speed, and a full stop before crossing."

Nov 1889: The Adjutant gave Mr Watkins permission to move his shed from the lighthouse wharf to the new wharf since requested sheds were never approved. He was warned he might have to remove the shed.

Dec 1889: Adjutant to Hackmen: "The hackstand is located on the site of the new extension of the C&O railroad and depot, and you must move it by 20 December. You may apply to relocate the stand if you promise to maintain suitable hacks, horses, and harnesses of a standard equal to the best class of vehicles elsewhere."

Dec 1889: Col Frank to the AGO: "Permission has been granted for 35 hacks (Mr Sheets has 15 to supply the Hygeia Hotel) and 20 others of all shades of color and conditions."

May 1891: Col Frank to the AGO: "The steamer *General Wool* was moved to New York on 12 January, and the fort has no way to tow targets."

Oct 1891: Col Frank to Hampton and Old Point Comfort Railway Company: "Permission has been granted for an electric rail across this reservation."

Nov 1891: Col Frank to the AGO: "There is no military necessity for the electric railroad to go to the wharf, but it would facilitate heavy travel and commerce. I propose the route be from the C&O railroad, down the west side of the causeway, thence to the rear of the stables, thence on trestles inside the bulkhead in front of the Arsenal ground, thence near the Sherwood, and thence by main road to the wharf."

Aug 1892: Col Frank asks the president of the Hampton and Old Point Comfort Railway Company if there could be a special rate to transport children to schools in Hampton to alleviate running a school on post. He notes that Hampton is but twenty minutes distant, and Chesapeake City but five or ten minutes away.

Dec 1892: Col Frank to the President of the Hampton & Old Point Comfort Railway Company: "Due to the recent death of Sergeant Kahn's child [hit by a train], it is suggested that further safeguards be provided against such accidents." [Sergeant Kahn retired in March 1893.]

Nov 1896: The Adj to the QM: "You are directed to repair the roads with three inches of clay in the central portion, two-thirds of the width, and cover same with gravel. The clay can be brought from the government farm across Mill Creek with the four-mule team. You are to start at the 3d Front and [move] on toward the Postern Gate, and continue on around to the start point."

Dec 1896: Col Frank to the Secretary of War: "The Act authorizes one-half of actual cost of repairs on the wharf to be charged against vessels using the wharf, and the other half by the government. The Hampton and Old Point Comfort Railway Company complains of the charge for running their trolley across the entire reservation every fifteen minutes until midnight and requests lighting on the wharf."

Apr 1901: Col Guenther to the AGO: "I have delivered the notice of the revocation of license to the president of the Newport News and Old Point Comfort Railway and Electric Company."

Apr 1905: The government ordered the hack stand to be removed within 60 days to make room for the new Artillery School building.

Jun 1905: Col Ramsey Potts to the AGO: "The Washington and Norfolk Steamship Company runs boats twice daily to Norfolk and Portsmouth. The Old Dominion Steamship Company has steamers to New York once a day. (A small steamer of the same company [stops] three times a day.) The Baltimore Steam Packet Company comes once a day. The steamer *Ocean View* runs hourly from 8:20 AM to 8:20 PM to Willoughby Spit and the trolley to Norfolk. The Virginia Navigation Company stops once a day enroute to Norfolk. The C&O depot is on the west side, 80 yards from the QM storehouse. The terminus for the Newport News and Old Point Comfort Railway and Electric Trolley is on the main wharf 300 yards from the QM storehouse. The Hampton Roads Railroad and Electric Trolley is the same."

Dec 1905: The Old Dominion steamship *Monroe* collided with the wharf and did considerable damage.

May 1906: The ammunition train frequently ran off the track due to settling of the track, spreading of rails, etc. Guns and carriages installed at Battery Parrott were damaged in this manner.

1919: Frank Clark, *Aunt Lena*: "...at Old Point wharf were the steamships *Washington, Baltimore*, and *Cape Charles.*"

1935: Frank Clark, *Aunt Lena*: "Norfolk could be reached by the seven-mile bridge over the James River at Newport News, Virginia, running thence through Portsmouth to Norfolk."

1951: Frank Clark, *Aunt Lena*: "The present underwater highway from Old Point Comfort to Willoughby Spit was built in 1951. From the main dock in front of the Chamberlin Hotel, four Chesapeake Bay ships sailed each evening: The NYP&N from Norfolk to Cape Charles left at 6:00 PM; the Washington ship from Norfolk to DC left at 6:45 PM; and two Chesapeake Line ships from Norfolk to Baltimore left about 7:15 PM; the Old Bay Line ship from Norfolk to Baltimore left at 7:30 PM. Sister ships of each of those lines arrived at that same dock early each morning on their way back to Norfolk."

APPENDIX IV. COMMUNICATIONS

Feb 1887: Report for the Artillery School Telegraph Line: "During the month of January, the line has been open from some cause on 13 out of 27 days, or nearly 50 percent of the time. It did not work continuously more than four days at a time. Causes for breaks were: once from weight of ice; four times open switches; nine times unknown. Five times it appeared that some person, from sheer malice, interrupted conversations, but no clue is as yet available."

May 1887: "There are twelve telephones and six call-boxes used in connection with the guard and fire systems and hospital services."

Oct 1888: The Signal Office forwarded a manual of instructions to Fort Monroe describing how to construct telegraph lines.

May 1892: The York Telephone and Telegraph Company was granted the right to put lines across the reservation and Fort Wool, between Newport News and Norfolk.

May 1894: The United States Express Company, the Western Union Telegraph Company, and the York Telephone and Telegraph Company have offices in the Hygeia Hotel.

Oct 1895: The Commanding Officer to Frank Holtzclaw: "In exchange for extending your line across the reservation, we gladly accept a telephone station for the free use of officers of the post, and suggest that the Officers' Club is the most convenient place to locate it."

Jun 1905: CO to the Adjutant General's Office: "The following communication facilities are installed: Western Union at the Sherwood Inn; Postal Telegraph at the Chamberlin; and Southern Bell Telephones at the Chamberlin, Sherwood, and QM office."

Aug 1905: CO to the AGO: "There are 49 phones installed, in addition to 12 authorized for administrative use. Eleven more should be added, as well as a reserve of six for replacement. Alibis and excuses i.e., failure to meet train to unload fresh beef, reports not forwarded to Washington, etc. are laid to telephones not working."

APPENDIX V. CANTEEN OR PX

Nov 1832: The Adjutant General's Office to the Commanding Officer of Fort Monroe: "(1) No ardent spirits will be issued to US troops, and no commutation in money will be paid. (2) No ardent spirits will be introduced into any fort, camp or garrison, nor sold by any sutler to the troops, nor will any permit be granted for their purchase. As a substitute for ardent spirits previously issued, for every 100 rations there shall be issued eight pounds of sugar, four pounds of coffee, and ten pounds of rice (or) eight quarts of beans."

1843: Robert Archer is listed as post trader.

1856: G C Mellen, post trader, died.

Jan 1862: Order #14: "There shall be no beer sold at the sutler's store."

Dec 1872: Quartermaster (QM) Captain T J Ekerson to the Adjutant of the Artillery School and Post Adj: "I have not at any time understood the CO as directing me to procure alcohol, or I should have lost no time in doing so. Up to this time, alcohol has only been furnished to this Post among other Horse Medicines, but pursuant to the instructions contained in your letter, I herewith enclose for the approval of the Post CO a special estimate for 30 gallons, for the use named in said letter."

Jul 1876: William Baulch appointed post trader by the Secretary of War.

Jan 1877: Letter from a soldier to the Secretary of War: "to tell you of the wrong going on here in the Post Settler's Store. That prices for the things ar' most extargable, for instance, for a pair of white coton gloves that we ware on duty that are worth .25 cents he charges us .75 cents, and all other clothes we are chared in like manner. This sitter is a new one and this Settler Store is carried on a most diapated maner they are allowend to carry it on as they like it is kept open from daylight until late hours at night and it is a great annoyance to Parties living in that visinity and above this allowed to keep open on Sunday morning and Evenings and that is morrowly wrong as the Sabath and there ought to be a government store for this artiley school solgers it is a very wrong to have sutch drinking place in this fort they oughter be in church when they are in the Settlers drinking at times the solger can be seen rolling kegs of beer acros the parade ground to there Quarters I feel confident most Hon Sir if you investigate this and you will find my words true it is the honest trouth.
[signed] A Solger of this Post."

Jan 1877: Trader Baulch replied through the post commander that "complaints against him were malodorous and malicious lies; that he was never open on Sunday; that he charged only .15 cents for gloves; and that he was restricted by post order on the amount of malt liquor sold, and abided by it."

Feb 1889: Col Frank to the AGO: "I have investigated establishing a canteen, as directed by your office, and discussed it with the officers and the Post Trader, and enclose a tracing showing the casemate rooms now used by the trader with such additional rooms as can be made available for a canteen, or used in connection with his store. I approve of the principle, and believe if the rooms are made comfortable with reading matter and means for games and sports, and if light wines, beer, cigars and refreshments like ham, tongue, and cheese sandwiches with coffee can be provided at a moderate charge it would prove very attractive to enlisted men. It would make the post more attractive to them, would create a feeling of self-respect and good fellowship, and mitigate the evils of intemperance and help break up the low groggeries and other objectionable resorts which spring up in the neighborhood of military posts. I recommend casemates 5, 6, 7, 8 and 9, and that the QM ceil and floor them to be used as a social resort. The Post Trader already has two billiard and two pool tables, and could probably furnish the refreshments. He could charge for pool, but not for cards and dominoes."

Sep 1889: Col Frank to the AGO: "There is no want so much felt at the post as proper means of social entertainment for the enlisted men. All others have social measures. The soldier has none except those found in saloons and resorts of the lowest character which have grown up on the other side of Mill Creek, attracted there by the patronage of the Soldiers' Home and this post. The absence of social resources is the principal cause of desertion and disinclination of soldiers to reenlist.

"Mr Baulch [post trader or sutler] is a man who exercises a wholesome influence over the enlisted men, conducts all his business in a satisfactory way and on small profit. I believe the plan here proposed superior to the Canteen, and I think it would be generally preferred, the same control and supervision being exercised over it as in the case of the canteen. It would be better that the QM Dept ceil and floor the [casemate] rooms, thus enabling the men to obtain refreshments at more reasonable rates, and the government to resume possession of the rooms at any time. If done, the post needs a special allotment."

Nov 1889: "The only casemates available for a canteen are those between the bakery and the post trader, or those occupied by Lieutenants Bartlett and Humphreys."

Apr 1890: AGO to the CO, Fort Monroe: "Has a canteen been established at the post under the provisions of Pp 328, et seq. of the Regulations?"

Jul 1891: Col Frank to the AGO: "The canteen was established on 1 March 1891 in rooms formerly occupied by the Post Trader. There are four casemates divided into eight rooms: one for beer, one for lunch, one for billiards, one for chess, one for reading, one for an office, one for storage, and one for a urinal.

"An assessment of $25 was made upon the six batteries to outfit, plus $33 for fixtures. There are four enlisted men and one steward employed.

"In stock are beer, soda, coffee, milk, cold ham, bologna, herring, sardines, tongue, pig's feet, crackers, cheese, bread, pies, tobacco and cigars. It is open weekdays from 8:00 to 11:45 AM, and from 1:00 to 10:30 PM (except for retreat).

"During the four months, there has been a profit of $2,259 (or $1.80 per man per month). $1,600 has been apportioned to the band, the hospital, and to the six batteries. The revenue derived allows the companies to add to the comfort of the men, especially to the rations. The rooms are attractive, afford agreeable amusement, and the best qualities of supplies.

"It is requested that toweling, brushes, and blackening soap be added for sale. Also a better bar, not a gaudy thing with mirrors and displays of glassware and alluring pictures, just a plain bar to sell beer."

Feb 1892: Col Frank to the AGO: "It has been agreed to change the name of the canteen to Post Exchange [PX]."

Dec 1894: Post Exchange Report:

Sale of beer = $8,253.15.
Merchandise = $6,243.78.
Strength of garrison = 453, with 120 non-drinkers.
Sales increased by members of Washington Barracks and
Fort McHenry at Fort Monroe for artillery practice.

Sep 1901: CO Guenther to the AGO: "A list of liquor saloons within one mile of Fort Monroe prepared 15 February 1901 and again in August shows a decrease of five saloons. Abolishment of the canteen has had little effect as to drunkenness among the enlisted men, the number of Courts Martial being the same before and after. The abolition of the sale of beer has had no effect upon the morality or discipline, nor on the health. It has been the cause of some discontent, but accepted without much complaint."

1903: Electric lights requested for rooms being used as a PX.

Dec 1903: Col Story to Massachusetts Brewers Company of Boston: "I acknowledge the letter and receipt of three bottles of 'Leisester Malt.' The surgeon of the post informs me this malt is obnoxious to the law prohibiting sale of beer at the PX. I cannot authorize it in our exchange. Also, the Christian Temperance Ladies of this nation have driven our soldiers into the dens of iniquity near post installations by not allowing comfort and companionship in the post PX."

APPENDIX VI. HYGEIA HOTEL

In 1821, Major Gratiot (commanding engineer for the construction of Fort Monroe) permitted William Armistead to build a hotel-restaurant to accommodate workmen and officers without quarters. The Secretary of War approved the request 17 June 1822. Gradual enlargement and improvements were made as social needs demanded, and as the garrison increased in size and mission. Public facilities operated on government land under a revokable license that required the buildings be razed and the land returned to the original state if military needs demanded. The Civil War caused the demolition in 1862 of the first Hygeia, which occupied most of the land between the present YMCA and the Postern Gate. One building was retained to be used as a hospital.

In 1863, C C Willard was given permission to erect a one-story Hygeia Dining Saloon on the waterfront at the site of the present Continental Park. Ownership passed from Willard to C T Norris, to Mr Pratt, to Henry Clark. Clark's right to operate the facility was recognized by a Joint Resolution of Congress in June 1868.

In 1871, Clark formed a partnership with J M West, and they sold their interest to S M Shoemaker, who received congressional approval to enlarge the facility in February, 1875. Shoemaker sold his right to Harrison Phoebus in February, 1877, without obtaining the permission of the Secretary of War. Phoebus eventually was sanctioned the right in February 1884, and modernized and increased the hotel in size.

When Phoebus died in 1886, his heirs formed a joint stock company, the Hygeia Hotel Company, but again without governmental approval. By this time the room capacity had doubled, and with the construction of an annex, doubled again, now extending from the present Post Office to the Flag Bastion. A billiard room and bar was permitted to sell alcoholic beverages to guests. A large ballroom accommodated lavish galas for which the post's band frequently performed. A lamp-lit promenade extended along the waterfront leading to surf bathing dressing rooms, and a short wharf terminated with a covered pavilion. A private carriage service supplanted the public hacks which met the trains and steamers. The post commander requested to be notified of the presence of distinguished visitors so that the post could render appropriate honors.

By the close of the century, the Hygeia Hotel at Old Point Comfort was the favorite spa of the elite. Designing mothers maneuvered to show off their eligible daughters to the Army and

84

Navy officers in their handsome uniforms. Steamboats, overnight ferries from Washington and Baltimore, and Palace Pullman cars transported their elegant guests to "take the sea air."

After the Spanish-American War, Congress approved a vast sum of money for expansion of Fort Monroe and to update the quarters and facilities for the Harbor Defense Command and the Artillery School. With adequate military housing forecast, and the need to clear the waterfront of this monstrous edifice which blocked the guns from protecting the shipping lanes to the harbor, the hotel was notified to vacate the property by the end of 1902. Within a few months, all traces of the grande dame of Hampton Roads had disappeared.

APPENDIX VII. CHAMBERLIN HOTEL

Jul 1886: Colonel Tidball to the Adjutant General's Office: "...regarding the request of J F Chamberlain for authority to erect a hotel on land of the US, the most eligible site is that on the Quartermaster's blueprint enclosed. Most of the area is new beach made within the last 15 years, but the QM's residence is on one corner. To replace it would cost about $7,000. Immediately adjoining this site to the north are two private buildings: Adams Express Office, with a family residence over it, and Kimberly's Mercantile (groceries and dry goods) with a residence above. These buildings occupy public ground by authority of the Secretary of War.

"The next eligible site is that marked 'Old Hygeia.' This hotel was removed during the war, but is now occupied by a new building, the quarters of the Post Commissary [#55] which is valued at $4,000. In addition, the ground is occupied by the quarters of the Post QM Sergeant, the Post Office, and a schoolhouse for enlisted men's children--all old and dilapidated, but to replace them would cost at least $5,000.

"Another, the least objectionable to the post, site is marked Mill Creek. Upon this site is a building occupied by the captain of the government steamer, *General Wool*. It is necessary to provide him quarters, and to replace this building would cost $1,200. Soon after the war, the Willards were granted permission to erect a hotel on this site, but failed to do so.

"There is an area marked Mrs Eaton's which might be used for a hotel without detriment to government interests. It has a boarding house which might be purchased for $12,000 to $15,000. Adjoining this are a couple of old buildings belonging to the government: one occupied as a residence by the Commissary Ser-

85

geant, and the other by the QM storekeeper. Next to these are two buildings: the parsonage, and a schoolhouse belonging to the Catholic Church. They are worth about $1,200. There are insuperable objections to use of any land eastward of the present Hygeia, which occupies a space of about 700' x 250', ample for a first-class house. Most of the land outside the fort belongs to either the Engineers or Ordnance, and is so mixed in with that belonging to the post that I cannot discuss the relative merits of the area."

[A hotel privilege was granted to J F Chamberlain by a Joint Resolution of Congress dated 3 March 1887. The concession was granted for two years.]

Mar 1887: Col Tidball to the AGO: "The site proposed for a hotel, in my opinion, is not available for many reasons: (1) Such a building would completely mask the lighthouse to the eastward, the most important approach to Hampton Roads. To raise the lighthouse sufficiently to overlook the hotel would require an entire new structure, and would have to be done before the hotel is built. (2) The hotel would shut off fire from a very important part of the fort upon the ship channel leading into Hampton Roads. The force of this objection is enhanced by what is understood to be the intent of the government--to construct turrets and other modern defenses upon the parts of the fort thus marked. (3) The ground proposed for the hotel includes the site of a projected exterior battery for heavy guns to enfilade the ship channel. (4) A due regard to the guests of a hotel on this site would entirely prevent firing from the guns of the waterfront of the fort, and thus deprive the Artillery School of the most important object of its existence. Even with the present hotel, firing has occasionally been suspended on account of the illness of some guest."

Nov 1889: Col Frank to the AGO: "The site delegated for the Chamberlin hotel is occupied by the quarters of the Post QM and one civilian employee. Whereas they are adequate, it is doubtful they could be moved without destroying them. Chamberlain has not exercised his option for over two and a half years, and it was assumed he had abandoned the project. The site was indicated as the probable location of new quarters for the Commanding Officer, and two sets of field grade [major and above] quarters. It would be injurious to the school to make this place into a pleasure resort, and I recommend his privilege be cancelled.

"As it is, the Hygeia Hotel towers above everything around it, and covers as with a screen nearly the whole southern front, practically throwing into its backyard the old line of Engineer quarters, the best line of site for officers' quarters, cutting them off entirely from any view of the bay and the prevailing winds of summer, and affording in lieu the fragrance of the kitchens, boiler rooms, etc. The construction of this hotel will continue this screen around toward the west with similar effect, leaving few or no desirable building sites outside the fort except those belonging to the Arsenal."

Feb 1890: Col Frank to the AGO: "The hotel plan abuts closely against the rear of Mr Kimberly's lot and that of the Adams Express. It also abuts close up to the edge of the narrow road leading to the Quartermaster wharf and extends nearly to the new iron pier known as the Baltimore Wharf."

Jan 1891: Col Frank to the AGO: "The framework of the Chamberlin Hotel has reached the second story, part of which is roofed. It is to be completed by May."

Mar 1891: A letter from the post adjutant to the architect denies the request to enlarge the hotel with an additional floor. He stated that the plans call for four stories, with 40 rooms on the first floor, and 129 rooms on the other floors.

Sep 1892: Col Frank to the AGO: "Work on Chamberlin Hotel started in May 1890, and continued sporadically until several months hence when work ceased for lack of funds, and the building is incomplete."

Mar 1893: Col Frank to the AGO: *The Washington Star* states the hotel is to be sold under US Court order. I suggest it be torn down instead."

Aug 1902: Col Story to the Judge Advocate General in Washington, DC: "When the Chamberlin raised the price of meals per month for officers this winter, a successful movement was made to inaugurate an officers' mess. It has had beneficial results and improved morale. I do not favor reduction in price of meals at the hotel. I am inclined to recommend $40 for single officers, with a 25 percent reduction for married officers and families ($30/month--the old rate at the Hygeia)."

May 1965: Newspaper account of the 1920 Chamberlin Hotel fire, as reported in the *Daily News* [Newport News, VA, pp. 1, 21]. "The origin of the fire which started late afternoon of March 7, 1920 was never determined. The 675 people in the hotel were brought to safety and there was no loss of life or serious injury. Estimated loss to the hotel and furnishings was nearly $2-1/2 million, and an additional $1 million in jewelry was lost by guests. Other losses included J B Kimberly's General Merchandise Store ($53,000) and Adams' Express Company ($10,000). Two Army classrooms were gutted by flames. Insurance on the hotel was only $350,000."

The Chamberlin-Vanderbilt Hotel was erected in 1928 by Richmond restauranteur, L W Noland, on the same site as the hotel which burned. The indoor swimming pool remains, as does some of the interior detailing, but when the name Vanderbilt was dropped is unknown.

Retired Colonel C N Myers wrote: "Fort Monroe was an overnight boat trip from Washington, and it was a favorite spot for military attaches and others from the embassies and other high-ranking VIPs. They were given the usual honors, and they could sort of dry out in the Hotel Chamberlin."

Retired Colonel S W Berliner served at Fort Monroe as a first lieutenant from 1931 to 1932. "Many single officers lived at the Chamberlin Hotel. Since this was depression times, the rather new hotel had many, many vacancies. I recall that they rented a nice large room for two for $40/month. As the allowance for officers to occupy quarters off post was $60/month for lieutenants, and $80/month for captains, this would account for some of the officers deciding to live there."

APPENDIX VIII. DeRUSSY HOUSE

Behind the post office, in the back garden area of the commanding general's quarters, the engineers constructed a storage building in 1817 which was later converted into a barracks or prison for slaves and military prisoners employed in building the fort. Around 1842 this structure was remodeled and made into a dwelling house for engineer personnel. It was here where Colonel Rene E. DeRussy lived with his family.

When the Colonel died in 1876, his widow petitioned the Secretary of War to allow her and her invalid mother to remain in the house "during their state of overwhelming bereavement." The ladies lived there, rent free, from 1876 to 1891.

Sep 1876: Quartermaster to the Office of the QM General: "A terrific storm has prevailed here for two days, partially destroying slate roofing and gutters of quarters and cisterns. A falling tree crushed a portion of the wall of General Barry's quarters [Quarters #1 by the East Sallyport]; damaged the DeRussy house...and total-ly destroyed the Engineer's frame building by the artesian well."

Dec 1887: The Adjutant General's Office to Colonel Tidball: "I am instructed by the Secretary of War to say that he will be very glad if you will permit Mrs DeRussy, the widow of Colonel Rene E DeRussy, to continue to reside in the quarters in which she is now living at Old Point Comfort, if the convenience of the public service will permit."

Dec 1887: Col Tidball to the AGO: "With reference to the occupancy of a house at this post by Mrs DeRussy, I have no desire to dispossess her or any of the widows occupying Engineer buildings, and for that reason [I] have told the Quartermaster not to receive the buildings while so occupied, as in that case, the buildings were not available 'exclusively for post purposes'--the conditions required in the order directing the transfer. Your concurrence is gratifying, as it relieves me from the necessity of distressing Mrs DeRussy, and gives me pleasure to carry out the wishes of the Secretary of War."

May 1891: Post QM to QM General: "The Engineer quarters occupied by Mrs DeRussy were transferred to the post about five years ago [1887], but have never been used by the post authorities. The DeRussy house has since been retransferred back to the Engineers on 4 May 1891."

Feb 1907: Fort Monroe Post Engineer to the Chief Engineer, Washington, DC: "Of the numerous Engineer buildings at Fort Monroe there are now but three. The DeRussy house with two out-buildings, the Engineer office, and a small brick storehouse. The DeRussy house has been occupied for a number of years by Mr James Ware, Superintendent of Construction; his salary is based on being given quarters. Therefore, his salary will have to be raised as there are no other quarters available. While interesting for its historical association, the DeRussy house is falling into decay and no longer harmonizes with the new surroundings. The QM should remove it."

Sep 1908: The Fort Monroe QM states: "The DeRussy house has heavy rubble stone walls to the level of the second story, with framework above. To duplicate this building would cost $10,000."

No record was found of the demolishment of this building, but if it stood until around 1908 it can be assumed that when senior officer quarters were to be constructed on the Gold Coast, the demise of the DeRussy House was simply a matter of clearing the area for planned construction.

APPENDIX IX. FRATERNAL LODGES

Dec 1892: Colonel Frank to the Adjutant General's Office regarding the Monitor Lodge #197, Ancient Free and Accepted Masons, and the Old Point Lodge #144, Independent Order of Odd Fellows: "These lodges were established during the war in a room over the stables, which was torn down. The present one [was] built in 1865. Of the 50 members of the Masonic Lodge, eight men are soldiers; of the 139 members of the Odd Fellows Lodge, 60 are soldiers. The men like having the lodges. A site could be designated on the part of the post near the present stables for lodge rooms."

The Army and Navy Lodge, No. 306, Fort Monroe, was conceived at a meeting held in the quarters of First Lieutenant Adelno Gibson, Coast Artillery Corps, in Casemate #1, First Front, on 19 March 1909. Organized under a dispensation dated 2 April 1909, chartered 10 February 1910, and constituted and consecrated 11 March 1910. Called "the only lodge that met underground," the casemate was used for meetings until 1977.

In 1915, a member of the Lodge ran across an item concerning an earlier Masonic Order which had been established at Old Point Comfort. A report of 13 December 1825 indicated that a charter would be issued for establishment of a Lodge at Old Point, Fortress Monroe, in the County of Elizabeth City, by the name of Comfort Lodge, #143. Robert Archer was appointed master, Charles Gratiot as senior warden, and J F Heileman as junior warden. Mordecai Cooke was grand master in 1825. Fourteen members were listed: W T Bainbridge, G S Drane, S McKenzie, C Mellon, W W Morris, W S Newton, S Ringgold, H Saunders, H Whiting, R H Zantziner, J Bosworth, J R Ingalls, J M W Licton, and T C Randolph. The Lodge was reported as "dormant" from 1827 to 1831, and it remained so until it disappeared from the roster in 1848. The following biographies are given of original members:

Robert Archer: Hospital Surgeon's Mate in May 1814; post surgeon in 1818; resigned as a major in 1840; died 1877.

Charles Gratiot: West Point Class of 1804; lieutenant colonel 1819; brevet brigadier general 1828; dismissed December 1838 for refusing to settle his accounts with Van Buren's Secretary of the Treasury; died 1855.

J F Heileman: West Point Class of 1803; died in Florida as a lieutenant colonel in 1836.

Captain McKenzie died in the Mexican War in 1847.

Captain Mellon was killed in the Seminole War at Lake Monroe, Florida, 8 February 1837.

S Ringgold was mortally wounded at Palo Alto in the Mexican War. Ringgold "met a soldier's death amidst his guns; and should the sight of the mineplanter bearing his name awaken an enquiry, let the answer be that it was named after one of the best officers in the splendid body now known as the 'old Army,' and was also a brother of the Craft."

Retired Colonel D C Tredennick shared this memory: "I gave a speech at the Fort Monroe Army and Navy Lodge dinner for West Point graduates on 22 March 1924. The following gentlemen attended [the year following the name indicates date of graduation from the US Military Academy]:

Swift E S	1876	Giffin S S	1913
Rees T H	1886	Gillespie J B	1913
Smith W R	1892	Villaret E	1914
Jervey J P	1892	McNarney J T	1915
Cloke H E	1897	Kahle J F	1915
Pope F A	1900	Lyon E B	1915
Fenner R H	1900	Naiden E L	1915
Prentice J	1901	Walbach J D	1916
Smith F H	1903	Ruddell J C	1916
Bunker P D	1903	Patterson W E	1916
Fenton C L	1904	Gallagher F F	1916
Singles W	1904	Sackville W	1917
Dusenbury J S	1905	Butler W O	1917
Horsfall L P	1906	Lohmann L H	1917
Green J A	1906	Fleming W R	1918
Pendleton A J	1906	Barnes H C Jr	1918
Westover O	1906	Wilson C F	1918
Loughry H K	1906	Pichel J F	1919
Shedd W E	1907	Patterson W J	1919
Horton P J	1907	Dolph E A	1920
Arthur R	1907	Slifer B W	1920
Coleman F H	1907	Flory L D	1921
Loustalot A L	1908	Williams J G	1921
Donovan R	1908	MacMillan A R	1920-A
Putney E W	1908	Goff J L	1922-20A
Pendleton L L	1908	Bartlett L W	1922-20A
Cunningham J	1908	Turnbull H T	1922-20A
Sneed A L	1908	Schuyler C V	1922
Kelly E L	1909	Leonard L C	1922
Milling T D	1909	Miller S M	1922
Gage P S	1909	Anderson G	1922
McKinney C F	1911	Woods F J	1922
Homer J L	1911	Tyler H E	1922
Cramer R V	1912	Raymond A D	1923
Harms H W	1912	Osborne T M	1923

Tudor R A	1923	Gurley F K	1923
Barroll L S	1923	Imhof L H	1923
Heaney G F Jr	1923	Bates R E	1923
Savini S H	1923	Thomas W A D	1923
Farrow J H	1923	Carroll J B	1923
Pamplin D G	1923	McLean D	1923
Waldo G E	1923	Breitung H E C	1923
Shepard L	1923	Lutwack E E	1923
Burnett J R	1923	Jeffries J S	1923
Love E L	1923	Morton L M	1923
Stone R Jr	1923	Kreuger R H	1923
Vandersluis H	1923	Tredennick D C	1923
Breidster W F	1923	(Junior Officer)	

APPENDIX X. CEMETERY

Mar 1858: Commanding Officer to the Post Quartermaster: "The cemetery recently established will be known as Hollywood Cemetery, and is in the immediate charge of the Quartermaster who will assign spaces for graves and see to maintenance. No grave will be opened but by his direction."

Mar 1886: Colonel Tidball to the Adjutant General's Office: "It is important that graves in the cemetery at this post should be marked in a permanent manner. The cemetery is located in a pine grove upon a soil of pure sand, and owing to the shade and nature of the soil, the position of graves cannot be indicated by grass mounds. In locating new graves, danger exists of disturbing former ones. It would be desirable to have dressed stones...or ordinary rough stones about two feet long."

Mar 1886: Col Tidball to the AGO: "...250 headstones are needed for the cemetery. Marble blocks have been placed on graves of soldiers, but many others are buried there. The cemetery contains 87 officers and soldiers, 167 civilians, children, and Rebels."

Mar 1886: 1st Indorsement from the AGO: "Headstones have already been provided for officers and soldiers. There is no appropriation for marking graves of others. Persons without means or relatives should be assigned to a special part of the cemetery."

Jul 1886: Col Tidball to the Inspector General: "The records of this cemetery do not extend further back than 1861. It is presumed no records were kept previous to that. Since that date there have been 95 burials of enlisted men, and one officer. In addition, there have been buried 185 civilians, Confederate soldiers, and 409 Union soldiers. The Union soldiers were subsequently moved to the National Cemetery at Hampton. This cemetery was probably established as early as 1830 (or before). It is desired to mark the graves with some kind of stone so that the area can be laid out in plats. The Confederate graves also should be appropriately marked."

Mar 1892: Col Frank to the AGO: "It is requested that a road be built to the cemetery at the northern extremity of the reservation. It had been reached formerly by going on the beach on the channel front which now has jetties and a railroad track. The burnt headboards are due to fires started by local boys when the grass and leaves are dried and dead. Wooden headboards and fences are unsuitable."

Apr 1894: Col Frank to the AGO: "The cemetery contains some officers' families, sailors, bodies found on the beach, many government employees and civilians, and during the war, volunteers and some Confederate soldiers were buried there. The Quartermaster records are not complete, but show that exclusive of volunteers and Confederates, most of whom have been removed to the National Cemetery at Hampton, there is one officer, 112 soldiers, 211 civilians (including soldiers' families). Some graves have iron or wooden fences, some have headstones, but more graves have a wooden headboard, or a post, or nothing at all."

Feb 1897: QM General to CO, Fort Monroe: "By the direction of the Depot QM at Washington, DC, it has been decided to discontinue the cemetery and to move the bodies from there to the National Cemetery nearby."

May 1897: Col Frank to the Superintendent, Hampton National Cemetery: "The first death [since the discontinuation of the Fort Monroe cemetery] occurred on 20 May 1897, Private S L White. It is requested that instructions be given in regard to burial in Hampton."

BARS TO STARS

With the exception of the Civil War, when the rank of general was rather generously bestowed, the General Officer group was relatively small and select up to World War II. The fact that at least 265 artillerymen attained the rank of general is a distinct accomplishment.

The following Artillerymen rose to general officer rank during their service. They are listed by last name and initials, followed by their rank. Those who never lived in permanent quarters (only in the Old Hundred Building) are marked with asterisks (*). Dates they served in the general officer rank are shown, if known.

Abernethy R S BG 1928	Burnell N A MG * 1932
Alger J D LTG	Burton H S BG 1865
Allen H C BG *	Butler B F MG 1864
Allen R R MG	Butler W O MG 1942
Argo R W MG	Callan R E MG 1924
Armistead W K BG 1834	Campbell L H Jr BG *
Armstrong C H BG *	Carmichael R L MG
Armstrong D BG	Carter M S LTG
Aurand H S LTG * 1915	Case H B BG
Badger G M BG *	Cassevant A G MG *
Bailey C J MG	Cassidy J F BG *
Baker W C MG	Chamberlain E W BG
Bankhead J BG	Chamberlaine W BG 1919
Barber E BG * 1931	Chapin W M BG
Barnes H C BG	Chapman E A MG
Barrette J D BG	Clark F S BG 1940
Barry W F MG 1867	Cole W E MG
Bender A H MG *	Colladay E B BG *
Bennett I L MG	Colton R B MG * 1927
Berry R W MG * 1933	Connell R M BG
Berry J A MG	Corbin F P Jr BG
Betts T J BG * 1917	Corlett C R MG
Bishop P P MG	Cox R F BG *
Black E F BG * 1942	Crain J K MG
Blakelock D H MG *	Crawford J B BG
Blood K T MG	Crichlow R W Jr MG
Boatwright W P BG	Cronkhite A MG 1920
Boyd L R BG	Crowell E R BG
Bradshaw A Jr MG	Cunningham J H BG 1948
Brigham C E MG	Davis L L BG
Brucker W H BG *	Davis R P MG
Bucher O B BG	Devine J G BG

Dillon J V BG * 1921
Dix J A MG 1863
Donaldson W G Jr BG
Donovan R LTG 1947
Drewery G H BG
Duff C B LTG
Dunn C G BG
Devoe R G BG
Easterbrook E P MG, Chap
Edwards P W MG *
Embick S D LTG * 1930
Englehard A F BG
Erickson S BG * 1907
Eustis A BG 1837
Fellers B G BG * 1920
Fenton C L BG 1948
Fenwick J R BG 1825
Fergusson F K BG 1918
Flory L L BG 1949
Foote S M BG
Foster E M MG
Frank S H BG
Franke G H MG * 1911
Franklin A G Jr MG *
Frederick R T MG 1945
French A J BG
Gage P S BG * 1941
Galusha M H BG *
Gardner F Q C MG *
Garrett R C BG
Gerhardt H A MG
Getty G W MG 1867
Giffin S L BG
Gildart R C BG
Glasgow R I BG
Goodman W M MG *
Green J A MG 1940
Gulick J W MG 1936
Guyer L M BG
Hagood J MG 1919
Haines R E BG *
Handwerk M C BG
Hardaway F P BG * 1910
Harms H W BG 1940
Harriman J E BG
Harris C S BG
Harris W H BG
Hartman J L BG
Hasbrouck R W MG * 1918
Hayden F L BG *
Haynes I A BG 1918
Hays W BG 1867
Hendrix R R MG *

Hero A Jr MG
Herrick H N BG
Hesketh W BG
Hess W W Jr BG
Hewett H MG
Hickey D W Jr BG
Hines C BG
Hines F T BG
Hinman D D BG
Holmes H B Jr BG
Homer J L MG 1942
Hopkins J P BG
Irvine W W MG
Jablonsky H J MG *
Jackson H R BG
Jarman S BG
Jervey J P BG 1920
Johnson J C BG
Jones T H BG
Jordan R H BG
Kabrick W C BG
Keeler M G BG
Keeler G E Jr MG * 1935
Kelly P B BG
Kilborune C E MG
Kirk J MG *
Knerr H J BG
Kobbe W A MG
Kyster O H Jr MG
Lane J J MG * 1938
Lawton W S LTG
Leary J E BG
Lee R E GEN 1862
Lemnitzer L L GEN
Lewis J T LTG
Longino O H BG
Loomis H F BG
Loughry H K MG 1940
Luczak B R BG
Lutes L LTG * 1928
Lyster T C BG
Marquat W F MG
Mather J BG
Maynard J B BG
Mellnik S M BG
Metzger E H BG
Meyer R J MG
Meyer R D MG
Meyers H G BG
Michelet H E BG
Mickelsen S R LTG
Milburn B L MG
Miles N A MG

Miley H A Jr GEN * 1941

Milling T D BG 1940

Mitchell J B BG

Mitchell R M BG

Montgomery J E BG

Moore C R MG

Moore G F MG

Myer G R MG

Myers H F BG

MacMoreland E E MG *

McConnell F C BG * 1930

McCroskey S L BG *

McGoldrick F M MG *

McIntyre A MG

McKee W G GEN * 1936

McNarney J T GEN

McSherry F J BG

Nichols H F BG

Nugent G A BG

Oldfield H R MG

Osborne T M BG * 1948

Ostrom C D Y BG

Pape R B BG *

Parks H C MG

Pendleton R T BG

Perkins R M BG

Perry W A BG

Phillips T R BG *

Pickering J A BG * 1916

Potts R D BG

Rees T H BG 1930

Renshaw C BG

Reybold E LTG

Roberts J MG 1863

Robinson J S BG

Russell S C MG

Rutledge P W MG 1954

Schabacker C H BG *

Schmick P BG

Schuyler C V R GEN 1953

Shedd W E MG 1941

Shull H W BG

Skelton W G BG

Skidmore W M BG

Smith F H MG 1938

Smith J P MG

Smith R H BG

Smith W R MG 1923

Sneed A L BG 1946

Spalding S F MG * 1912

Spalding O L BG

Spiller O L BG

Starr R E BG

Stayton T V MG 1959

Steele H L MG

Stevens J D BG

Stockton E A Jr BG

Strong A G BG

Strong F S MG

Stuart L L BG

Sullivan J P MG * 1922

Sunderland A H MG

Swift E S Jr MG 1918

Taber A P BG

Tarrant L K BG

Taylor C K MG

Thiele C M BG

Thompson M R BG

Tidball J C MG 1883

Tiernon J L BG

Tilton R L BG 1940

Timberlake E N BG

Todd H D Jr MG

Toftoy H N MG

Townsend J R BG

Townsley C P MG

Tracy J P BG 1932

Vandersluis H J BG 1954

Vogel G H BG 1952

Walbach J D BG

Walker W H GEN

Waterman B S BG * 1940

Weeks L B BG 1942

Weld S L Jr BG

Wells G M MG *

West C W BG *

Westover O MG 1935

Williford F E BG

Wilson J H BG

Wilson W H MG

Wilson W K MG

Wood R J GEN

Wool J E MG 1861

QUARTERS OCCUPANTS

The following lists provide the names of occupants of Fort Monroe officers' and noncommissioned officers' quarters. The occupants are listed by their last name, initials, rank, quarters number, street address, year and month they moved in, year and month they moved out, and the source of the information. The quarters number is the number assigned by the Post Engineers; the street address is that given by the Post Office.

The supplementary information given after the dates of residence may include ranks, branches of service, positions held or attained, school courses attended and personal notes; also see the bibliography. Surnames appearing at the end of an entry indicate occupants, contemporaries, friends, or family who provided information. All abbreviations used in the lists are given in the key below.

In addition to the military occupants, some civilian occupants of Fort Monroe quarters are listed here as well. These were civilians who held some position on the post, such as fire chief, post electrician, contract surgeon, and post trader (or sutler).

Typographical errors are those of the author who tried valiantly not to alter history to justify entries. Research records are stored at the Casemate Museum, Fort Monroe, VA. Lists of quarters of officers and noncommissioned officers are also stored in the genealogical section of the National Archives. The US Army Office of Military History (presently located at the Washington, DC Navy Yard following a fire at their old address) also has a copy of all research records.

KEY TO ABBREVIATONS OF SUPPLEMENTARY INFORMATION

1SG First Sergeant
a National Archives (NA) Annex, Alexandria, VA, Drawer 57, + sheet #
Adj Adjutant
AdvC CAS Advanced Course
AF Air Force
AGO Adjutant General's Office
AN306 Masonic Lodge
Ar Avia Army Aviation
Arty Bd Artillery Board
b NA, RG-393, Part V, Entry 3, + Volume #
BG Brigadier General
BEO1c Navy enlisted rank

BM1 USN Bosun's Mate
BOQ Bachelor Officers' Quarters
BtryOCs Battery Officer's Course
c NA, RG-393, Part V, Entry 9, + Box #
CAS Coast Artillery School + Year
Cav Cavalry
cd Class Directories, Fort Monroe, VA
CG Commanding General
CGH Coast Guard House
Chap Chaplain
cl Class + year
Co Company
CO Commanding Officer

Col Colonel
Con Contract Surgeon
CSM Command Sergeant Major
CW+# Chief Warrant Officer (1, 2, 3, or 4)
CWO Chief Warrant Officer
D Died
d NA, RG-92, Entry 225, + Box #
DC Dental Corps
DCSPER Deputy Chief of Staff, Personnel
doc NA, RG-92, Entry 225, + document number
DR Doctor
DSM Distinguished Service Medal
E+# Army enlisted rank
ENGR Engineer Corps
f Fort Monroe Facilities Engineer Office
FE+# US Coast Guard enlisted rank
FOcs CAS Field Officers' Course
GEN Four-star general
GS+# Civil Service Rating
HABS Historical American Buildings Survey. *The Architectural Heritage of Fort Monroe*
Inf Infantry
Instr Instructor
JHC J H Cochran
KIA Killed in Action
LNO Liaison Officer
LTC Lieutenant Colonel
LTG Lieutanant General
MedC Medical Corps
mfh Military Family Housing Records, Fort Monroe, VA
MG Major General
micro NA, Microfilm, + Box #
MOH Medal of Honor
MSG Master Sergeant
NA doc National Archives document + document #
NCO Noncommissioned Officer
nd No date
ORD Ordnance Corps
OPC Old Point ComfortPhBk Phone Book(s), + year when known
Pioneer Troops Construction engineer troops

PMc McClellan, P. "Fort Monroe Historic Quarters Research Report" (Casemate Museum, Fort Monroe, VA: 1974.)
POW Prisoner of War
PubH Public Health House
QM Quartermaster Corps
qm NA, RG-92, Entry 89, Box # + Document #
RegC Regular Course
REL General Robert E Lee
Ret Retired
Rev Reverend
RLT Rollin L Tilton
rm(s) Room(s) in quarters
rq NA, Quartermaster "Report of Quarters"
RVN Republic of South Vietnam
S&F Staff and Faculty
SC South Carolina
Secy Secretary
SFC Sergeant First Class
SGM Sergeant Major
SNCB US Navy enlisted rank
SP+# Army Specialist + grade number
SSG Staff Sergeant
Surg Surgeon
TRADOC US Army Training and Doctrine Command
T/Sgt of TSG Technical Sergeant
unk Unknown
USAC US Air Corps
usacc US Army Communications Center, Fort Monroe, VA
USN US Navy
USMC US Marine Corps
VEQ Visiting Enlisted Quarters
Vet Veterinarian
VIP Very important personages
w Weinert & Arthur, *Defender of the Chesapeake*
WO Warrant Officer
WOJG Warrant Officer Junior Grade
WWI World War I
WWII World War II
XO Executive Officer
YNC US Navy enlisted rank
+ Supporting sources

NONCOMMISSIONED OFFICERS

Abbott O SGT 149-S 9 Moat Walk 1977.10 1978.9 mfh
Abbott H L SGT 112-E 32 Tidball 1945.10 1946.9 AN306
Abbott J M SGT 71-W 17 Harrison 1954.7 1954.9 usacc
Abbott H L SGT 136-N 17 Hatch 1944.9 1945.9 PhBk
Abell S SGT 132-W 13 Tidball 1926 1929 '27-29cds
Ackerman D E SSG 152-W 12 Patch 1984.3 1986.7 mfh
Acosta SFC 192-S 6 Pratt 1975.2 1975.11 mfh
Acosta F W SFC 149-N 11 Moat Walk 1974.8 1975.2 mfh
Adams J T SFC 150-S 13 Moat Walk 1955.2 1955.5 usacc
Adams J T SFC 72-W 21 Harrison 1954.7 1955.2 usacc
Adams E T TSG 71-W 17 Harrison 1950 1931 '31cd
Adams L SP4 136-N 17 Hatch 1963.9 1964.2 mfh
Adams J W WOJG 113-W 26 Tidball 1943 1945 '44-5 PhBks
Adams H M SSG 150-S 13 Moat Walk 1961.4 1963.3 mfh
Adkins J D Jr MSG 156-N 181 Bernard 1954.12 1955.1 usacc
Aeillo D J SFC 156-N 181 Bernard 1953.3 1953.5 usacc
Aeillo D J MSG 195-N 7 Pratt 1953.5 1955.9 usacc
Agee J SP4 5 Big Bethel 1979.8 1980.2 mfh
Agosto I E-7 151-W 8 Patch 1969.2 1971.4 mfh
Akkerman M E-6 151-E 10 Patch 1971.11 1975.6 mfh
Ala L SSG 6 Big Bethel 1976.11 1977.6 mfh
Alberico F A SSG 148-N 5 Moat Walk 1963.10 1966.4 mfh
Albert R L SFC 155-S 183 Bernard 1969.7 1972.2 mfh
Albright K SSG 150-N 15 Moat Walk 1979.10 1980.6 mfh
Aldrich R E-7 71-E 19 Harrison 1969.11 1973.5 mfh
Alexander S F SP4 111-E 36 Tidball 1982.6 1984.11 mfh
Alion D 1SG 115-W 18 Harrison 1940 1941 '40-41PhBks
Allen J SSG 132-W 13 Tidball 1978.6 1981.11 mfh
Allison R E CPT 31-N 40 Hampton 1986.6 1986.12 mfh
Allred H SGT 140-N 19 Moat Walk 1950.10 1952.5 usacc
Almeida J MSG 132-E 15 Tidball 1967.3 1969.5 mfh
Alston T C SSG 71-E 19 Harrison 1928 1933 '29-33cds
Ambler L J SGM 3-F Casemate 1919.10 ? AN306
Ambrose S TSG 109-N 3 Frank Lane 1930 1931 '31cd
Ambrose M P SGM 195-S 5 Pratt 1963.9 1967.10 mfh
Ammons R M SGM 30-N 36 Hampton 1968.5 1969.12 mfh
Anderson J R SP5 148-S 7 Moat Walk 1975.8 1979.3 mfh
Anderson G LTC 61-S 43 Ingalls 1940.9 1943.11 S&F Anderson
Anderson L SFC 192-N 8 Pratt 1980.2 1981.12 mfh
Anderson J H E-7 90 21 Moat Walk 1968.11 1971.6 mfh
Apfelbeck K SP5 167-B 9 Patch 1981.1 1983.7 mfh
Apponi P A SFC 149-N 11 Moat Walk 1951.11 1952.11 usacc

Archer R C MSG 152-E 14 Patch 1948.4 1948.11 usacc
Armellino R L E-6 154-N 15 Murray 1970.5 1971.4 mfh
Armstrong G J TSG 115-E 20 Harrison 1939 1940 '40PhBk
Armstrong H W SSG 137-E 23 Hatch 1969.9 1972.1 usacc
Arnold K P SSG 114-W 22 Harrison 1967.12 1968.7 mfh
Arthur R H TSG 154-N 15 Murray 1943.11 1944.6 '43PhBk
Arthurs R E GS10 187-S 21 Murray 1963.7 1966.5 mfh
Ashe S ? 6 Big Bethel 1980.1 1980.12 mfh
Ashe S SSG 130-S 22 Tidball 1976.2 1977.11 mfh
Ashton L G SGT 136-N 17 Hatch 1966.4 1967.9 mfh
Askew T L E-6 112-W 30 Tidball 1965.4 1966.3 mfh
Askey D SGM 25-E 35 Tidball 1970.6 1971.8 mfh
Austin T E 1SG 110-W 38 Tidball 1930 1932 '31cd
Austin D R SFC 155-N 185 Bernard 1952.3 1952.10 usacc
Austin O W BM1 33 67 Fenwick 1961.7 1964.6 usacc
Ayers C F SSG 113-E 28 Tidball 1930 1931 '31cd
Ayers L G 1LT 71-E 19 Harrison 1918.12 1919.12 '19cd
Backstrom J SP5 167-B 9 Patch 1980.7 1981.1 mfh
Backstrom G A MSG 72-E 23 Harrison 1942 1945 '43-45PhBks
Backues R L SSG 114-E 24 Harrison 1930 1932 '31cd
Baege L Clerk 61-N 45 Ingalls 1900 1912 '00-12cds QMC
Bagley G G SFC 153-N 13 Hatch 1956.4 1960.12 usacc
Bailey R H SFC 137-E 23 Hatch 1952.2 1952.4 usacc
Bailey R SP5 150-N 15 Moat Walk 1977.3 1978.5 mfh
Bailey E M SGT 112-E 32 Tidball 1959.7 1961.6 usacc
Bailey E A Mr 115-E 20 Harrison 1945-3 1947.1 usacc
Bailey R H MSG 149-N 11 Moat Walk 1956.2 1962.10 mfh
Bailey R H MSG 148-S 7 Moat Walk 1952.4 1955.11 usacc
Bailey G C SGT 71-E 19 Harrison 1956.9 1958.3 usacc
Bair L W CWO 25-W 33 Tidball 1944.11 1945.12 '44PhBk
Bair L W CWO 26-W 29 Tidball 1943.9 1944.11 '43-45PhBks
Bais J A SP5 151-E 10 Patch 1975.6 1976.7 mfh
Baker T B TSG 115-E 20 Harrison 1930 1931 '31cd
Baker L E Sr MSG 112-E 32 Tidball 1953.1 1953.6 usacc
Baker L E Sr MSG 25-W 33 Tidball 1953.6 1953.12 usacc
Baldwin E SP5 131-E 18 Tidball 1978.5 1979.1 mfh
Ball E N MSG 186-S 17 Murray 1957.4 1959.7 usacc
Ballou C G MSG 136-E 19 Hatch 1937.6 1938.8 Ballou
Ballou C G MSG 130-N 24 Tidball 1940.11 1942.5 Ballou
Ballou C G SSG 131-E 18 Tidball 1930 1931 '31cd
Bander M SSG 113-E 28 Tidball 1919 1930 '29cd
Bander M MSG 131-W 20 Tidball 1938 1939.6 '39PhBk
Bander M TSG 149-N 11 Moat Walk 1939.6 1940 '40PhBk
Banks R J MSG 140-S 17 Moat Walk 1958.5 1965.2 mfh
Banks S SGT 148-N 5 Moat Walk 1981.8 1982.11 mfh
Banks S W SSG 110-E 40 Tidball 1983.7 1986.8 mfh
Barham D W SP4 136-E 19 Hatch 1964.4 1965.10 usacc
Barker A J SSG 132-W 13 Tidball 1930 1931 '31cd
Barkley R P SSG 136-E 19 Hatch 1942.6 1945.10 '43-45PhBks
Barlow D SFC 194-S 1 Pratt 1976.8 1977.8 mfh
Barnes R H SFC 194-S 1 Pratt 1953.1 1953.12 usacc
Barnes R H SFC 154-N 15 Murray 1953.1 1953.1 usacc
Barnes C W 1SG 196-N 11 Pratt 1973.7 1975.7 mfh

Barnes C A MSG 115-W 18 Harrison 1949.6 1950.2 usacc
Barrett E S WOJG 192-S 6 Pratt 1943 1946 '43-45PhBks
Barrett E S SSG 71-W 17 Harrison 1936.6 1938 '37PhBk
Barrett E S SSG 111-W 34 Tidball 1938 1940 '39-40PhBks
Barron D E-7 71-W 17 Harrison 1965.4 1966.9 mfh
Barron D K SSG 136-E 19 Hatch 1967.4 1968.3 usacc
Barron D SFC 149-N 11 Moat Walk 1966.9 1967.10 mfh
Bartok L J MAJ 31-S 38 Hampton 1983.7 1985.6 mfh
Barwig D L E-7 90 21 Moat Walk 1972.11 1973.5 mfh
Bashow E F SGM 196-N 11 Pratt 1960.10 1963.3 mfh
Bashow E F MSG 150-S 13 Moat Walk 1960.8 1960.10 usacc
Batton R M SGM 30-S 34 Hampton 1965.7 1966.3 mfh
Baty P L SFC 150-N 15 Moat Walk 1953.4 1954.9 usacc
Baumgarner O R CWO 25-E 35 Tidball 1948.8 1950.6 usacc
Bautz M SFC 193-N 12 Pratt 1982.3 1982.9 mfh
Bavaria E A MSG 149-N 11 Moat Walk 1946.8 1949.1 usacc
Beale R SGT 71-W 17 Harrison 1900 1904 '00-03cd QMC
Beall L N E-8 30-S 34 Hampton 1968.12 1970.3 mfh
Beall C E Jr SGT 136-E 19 Hatch 1974.11 1974.11 mfh
Beall C E Jr E-3 90 21 Moat Walk 1974.11 1975.4 mfh
Bear C D SSG 154-S 13 Murray 1926 1927 '27cd
Beattie J TSG 114-E 24 Harrison 1933 1938 '33-7cd Pugh
Beck R B MSG 31-N 40 Hampton 1972.7 1973.6 mfh
Beckelhimer A TSG 140-N 19 Moat Walk 1946.8 1950.1 usacc
Beckman H E MSG 149-N 11 Moat Walk 1951.9 1951.11 usacc
Beckman C W SFC 153-N 13 Hatch 1952.10 1955.11 usacc
Beer C Mr 114-E 24 Harrison 1912 1914 '13-14PhBks
Beever R CWO 26-W 29 Tidball 1953.3 1953.7 usacc
Beever R MSG 151-E 10 Patch 1953.2 1953.3 usacc
Belding C E SGT 152-E 14 Patch 1926 1927 '27cd
Bell J SP4 131-W 20 Tidball 1981.12 1982.5 mfh
Bell E H E-7 113-W 26 Tidball 1969.12 1971.10 mfh
Bellamy J A SP5 90 21 Moat Walk 1985.5 1986.6 mfh
Beller S J E-6 140-N 19 Moat Walk 1970.6 1971.11 mfh
Beller S J SP6 136-E 19 Hatch 1969.8 1970.6 usacc
Bell L Jr MSG 192-S 6 Pratt 1964.8 1965.8 mfh
Belton N L SP5 137-E 23 Hatch 1975.8 ? mfh
Bender M TSG 186-N 19 Murray 1941 1942 '40-41PhBks
Bender R A SFC 25-W 33 Tidball 1984.12 1985.2 mfh
Bendos E SFC 71-W 17 Harrison 1960.1 1960.7 usacc
Benfer E L SSG 136-E 19 Hatch 1930 1931 '31cd
Benhoff J T SP5 111-E 36 Tidball 1974.12 1975.7 mfh
Bennett F J CSM 30-N 36 Hampton 1970.1 1973.1 mfh
Bennett F J SGM 26-W 29 Tidball 1967.6 1968.2 mfh
Bennett J D MSG 109-N 3 Frank Lane 1963.12 1965.9 mfh
Benson C N SFC 114-E 24 Harrison 1969.9 1970.8 mfh
Bentz O SGT 151-W 8 Patch 1926 1927 '27cd
Beranek J E SFC 152-E 14 Patch 1966.10 1967.7 mfh
Berberick S G E-6 130-N 24 Tidball 1968.7 1969.1 mfh
Bergbon C E ? 112-W 30 Tidball 1916 1917 '17cd rms?
Bergman R P SGT 137-E 23 Hatch 1969.4 1969.6 usacc
Berlin N R SFC 114-W 22 Harrison 1969.8 1970.7 mfh
Bernard J SGT 149-N 11 Moat Walk 1979.3 1980.2 mfh

Berney T J SGT 71-W 17 Harrison 1912 1914 '13-14cds
Berrios E MSG 131-E 18 Tidball 1956.11 1962.8 mfh
Berrios-Miranda A A E-6 148-S 7 Moat Walk 1968.6 1969.9 mfh
Berry W MSG 33 E-2 63 Fenwick 1978.8 1979.3 mfh
Berry W G SGT 151-E 10 Patch 1926 1927 '27cd
Bethea A H E-7 112-E 32 Tidball 1969.3 1970.5 mfh
Betten S D SSG 72-W 21 Harrison 1968.11 1969.6 usacc
Bettis J SGM 35 W-2 2 Reeder Cir 1982.5 1986.1 mfh
Bevers R E-6 153-N 13 Hatch 1972.1 1972.8 mfh
Bevilacqua J E-8 154-S 13 Murray 1969.4 1970.3 mfh
Beylickjian G G E-8 195-S 5 Pratt 1970.9 1973.6 mfh
Bibal J E SP4 114-W 22 Harrison 1983.4 1984.5 mfh
Bickley J A SGT 137-E 23 Hatch 1967.8 1969.4 usacc
Biegler D SSG 153-S 15 Hatch 1977.6 1978.8 mfh
Biggs K W TSG 71-W 17 Harrison 1947.1 1950.1 usacc
Bigler W R SGT 154-N 15 Murray 1916 1917 '17cd
Billingsley W P ? 137-W 21 Hatch 1915 1919 '17-19cds
Binau J B SFC 136-N 17 Hatch 1956.9 1958.1 usacc
Binau P I SGT 136-N 17 Hatch 1953.2 1956.7 usacc
Binau P J E-7 150-N 15 Moat Walk 1959.6 1963.4 mfh
Bingham B L SGT 156-S 179 Bernard 1916 1917 '17cd
Bingham B L SGT 136-N 17 Hatch 1912 1914 '13-14cds
Biondi L F MSG 30-S 34 Hampton 1962.5 1963.5 mfh
Biondi L F MSG 113-W 26 Tidball 1962.4 1962.5 mfh
Birckhead S SSG 115-E 20 Harrison 1979.7 1983.2 mfh
Bittle D TSG 30-S 34 Hampton 1940 1942 '40-44PhBks
Bivens W Jr SFC 194-N 3 Pratt 1978.6 1981.6 mfh
Bixler M SFC 192-S 6 Pratt 1981.3 1982.6 mfh
Black J M SGT 153-S 15 Hatch 1915 1916 '16cd
Black J M SGT 155-N 185 Bernard 1912 1915 '13-14cds
Black J E SSG 114-E 24 Harrison 1968.9 1969.4 mfh
Blackham K A SGT 140-N 19 Moat Walk 1982.9 1984.3 mfh
Blackwell M D MSG 113-W 26 Tidball 1957.7 1959.6 usacc
Blair P W TSG 136-N 17 Hatch 1939.6 1940.6 '39cd '40PhBk
Blake J SP4 140-N 19 Moat Walk 1980.6 1982.4 mfh
Blakeman C SP5 115-W 18 Harrison 1974.3 1979.8 mfh
Blalock W W SSG 136-N 17 Hatch 1939.6 1940.6 '39 cd '40 PhBk
Bland T R MSG 148-S 7 Moat Walk 1947.1 1949.1 usacc
Blandford D SGT 71-E 19 Harrison 1913 1915 '13-14cds
Blandford D SGT 156-N 181 Bernard 1916 1917 '17cd
Bledsoe B R SP4 151-E 10 Patch 1985.11 1987.12 mfh
Bledsoe B L MSG 152-W 12 Patch 1962.8 1964.6 mfh
Bloomstrom G SGM 30-N 36 Hampton 1960.8 1962.6 mfh
Bogard S B SGM 72-E 23 Harrison 1906.6 ? b-25
Bogardus W WOJG 90 21 Moat Walk 1942 1943 '43PhBk
Boles C L SSG 137-E 23 Hatch 1930 1931 '31cd
Boley R M SFC 114-E 24 Harrison 1969.5 1969.9 mfh
Bond B E SGT 148-S 7 Moat Walk 1985.10 1987.2 mfh
Bond C C SSG 5 Big Bethel 1985.7 1987.7 mfh
Bonner L ? 156-S 179 Bernard 1976.12 1978.7 mfh
Booe W TSG 115-E 20 Harrison 1947.1 1948.3 usacc
Boofter J E E-7 113-W 26 Tidball 1972.9 1973.10 mfh
Borden L A 1SG 132-W 13 Tidball 1932 1933 '33cd

104

Bores M E SP4 137-E 23 Hatch 1972.1 1972.2 mfh
Bosko S MSG 136-N 17 Hatch 1948.8 1949.2 usacc
Boullianne C J SFC 72-W 21 Harrison 1955.5 1958.3 usacc
Boullianne C J SFC 152-E 14 Patch 1958.3 1961.10 usacc
Bowen F L WO 150-S 13 Moat Walk 1946.12 1948.9 usacc
Bowick H B E-6 110-W 38 Tidball 1969.6 1970.4 mfh
Bowling L G Jr SGM 194-S 1 Pratt 1966.2 1966.9 mfh
Boyce V M MSG 154-S 13 Murray 1955.2 1956.4 usacc
Boyer G W MSG 26-E 31 Tidball 1954.5 1958.2 usacc
Boyer R W SFC 136-N 17 Hatch 1962.6 1963.7 mfh
Boyer P E SSG 112-E 32 Tidball 1973.10 1975.10 mfh
Boykin C B SFC 155-N 185 Bernard 1959.8 1960.9 usacc
Bracken F J SSG 140-N 19 Moat Walk 1930 1931 '31cd
Bradley L MSG 191-S 2 Pratt 1956.12 1958.7 usacc
Bradley J M MSG 188-S 25 Murray 1955.5 1961.11 usacc
Bradsher L A SP5 150-S 13 Moat Walk 1973.6 1973.9 mfh
Branham P SFC 131-W 20 Tidball 1978.10 1981.12 mfh
Brashear M G CWO 31-S 38 Hampton 1942.6 1946.9 '43-45PhBks
Braswell C W MSG 131-E 18 Tidball 1968.10 1974.4 mfh
Brayboy A M E-6 153-N 13 Hatch 1972.8 1973.3 mfh
Brett J K SFC 193-N 12 Pratt 1980.7 1982.3 mfh
Brickhouse J ? 6 Big Bethel 1980.12 1983.4 mfh
Bridwell H L SFC 115-W 18 Harrison 1951.7 1952.5 usacc
Brill R W SFC 154-S 13 Murray 1958.2 1959.3 usacc
Brinkman E X SFC 131-E 18 Tidball 1966.10 1968.9 mfh
Broadrick N C SSG 148-N 5 Moat Walk 1930 1932 '31cd
Brobson W H SSG 132-E 15 Tidball 1985.10 1986.12 mfh
Brook W H 1SG 131-E 18 Tidball 1948.9 1949.1 usacc
Brooks I W SSG 132-W 13 Tidball 1939.9 1942.6 '39-40PhBks
Brooks H J 1SG 131-E 18 Tidball 1940.9 1942.6 '40-41PhBks
Brooks W R SFC 140-S 17 Moat Walk 1950.1 1950.6 usacc
Brooks W D MSG 110-W 38 Tidball 1952.2 1952.5 usacc
Brooks I W 1SG 149-N 11 Moat Walk 1944.10 1946.8 '44-45PhBks
Brooks W D MSG 186-N 19 Murray 1952.5 1952.10 usacc
Brooks I W SSG 148-S 7 Moat Walk 1930 1931 '44-45PhBks
Brookshire F E SGM 30-S 34 Hampton 1966.4 1967.4 mfh
Brosseau H CPT 30-N 36 Hampton 1984.6 1985.5 mfh
Brown C E MSG 188-S 25 Murray 1962.1 1962.8 mfh
Brown V L SFC 132-E 15 Tidball 1961.8 1961.11 usacc
Brown R P SP6 110-E 40 Tidball 1974.3 1977.6 mfh
Brown L L CW3 30-N 36 Hampton 1985.5 1987.7 mfh
Brown J S SSG 131-E 18 Tidball 1938.9 1939.9 AN306
Brown J O 1SG 151-E 10 Patch 1930 1931 '31cd
Brown J W E-8 61-N 45 Ingalls 1967.3 1967.3 mfh
Brown H W TSG 150-N 15 Moat Walk 1919 1933 '31cd
Brown A P SSG 149-S 9 Moat Walk 1930 1932 '31cd
Brownell R J MSG 195-N 7 Pratt 1955.10 1957.3 usacc
Brownell R J MSG 111-E 36 Tidball 1954.2 1955.10 usacc
Brownell R MSG 154-S 13 Murray 1949.8 1951.3 usacc
Brownell R J MSG 111-E 36 Tidball 1954.2 1955.10 usacc
Browning D W MSG 140-N 19 Moat Walk 1957.4 1958.8 usacc
Browning R E 1SG 195-S 5 Pratt 1967.11 1969.2 mfh
Browning R E MSG 148-S 7 Moat Walk 1965.8 1966.6 mfh

Brown H I Jr MSG 148-N 5 Moat Walk 1952.9 1953.10 usacc
Brown R A Jr SGT 151-E 10 Patch 1953.4 1954.2 usacc
Brown R A Jr SGT 137-W 21 Hatch 1952.5 1953.4 usacc
Brown W B Sr MSG 90 21 Moat Walk 1953.1 1954.6 usacc
Brown H I Sr MSG 187-N 23 Murray 1953.10 1954.3 usacc
Bruce E H MSG 31-S 38 Hampton 1954.8 1955.8 usacc
Bruce H A SGT 110-E 40 Tidball 1953.2 1953.6 usacc
Brush A P MSG 115-W 18 Harrison 1950.2 1951.6 usacc
Bruton J SP5 114-E 24 Harrison 1976.4 1979.2 mfh
Brye J C SP5 156-S 179 Bernard 1974.10 1976.12 mfh
Bryles H C 1SG 156-N 181 Bernard 1936 1938 '37 PhBk
Bryles H C 1SG 186-S 17 Murray 1938 1940 '40 PhBk
Bublich J F SP1 113-E 28 Tidball 1957.2 1958.7 usacc
Bucheli J MSG 193-N 12 Pratt 1944.6 1946.9 '44-45PhBks
Buderer G L SSG 137-W 21 Hatch 1928 1931 '29-31cds
Bufter W S WO 187-S 21 Murray 1938 ? '37cd
Buhl F P SSG 153-S 15 Hatch 1940 1941 '40-41PhBks
Bullard F H WO 155-S 183 Bernard 1924 1925 AN306
Bunting C 1SG 152-E 14 Patch 1930 1931 '31cd
Burden P A SP4 148-S 7 Moat Walk 1985.4 1985.10 mfh
Burford A N E-6 151-E 10 Patch 1970.12 1971.10 mfh
Burke R H E-7 149-S 9 Moat Walk 1969.8 1971.9 mfh
Burnett F M MSG 49 49 Bernard 1951.6 1952.5 usacc
Burnett C V SSG 140-S 17 Moat Walk 1965.3 1965.8 mfh
Burnham R L MSG 30-N 36 Hampton 1955.6 1958.4 usacc
Burns B S SP5 151-W 8 Patch 1983.12 1984.2 mfh
Burns R E MSG 154-S 13 Murray 1957.5 1958.2 usacc
Burns C E E-5 71-W 17 Harrison 1967.5 1968.1 mfh
Burns R E MSG 193-S 10 Pratt 1958.2 1961.3 usacc
Burns L 1SG 150-S 13 Moat Walk 1940 1943.6 '40-41PhBks
Burwell C R Mr 195-N 7 Pratt 1962.9 1963.6 mfh
Burwell C R Mr 156-S 179 Bernard 1961.11 1962.9 usacc
Busisy A D SGT 109-S 1 Frank Lane 1953.3 1953.4 usacc
Busker W M TSG 153-S 15 Hatch 1937 1940 '37cd '39-40PhBks
Butkiewicz J K Clerk 71-E 19 Harrison 1907 1908 '08cd QMC
Butler P D SSG 115-E 20 Harrison 1970.6 1970.8 mfh
Butler J A TSG 150-N 15 Moat Walk 1938 1941 '39cd '40-41PhBks
Butler R J MSG 149-S 9 Moat Walk 1944.9 1946.9 '44-45PhBks
Butters F H CWO 25-E 35 Tidball 1944.9 1946.8 '45PhBk
Butters F H CWO 193-S 10 Pratt 1942 1943.10 '43PhBk
Butters F H CWO 151-E 10 Patch 1943.10 1944.9 AN306
Button A M SSG 156-S 179 Bernard 1926 1929 '27-29cds
Byrd O W SGM 25-W 33 Tidball 1964.9 1966.8 mfh
Byrne A W TSG 191-S 2 Pratt 1939 1940 '40PhBk
Byrne D H SP5 72-E 23 Harrison 1965.6 1966.10 mfh
Byrne D H E-6 151-W 8 Patch 1966.10 1968.1 mfh
Cabal M P SP5 136-E 19 Hatch 1963.1 1963.3 usacc
Cable L J ? 137-E 23 Hatch 1914 1917 '14-17cds
Caccia O J SFC 115-W 18 Harrison 1952.9 1954.5 usacc
Caldwell J H E-8 193-N 12 Pratt 1970.12 1971.6 mfh
Calhoun L N SFC 113-W 26 Tidball 1952.6 1954.11 usacc
Callis R S MSG 109-S 1 Frank Lane 1950.8 1950.11 usacc
Calnon K K E-6 114-E 24 Harrison 1972.1 1973.7 mfh

Calvert L R SSG 109-S 1 Frank Lane 1936 1941 '37-41PhBks
Cambell G MSG 187-N 23 Murray 1947.8 1949.6 usacc
Campbell R WO 188-N 27 Murray 1937 1939 '37 PhBk
Campbell W SP5 148-S 7 Moat Walk 1979.3 1980.10 mfh
Campbell J J CWO 25-E 35 Tidball 1950.6 1952.8 usacc
Campbell D T SGT 90 21 Moat Walk 1951.11 1953.1 usacc
Carenbauer G H SFC 136-E 19 Hatch 1950.6 1950.10 usacc
Carenbauer G H SFC 148-N 5 Moat Walk 1950.10 1952.8 usacc
Carhart S W MSG 148-N 5 Moat Walk 1959.7 1962.6 mfh
Carmical J SP5 140-S 17 Moat Walk 1972.8 1973.7 mfh
Carpenter J SGT 109-N 3 Frank Lane 1915 1916 '16cd
Carpenter G L SFC 30-S 34 Hampton 1974.8 1977.8 mfh
Carpenter J R SSG 71-E 19 Harrison 1926 1927 '27cd
Carr M SFC 192-S 6 Pratt 1979.8 1981.1 mfh
Carroll E S SFC 111-W 34 Tidball 1952.4 1952.12 usacc
Carrow F N SFC 150-N 15 Moat Walk 1964.8 1965.7 mfh
Carter R B SFC 192-N 8 Pratt 1963.6 1965.6 mfh
Carter W N SGT 71-W 17 Harrison 1907 1908 '08cd
Carter W SSG 110-W 38 Tidball 1977.1 1979.6 mfh
Carter G SP4 114-E 24 Harrison 1973.11 1976.3 mfh
Carter E C Jr MSG 148-N 5 Moat Walk 1954.11 1955.7 usacc
Cartright C D SSG 132-E 15 Tidball 1965.9 1967.3 mfh
Case W H YNC 112-W 30 Tidball 1961.9 1962.8 mfh
Casey M W MSG 187-N 23 Murray 1969.8 1971.5 mfh
Casey M W SFC 150-S 13 Moat Walk 1963.4 1964.10 mfh
Cassim-Garcia O J SFC 71-W 17 Harrison 1952.5 1952.9 usacc
Castele A H SGM 26-W 29 Tidball 1965.8 1967.5 usacc
Catron J R MSG 131-E 18 Tidball 1956.2 1956.10 usacc
Cauddill L F 1SG 188-N 27 Murray 1975.9 ? mfh
Cavalli R PFC 71-W 17 Harrison 1974.5 ? mfh
Cavanaugh MAJ 30-S 34 Hampton 1981.6 1983.11 mfh
Chadwick A W SGT 149-S 9 Moat Walk 1963.10 1966.4 mfh
Chang C C MSG 150-N 15 Moat Walk 1965.7 1967.5 mfh
Chang C C MSG 153-N 13 Hatch 1968.8 1970.2 usacc
Chapman H SP5 140-N 19 Moat Walk 1977.3 1978.10 mfh
Chapman S I MSG 131-E 18 Tidball 1928 1929 '29cd
Chase G MSG 114-E 24 Harrison 1946.10 1948.12 usacc
Chaves-Deliz R A E-6 110-W 38 Tidball 1967.8 1968.4 mfh
Chestnut M L Jr E-8 193-S 10 Pratt 1972.10 1976.10 mfh
Childress W A SSG 167-B 9 Patch 1983.7 1984.8 mfh
Childress W A SFC 26-E 31 Tidball 1986.5 ? mfh
Christensen G M E-5 136-N 17 Hatch 1968.6 1969.1 mfh
Christensen W SP4 152-W 12 Patch 1977.12 1979.3 mfh
Christenson E SGM 155-N 185 Bernard 1916 1917 '17cd
Christenson H SFC 132-E 15 Tidball 1950.1 1952.9 usacc
Christenson A W WO 152-W 12 Patch 1930 1931 '31cd
Christian B H CWO 26-E 31 Tidball 1944.10 1945.9 '44-45PhBks
Christofferson C G SSG 140-N 19 Moat Walk 1936 1937 '37PhBk
Clark R G I MSG 109-N 3 Frank Lane 1952.3 1953.2 usacc
Clark M J SGT 130-N 24 Tidball 1984.9 1986.2 mfh
Clark H L SFC 140-S 17 Moat Walk 1956.4 1958.5 usacc
Clark J E SFC 111-E 36 Tidball 1968.7 1969.7 mfh
Clark C G E-8 193-S 10 Pratt 1970.11 1972.9 mfh

Clark C W MSG 112-E 32 Tidball 1959.2 1959.7 usacc
Clark G L SFC 195-N 7 Pratt 1973.7 1973.12 mfh
Clauson J Jr ? 187-N 23 Murray 1980.8 1981.7 mfh
Clement W L 1SG 131-W 20 Tidball 1946.10 1948.1 usacc
Clements W J SGT 167-B 9 Patch 1985.10 1986.2 mfh
Cleveland S T MSG 191-N 4 Pratt 1950.8 1953.12 usacc
Clevenger V E SP6 155-N 185 Bernard 1971.8 1972.8 mfh
Clifton W H SP5 153-N 13 Hatch 1973.12 1974.6 mfh
Clifton M SGM 192-S 6 Pratt 1963.2 1964.8 mfh
Clifton P E SP5 155-S 183 Bernard 1973.11 1973.12 mfh
Cochran W N SFC 156-N 181 Bernard 1949.12 1952.12 usacc
Cochran D S SP4 152-W 12 Patch 1986.7 1987.11 mfh
Cockrum G SP5 114-E 24 Harrison 1979.2 1979.12 mfh
Coder R H MSG 71-E 19 Harrison 1942 1946 '41-45PhBks
Coe C A SSG 114-W 22 Harrison 1936 1939 '37-39PhBks
Cogburn N W SFC 114-W 22 Harrison 1968.7 1969.7 mfh
Coile C R MSG 131-E 18 Tidball 1912 1914 '13-14cds
Coile C R MSG 186-S 17 Murray 1935 1938 '37PhBk
Colbaugh D E MSG 115-E 20 Harrison 1957.2 1957.6 usacc
Cole H R MSG 155-N 185 Bernard 1928 1933 '29-33cds
Cole W H SFC 149-N 11 Moat Walk 1950.2 1951.8 usacc
Cole A E SGT 151-W 8 Patch 1914 1916 '14-16cds
Coleman G N CWO 194-N 3 Pratt 1942 1944 AN306 '43PhBk
Collier SNCB 33 67 Fenwick 1957.10 1961.7 usacc USN
Collins J SP6 110-E 40 Tidball 1967.10 1968.11 mfh
Collins A C SGT 155-S 183 Bernard 1954.7 1955.3 usacc
Collins F B E-7 140-N 19 Moat Walk 1971.12 1973.8 mfh
Collins F B SFC 187-N 23 Murray 1973.8 1974.11 mfh
Colombo J A MSG 196-S 9 Pratt 1953.1 1953.10 usacc
Colon R SP4 150-S 13 Moat Walk 1982.1 1982.9 mfh
Colraine J B MSG 196-S 9 Pratt 1972.6 1974.5 mfh
Colyer W C MSG 132-W 13 Tidball 1954.6 1955.10 usacc
Colyer W C MSG 109-N 3 Frank Lane 1955.10 1957.9 usacc
Condron P H SFC 155-N 185 Bernard 1954.3 1956.3 usacc
Conklin H W SSG 112-W 30 Tidball 1937 1938 '37cd
Conklin H W SSG 155-S 183 Bernard 1938 1941 '39-41PhBks
Conley G W MSG 130-S 22 Tidball 1969.9 1971.6 mfh
Conner W B SFC 130-S 22 Tidball 1967.7 1968.12 mfh
Conner J P SP4 6 Big Bethel 1985.12 1986.6 mfh
Conner A V E-8 193-N 12 Pratt 1971.6 1973.7 mfh
Conner J A Clerk 61-S 43 Ingalls 1908 ? '08PhBk QMC
Conrad L L SFC 152-E 14 Patch 1964.3 1965.6 mfh
Conroy R 1LT 156-N 181 Bernard 1919 ? '19cd rms?
Conroy F SGT 72-E 23 Harrison 1915 1916 '16cd
Conway G SP6 152-W 12 Patch 1979.3 1984.2 mfh
Cook J Jr SSG 156-N 181 Bernard 1944.11 1946.9 '44-45PhBks
Cook J W SGT 136-N 17 Hatch 1951.4 1952.12 usacc
Cook D W SSG 111-E 36 Tidball 1984.12 1986.5 mfh
Cook O R SFC 156-S 179 Bernard 1956.9 1957.10 usacc
Cook J E SP5 156-N 181 Bernard 1971.11 1972.1 mfh
Cook J S TSG 136-E 19 Hatch 1932 1933 '33cd
Cooke E W MSG 148-N 5 Moat Walk 1956.12 1958.8 usacc
Cool H M 1LT 156-N 181 Bernard 1919 ? '19cd rms?

Copeland S A SFC 153-S 15 Hatch 1960.7 1961.2 usacc
Corbin A T MSG 194-N 3 Pratt 1952.6 1953.3 usacc
Corbin A T TSG 109-N 3 Frank Lane 1942.2 1946.12 usacc
Corbin A T MSG 151-E 10 Patch 1949.7 1952.6 usacc
Corcoran W F SFC 114-W 22 Harrison 1951.12 1953.4 usacc
Corley B W MSG 154-S 13 Murray 1948.7 1949.7 usacc
Corley R C SGT 154-N 15 Murray 1973.7 1973.10 mfh
Corley S C Jr SFC 111-W 34 Tidball 1952.1 1952.3 usacc
Costello F SSG 154-N 15 Murray 1930 1931 '31cd
Counts D G SFC 111-E 36 Tidball 1961.11 1962.12 mfh
Cournouer J B M MSG 140-N 19 Moat Walk 1953.10 1954.1 usacc
Courtney J CPT 148-S 7 Moat Walk 1917 1920 '17-20cd AN306
Couzynbe B MSG 193-S 10 Pratt 1951.9 1953.4 usacc
Covola J SSG 155-S 183 Bernard 1944.12 1948.3 usacc
Cox A P SGM 188-S 25 Murray 1968.7 1969.11 mfh
Cox L D MSG 153-N 13 Hatch 1948.7 1949.1 usacc
Cox T G MSG 25-E 35 Tidball 1968.5 1970.5 mfh
Cox D Z SSG 131-W 20 Tidball 1933 1937 '37cd
Cox R E SSG 114-W 22 Harrison 1974.1 1975.9 mfh
Coyle J W MSG 153-N 13 Hatch 1947.2 1947.6 usacc
Craft C E SSG 149-S 9 Moat Walk 1971.10 1972.3 mfh
Craft J CSM 64 71 Fenwick 1980.8 1981.7 mfh
Cramer H W MSG 25-W 33 Tidball 1951.10 1953.4 usacc
Cramer H W MSG 112-E 32 Tidball 1950.6 1951.10 usacc
Craven R SP4 151-W 8 Patch 1980.3 1981.11 mfh
Crawford H J MSG 90 21 Moat Walk 1958.8 1962.11 mfh
Crawford A M SGM 149-N 11 Moat Walk 1911.6 1917.6 '11-17cds
Crawford A M 1LT 149-N 11 Moat Walk 1917.6 1919.4 S&F '19cd Arthur
Creagan J P 1SG 153-S 15 Hatch 1967.4 1968.4 mfh
Crider E H MSG 151-E 10 Patch 1963.5 1964.12 mfh
Crisel C E-5 149-S 9 Moat Walk 1972.3 1972.9 mfh
Crocker J R SGM 31-S 38 Hampton 1967.6 1969.10 mfh
Crocker J R MSG 154-S 13 Murray 1959.4 1959.6 usacc
Crocker J R MSG 31-N 40 Hampton 1959.6 1961.7 usacc
Crosby W O MSG 187-N 23 Murray 1953.3 1953.10 usacc
Crosby W O MSG 149-S 9 Moat Walk 1953.2 1953.3 usacc
Cross T L E-9 192-S 6 Pratt 1966.11 1969.7 mfh
Crossett D C E-8 110-W 38 Tidball 1970.4 1971.8 mfh
Crossett D C MSG 25-E 35 Tidball 1971.8 1973.4 mfh
Crothers T G SP6 152-W 12 Patch 1967.8 1968.11 mfh
Crowe M L SSG 115-W 18 Harrison 1963.10 1964.4 mfh
Crowley F MSG 196-N 11 Pratt 1972.7 1973.7 mfh
Cruz-Santiago F SGM 35-E-2 8 Reeder 1982.6 1985.6 mfh
Cuevas H SGT 115-E 20 Harrison 1978.3 1979.7 mfh
Cuha T SP6 90 21 Moat Walk 1977.12 1980.3 mfh
Cummings T V E-7 148-S 7 Moat Walk 1966.8 1967.7 mfh
Cunningham D R SP4 151-W 8 Patch 1986.4 1986.9 mfh
Cunningham C P Mr 109-S 1 Frank Lane 1911 1917 '12-17cds
Cunningham W C ? 109-S 1 Frank Lane 1906 1909 '06-09cd ENGR
Cunningham C C ? 72-E 23 Harrison 1900 1907 '00-07cd
Curry G W SP4 167-B 9 Patch 1984.8 1985.10 mfh
Dahlquist G W WO 187-S 21 Murray 1931 1933 '31-33cds
Dailey W T MSG 196-S 9 Pratt 1955.5 1962.11 mfh

Dailly J F SSG 113-W 26 Tidball 1967.8 1969.11 mfh
Dailly J F SSG 137-E 23 Hatch 1967.5 1967.8 usacc
Dale G TSG 109-N 3 Frank Lane 1930 1940 '40PhBk
Dale G MSG 25-W 33 Tidball 1943.6 1944.9 '43PhBk
Dale G TSG 25-W 33 Tidball 1940 1942 '40-41PhBks
Dalrymple D MSG 195-S 5 Pratt 1982.6 1983.6 mfh
Damrath G J SP5 136-E 19 Hatch 1959.10 1960.9 usacc
Daniels L H 1SG 150-N 15 Moat Walk 1943.6 1946.11 '43-46PhBks
Daniels W F MSG 31-N 40 Hampton 1963.6 1965.9 mfh
Danko F S E-7 71-W 17 Harrison 1969.6 1969.10 mfh
Darling J ? 5 Big Bethel 1973.8 1976.8 mfh
Darneille J G MSG 130-N 24 Tidball 1912.6 1917.6 '13-17cds
Darneille J F 2LT 130-N 24 Tidball 1917.6 1918.3 S&F Arthur
David L H SSG 131-W 20 Tidball 1928 1933 '29-33cds
Davidson R MSG 130-S 22 Tidball 1951.11 1951.11 usacc
Davidson R MSG 194-S 1 Pratt 1951.11 1953.1 usacc
Davies F MSG 188-N 27 Murray 1955.11 1956.8 usacc
Davies R T MSG 115-E 20 Harrison 1948.5 1950.6 usacc
Davies F MSG 131-E 18 Tidball 1955.3 1955.11 usacc
Davis B E SGT 115-E 20 Harrison 1985.6 1986.6 mfh
Davis H L 1SG 156-S 179 Bernard 1936 1939 '37cd
Davis R H SFC 156-S 179 Bernard 1951.9 1952.10 usacc
Davis R T TSG 136-E 19 Hatch 1947.2 1947.10 usacc
Davis J L MSG 115-W 18 Harrison 1912 1917 '13-17cds
Davis R W SGT 111-E 36 Tidball 1913 1916 '14-15cds
Davis H L 1SG 26-W 29 Tidball 1939 1943 '39-41PhBks
Deal R MSG 131-E 18 Tidball 1949.5 1951.6 usacc
Deal A P MSG 150-N 15 Moat Walk 1933 1938 Pugh
Dearing A W SP6 115-E 20 Harrison 1972.9 1973.7 mfh
Deavy J 1SG 148-N 5 Moat Walk 1911 1912 '12cd
Decker E A MSG 156-S 179 Bernard 1959.5 1961.11 usacc
DeEntremont C E MSG 132-E 15 Tidball 1952.11 1955.11 usacc
DeHaan J MSG 188-S 25 Murray 1965.6 1965.11 mfh
DeHaven G SGM 194-N 3 Pratt 1976.4 1978.6 mfh
Dehner K E MSG 31-N 40 Hampton 1953.9 1954.10 usacc
DeJesus Fuentes A A SSG 149-N 11 Moat Walk 1968.9 1970.4 mfh
DeJesus Santana S SP6 153-S 15 Hatch 1968.4 1969.3 mfh
Del-Colle E F MSG 191-S 2 Pratt 1961.1 1962.6 mfh
Del-Colle E F MSG 150-S 13 Moat Walk 1960.10 1961.1 usacc
Delk H L SSG 152-E 14 Patch 1974.11 1975.9 mfh
Delo C P CWO 188-N 27 Murray 1948.2 1953.6 usacc
Dennis J F SGT 131-W 20 Tidball 1917 1918 '17cd
D'Entremont C E MSG 130-S 22 Tidball 1955.11 1956.3 usacc
DesLaurier J SFC 196-N 11 Pratt 1978.6 1980.10 mfh
Desrochers A TSG 26-E 31 Tidball 1939 1941 '39-41PhBks
Devlin R R SFC 149-S 9 Moat Walk 1952.12 1953.1 usacc
DeWalt F ? ll4-W 22 Harrison 1943.12 1944.10 Chapel Records
Dewitt E M SFC 113-E 28 Tidball 1952.10 1953.12 usacc
Diaz R SFC 71-E 19 Harrison 1954.10 1956.7 usacc
Dicarle P A TSG 72-W 21 Harrison 1946.12 1948.10 usacc
Dickman V L MSG 148-S 7 Moat Walk 1959.6 1959.10 usacc
Dickman B L MSG 155-S 183 Bernard 1949.10 1950.5 usacc
Dickson J P E-6 136-N 17 Hatch 1965.8 1965.10 mfh

Diehl J P SSG 150-N 15 Moat Walk 1911.6 1917 '13-17cds
Diehl J P SGM 72-E 23 Harrison 1907 1911.6 '08cd
Diehl J P WO 194-S 1 Pratt 1937 1939 '37cd Pugh
Diehl J P MSG 150-S 13 Moat Walk 1931 1933 '33cd
DiMarino N J MSG 153-N 13 Hatch 1948.1 1948.7 usacc
Dinger R L SFC 114-E 24 Harrison 1963.10 1965.4 mfh
Diolosa J SFC 26-W 29 Tidball 1976.12 1979.10 mfh
Disanti A SFC 4 Big Bethel 1975.11 1976.7 mfh
Disney C S SGT 130-N 24 Tidball 1983.7 1984.8 mfh
Dixon L E SFC 111-E 36 Tidball 1967.9 1968.7 mfh
Dixon SFC 193-S 10 Pratt 1976.10 1981.7 mfh
Dixon D C Mr 154-S 13 Murray 1930 1933 '31-33cds
Dolan R S SFC 113-W 26 Tidball 1949.11 1951.6 usacc
Dolley A W Jr SP6 113-W 26 Tidball 1974.5 1977.9 mfh
Donaldson M A SP5 151-W 8 Patch 1968.5 1969.2 mfh
Donnell J A SSG 153-N 13 Hatch 1985.7 1986.6 mfh
Dore B C Mr 61-N 45 Ingalls 1946.8 1955.11 usacc D V Lewis
Dore B C Mr 113-E 28 Tidball 1945.1 1946.8 '45 PhBk
Dorman J V E-6 149-S 9 Moat Walk 1972.10 1974.5 mfh
Dorsett C C MSG 111-W 34 Tidball 1951.11 1952.1 usacc
Dorsey J R CWO 193-S 10 Pratt 1946.9 1949.11 usacc
Doster H H MSG 191-S 2 Pratt 1949.3 1950.1 usacc
Doster H H MSG 140-S 17 Moat Walk 1946.12 1949.3 usacc
Dowell C O MSG 31-S 38 Hampton 1936 1942 '37-39cds 40-41PhBk
Dowell C O TSG 110-E 40 Tidball 1928 1936 '29-35cds
Dowell J SGM 196-N 11 Pratt 1969.3 1972.5 mfh
Downey L A SP4 155-N 185 Bernard 1972.9 1974.2 usacc
Downs W SSG 4 Big Bethel 1979.10 1984.7 mfh
Doyle E M MSG 130-N 24 Tidball 1946.10 1947.8 usacc
Drake R D SGT 140-N 19 Moat Walk 1952.5 1953.8 usacc
Drake D C MSG 195-S 5 Pratt 1983.6 1985.3 mfh
Draper M G MSG 110-E 40 Tidball 1955.12 1956.8 usacc
Dressler C B Mr 61-N 45 Ingalls 1912 1943.7 PhBk Fire Chief
Drexel C G SSG 140-N 19 Moat Walk 1937 1940 AN306
Drexel C G SSG 112-W 30 Tidball 1928 1929 '29cd
Drexel C G TSG 148-S 7 Moat Walk 1940 1943 '40-41PhBks
Driskill G A MSG 187-N 23 Murray 1947.1 1947.8 usacc
Duerod D SP4 154-N 15 Murray 1979.7 1980.12 mfh
Dugon J P TSG 131-E 18 Tidball 1942.6 1944.9 '43PhBk
Dula J A SGT 132-E 15 Tidball 1926 1929 '27-29cds
Dunlap G C TSG 110-E 40 Tidball 1946.9 1948.9 usacc
Dunn W A MSG 186-S 17 Murray 1982.6 1985.12 mfh
Dupont L J MSG 72-E 23 Harrison 1955.3 1955.9 usacc
Dupuy H A CWO 61-N 45 Ingalls 1956.1 1958.11 usacc
Duquette T S MSG 195-N 7 Pratt 1963.12 1965.4 mfh
Dutton C L SSG 71-E 19 Harrison 1938 1939 '37cd
Dutton C L TSG 140-S 17 Moat Walk 1939 1940 '39cd '40PhBk
Dutton C L SSG 132-W 13 Tidball 1933 1935 Farley
Dutton C L TSG 195-N 7 Pratt 1940 1941 '40-1PhBks
Duval C 1SG 136-N 17 Hatch 1932.5 1933.? '33cd
Duval C 1SG 192-N 8 Pratt 1937 1939 '37cd
Duval C MSG 192-S 6 Pratt 1939 1940 '40PhBk
Duvall R A SP5 110-W 38 Tidball 1975.10 1976.8 mfh

Dwyer G T SFC 72-W 21 Harrison 1950.3 1950.10 usacc
Dwyer G T SFC 130-S 22 Tidball 1951.11 1953.4 usacc
Dwyer G T SFC 152-E 14 Patch 1950.10 1951.3 usacc
Dykeman H A 1SG 115-E 20 Harrison 1940 1941 '40-41PhBks
Eastin J T SSG 149-N 11 Moat Walk 1963.10 1965.9 mfh
Ebzery W C MSG 150-N 15 Moat Walk 1946.11 1949.12 usacc
Eckert H E SFC 151-W 8 Patch 1951.2 1952.11 usacc
Ecoff J M MSG 187-N 23 Murray 1949.7 1950.1 usacc
Ecoff J M SSG 136-E 19 Hatch 1938.8 1938.8 usacc
Ecoff J M MSG 156-N 181 Bernard 1948.4 1949.7 usacc
Edward F SGT 148-S 7 Moat Walk 1973.11 1975.7 mfh
Edwards J L MSG 151-E 10 Patch 1954.9 1955.10 usacc
Edwards A SSG 112-E 32 Tidball 1976.1 1976.6 mfh
Edwards K T SSG 114-W 22 Harrison 1987.1 1988.2 mfh
Egert P D E-8 156-S 179 Bernard 1969.6 1971.7 mfh
Ehrgood J CSM 33-E-1 61 Fenwick 1978.7 1981.12 mfh
Einarsen E SP4 167-A 7 Patch 1973.2 1973.3 mfh
Elam G SGT 136-E 19 Hatch 1953.2 1955.4 usacc
Elbin E F MSG 112-W 30 Tidball 1943 1945 '43-45PhBks
Elkins J T MSG 72-W 21 Harrison 1942 1944 '43-44PhBks
Ellenbast H L CWO 188-N 27 Murray 1946.11 1948.1 usacc
Ellington G WO1 196-N 11 Pratt 1982.5 1984.6 mfh
Elliott B M SFC 115-E 20 Harrison 1953.1 1955.8 usacc
Elliott D SP5 153-N 13 Hatch 1974.7 1974.8 mfh
Elliott C D SP5 90 21 Moat Walk 1973.7 1974.11 mfh
Ellis J G SFC 192-S 6 Pratt 1974.4 1975.1 mfh
Ellis R SGT 137-W 21 Hatch 1946.11 1946.12 usacc
Ellis J G E-7 150-N 15 Moat Walk 1970.12 1974.4 mfh
Ellsworth L K MSG 26-W 29 Tidball 1957.5 1960.3 usacc
Elston W SGM 195-N 7 Pratt 1982.6 1982.6 mfh
Emans M E SP4 111-W 34 Tidball 1984.7 1985.9 mfh
Emerick J B SSG 110-E 40 Tidball 1936 1938 '37cd
Emery S SP5 153-N 13 Hatch 1976.8 1978.2 mfh
Emmick P A SP6 156-N 181 Bernard 1966.9 1967.3 mfh
Emmons E MSG 111-W 34 Tidball 1932 1943 '43PhBk
Emmons L SSG 149-N 11 Moat Walk 1926.9 1937.8 Emmons '33-37cd
Emory J P MSG 156-S 179 Bernard 1948.12 1950.1 usacc
England C L E-5 154-N 15 Murray 1972.7 1973.2 mfh
Engleman W SGT 131-E 18 Tidball 1915 1917 '16-17cds
English J J MSG 26-E 31 Tidball 1967.6 1968.5 mfh
Engs R N MSG 131-E 18 Tidball 1949.1 1949.5 usacc
Epperson D M E-7 150-N 15 Moat Walk 1963.5 1964.7 mfh
Erbin L A SP5 137-E 23 Hatch 1972.2 1972.8 mfh
Erbin L A E-5 72-W 21 Harrison 1972.8 ? mfh
Erert P MSG 187-N 23 Murray 1971.7 1973.6 mfh
Erhard J SP5 115-E 20 Harrison 1972.6 1972.8 mfh
Erickson D H CW2 30-S 34 Hampton 1984.12 1987.7 mfh
Erno E H MSG 195-S 5 Pratt 1960.7 1961.12 mfh
Erno E H MSG 150-S 13 Moat Walk 1957.1 1958.8 usacc
Ernst M J MSG 188-S 25 Murray 1984.1 1985.6 mfh
Ertel R E SFC 90 21 Moat Walk 1962.12 1963.9 mfh
Escalante A SFC 156-S 179 Bernard 1962.9 1963.8 mfh
Etheridge W L MSG 156-S 179 Bernard 1942 1944.6 '43PhBk

Etheridge W L MSG 191-S 2 Pratt 1944.6 1949.3 usacc
Evans M SGT 110-E 40 Tidball 1981.1 1983.7 mfh
Evans F TSG 110-W 38 Tidball 1932 1937 '32-37cds
Evans T L E-7 111-W 34 Tidball 1968.8 1970.9 mfh
Everett G E MSG 154-N 15 Murray 1956.3 1958.6 usacc
Ewing W R MSG 186-S 17 Murray 1952.4 1952.7 usacc
Ewing W R MSG 150-N 15 Moat Walk 1952.1 1952.4 usacc
Fagan Q E WOJG 130-N 24 Tidball 1951.2 1953.5 usacc
Fanning R M E-6 154-N 15 Murray 1971.5 1972.7 mfh
Farley W P SSG 130-N 24 Tidball 1931.6 1935.4 Farley '31cd
Farmer F CPT 153-S 15 Hatch 1917 1920 '17-20cds
Farmer R MSG 132-E 15 Tidball 1962.8 1962.8 mfh
Farmer R 1SG 188-S 25 Murray 1962.8 1964.4 mfh
Farmer R MGnr 153-S 15 Hatch 1912 1914 '12-14cd AN306
Farmer L H SP5 131-W 20 Tidball 1973.7 1974.9 mfh
Farrar J SSG 114-W 22 Harrison 1981.1 1981.10 mfh
Farrar J SSG 154-N 15 Murray 1979.4 1979.7 mfh
Faulhaber E C Mr 132-E 15 Tidball 1961.11 1962.8 mfh
Faulhaber E C Mr 31-S 38 Hampton 1962.8 1963.2 mfh
Fay D E SSG 151-E 10 Patch 1967.8 1968.2 mfh
Fearing M A SP4 112-W 30 Tidball 1984.3 1984.7 mfh
Felse J E SGM 132-E 15 Tidball 1912 1917 '13-17cds
Fender W E SGT 156-S 179 Bernard 1915 1916 '16cd
Ferchak M P 1SG 150-S 13 Moat Walk 1943.6 1944.9 '43PhBk
Ferrare R V MSG 71-W 17 Harrison 1955.5 1956.3 usacc
Ferrare R V MSG 148-N 5 Moat Walk 1956.3 1956.11 usacc
Ferrecchia J A MSG 188-N 27 Murray 1965.9 1968.10 mfh
Ferris A L SSG 155-S 183 Bernard 1967.12 1968.5 usacc
Ferry B E MSG 156-S 179 Bernard 1953.11 1956.7 usacc
Fields J D TSG 153-S 15 Hatch 1942 1944 '43PhBk
Fields J H 1SG 150-S 13 Moat Walk 1938 1940 '39cd '40PhBk
Fields S A ? 110-E 40 Tidball 1986.8 1987.11 mfh
Filicko R M SP5 136-E 19 Hatch 1974.12 1975.9 mfh
Filicko R M SP5 154-S 13 Murray 1975.9 1979.4 mfh
Finkelstein I 1SG 153-N 13 Hatch 1930 1931 '31cd
Finley B G SSG 154-S 13 Murray 1963.10 1964.9 mfh
Fiscus K MSG 194-N 3 Pratt 1981.6 1987.12 mfh
Fisher J CWO 25-W 33 Tidball 1942.6 1943.6 AN306
Fisher J ? 109-N 3 Frank Lane 1912 1914 '13-14cds
Fisher B 1LT 156-N 181 Bernard 1919 ? '19cd rms?
Fitting A K SFC 72-W 21 Harrison 1962.8 1963.4 usacc
Fittro D L SFC 26-W 29 Tidball 1986.2 1987.4 mfh
Flanders G SSG 131-W 20 Tidball 1976.8 1978.10 mfh
Fleming V L SFC 114-E 24 Harrison 1967.4 1968.8 mfh
Fleming D O MSG 110-W 38 Tidball 1946.9 1950.4 usacc
Fletcher R C MSG 110-W 38 Tidball 1955.10 1956.2 usacc
Fletcher C S SFC 114-W 22 Harrison 1958.9 1959.8 usacc
Flint R B MSG 192-N 8 Pratt 1965.6 1968.7 mfh
Flint C C MSG 150-S 13 Moat Walk 1964.10 1965.6 mfh
Flower L B E SFC 152-E 14 Patch 1951.10 1951.7 usacc
Floyd J M SGT 115-E 20 Harrison 1914 1917 '14-17cds
Flynn D W MSG 113-E 28 Tidball 1948.4 1948.10 usacc
Flynn J W SGM 152-E 14 Patch 1966.4 1966.5 mfh

Flynn C E SGT 72-W 21 Harrison 1907 ? '08cd
Flynn J W SGM 26-E 31 Tidball 1966.5 1967.6 mfh
Forbes J H MSG 30-N 36 Hampton 1958.4 1958.4 usacc
Forbes J H MSG 111-W 34 Tidball 1957.7 1958.4 usacc
Forbes W J E-7 115-E 20 Harrison 1962.9 1965.11 mfh
Forbes H G SGM 71-E 19 Harrison 1918.12 1919.12 '19cd 1/2 house
Ford L B SFC 152-W 12 Patch 1949.10 1952.5 usacc
Ford L B MSG 187-S 21 Murray 1952.5 1952.11 usacc
Forsyth W A MSG 148-S 7 Moat Walk 1943.6 1946.11 '43-45PhBks
Fortino L J SGT 72-E 23 Harrison 1971.10 1972.6 mfh
Fosse E J MSG 112-W 30 Tidball 1949.10 1951.9 usacc
Foster M E MSG 111-W 34 Tidball 1946.9 1949.4 usacc
Foster M E MSG 187-S 21 Murray 1943.6 1944.12 '43-44PhBks AN306
Fournier W L MSG 155-S 183 Bernard 1960.1 1967.12 usacc
Foutain R H SGT 137-E 23 Hatch 1951.9 1952.1 usacc
Francis S J MSG 25-W 33 Tidball 1985.2 1987.1 mfh
Francis F SSG 136-E 19 Hatch 1936 1937 '37cd
Franklin C T MSG 186-N 19 Murray 1971.9 1974.5 mfh
Freeman W H Mr 136-E 19 Hatch 1915 1916 '16cd
Freeman J E SP5 140-S 17 Moat Walk 1975.9 1976.4 mfh
Freese M SP4 113-W 26 Tidball 1978.3 1979.10 mfh
Frisbie W E SGM 71-W 17 Harrison 1914 1917 '14-17cds
Frisbie F TSG 72-E 23 Harrison 1933 1937 Pugh
Frisbie W E MSG 151-E 10 Patch 1917 1918 Colgan
Funk C A R CWO 30-S 34 Hampton 1950.2 1955.5 usacc
Funk E E SGT 154-S 13 Murray 1951.6 1952.3 usacc
Funk J SFC 131-W 20 Tidball 1960.6 1961.4 usacc
Funk D SP4 112-W 30 Tidball 1982.1 1983.2 mfh
Funk J SSG 193-S 10 Pratt 1961.4 1961.10 usacc
Furches C MSG 148-S 7 Moat Walk 1955.11 1959.6 usacc
Furnas J M SP5 115-W 18 Harrison 1983.12 1987.10 mfh
Furtado F S SGM 195-N 7 Pratt 1970.6 1972.5 mfh
Futhridge J G SSG 136-N 17 Hatch 1946.9 1948.8 usacc
Futrell C V 1SG 195-S 5 Pratt 1946.6 1949.9 usacc
Futrell C V 1SG 148-N 5 Moat Walk 1943.10 1946.6 '44-45PhBk AN306
Futrell D R MSG 154-S 13 Murray 1964.9 1964.11 mfh
Fyock E E SFC 132-E 15 Tidball 1962.8 1962.8 mfh
Gabriel G MSG 187-S 21 Murray 1944.12 1946.10 '45PhBk
Gabriel G MSG 151-W 8 Patch 1943.6 1944.12 '44PhBk
Gabriel G MSG 194-S 1 Pratt 1948.1 1951.4 usacc
Gagan J A MSG 130-N 24 Tidball 1964.7 1967.8 mfh
Gainer A E SFC 115-E 20 Harrison 1969.1 1970.6 mfh
Gallagher R E-7 111-E 36 Tidball 1969.8 1972.1 mfh
Gammon F M MSG 113-E 28 Tidball 1950.1 1950.10 usacc
Garcia L PVT 7 Big Bethel 1980.2 1982.8 mfh
Gardapee L H SSG 110-W 38 Tidball 1940 1941.6 '40-41PhBks
Gardapee L H CWO 186-S 17 Murray 1943.5 1945.9 Gardapee
Gardapee L H MSG 137-W 21 Hatch 1941.6 1943.6 Gardapee
Gardner G SP4 167-A 7 Patch 1984.6 1985.5 mfh
Garmilla D D E-7 132-W 13 Tidball 1970.10 1971.2 mfh
Garrett SP4 153-S 15 Hatch 1976.6 1977.6 mfh
Garris J F SGT 137-W 21 Hatch 1953.5 1957.12 usacc
Gartland J B MSG 196-N 11 Pratt 1957.11 1960.9 usacc

Gaunce H M SFC 113-W 26 Tidball 1955.8 1956.1 usacc
Gee W H TSG 153-S 15 Hatch 1926 1927 '27cd
Gehrmann W SGT 156-S 179 Bernard 1912 1914 '13-14cds
Genson P E SSG 137-E 23 Hatch 1940.2 1942.7 '40-41PhBks
Gentile R G TSG 49 49 Bernard 1943 ? '43PhBk rms?
George A M SSG 61-S 43 Ingalls 1937 1939 '37cd
George A M TSG 110-E 40 Tidball 1939 1941 '40-41PhBks
Gepfert E M MSG 30-N 36 Hampton 1964.8 1968.4 mfh
Gertney M SSG 153-N 13 Hatch 1926 1929 '27-29cds
Giacchetti F J SGT 111-W 34 Tidball 1907 1914 '09-14cds
Giannattasio J Jr MSG 112-E 32 Tidball 1961.6 1963.1 mfh
Gibson S C MSG 114-W 22 Harrison 1955.12 1957.12 usacc
Gibson J SSG 110-W 38 Tidball 1979.6 1980.8 mfh
Gilley J W SGM 26-W 29 Tidball 1963.9 1964.8 mfh
Gilmore R L SFC 195-S 5 Pratt 1973.8 1974.2 mfh
Givens D L E-6 137-W 21 Hatch 1967.11 1970.6 mfh
Glass H B SFC 111-W 34 Tidball 1956.4 1956.7 usacc
Glass L R Mr 61-N 45 Ingalls 1943.7 1948.7 PhBk Fire Chief
Glass L R Mr 150-S 13 Moat Walk 1948.7 1955.1 usacc Fire Chief
Glover R SSG 7 Big Bethel 1985.1 1985.6 mfh
Gloxner J A MSG 156-N 181 Bernard 1956.3 1959.4 usacc
Gloxner J A MSG 155-N 185 Bernard 1953.5 1954.1 usacc
Goda R F SGT 72-E 23 Harrison 1953.1 1953.5 usacc
Goda R F SGT 130-S 22 Tidball 1953.5 1955.4 usacc
Gomez F E E-8 132-E 15 Tidball 1969.11 1971.7 mfh
Gonzalez P SP5 7 Big Bethel 1984.5 1976.11 mfh
Good H H E-7 140-S 17 Moat Walk 1966.1 1967.2 mfh
Goodman O F MSG 156-S 179 Bernard 1957.10 1959.3 usacc
Goodner C SSG 72-E 23 Harrison 1937 1939 '37-39cds
Goodwin SFC 90 21 Moat Walk 1950.10 1951.10 usacc
Gordon R B SGT 71-E 19 Harrison 1952.9 1952.12 usacc
Gordon R E 1LT 156-N 181 Bernard 1919 ? '19cd rms?
Gordon J R MSG 140-S 17 Moat Walk 1949.3 1950.1 usacc
Gorjup J G MSG 191-S 2 Pratt 1950.2 1951.3 usacc
Gorjup J G MSG 192-S 6 Pratt 1954.11 1955.5 usacc
Gorjup J G MSG 151-E 10 Patch 1957.9 1958.2 usacc
Gorjup J G MSG 109-N 3 Frank Lane 1947.9 1950.2 usacc
Gorjup J G MSG 187-N 23 Murray 1958.2 1962.10 mfh
Gosser W G MSG 25-E 35 Tidball 1940 1942 '40-41PhBkss
Gradillas G 1SG 195-N 7 Pratt 1961.4 1962.8 mfh
Grafe H R MSG 195-N 7 Pratt 1939 1940 '40PhBk
Grafe H R TSG 140-S 17 Moat Walk 1930 1933 '31-33PhBks
Grant E P CPT 30-S 34 Hampton 1983.11 1984.12 mfh
Graves R L SSG 156-S 179 Bernard 1973.9 1974.9 mfh
Gray J SSG 140-S 17 Moat Walk 1982.11 1986.12 mfh
Gray F SFC 115-E 20 Harrison 1970.11 1972.5 mfh
Gray W R SFC 111-E 36 Tidball 1965.6 1967.9 mfh
Gray W R SFC 110-E 40 Tidball 1963.5 1963.8 mfh
Graziano S A SFC 196-N 11 Pratt 1964.1 1964.7 mfh
Green L D SFC 110-W 38 Tidball 1952.5 1953.3 usacc
Green W C SGT 6 Big Bethel 1984.1 1985.12 mfh
Green O L SGT 111-W 34 Tidball 1917 1918 '17cd
Green W SP5 132-E 15 Tidball 1972.2 1972.7 mfh

Green O L SGT 72-E 23 Harrison 1912 1915 '13-14cds
Green L S MSG 151-E 10 Patch 1954.2 1954.9 usacc
Green O L SGT 131-W 20 Tidball 1915 1917 '16cd
Green F M MSG 109-S 1 Frank Lane 1942.7 1943.11 AN306
Green L D SFC 72-W 21 Harrison 1952.5 1952.5 usacc
Greene C F MSG 140-N 19 Moat Walk 1958.8 1958.10 usacc
Greenleaf R M E-5 71-E 19 Harrison 1973.6 1975.7 mfh
Green W Jr E-7 113-E 28 Tidball 1971.3 1971.4 mfh
Gregory G SGT 156-S 179 Bernard 1952.11 1953.11 usacc
Gregory W MSG 109-N 3 Frank Lane 1957.10 1958.8 usacc
Gresham G D SGT 111-E 36 Tidball 1975.8 1979.4 mfh
Grice C F TSG 113-W 26 Tidball 1931 1933 '33cd
Grier C V SSG 112-E 32 Tidball 1928 1936 '29-33cds
Grier C V MSG 193-N 12 Pratt 1936 1937 '37cd
Griffin M P SSG 156-N 181 Bernard 1926 1929 '27-29cds
Griffin B SP4 154-S 13 Murray 1980.11 1982.6 mfh
Griffith J MSG 193-N 12 Pratt 1980.4 1980.7 mfh
Griggs W T 1SG 114-W 22 Harrison 1939 1940 '40PhBk
Gronquist W A MSG 153-S 15 Hatch 1964.8 1965.10 mfh
Gross T L MSG 148-N 5 Moat Walk 1966.8 1966.11 mfh
Grossman W H E-8 25-W 33 Tidball 1972.11 1973.12 mfh
Gudonsky A R SSG 111-E 36 Tidball 1944.11 1945.6 '44-45PhBks
Guenther T SSG 109-N 3 Frank Lane 1932 1933 '33cd
Guenther T MSG 25-E 35 Tidball 1937 1940 '37-40cd
Guenther T MSG 112-W 30 Tidball 1933 1937 Pugh
Guerassio V J SGT 136-E 19 Hatch 1960.11 1963.1 usacc
Gunter L E MSG 111-E 36 Tidball 1959.12 1961.11 usacc
Gustafson L P TSG 140-N 19 Moat Walk 1944.12 1945 '45PhBK
Gustafson L P SSG 114-W 22 Harrison 1944.11 1944.12 '44PhBk
Guston H W CWO 30-S 34 Hampton 1946.9 1947.5 usacc
Guyer J R MSG 90 21 Moat Walk 1949.5 1950.10 usacc
Guymon C M TSG 90 21 Moat Walk 1937.9 1940.6 '39PhBk
Hablutzel R R SP6 132-W 13 Tidball 1963.5 1966.5 mfh
Hack R B SSG 154-N 15 Murray 1926 1929 '17-19cds
Hackett W M 1SG 111-E 36 Tidball 1943.1 1944.11 '43PhBk
Hackett SGT 61-S 43 Ingalls 1945.4 1946.7 D V Lewis
Hackworth F D TSG 156-S 179 Bernard 1944.10 1946.12 '44-45PhBks
Hagan C J 1SG 155-S 183 Bernard 1928 1938 '29-37cds
Hagan C J 1SG 195-S 5 Pratt 1938 1939 '39PhBk
Hager J C CSM 26-E 31 Tidball 1976.8 1977.10 mfh
Haggerty J E MSG 193-N 12 Pratt 1961.4 1962.9 mfh
Haggerty J E SGM 186-N 19 Murray 1966.6 1967.6 mfh
Hagler R D SFC 188-N 27 Murray 1984.9 1986.9 mfh
Hahn O S SGT 113-E 28 Tidball 1912 1914 '13-14cds
Hahn R SSG 90 21 Moat Walk 1982.2 1983.10 mfh
Hahn O S SGT 111-E 36 Tidball 1917.5 1918.9 '17cd
Hahn O S 2LT 111-E 36 Tidball 1917.6 1918.9 S&F
Hahn G H SGT 150-S 13 Moat Walk 1915 1916 '16cd
Hahn R SSG 90 21 Moat Walk 1982.2 1983.10 mfh
Haines V MSG 188-N 27 Murray 1962.2 1963.3 mfh
Haines V MSG 152-W 12 Patch 1956.1 1962.2 mfh
Haire J R E-7 132-W 13 Tidball 1969.1 1969.12 mfh
Hale T L SP5 137-E 23 Hatch 1973.5 1975.7 mfh

Haley H H SFC 195-N 7 Pratt 1974.1 1979.9 mfh
Halfrick J MSG 114-W 22 Harrison 1949.9 1950.10 usacc
Hall R SGT 154-N 15 Murray 1980.12 1982.6 mfh
Hall N SFC 110-W 38 Tidball 1951.5 1952.1 usacc
Hall D R SGT 115-E 20 Harrison 1983.5 1985.6 mfh
Hall M SP5 114-W 22 Harrison 1984.5 1985.5 mfh
Hall G S SSG 140-N 19 Moat Walk 1984.4 1986.2 mfh
Hall R SFC 191-S 2 Pratt 1979.8 1982.5 mfh
Hall E P SGT 131-W 20 Tidball 1912 1914 '13-14cds
Hall E P MSG 192-S 6 Pratt 1940 1943 '40-41PhBks
Halla M J SP4 132-E 15 Tidball 1981.12 1982.1 mfh
Haller E D MSG 140-S 17 Moat Walk 1951.7 1951.9 usacc
Haller E D MSG 110-E 40 Tidball 1949.8 1950.12 usacc
Halloran J J E-7 72-E 23 Harrison 1969.10 1970.1 mfh
Halloway K E CWO 193-S 10 Pratt 1949.11 1951.4 usacc
Halls M J SGT 110-W 38 Tidball 1984.4 1985.10 mfh
Halverson S E SFC 114-E 24 Harrison 1953.1 1955.11 usacc
Hamerstrom W B E-7 149-S 9 Moat Walk 1963.4 1963.10 mfh
Hamilton J F E-9 187-S 21 Murray 1969.3 1973.1 mfh
Hammond O E-7 115-E 20 Harrison 1965.3 1966.5 mfh
Hamrick R J SP5 136-N 17 Hatch 1968.2 1968.5 mfh
Hamrick R J SP5 156-S 179 Bernard 1968.5 1969.6 mfh
Hamrick G SP4 155-S 183 Bernard 1976.9 1978.1 mfh
Hamrick T G MSG 193-N 12 Pratt 1952.1 1955.10 usacc
Hamrick T G SSG 150-N 15 Moat Walk 1950.1 1952.1 usacc
Hanh R SP5 6 Big Bethel 1976.4 1976.11 mfh
Hannah J W SGM 31-S 38 Hampton 1973.5 1976.12 mfh
Hannon P E MSG 26-W 29 Tidball 1955.11 1957.3 usacc
Hanson R SFC 191-S 2 Pratt 1977.9 1978.7 mfh
Hapli L J MSG 26-E 31 Tidball 1951.8 1953.6 usacc
Hapli L J MSG 72-E 23 Harrison 1946.10 1951.8 usacc
Harden R SSG 136-N 17 Hatch 1973.11 ? mfh
Harding T W SP5 71-W 17 Harrison 1968.1 1968.6 mfh
Hardshaw F W SGT 152-W 12 Patch 1926 1929 '27-29cds
Hare R SGT 154-N 15 Murray 1912 1914 '13-14cds
Hargrave J T Jr E-8 187-S 21 Murray 1962.4 1963.7 mfh
Harley R SFC 130-S 22 Tidball 1958.4 1959.5 usacc
Harmon W T MSG 187-N 23 Murray 1955.12 1957.4 usacc
Harmon P C MSG 153-N 13 Hatch 1949.9 1950.12 usacc
Harness T M SSG 140-N 19 Moat Walk 1926 1927 '27cd
Harness T M SSG 152-W 12 Patch 1936 1938 '37cd
Harp R SFC 30-S 34 Hampton 1978.4 1981.6 mfh
Harpool M R SGM 130-N 24 Tidball 1957.2 1964.2 mfh
Harrell G H SGT 111-W 34 Tidball 1915 1917 '16-17cds
Harrell F SP5 6 Big Bethel 1974.2 1976.3 mfh
Harrell B SP4 130-N 24 Tidball 1975.12 1976.10 mfh
Harrington R P SP6 113-W 26 Tidball 1973.12 1974.5 mfh
Harrington F MSG 195-N 7 Pratt 1980.4 1981.6 mfh
Harris C A E-9 192-S 6 Pratt 1969.8 1970.2 mfh
Harris H B 1SG 130-S 22 Tidball 1939 1940 '40PhBk
Harris J A SP4 151-W 8 Patch 1984.2 1984.6 mfh
Harris R W MSG 188-S 25 Murray 1964.4 1965.5 mfh
Harris S D SP5 90 21 Moat Walk 1975.4 1976.3 mfh

117

Harris C E MSG 196-S 9 Pratt 1953.10 1953.12 usacc
Harris S D SP5 90 21 Moat Walk 1975.4 1976.3 mfh
Harris C E MSG 153-N 13 Hatch 1951.1 1951.2 usacc
Harrison R N SFC 112-E 32 Tidball 1953.7 1956.1 usacc
Harsch J I E-9 188-N 27 Murray 1969.9 1971.7 mfh
Harsch J I MSG 188-N 27 Murray 1965.5 1965.9 mfh
Harsh W S E-5 151-W 8 Patch 1973.8 1974.4 mfh
Hartley W C SSG 137-W 21 Hatch 1926 1927 '27cd
Hartwell R E-7 132-E 15 Tidball 1971.7 1972.1 mfh
Hartwell M E SFC 152-W 12 Patch 1962.3 1962.7 mfh
Harville SP5 156-N 181 Bernard 1976.11 1977.5 mfh
Hash H L 1SG 132-W 13 Tidball 1944.1 1946.9 '45PhBk
Haskins K R SGT 131-E 18 Tidball 1982.8 1984.9 mfh
Hassler D L SP5 114-W 22 Harrison 1975.9 1977.2 mfh
Hastee J F WO 156-N 181 Bernard 1930 1931 '31cd
Hastee J F WO 109-N 3 Frank Lane 1926 1927 '27cd AN306
Hatcher P L 1SG 187-N 23 Murray 1940 1943 '40-42PhBk
Hatcher P L MSG 188-N 27 Murray 1934 1937 Pugh
Hatton C E 1SG 191-N 4 Pratt 1937 1939 '37cd '39PhBk
Hatton C E 1SG 148-N 5 Moat Walk 1933 1944 '33cd Pugh
Hauger L M TSG 152-W 12 Patch 1944.6 1946.11 '45-46PhBks
Hauger L M TSG 193-N 12 Pratt 1942 1944.6 '43PhBk
Haveman L G Jr SP7 111-W 34 Tidball 1967.6 1968.8 mfh
Haveman L G Jr SP8 191-S 2 Pratt 1968.8 1969.6 mfh
Havey S F WO 188-S 25 Murray 1933 1934 '33cd
Haw J R SGT 153-N 13 Hatch 1915 1916 '16cd
Hawk L SFC 25-W 33 Tidball 1975.12 1977.8 mfh
Hawkins W E E-8 191-S 2 Pratt 1971.1 1971.7 mfh
Hawkins J Q SGT 154-N 15 Murray 1951.8 1952.5 usacc
Haycox J I SFC 112-W 30 Tidball 1967.1 1968.10 mfh
Hayes F H SSG 49 49 Bernard 1943 ? '43PhBk rooms?
Hayward G E MSG 31-N 40 Hampton 1957.6 1958.9 usacc
Hayward G E MSG 111-W 34 Tidball 1956.7 1957.6 usacc
Hazel E D CPL 72-W 21 Harrison 1958.4 1959.11 usacc
Hazel E D CPL 136-E 19 Hatch 1957.10 1958.4 usacc
Headen H L SSG 113-W 26 Tidball 1971.10 1972.6 mfh
Healy D J SFC 114-E 24 Harrison 1965.6 1967.4 mfh
Heater R L MSG 112-W 30 Tidball 1966.4 1966.12 mfh
Heater R L MSG 196-S 9 Pratt 1966.12 1967.8 mfh
Heaton H MSG 186-N 19 Murray 1948.12 1952.4 usacc
Hefley R E TSG 113-W 26 Tidball 1928 1930 '29cd
Helm M M SFC 111-E 36 Tidball 1956.4 1958.7 usacc
Helmer W J MSG 72-E 23 Harrison 1916 1917 '17cd
Hemmelgarn A B MSG 186-S 17 Murray 1961.12 1965.9 mfh
Hemphill B SFC 188-S 25 Murray 1979.12 1984.1 mfh
Henderson E SFC 186-S 17 Murray 1979.2 1980.2 mfh
Henderson B A SP4 149-S 9 Moat Walk 1985.10 1986.12 mfh
Hendrix J SP5 140-S 17 Moat Walk 1981.4 1982.11 mfh
Henley T SSG 149-S 9 Moat Walk 1980.3 1981.4 mfh
Henley C R SFC 136-N 17 Hatch 1959.1 1959.9 usacc
Henley E L MSG 114-E 24 Harrison 1958.4 1960.6 usacc
Henness A K MSG 115-W 18 Harrison 1945.4 1946.11 '45PhBk
Henness A K MSG 115-E 20 Harrison 1943 1945.4 '43-44PhBks

Henry B G SSG 90 21 Moat Walk 1983.10 1984.7 mfh
Henry R L MSG 130-N 24 Tidball 1954.9 1955.4 usacc
Henry B J SSG 90 21 Moat Walk 1983.10 1984.7 mfh
Henry R L MSG 193-S 10 Pratt 1955.4 1955.12 usacc
Herbert R A SGT 72-E 23 Harrison 1951.10 1952.6 usacc
Herbert R A SGT 188-S 25 Murray 1952.6 1952.11 usacc
Herbert R A 1SG 136-E 19 Hatch 1950.11 1951.10 usacc
Herondorf S MSG 131-W 20 Tidball 1965.9 1967.12 mfh
Herondorf S SFC 130-S 22 Tidball 1959.6 1964.8 mfh
Hess W R MSG 196-S 9 Pratt 1967.8 1968.6 mfh
Hess W R MSG 112-E 32 Tidball 1965.7 1967.8 mfh
Hess H H MSG 187-S 21 Murray 1953.11 1955.2 usacc
Hess J SGT 137-E 23 Hatch 1912 1914 '13-14cds
Hester L K SFC 136-N 17 Hatch 1960.4 1962.2 mfh
Hichle E T SGM 153-N 13 Hatch 1912 1914 '13-14cds
Hickey V J MSG 140-N 19 Moat Walk 1954.2 1955.3 usacc
Hicks G H SGT 90 21 Moat Walk 1907 1911 '08-11cds
Higa S AFC 90 21 Moat Walk 1963.9 1965.7 mfh
Higgins E J SGT 154-N 15 Murray 1951.8 1952.5 usacc
Hildebrand G W MSG 31-S 38 Hampton 1955.9 1962.7 mfh
Hildebrand G W MSG 154-N 15 Murray 1954.9 1955.9 usacc
Hill G F SFC 154-S 13 Murray 1953.2 1954.6 usacc
Hill K M E-7 112-E 32 Tidball 1963.2 1963.5 mfh
Hill J M MSG 130-N 24 Tidball 1955.11 1957.1 usacc
Hill R G E-6 136-N 17 Hatch 1969.2 1971.12 mfh
Hill J M MSG 192-N 8 Pratt 1952.11 1952.12 usacc
Hillman R SFC 192-S 6 Pratt 1983.4 1983.10 mfh
Hines V J MSG 154-N 15 Murray 1948.6 1948.11 usacc
Hinkley C WO 153-N 13 Hatch 1932 1933 '33cd
Hinshaw B A SP4 109-N 3 Frank Lane 1985.3 1985.12 mfh
Hinson B F TSG 30-S 34 Hampton 1936 1937 '37cd
Hinton A SFC 192-S 6 Pratt 1978.7 1979.8 mfh
Hinton R L 1SG 115-W 18 Harrison 1943.11 1944.6 '43PhBk
Hipshman J TSG 154-N 15 Murray 1940.5 1942.6 '40-41PhBks
Hobbs Q L E-7 153-S 15 Hatch 1969.4 1971.2 mfh
Hobling D SGT 156-S 179 Bernard 1980.5 1983.9 mfh
Hobort SP5 136-E 19 Hatch 1972.1 1972.10 mfh
Hochgeryle J K MSG 156-N 181 Bernard 1953.8 1954.6 usacc
Hodgins J B 1SG 90 21 Moat Walk 1912 1914 '13-14cds
Hodgkins L M CWO 188-S 25 Murray 1950.5 1952.5 usacc
Hofheinz W J E-4 33 67 Fenwick 1970.7 1972.3 usacc
Hohenthal W D 2LT 112-W 30 Tidball 1918.4 1919.1 Hennessy rms?
Hoke C H SP4 71-E 19 Harrison 1959.9 1960.5 usacc
Holden J E MSG 26-E 31 Tidball 1968.6 1969.2 mfh
Holland R SP5 154-S 13 Murray 1971.10 1974.10 mfh
Hollifield H G SSG 113-E 28 Tidball 1937 1938 '37cd
Hollifield H G SSG 154-S 13 Murray 1938 1939 '39PhBk
Holloman E V MSG 155-S 183 Bernard 1955.4 1956.9 usacc
Holloman E V MSG 188-N 27 Murray 1956.9 1959.7 usacc
Holman C SFC 148-N 5 Moat Walk 1953.12 1954.10 usacc
Holman G C SSG 115-W 18 Harrison 1981.7 1983.12 mfh
Holmbert F A 1SG 153-S 15 Hatch 1927 1931 '27-31cd
Holmes M J SSG 109-S 1 Frank Lane 1926 1933 '27-33cds

Holmes J D SGT 153-N 13 Hatch 1983.9 1985.7 mfh
Holmes H H MSG 109-N 3 Frank Lane 1962.5 1963.2 mfh
Holmes H H MSG 195-S 5 Pratt 1963.2 1963.9 mfh
Holy A D SFC 71-W 17 Harrison 1960.7 1962.2 mfh
Hooks J A SFC 110-E 40 Tidball 1951.3 1951.7 usacc
Hooley T P E-7 153-S 15 Hatch 1961.3 1964.2 mfh
Hoops D L E-2 33 67 Fenwick 1972.3 1973.11 usacc
Hopkins J SGT 154-N 15 Murray 1977.10 1979.4 mfh
Hopkins D C SFC 26-E 31 Tidball 1981.6 1982.11 mfh
Hopson J E ? 149-N 11 Moat Walk 1965.12 1966.8 mfh
Hopson C W 1SG 136-N 17 Hatch 1926 1927 '27cd
Horey I N SGT 152-E 14 Patch 1928 1929 '29cd
Horey I N SSG 131-W 20 Tidball 1926 1928 '27cd
Horne R D SGT 155-S 183 Bernard 1916 1917 '17cd
Horne J MSG 112-W 30 Tidball 1962.8 1963.11 mfh
Horne C S SSG 152-E 14 Patch 1972.7 1974.10 mfh
Horning G J MSG 191-N 4 Pratt 1949.10 1950.8 usacc
Horning G J MSG 113-W 26 Tidball 1948.4 1949.10 usacc
Hornsey J W LTC 61-N 45 Ingalls 1963.10 1966.10 mfh
Horstmann O SSG 114-W 22 Harrison 1931 1933 '31-33cds
Horstmann O SGT 113-W 26 Tidball 1914 1916 '14-16cd
Horstmann O MSG 113-W 26 Tidball 1933 1937 Pugh
Hough H P TSG 109-N 3 Frank Lane 1906 1912 '08-12cds Son
Hough H P TSG 109-N 3 Frank Lane 1916 1917 '17cd
Hounshell P 1SG 151-E 10 Patch 1927 1929 '27-29cd
House J TSG 130-N 24 Tidball 1939 1940.11 '40-41PhBks
Houser D SP5 148-S 7 Moat Walk 1980.10 1981.1 mfh
Houston R W SP4 71-E 19 Harrison 1975.8 ? mfh
Houston R SGT 115-E 20 Harrison 1976.8 1978.3 mfh
Howard S W Mr 195-N 7 Pratt 1942 1943.11 '43PhBk
Howe T B CPT 31-N 40 Hampton 1982.8 1986.6 mfh
Howe H M MSG 194-N 3 Pratt 1963.3 1965.2 mfh
Howe H M MSG 148-S 7 Moat Walk 1962.11 1963.3 mfh
Hricinak W H CWO 195-S 5 Pratt 1950.2 1954.2 Hricinak usacc
Hubbard C SP5 149-N 11 Moat Walk 1976.9 1979.3 mfh
Hubbard R S MSG 31-N 40 Hampton 1967.10 1969.12 mfh
Hubbard J F Jr E-7 114-W 22 Harrison 1966.10 1967.11 mfh
Hubbard J F Jr SP7 131-W 20 Tidball 1969.2 1970.2 mfh
Hudson L V SFC 136-N 17 Hatch 1949.3 1950.1 usacc
Hudson L V SFC 156-S 179 Bernard 1950.1 1950.4 usacc
Hudson J W Jr SP5 154-N 15 Murray 1968.2 1969.5 mfh
Hudson J W Jr SP5 136-N 17 Hatch 1967.10 1968.2 mfh
Huff M G SFC 149-N 11 Moat Walk 1962.10 1963.9 mfh
Huffman F W MSG 132-W 13 Tidball 1946.9 1950.4 usacc
Huffman F W MSG 186-S 17 Murray 1954.6 1957.4 usacc
Hughes B E SP1 136-N 17 Hatch 1958.3 1958.9 usacc
Hughes T R SFC 110-E 40 Tidball 1966.9 1967.9 mfh
Hughes T R SFC 156-N 181 Bernard 1966.4 1966.9 mfh
Hughes A T WOJG 31-S 38 Hampton 1952.9 1954.7 usacc
Humphries E G MSG 187-N 23 Murray 1943.10 1947.1 '43-44PhBks
Humphries J W E-6 153-N 13 Hatch 1970.2 1972.1 mfh
Huneycutt S D SP4 156-N 181 Bernard 1972.1 1972.9 mfh
Hunker K SSG 109-S 1 Frank Lane 1976.7 1977.3 mfh

Hunt C E SP5 136-N 17 Hatch 1964.2 1965.8 mfh
Hunt D L SP5 4 Big Bethel 1974.9 1975.10 mfh
Hunt C R E-6 130-N 24 Tidball 1969.1 1971.8 mfh
Huskins C W SP6 151-W 8 Patch 1974.6 1977.12 mfh
Huston O C SGT 115-E 20 Harrison 1912 1914 '13-14cds
Hutcheson W L SGT 155-S 183 Bernard 1953.1 1954.7 usacc
Hutson R SGT 130-N 24 Tidball 1926 1927 '27cd
Huttlinger W O MSG 130-N 24 Tidball 1949.10 1950.7 usacc
Huyck W SFC 149-N 11 Moat Walk 1970.5 1970.12 mfh
Iles L SGT 136-N 17 Hatch 1959.9 1960.3 usacc
Inano T SFC 156-N 181 Bernard 1955.8 1956.1 usacc
Inman J H SFC 109-S 1 Frank Lane 1952.6 1952.8 usacc
Ivanick P TSG 131-E 18 Tidball 1944.9 1946.9 '44-45PhBks
Jackson R A SP6 112-W 30 Tidball 1974.3 1976.4 mfh
Jackson R L SFC 109-S 1 Frank Lane 1964.1 1967.1 mfh
Jackson P MSG 26-E 31 Tidball 1982.12 1983.7 mfh
Jackson G G MSG 137-W 21 Hatch 1958.1 1958.8 usacc
Jackson W H E-7 153-S 15 Hatch 1971.3 1973.8 mfh
Jackson G G MSG 113-E 28 Tidball 1958.8 1958.11 usacc
Jackson R B SP5 130-S 22 Tidball 1983.11 1984.9 mfh
Jackson P SGT 114-E 24 Harrison 1979.12 1982.12 mfh
Jacobs W J SP5 72-E 23 Harrison 1966.11 1969.10 mfh
Jacobson D W E-7 72-E 23 Harrison 1970.1 1970.11 mfh
Jaegers M L B PFC 131-W 20 Tidball 1987.2 1988.2 mfh
Jambard J SP6 149-N 11 Moat Walk 1975.2 1976.2 mfh
Jamison C R MSG 152-E 14 Patch 1949.8 1950.8 usacc
Janack J SGT 140-S 17 Moat Walk 1987.2 1981.4 mfh
Jans A J SP5 137-E 23 Hatch 1966.9 1967.4 usacc
Jayne W A SSG 150-S 13 Moat Walk 1986.10 1987.12 mfh
Jenkins M SFC 35 E-1 6 Reeder Cir 1980.8 1984.5 mfh
Jenkins T B SP4 131-E 18 Tidball 1984.9 1986.3 mfh
Jenkins D R SSG 131-W 20 Tidball 1968.1 1969.1 mfh
Jenkins B L E-7 154-S 13 Murray 1959.6 1963.7 mfh
Jennings W W SP5 136-E 19 Hatch 1970.6 1971.1 mfh
Jennings R W SP5 112-W 30 Tidball 1984.7 1985.10 mfh
Jennings W W E-5 112-E 32 Tidball 1971.1 1971.12 mfh
Jesus F A E-7 132-E 15 Tidball 1972.7 1973.4 mfh
Jinkens M E MSG 152-E 14 Patch 1948.11 1949.7 usacc
Jinks D MSG 112-W 30 Tidball 1966.3 1966.4 mfh
Jinks D SGM 193-N 12 Pratt 1965.4 1967.7 mfh
Jinks D E-9 193-S 10 Pratt 1969.6 1970.10 mfh
Joga C S E-6 72-W 21 Harrison 1964.5 1965.9 usacc
Johnson A F TSG 131-E 18 Tidball 1932 1933 '33cd
Johnson L W SGT 137-W 21 Hatch 1947.1 1951.2 usacc
Johnson A J SGM 152-W 12 Patch 1912 1917 '13-17cds
Johnson L W MSG 194-N 3 Pratt 1959.5 1961.6 usacc
Johnson J P SGT 140-S 17 Moat Walk 1951.10 1952.7 usacc
Johnson F E TSG 114-E 24 Harrison 1944.11 1945.10 '44-45PhBks
Johnson R D SP5 112-W 30 Tidball 1976.4 1982.1 mfh
Johnson C H SFC 132-W 13 Tidball 1952.10 1954.3 usacc
Johnson J E MSG 49 49 Bernard 1943 ? '43PhBk rms?
Johnson C A SGT 151-W 8 Patch 1953.5 1958.2 usacc
Johnson L W SSG 30-S 34 Hampton 1952.10 1953.1 usacc

Johnson D L E-6 140-N 19 Moat Walk 1969.7 1970.6 mfh
Johnson L W SSG 153-N 13 Hatch 1951.3 1952.10 usacc
Johnson C A SGT 150-N 15 Moat Walk 1974.5 1974.10 mfh
Johnson C H MSG 156-N 181 Bernard 1962.1 1966.2 mfh
Johnson H K MSG 192-N 8 Pratt 1968.7 1971.2 mfh
Johnson J P MSG 187-N 23 Murray 1957.5 1958.2 usacc
Johnson L W MSG 115-W 18 Harrison 1954.11 1959.5 usacc
Johnson J SSG 154-N 15 Murray 1973.10 1977.9 mfh
Johnson J P SFC 186-S 17 Murray 1952.7 1954.6 usacc
Johnson R SP5 140-S 17 Moat Walk 1976.4 1978.2 mfh
Johnson W III SGT 131-W 20 Tidball 1963.10 1965.7 mfh
Johnston S D 1SG 130-N 24 Tidball 1942.5 1944.10 '43PhBk
Johnston W L SSG 72-W 21 Harrison 1944.11 1946.11 '45PhBk
Jolley R F MSG 154-N 15 Murray 1949.12 1950.9 usacc
Jones W E WO 137-W 21 Hatch 1931 1933 '31-33cds
Jones M E MSG 194-N 3 Pratt 1945.2 1949.11 usacc
Jones C E-7 112-E 32 Tidball 1970.6 1971.1 mfh
Jones M E MSG 71-W 17 Harrison 1952.2 1952.3 usacc
Jones S W MSG 49 49 Bernard 1952.9 1954.3 usacc
Jones D J TSG 90 21 Moat Walk 1940.6 1941 '40-41PhBks
Jones F SGT 113-E 28 Tidball 1907 ? '08cd ORD
Jones H W SSG 114-W 22 Harrison 1944.12 1946.11 '45PhBk
Jones S W MSG 195-S 5 Pratt 1954.3 1956.10 usacc
Jones S M MSG 196-S 9 Pratt 1953.12 1955.5 usacc
Jones W C SP5 140-S 17 Moat Walk 1971.9 1972.7 mfh
Jones J D SSG 115-W 18 Harrison 1926 1933 '27-33cds
Jones G SSG 156-N 181 Bernard 1980.6 1986.2 mfh
Jones S M MSG 111-E 36 Tidball 1951.12 1953.1 usacc
Jones J H MSG 154-N 15 Murray 1958.6 1961.2 mfh
Jones E W Jr SGM 186-S 17 Murray 1966.4 1968.8 mfh
Jones E W Jr MSG 156-N 181 Bernard 1966.2 1966.4 mfh
Jordon H E-4 110-W 38 Tidball 1972.4 1972.9 mfh
Joyner J SFC 114-E 24 Harrison 1982.12 1987.1 mfh
Judd O A E-8 188-S 25 Murray 1969.11 1973.7 mfh
Judge M SFC 187-N 23 Murray 1981.7 1985.10 mfh
Jula J MSG 186-S 17 Murray 1948.11 1952.3 usacc
Juliano J R SGT 110-E 40 Tidball 1953.6 1954.1 usacc
Jungblyth A E E-7 109-N 3 Frank Lane 1969.2 1970.3 mfh
Jurutka E T MSG 192-S 6 Pratt 1983.10 1986.1 mfh
Kaap SFC 26-E 31 Tidball 1978.3 1979.8 mfh
Kahl C MSG 194-S 1 Pratt 1982.4 1983.2 mfh
Kalakikos G M MSG 149-S 9 Moat Walk 1957.2 1958.7 usacc
Kalin K L SFC 112-W 30 Tidball 1953.8 1955.1 usacc
Kama J N SSG 132-W 13 Tidball 1966.6 1968.5 mfh
Kammerdiener R E E-5 155-N 185 Bernard 1968.1 1968.10 mfh
Kanda G M SFC 111-W 34 Tidball 1962.11 1964.12 mfh
Kaufman R F 1SG 193-S 10 Pratt 1941 1942 '40-41PhBks
Kearse W SP6 72-W 21 Harrison 1963.6 1964.5 usacc
Keating G P SFC 151-E 10 Patch 1965.4 1966.12 mfh
Keating P J SP4 112-E 32 Tidball 1987.4 1987.11 mfh
Keen T M 1SG 132-E 15 Tidball 1940.5 1946.10 '40-45PhBks
Keicer R H SFC 155-N 185 Bernard 1949.7 1950.6 usacc
Kelley W L SFC 155-S 183 Bernard 1957.5 1959.12 usacc

Kelley J E SP4 115-E 20 Harrison 1973.8 1976.6 mfh
Kelley M SGT 90 21 Moat Walk 1916 1917 '16-17cds
Kelley R C SGT 5 Big Bethel 1984.6 1985.7 mfh
Kelley C M MSG 196-N 11 Pratt 1963.4 1964.1 mfh
Kelly J W SSG 6 Big Bethel 1986.6 1986.10 mfh
Kelly W F SSG 149-S 9 Moat Walk 1937.5 1942.6 '37-39cd '40-41PhBks
Kelly J B ? 136-N 17 Hatch 1914 1915 '14cd
Kelly J G MSG 148-S 7 Moat Walk 1933 1938 '33cd Pugh
Kelly J G SGT 148-N 5 Moat Walk 1916 1917 '17cd
Kelly J SFC 114-W 22 Harrison 1951.6 1951.11 usacc
Kelly J E Sr SP2 71-W 17 Harrison 1958.6 1958.8 usacc
Kennah W L ? 6 Big Bethel 1983.4 1984.1 mfh
Kennedy W SGT 132-E 15 Tidball 1983.3 1984.6 mfh
Kennedy B F ? 72-E 23 Harrison 1911 1912 '12cd
Kennedy H C Jr SGM 193-N 12 Pratt 1963.1 1963.8 mfh
Kenney G N MSG 110-E 40 Tidball 1950.12 1951.3 usacc
Kerley T J SP4 151-W 8 Patch 1986.10 1987.7 mfh
Kern F SSG 110-W 38 Tidball 1943 1945 '43-45PhBk
Kerr C MSG 151-E 10 Patch 1916 1917 '17cd
Kerr C SGM 140-S 17 Moat Walk 1918 1919 '19cd
Kerr J H CWO 193-S 10 Pratt 1951.4 1951.9 usacc
Kilgour H C 1SG 155-S 183 Bernard 1948.3 1949.10 usacc
Killinger R E-6 112-E 32 Tidball 1972.1 1973.7 mfh
King C M E-5 72-W 21 Harrison 1971.5 1971.9 mfh
King E L E-7 140-N 19 Moat Walk 1968.5 1969.6 mfh
King J D MSG 49 49 Bernard 1954.3 1955.1 usacc
Kinsey P L E-7 112-E 32 Tidball 1967.10 1969.2 mfh
Kinton C W SP5 109-N 3 Frank Lane 1973.11 1974.12 mfh
Kirby O O SGT 72-W 21 Harrison 1952.6 1952.12 usacc
Kirk SP5 136-N 17 Hatch 1973.7 1973.10 mfh
Kirn H R SP4 140-N 19 Moat Walk 1974.9 1976.11 mfh
Kishler C L MGnr 148-N 5 Moat Walk 1912 1914 '13-14cds
Kleeman W T E-5 71-E 19 Harrison 1969.6 1969.10 mfh
Kleinman F K SFC 72-E 23 Harrison 1956.5 1960.4 usacc
Kline J A SGT 148-S 7 Moat Walk 1987.2 1987.9 mfh
Klinefelter M C SFC 26-E 31 Tidball 1983.7 1986.4 mfh
Klusmann G SP5 153-S 15 Hatch 1978.8 1979.2 mfh
Knowlton L R SFC 152-E 14 Patch 1961.11 1962.3 mfh
Knutson W E MSG 31-S 38 Hampton 1963.3 1966.2 mfh
Knutson W E SFC 114-W 22 Harrison 1962.2 1963.3 mfh
Kohl D W MSG 30-N 36 Hampton 1962.7 1964.7 mfh
Kohl D W MSG 131-W 20 Tidball 1958.5 1959.2 usacc
Kohl D W MSG 110-W 38 Tidball 1953.6 1953.7 usacc
Kohl D W MSG 26-E 31 Tidball 1953.7 1954.5 usacc
Kohlmann H J SFC 194-S 1 Pratt 1975.8 1976.8 mfh
Kohn E O E-9 186-S 17 Murray 1970.7 1973.5 mfh
Kolarik L G MSG 150-S 13 Moat Walk 1970.2 1972.4 mfh
Konz M F SSG 191-N 4 Pratt 1945.4 1946.9 AN306
Kot J H SGT 137-E 23 Hatch 1951.1 1951.5 usacc
Kowar F SSG 111-W 34 Tidball 1928 1930 '29cd
Kral D E YNC 109-S 1 Frank Lane 1969.1 1973.8 mfh USN
Kramer F C MSG 49 49 Bernard 1952.5 1952.9 usacc
Kramer K D E-6 72-W 21 Harrison 1971.1 1971.5 mfh

Kramp M W MSG 115-W 18 Harrison 1959.6 1962.9 mfh
Kravitz J D SSG 71-W 17 Harrison 1931 1932 AN306
Kravitz J B SGT 113-E 28 Tidball 1940 1941 '40-41PhBks
Kravitz SP5 136-E 19 Hatch 1972.11 1973.6 mfh
Kropczynski R SSG 152-W 12 Patch 1964.6 1966.10 mfh
Krouse T W SSG 150-N 15 Moat Walk 1926 1929 '27-29cds
Kryworuck E 1SG 114-E 24 Harrison 1940.10 1944.11 '40-43PhBks
Kubitz S A SSG 112-W 30 Tidball 1940 1942 '40-41PhBks
Kubitz S A SSG 72-W 21 Harrison 1938 1940 '39cd '40PhBk
Kuehne A TSG 140-N 19 Moat Walk 1942 1943 '43PhBk
Kulper A L TSG 194-N 3 Pratt 1940 1941 '40-41PhBks
Kushi L J E-7 140-S 17 Moat Walk 1969.2 1971.9 mfh
Kuss F J TSG 151-E 10 Patch 1944.9 1946.12 '44-45PhBks
Kuttenberg J SP4 112-W 30 Tidball 1983.2 1984.3 mfh
Kuykendall V L WOJG 191-S 2 Pratt 1940.5 1941.5 Kuykendall
Kuykendall V L MSG 132-E 15 Tidball 1936.6 1940.3 Kuykendall '37cd
Kuykendall V L SSG 71-W 17 Harrison 1932.5 1936.6 Kuykendal '33cd
Kuykendall V L SSG 136-N 17 Hatch 1932.1 1932.5 Kuykendall
La Voie J F CSM 30-N 36 Hampton 1973.6 1977.5 mfh
Lackey C L 1LT 154-N 15 Murray 1918 1919 '19cd
Lackmiller R A MSG 188-N 27 Murray 1953.8 1955.11 usacc
Lackmiller R A MSG 110-W 38 Tidball 1953.7 1953.8 usacc
LaClair C SP5 71-W 17 Harrison 1972.9 1974.5 mfh
LaClair C SP5 137-W 21 Hatch 1972.3 1972.9 mfh
Lacombe L L SGT 109-S 1 Frank Lane 1953.4 1955.5 usacc
LaFrancis C CWO 31-S 38 Hampton 1947.4 1949.2 usacc
Lamb E B MSG 193-N 12 Pratt 1964.8 1964.11 mfh
Lambka L L MSG 31-N 40 Hampton 1954.10 1957.5 usacc
Lambka L L 1SG 149-N 11 Moat Walk 1942.6 1944.10 '43PhBk
Lamneck W E SGT 137-E 23 Hatch 1955.4 1955.8 usacc
Lamoreaux F E E-8 30-S 34 Hampton 1963.5 1965.7 mfh
Lampman F M E-6 140-S 17 Moat Walk 1967.2 1968.5 mfh
Lampp M L SGT 110-W 38 Tidball 1907 ? '08cd
Lance G W Jr TSG 115-W 18 Harrison 1944.6 1945.4 AN306
Lange J A SGM 148-S 7 Moat Walk 1911.6 1917 '13-17cds
Langley J E SGM 192-S 6 Pratt 1965.8 1966.10 mfh
Langley J E SGM 90 21 Moat Walk 1965.7 1965.8 mfh
Larkins C D SSG 112-W 30 Tidball 1938 1939 '29PhBk
Larue G L TSG 113-W 26 Tidball 1937 1940 '37cd '40PhBk
Larue G L TSG 191-N 4 Pratt 1940 1943 '40-43PhBks
Lastooka J R WO 188-N 27 Murray 1931 193? '31cd
Lathrum O O MSG 194-S 1 Pratt 1968.7 1969.8 mfh
Lathrum O O SFC 109-S 1 Frank Lane 1967.2 1968.7 mfh
Latona N J SGT 152-W 12 Patch 1966.11 1967.8 mfh
Laughlin E Mr 140-S 17 Moat Walk 1912 1914 '13-4cds
Lausch J E SP5 72-W 21 Harrison 1969.6 1969.6 usacc
Lavalle R H YNC 71-E 19 Harrison 1961.2 1963.1 mfh USN
Lavin J J MSG 148-N 5 Moat Walk 1958.8 1959.6 usacc
Lavoie R J SFC 72-W 21 Harrison 1965.9 1965.10 usacc
Law A L SFC 112-W 30 Tidball 1971.12 1972.11 mfh
Lawler J D Mr 110-E 40 Tidball 1956.8 1959.5 usacc
Lawrence W A TSG 152-E 14 Patch 1946.11 1948.4 usacc
Lawrence G E SSG 111-W 34 Tidball 1936 1937 '37cd

Lawrie B C MSG 195-S 5 Pratt 1942.8 1944.8 '43PhBk Chapel
Lawson W R MSG 192-S 6 Pratt 1952.7 1952.12 usacc
Lay R G MSG 130-S 22 Tidball 1942.2 1943.10 AN306
Lay M D SFC 191-S 2 Pratt 1984.5 1986.1 mfh
Learnihan J T MSG 132-E 15 Tidball 1946.10 1948.6 usacc
Lee S MSG 191-S 2 Pratt 1971.12 1977.8 mfh
Lee W H 1SG 112-E 32 Tidball 1942 1944.10 '43-44PhBks
Lee F G TSG 115-E 20 Harrison 1932 1937 '33cd Pugh
Lee F G MSG 25-W 33 Tidball 1937 1939 '37cd
Leedy D W E-9 192-S 6 Pratt 1970.2 1971.8 mfh
Lehman K W SSG 72-E 23 Harrison 1939 1940.6 '40PhBk
Lehman K W SSG 130-S 22 Tidball 1940.6 1942.2 '40-41PhBks
Lemaster T A TSG 71-E 19 Harrison 1933 1937 Pugh
Lemaster T A CPT 110-W 38 Tidball 1917.11 1920.8 '20cd
Lemaster T A SGT 110-W 38 Tidball 1912.11 1917.11 '13-17cds
Lemaster T A SSG 112-W 30 Tidball 1930 1933 '31-33cds
Lenhart G R MSG 111-W 34 Tidball 1955.8 1955.12 usacc
Lenhart G R MSG 112-E 32 Tidball 1956.1 1959.1 usacc
Leonard E SSG 132-E 15 Tidball 1976.4 1978.2 mfh
Lesure S SP5 137-E 23 Hatch 1972.8 1973.4 usacc
Leverett C C MSG 196-N 11 Pratt 1966.10 1969.2 mfh
Leverett C C MSG 152-E 14 Patch 1966.5 1966.10 mfh
Levy F H SGM 191-N 4 Pratt 1953.12 1965.9 mfh
Lewis J MSG 131-W 20 Tidball 1948.2 1952.5 usacc
Lewis H C SGM 136-E 19 Hatch 1966.8 1966.9 usacc
Lewis D C SFC 148-N 5 Moat Walk 1966.11 1967.12 mfh
Lewis R SSG 151-E 10 Patch 1981.10 1982.9 mfh
Lewis D V Mr 61-S 43 Ingalls 1946.7 1973.10 Lewis usacc
Lieth W Jr W SGM 194-N 3 Pratt 1970.3 1976.3 mfh
Lind E R MSG 31-N 40 Hampton 1939 1940 '39cd
Lind E R TSG 130-S 22 Tidball 1934 1937 '37cd
Lindsay C SP6 152-W 12 Patch 1970.4 1972.11 mfh
Link MSG 5 Big Bethel 1976.9 1977.7 mfh
Lipus MSG 194-S 1 Pratt 1977.8 1981.4 mfh
List M P SSG 155-S 183 Bernard 1984.7 1985.11 mfh
Liverman F C MSG 115-E 20 Harrison 1950.7 1952.12 usacc
Liverman G A SFC 152-W 12 Patch 1952.6 1955.7 usacc
Llopis E B Jr SFC 154-S 13 Murray 1970.4 1971.10 mfh
Llopis E B Jr SSG 115-W 18 Harrison 1967.10 1968.7 mfh
Locke W J CWO 31-N 40 Hampton 1942 1944 '43PhBk
Locklear J SGT 114-W 22 Harrison 1977.2 1977.9 mfh
Loew C SP5 130-S 22 Tidball 1977.11 1978.12 mfh
Logan R S SFC 115-W 18 Harrison 1962.11 1963.10 mfh
Logan J T SP5 136-E 19 Hatch 1973.6 1974.4 mfh
Lomax J P SGM 186-S 17 Murray 1970.3 1970.7 mfh
Long F H MSG 72-E 23 Harrison 1954.5 1954.10 usacc
Long R E SSG 4 Big Bethel 1984.8 1986.2 mfh
Long D M SP4 155-N 185 Bernard 1974.7 1975.5 mfh
Long C M 1SG 131-W 20 Tidball 1939 1940 '40PhBk
Long P B SFC 132-E 15 Tidball 1964.6 1965.9 mfh
Long P B SFC 109-N 3 Frank Lane 1960.6 1962.5 mfh
Longmire B H MSG 130-N 24 Tidball 1947.8 1948.9 usacc
Longmire B H MSG 136-E 19 Hatch 1949.4 1950.4 usacc

Lorusso J G SP4 109-N 3 Frank Lane 1986.10 1988.3 mfh
Loth R W SFC 150-S 13 Moat Walk 1955.11 1957.1 usacc
Louis E D SGT 137-W 21 Hatch 1951.12 1952.5 usacc
Lounsbury E A E-6 132-W 13 Tidball 1971.2 1972.4 mfh
Love K SP4 115-E 20 Harrison 1983.2 1983.3 mfh
Lowe E L 1LT 71-W 17 Harrison 1942 1943 '39-41PhBks
Lucas J A TSG 195-S 5 Pratt 1939.6 1942.7 '40-41PhBks
Lucas J A TSG 149-N 11 Moat Walk 1937.8 1939.6 '39PhBk
Lucas C C SFC 191-N 4 Pratt 1982.1 1983.12 mfh
Luckett E L SFC 31-N 40 Hampton 1973.7 1975.7 mfh
Luebbe C L SSG 111-E 36 Tidball 1928 1929 '29cd
Lugo-Avila L SP5 112-E 32 Tidball 1983.11 1984.7 mfh
Lukas J B E-8 193-N 12 Pratt 1967.8 1968.9 mfh
Luptowski C E SFC 72-E 23 Harrison 1956.4 1956.4 usacc
Luptowski C E AFC 114-E 24 Harrison 1956.4 1958.4 usacc
Luzano G G SFC 186-N 19 Murray 1974.6 ? mfh
Lydic R F SP5 137-W 21 Hatch 1971.2 1971.11 mfh
Lynch N J MSG 115-W 18 Harrison 1947.7 1948.2 usacc
Lynch F C SSG 130-N 24 Tidball 1937 1939 '37-39cds
Lyon G SGT 4 Big Bethel 1977.6 1978.6 mfh
Lyon A G Mr 112-W 30 Tidball 1958.8 1961.8 usacc
Mace J W CWO 196-N 11 Pratt 1947.10 1949.4 usacc
MacGuire W H MSG 25-E 35 Tidball 1952.9 1956.10 usacc
Machle J B Mr 61-S 43 Ingalls 1911 1914 '12-14cd PhBk
MacQueen R O SGT 90 21 Moat Walk 1946.12 1949.4 usacc
Macrae R L SFC 130-N 24 Tidball 1971.10 1974.7 mfh
Malone K SGT 71-E 19 Harrison 1958.5 1959.7 usacc
Malone W E MSG 186-N 19 Murray 1962.3 1962.12 mfh
Malone W E MSG 110-E 40 Tidball 1959.6 1962.3 mfh
Malo D Jr D MSG 113-W 26 Tidball 1962.5 1963.4 mfh
Malton C W MSG 154-N 15 Murray 1950.11 1951.6 usacc
Manious T D SFC 137-W 21 Hatch 1960.3 1963.4 usacc
Manious T D SFC 148-S 7 Moat Walk 1963.4 1964.4 mfh
Manley T SP5 113-W 26 Tidball 1979.10 1982.3 mfh
Manoso E E-9 191-N 4 Pratt 1969.6 1971.5 mfh
Maples J C MSG 156-S 179 Bernard 1930 1931 Hricinak '31cd
Maples J C MSG 195-N 7 Pratt 1934 1939 Hrncinak '37cd
Marcell D E SFC 149-S 9 Moat Walk 1951.6 1952.11 usacc
Marcoux L D TSG 109-S 1 Frank Lane 1943.11 1944.11 '43PhBk
Marinis D E SGM 195-N 7 Pratt 1969.8 1970.6 mfh
Mark J L SP4 149-N 11 Moat Walk 1986.7 1987.5 mfh
Marker J A Jr MSG 193-N 12 Pratt 1955.11 1961.3 usacc
Marker J A Jr MSG 151-E 10 Patch 1946.12 1948.8 usacc
Markham J W MSG 71-W 17 Harrison 1952.9 1952.10 usacc
Marrero J L SGT 112-W 30 Tidball 1985.10 1987.10 mfh
Marrero C M SGM 187-N 23 Murray 1967.3 1969.8 mfh
Marrero C M MSG 153-S 15 Hatch 1967.1 1967.3 mfh
Marsee R E SFC 152-W 12 Patch 1970.3 1970.4 mfh
Marshall W SGT 72-W 21 Harrison 1903 1905 '03cd
Marshall T R E-9 26-W 29 Tidball 1973.8 1976.12 mfh
Martin S SSG 112-E 32 Tidball 1946.9 1948.12 usacc
Martin T E MSG 130-N 24 Tidball 1950.9 1951.2 usacc
Martin M SSG 131-W 20 Tidball 1982.6 1984.8 mfh

Martin E SFC 150-S 13 Moat Walk 1972.5 1973.5 mfh
Martin R SP5 150-N 15 Moat Walk 1975.12 1977.3 mfh
Martin J SGT 131-E 18 Tidball 1979.1 1980.8 mfh
Martin B SP5 155-N 185 Bernard 1975.5 ? mfh
Martin D L SFC 191-N 4 Pratt 1984.1 1985.12 mfh
Martin R L SGT 130-S 22 Tidball 1985.8 1986.7 mfh
Martone V SGT 156-N 181 Bernard 1912 1914 '13-14cds
Mason R Mr 136-E 19 Hatch 1912 1914 '13-14cd
Mason J V E-9 193-N 12 Pratt 1968.9 1970.10 mfh
Masters J W SGT 148-S 7 Moat Walk 1982.9 1985.4 mfh
Masuda H MSG 112-W 30 Tidball 1956.2 1958.8 usacc
Matheny L E SFC 137-E 23 Hatch 1959.7 1961.6 usacc
Matheson L H SFC 154-N 15 Murray 1965.10 1966.8 mfh
Mattox R SGT 152-E 14 Patch 1977.12 1978.9 mfh
Maupin P SGT 140-N 19 Moat Walk 1982.4 1982.9 mfh
Maxwell F T SGT 136-E 19 Hatch 1971.1 1972.1 mfh
May W F CWO 30-N 36 Hampton 1946.11 1947.9 usacc
Mayes D SSG 90 21 Moat Walk 1980.3 1981.5 mfh
Mayes D SSG 90 21 Moat Walk 1980.3 1981.5 mfh
Mayhugh B A SP4 111-W 34 Tidball 1983.11 1984.6 mfh
Mayo W CSM 60 67 Fenwick 1981.1 1984.8 mfh
Mays T SFC 195-S 5 Pratt 1974.2 1978.7 mfh
Mazerik R D SGT 114-W 22 Harrison 1963.10 1965.5 mfh
McAndrew T F SFC 113-E 28 Tidball 1960.7 1964.4 usacc
McAtamney J W MSG 113-E 28 Tidball 1959.7 1959.7 usacc
McAtamney J W MSG 186-S 17 Murray 1959.7 1961.10 usacc
McBride M MSG 194-N 3 Pratt 1953.4 1956.11 usacc
McBride M B SGM 31-N 40 Hampton 1967.3 1967.9 mfh
McBride M MSG 111-W 34 Tidball 1953.3 1953.4 usacc
McCall T E MSG 187-N 23 Murray 1953.1 1953.3 usacc
McCane G F MSG 114-W 22 Harrison 1957.12 1958.9 usacc
McCann J J MSG 149-S 9 Moat Walk 1946.9 1948.12 usacc
McCarthy E SGT 3-F Casemate 1900 1905 ORD b-23
McCarthy E SGT 71-W 17 Harrison 1905 1906 '06cd b-23 ORD
McCarty J C MSG 196-N 11 Pratt 1953.12 1957.10 usacc
McClain J L MSG 131-E 18 Tidball 1974.5 1975.12 mfh
McClaren S SFC 25-W 33 Tidball 1982.4 1984.12 mfh
McClellan H G E-9 191-S 2 Pratt 1969.6 1970.12 mfh
McComack SP5 140-N 19 Moat Walk 1976.11 1977.3 mfh
McCormick L M CWO 31-N 40 Hampton 1946.9 1950.3 usacc
McCoy R SSG 114-W 22 Harrison 1985.5 1987.1 mfh
McCoy H L SGM 148-S 7 Moat Walk 1961.9 1962.11 mfh
McCoy G V SGM 25-E 35 Tidball 1966.7 1968.5 mfh
McCoy D SP4 152-W 12 Patch 1977.1 1977.12 mfh
McCoy H L SGM 26-E 31 Tidball 1962.11 1966.5 mfh
McCracken M SGT 151-W 8 Patch 1981.11 1983.11 mfh
McCraner R C SP5 153-N 13 Hatch 1973.5 1973.10 mfh
McCreary M T SP4 112-E 32 Tidball 1984.8 1987.4 mfh
McCroskey J J SP4 111-W 34 Tidball 1982.9 1983.11 mfh
McCrum J C SGM 136-N 17 Hatch 1940.6 1942.7 '40-41PhBk Post SGM
McCuller J L MSG 156-S 179 Bernard 1963.8 1964.12 mfh
McCullough J M MSG 154-S 13 Murray 1954.7 1955.1 usacc
McDermott A R SGM 131-E 18 Tidball 1966.7 1966.10 mfh

McDermott A R SGM 194-S 1 Pratt 1966.10 1968.7 mfh
McDonald J S SGT 140-S 17 Moat Walk 1986.12 1988.2 mfh
McDorman D SGT 132-E 15 Tidball 1978.11 1981.5 mfh
McElroy A R SGM 109-N 3 Frank Lane 1967.6 1969.1 mfh
McGarry O A 1LT 114-E 24 Harrison 1918 1920 '19-20cds
McGarry O A SGT 61-S 43 Ingalls 1917 1918 '17cd
McGriff T L E-6 151-E 10 Patch 1970.6 1970.12 mfh
McGrody H N SFC 136-N 17 Hatch 1950.1 1950.5 usacc
McGuire P J SFC 131-W 20 Tidball 1953.1 1956.11 usacc
McGuire C SFC 186-S 17 Murray 1980.3 1981.6 mfh
McHargue F H MSG 109-S 1 Frank Lane 1956.11 1957.8 usacc
McIntyre J W SSG 112-E 32 Tidball 1936 1941 '37cd '41PhBk
McIntyre C 1SG 140-S 17 Moat Walk 1940.6 1943.11 '40-43PhBks
McIntyre C 1SG 195-N 7 Pratt 1944 1946 '44-45PhBks
McIntyre H J MSG 113-E 28 Tidball 1959.8 1960.7 usacc
McKeehan E D MSG 191-S 2 Pratt 1958.8 1959.7 usacc
McKeever P Mr 112-W 30 Tidball 1916 1917 '17cd rms?
McKeiver M SP4 167-A 7 Patch 1979.1 1979.1 mfh
McKenzie SGT 112-E 32 Tidball 1976.7 1977.11 mfh
McKenzie C R CWO 196-S 9 Pratt 1951.3 1952.12 usacc
McKeown W T E-7 113-E 28 Tidball 1971.4 1975.1 mfh
McKinley R J SGT 113-E 28 Tidball 1985.6 1986.7 mfh
McKinney W C MSG 25-E 35 Tidball 1973.6 1976.6 mfh
McLaughlin F J MSG 186-N 19 Murray 1952.11 1955.9 usacc
McLees D W SFC 113-W 26 Tidball 1959.6 1959.7 usacc
McManus T L SSG 155-S 183 Bernard 1985.11 1986.12 mfh
McMillan M C MSG 115-E 20 Harrison 1957.7 1958.2 usacc
McMillan M C MSG 137-E 23 Hatch 1957.4 1957.7 usacc
McMillian L A SSG 155-S 183 Bernard 1968.8 1969.4 usacc
McNarque F H MSG 149-S 9 Moat Walk 1955.3 1955.10 usacc
McNeil R B TSG 148-N 5 Moat Walk 1937 1941 '37-39cd '40-44PhBk
Meade J E-9 191-S 2 Pratt 1971.9 1971.12 mfh
Meade W H CSM 31-N 40 Hampton 1971.12 1972.6 mfh
Meagher T C 1SG 191-S 2 Pratt 1936 1939 '27-29cds
Means D T SGT 136-N 17 Hatch 1972.1 1973.7 mfh
Medley R SGT 5 Big Bethel 1981.2 1984.5 mfh
Meehan D SSG 109-N 3 Frank Lane 1979.7 1980.7 mfh
Meekins L AFC 90 21 Moat Walk 1954.8 1957.9 usacc
Meekins L SFC 152-E 14 Patch 1951.7 1952.10 usacc
Meekins I MSG 25-E 35 Tidball 1957.9 1959.11 usacc
Meinen G E MSG 71-W 17 Harrison 1957.6 1958.4 usacc
Melling T SP4 5 Big Bethel 1977.7 1979.4 mfh
Melocco J R MSG 132-E 15 Tidball 1958.5 1959.2 usacc
Melton C W MSG 194-S 1 Pratt 1948.6 1951.6 usacc
Menefee N SFC 148-N 5 Moat Walk 1971.5 1974.1 mfh
Mennen C H 1SG 187-N 23 Murray 1935 1939 '37-39cd AN306
Merrell J D SP5 7 Big Bethel 1984.4 1985.1 mfh
Merrit R SSG 72-W 21 Harrison 1933 1937 '37cd Pugh
Meyer A SSG 115-E 20 Harrison 1926 1927 '27cd
Mickle G E MSG 112-E 32 Tidball 1951.12 1951.12 usacc
Mikowicz J J SFC 110-E 40 Tidball 1951.7 1952.3 usacc
Miles M G SP5 71-E 19 Harrison 1966.6 1966.12 mfh
Miller J TSG 114-E 24 Harrison 1928 1930 '29cd

Miller R K SFC 110-E 40 Tidball 1963.11 1966.7 mfh
Miller W B SSG 72-W 21 Harrison 1930 1933 '31-32cds
Miller H SFC 153-S 15 Hatch 1964.3 1964.8 mfh
Miller S C E-7 132-W 13 Tidball 1972.5 1973.12 mfh
Miller J MSG 192-S 6 Pratt 1937 1939 '37cd
Miller J R SFC 188-S 25 Murray 1973.12 1974.8 mfh
Miller R G MSG 192-N 8 Pratt 1953.1 1955.12 usacc
Miller R G SFC 153-S 15 Hatch 1951.8 1953.1 usacc
Miller R F SSG 111-E 36 Tidball 1974.3 1974.11 mfh
Miller W C MSG 112-W 30 Tidball 1952.8 1953.5 usacc
Miller J MSG 151-W 8 Patch 1940 1941 '40-41PhBks
Miller J MSG 192-N 8 Pratt 1939 1940 '39-40PhBks
Miller J SSG 111-W 34 Tidball 1932 1933 '33cd
Miller D SP4 111-E 36 Tidball 1979.5 1982.6 mfh
Miller P D MSG 153-N 13 Hatch 1916 1917 '17cd
Miller P D MGnr 153-N 13 Hatch 1914 1916 '14cd
Miller G M SGT 149-N 11 Moat Walk 1976.2 1976.9 mfh
Milliken J T MSG 150-N 15 Moat Walk 1956.9 1959.5 usacc
Milliman R C MSG 196-S 9 Pratt 1962.12 1964.6 mfh
Milliman R C MSG 154-N 15 Murray 1962.4 1962.12 mfh
Mills D B MSG 155-N 185 Bernard 1950.6 1951.1 usacc
Mills J L SGT 136-N 17 Hatch 1953.1 1953.1 usacc
Mills G A 1LT 131-W 20 Tidball 1918.4 1919 '19cd
Mills G A SGT 130-S 22 Tidball 1914 1917.6 '14-17cds
Mills S W MSG 151-E 10 Patch 1968.4 1969.6 mfh
Mills G A 2LT 130-S 22 Tidball 1917.6 1918.4 S&F Arthur
Mills G A 2LT 130-S 22 Tidball 1917.6 1918.4 S&F cds Arthur
Mills B H Mr 140-S 17 Moat Walk 1915 1917 '15-17cds
Milton H E SP4 71-W 17 Harrison 1967.4 1967.5 mfh
Mincy W SGT 151-E 10 Patch 1977.5 1981.10 mfh
Minggia V SP5 90 21 Moat Walk 1984.7 1985.5 mfh
Minggia V SP5 90 21 Moat Walk 1984.7 1985.5 mfh
Mioduzewski B E-7 113-E 28 Tidball 1966.11 1968.9 mfh
Mitchell M E MSG 71-E 19 Harrison 1915 1917 '17cd
Mitchell O L SSG 114-W 22 Harrison 1926 1927 '27cd
Mitchell K W T/Sgt 136-E 19 Hatch 1947.10 1949.1 usacc
Mitchell K W SFC 114-E 24 Harrison 1949.1 1952.10 usacc
Mojarro M SSG 131-W 20 Tidball 1961.4 1963.9 mfh
Moller G J E-8 191-N 4 Pratt 1968.1 1969.6 mfh
Molovinsky D E MSG 131-W 20 Tidball 1959.2 1960.5 usacc
Monroe R H MSG 137-W 21 Hatch 1943.11 1946.11 '43-45PhBks
Monroe W L SFC 114-W 22 Harrison 1953.9 1955.5 usacc
Monroe W L SFC 154-S 13 Murray 1956.5 1957.4 usacc
Monsees E L MSG 153-N 13 Hatch 1949.1 1949.8 usacc
Montanez J L SGT 132-E 15 Tidball 1984.7 1985.10 mfh
Montgomery C J SSG 72-E 23 Harrison 1973.7 1974.4 mfh
Montgomery F SP6 131-E 18 Tidball 1980.8 1982.8 mfh
Montoya A MSG 149-N 11 Moat Walk 1954.10 1955.10 usacc
Montoya A 1SG 186-N 19 Murray 1958.3 1962.1 mfh
Moody W L TSG 131-E 18 Tidball 1939.9 1940.9 '40PhBk
Mooney G SGT 154-S 13 Murray 1980.2 1980.11 mfh
Moore W H SP4 137-W 21 Hatch 1959.8 1959.10 usacc
Moore E O SSG 153-S 15 Hatch 1931 1933 '33cd

Moore H L SSG 113-E 28 Tidball 1981.4 1983.7 mfh
Moore J W SP7 155-N 185 Bernard 1963.7 1964.4 mfh
Moore D E SGT 113-W 26 Tidball 1984.8 1985.10 mfh
Moore T O SGM 72-W 21 Harrison 1916 1917 '17cd
Moore D T SGT 188-N 27 Murray 1959.8 1960.4 usacc
Moore G SSG 115-W 18 Harrison 1979.8 1981.6 mfh
Moore C L SFC 196-N 11 Pratt 1981.8 1982.5 mfh
Moore C S SGM 132-W 13 Tidball 1913 1917 '14-17cds
Moorehead W P MSG 151-E 10 Patch 1948.8 1949.6 usacc
Moorehead W P MSG 186-N 19 Murray 1945.10 1945 '45PhBk
Moorehead W P MSG 130-S 22 Tidball 1943.10 1945.10 '43'44PhBks
Moran D SSG 149-S 9 Moat Walk 1983.3 1985.10 mfh
Morecock MSG 109-N 3 Frank Lane 1950.2 1950.12 usacc
Moree G A E-7 132-W 13 Tidball 1969.12 1970.9 mfh
Morehead E J SFC 111-E 36 Tidball 1963.1 1965.6 mfh
Moreland L SP5 151-W 8 Patch 1978.1 1978.8 mfh
Moreland SP5 7 Big Bethel 1978.8 1979.8 mfh
Moretz C O SGM 26-E 31 Tidball 1970.5 1976.6 mfh
Morgan J CWO 30-N 36 Hampton 1947.9 1948.7 usacc
Morgan J T Mr 25-E 35 Tidball 1959.12 1963.1 mfh
Morgan J SSG 113-W 26 Tidball 1982.4 1984.8 mfh
Morgan J T Mr 111-E 36 Tidball 1958.8 1959.11 usacc
Morgon C A MSG 111-E 36 Tidball 1945.6 1951.12 usacc
Moriarty T SP5 153-S 15 Hatch 1974.2 1976.6 mfh
Morrell C A TSG 156-S 179 Bernard 1946.12 1948.12 usacc
Morris W CWO 31-S 38 Hampton 1946.9 1947.4 usacc
Morris Mr 115-W 18 Harrison 1933 1937 Pugh
Morris T D SGM 113-E 28 Tidball 1964.4 1966.11 mfh
Morrison E E SSG 72-E 23 Harrison 1940.6 1941 '41PhBk
Morrison G W 1SG 188-S 25 Murray 1931 1933 '31cd
Morton R A E-8 195-S 5 Pratt 1969.2 1970.8 mfh
Morton W D MSG 153-S 15 Hatch 1958.6 1960.6 usacc
Motley T L SSG 110-W 38 Tidball 1968.5 1969.6 mfh
Mott C J Jr SFC 113-E 28 Tidball 1952.5 1952.5 usacc
Mott C J Jr SFC 71-W 17 Harrison 1952.3 1952.5 usacc
Moyer J A SP5 71-E 19 Harrison 1964.7 1966.1 mfh
Mucklevene J SP5 112-E 32 Tidball 1980.5 1983.11 mfh
Mulcahy J P SGM 195-N 7 Pratt 1965.4 1968.7 mfh
Mulcahy J P E-8 112-W 30 Tidball 1963.12 1965.4 mfh
Mulero G SP4 151-W 8 Patch 1984.6 1986.4 mfh
Mulick J SP4 148-N 5 Moat Walk 1977.5 1978.10 mfh
Mull S SP5 148-N 5 Moat Walk 1978.10 1980.2 mfh
Muller J G MSG 155-N 185 Bernard 1946.11 1947.10 usacc
Mullins H C MSG 137-E 23 Hatch 1946.1 1959.3 usacc
Munn D L Jr E-7 156-S 179 Bernard 1966.3 1967.3 mfh
Munn D L Jr E-9 186-S 17 Murray 1968.9 1968.9 mfh
Munn D L Jr E-9 186-N 19 Murray 1968.9 1969.6 mfh
Munroe C G SSG 149-S 9 Moat Walk 1928 1929 '29cd
Murphy MSG 110-W 38 Tidball 1958.5 1959.12 usacc
Murray P J SSG 148-S 7 Moat Walk 1926 1929 '27-29cds
Murray J E WO 187-N 23 Murray 1931 1934 '31-23cds
Musson A W SSG 152-W 12 Patch 1968.11 1969.2 mfh
Mutik A 1SG 191-N 4 Pratt 1946.9 1949.10 usacc

Mutters R 1SG 148-N 5 Moat Walk 1926 1929 '27-29cds
Myers D SP5 136-N 17 Hatch 1962.2 1962.5 mfh
Myers M E SFC 31-N 40 Hampton 1975.8 1982.5 mfh
Myers R K 1SG 132-W 13 Tidball 1942.6 1944.1 '43PhBk
Myrick J W MSG 196-S 9 Pratt 1938 1942 '39-41PhBks
Nabuda J MSG 155-N 185 Bernard 1960.10 1963.7 mfh
Nachbaur N T MSG 26-W 29 Tidball 1982.6 1984.8 mfh
Nagle R H SSG 150-N 15 Moat Walk 1968.6 1969.10 mfh
Nagorny S MSG 192-S 6 Pratt 1955.5 1961.3 usacc
Nagorny S MSG 71-E 19 Harrison 1946.9 1950.6 usacc
Nagorny S MSG 109-N 3 Frank Lane 1954.8 1955.5 usacc
Nance J SP4 7 Big Bethel 1979.8 1980.11 mfh
Nartowitz J MSG 192-N 8 Pratt 1941 1943 '43PhBk
Naylor W R MSG 194-S 1 Pratt 1939 1941 '39-41PhBks
Naylor W R TSG 109-N 3 Frank Lane 1936 1939 '37cd
Neal J R SP5 153-N 13 Hatch 1963.5 1964.2 usacc
Neidigh C D SGT 136-E 19 Hatch 1952.6 1952.8 usacc
Nelsen R F SP7 148-S 7 Moat Walk 1964.4 1965.8 mfh
Nelson G SGT 149-S 9 Moat Walk 1926 1927 '27cd
Nelson O H CWO 193-N 12 Pratt 1949.2 1951.12 usacc
Nersesian D SP4 156-N 181 Bernard 1977.5 1980.6 mfh
Neutzling J W E-5 137-W 21 Hatch 1970.6 1971.1 mfh
Newman J SSG 4 Big Bethel 1978.6 1979.10 mfh
Newman J SSG 132-W 13 Tidball 1976.7 1978.6 mfh
Newman R J Mr 111-W 34 Tidball 1964.12 1966.3 mfh
Nichols E A SGM 109-S 1 Frank Lane 1961.10 1963.12 mfh
Nichols P H E-7 140-S 17 Moat Walk 1968.6 1969.2 mfh
Nickerson E E CWO 26-W 29 Tidball 1949.6 1953.3 usacc
Niederauer J L SFC 191-S 2 Pratt 1986.1 1987.6 mfh
Niedferauer J L SFC 191-S 2 Pratt 1986.1 1987.6 mfh
Niedzielka B MSG 193-S 10 Pratt 1953.6 1955.3 usacc
Niedzielka B 1SG 150-S 13 Moat Walk 1944.9 1946.6 '44-45PhBk AN306
Niedzielka B 1SG 192-S 6 Pratt 1946.6 1950.1 usacc
Nikowicz J J SFC 72-W 21 Harrison 1950.10 1951.7 usacc
Nissen P R MSG 140-N 19 Moat Walk 1955.4 1955.11 usacc
Nissen P R MSG 113-W 26 Tidball 1956.2 1957.6 usacc
Nittinger E F SSG 150-S 13 Moat Walk 1965.6 1966.1 mfh
Noble L SFC 155-N 185 Bernard 1968.10 1970.6 mfh
Nolan A MSG 196-S 9 Pratt 1979.5 1982.8 mfh
Norman C W 1SG 186-N 19 Murray 1946.9 1948.12 usacc
Norris A L MSG 188-S 25 Murray 1965.11 1967.6 mfh
Norris J SFC 130-S 22 Tidball 1971.9 1972.8 mfh
Noteman H E-6 110-W 38 Tidball 1971.10 1972.4 mfh
Oatley E E MSG 140-N 19 Moat Walk 1958.10 1962.1 usacc
Oberseider J R C MSG 195-S 5 Pratt 1949.10 1950.1 usacc
Oberseider J R C SGT 130-N 24 Tidball 1948.9 1949.10 usacc
Oberseider J R C WOJG 110-E 40 Tidball 1943.11 1945.8 PhBks
O'Brien J H SGM 31-N 40 Hampton 1961.8 1962.8 mfh
O'Brien J H SGM 196-S 9 Pratt 1964.7 1966.11 mfh
O'Brien J H SGM 148-S 7 Moat Walk 1961.5 1961.8 usacc
O'Brien R D TSG 154-N 15 Murray 1944.6 1946.10 '44-45PhBks
Ochsenbein A R SFC 130-S 22 Tidball 1969.1 1969.8 mfh
O'Connell M J ? 72-E 23 Harrison 1974.5 ? mfh

Oczkowski F MSG 148-S 7 Moat Walk 1938 1939 '39PhBk
Oczkowski F MSG 140-S 17 Moat Walk 1937 1938 '37cd
Office Space 49 49 Bernard 1955.1 1975.12 usacc
Office Space 49 49 Bernard 1945 1950 usacc
O'Hearn J R SFC 72-W 21 Harrison 1959.12 1962.7 usacc
Oldham D C SGT 140-S 17 Moat Walk 1926 1929 '27-29cds
O'Leary J H ? 72-W 21 Harrison 1904 1907 '06cd b-23
Olivas P M SFC 71-E 19 Harrison 1952.12 1953.1 usacc
Olivas P M SFC 111-W 34 Tidball 1953.1 1953.3 usacc
Oliver E L SP5 111-W 34 Tidball 1972.1 1980.2 mfh
Oliver E SFC 25-E 35 Tidball 1980.2 1982.2 mfh
Olliver C W MSG 154-S 13 Murray 1942 1946 '43-45PhBks
O'Loughlin J A SFC 186-S 17 Murray 1973.7 1977.7 mfh
Olson J SGM 26-E 31 Tidball 1979.8 1981.5 mfh
O'Neal F D TSG 140-S 17 Moat Walk 1943.11 1946.12 '44-45PhBks
O'Quain R J SP5 113-E 28 Tidball 1958.11 1959.7 usacc
Orsellis T SP5 156-S 179 Bernard 1973.2 1973.8 mfh
Overstreet J H SGT 140-N 19 Moat Walk 1928 1929 '29cd
Owens O L SGT 155-S 183 Bernard 1912 1914 '13-14cds
Pabalate SSG 113-E 28 Tidball 1976.9 1980.1 mfh
Pace L A MSG 30-N 36 Hampton 1958.6 1960.8 usacc
Pace L A MSG 137-E 23 Hatch 1957.7 1958.6 usacc
Pace J H 1SG 152-E 14 Patch 1940 1941 '40-41PhBks
Page J W SSG 140-N 19 Moat Walk 1932 1933 '33cd
Palesky D E-9 25-W 33 Tidball 1969.12 1970.9 mfh
Palmer J C MSG 31-N 40 Hampton 1937 1939 '37cd
Palmer J M SSG 156-N 181 Bernard 1938 1939 '39PhBk
Palmer C MSG 111-W 34 Tidball 1933 1936 Pugh
Palmer J C SSG 111-E 36 Tidball 1930 1933 '30-33cds
Palmer G A SFC 152-E 14 Patch 1967.7 1968.9 mfh
Panunto A E-7 71-W 17 Harrison 1969.10 1970.4 mfh
Parent J H MSG 155-N 185 Bernard 1954.2 1954.3 usacc
Parent J H MSG 187-N 23 Murray 1954.3 1955.12 usacc
Parham F SP5 167-A 7 Patch 1976.10 1979.1 mfh
Park J SP5 131-E 18 Tidball 1976.3 1976.9 mfh
Parker M S TSG 90 21 Moat Walk 1944.11 1946.11 '44-45PhBk
Parker J W WO 151-W 8 Patch 1930 1931 '31cd
Parker P C 1SG 152-W 12 Patch 1946.11 1949.9 usacc
Parks G SSG 35 W-1 4 Reeder Cir 1982.5 1983.3 mfh
Parks H E SP6 113-W 26 Tidball 1965.3 1967.7 mfh
Parsons C W MSG 114-W 22 Harrison 1959.8 1961.1 usacc
Pate C P E-8 25-W 33 Tidball 1970.10 1972.9 mfh
Patterson H S SGM 130-N 24 Tidball 1964.2 1964.7 mfh
Patterson W L SGT 153-S 15 Hatch 1945.11 1951.8 usacc
Patterson H S SGM 196-N 11 Pratt 1964.7 1965.12 mfh
Pattison D SSG 149-N 11 Moat Walk 1980.2 1982.8 mfh
Paul H D MSG 25-W 33 Tidball 1960.7 1961.9 usacc
Payton A M MSG 194-S 1 Pratt 1954.1 1963.10 mfh
Pcola M J E-7 90 21 Moat Walk 1966.9 1968.11 mfh
Peabody R D SFC 71-W 17 Harrison 1958.8 1960.1 usacc
Pearson T D SGM 31-S 38 Hampton 1969.11 1970.7 mfh
Pearson R SP5 152-W 12 Patch 1975.11 1977.1 mfh
Peck J A MSG 154-N 15 Murray 1969.6 1970.5 mfh

Peck A E MSG 155-N 185 Bernard 1939.2 1942.6 '39-41cds
Peck A E MSG 25-E 35 Tidball 1942.6 1943.12 '43PhBk
Peck A E SSG 155-N 185 Bernard 1926 1927 '27cd
Pederson D L SSG 71-W 17 Harrison 1964.2 1965.4 mfh
Peed J E MSG 153-S 15 Hatch 1956.4 1957.8 usacc
Peek A R SGT 111-W 34 Tidball 1953.5 1955.8 usacc
Peek T Jr MSG 154-S 13 Murray 1963.7 1963.9 mfh
Pelis J A SFC 148-S 7 Moat Walk 1972.9 1973.6 mfh
Pellett C E SFC 155-N 185 Bernard 1952.11 1953.5 usacc
Pence M L 1SG 31-N 40 Hampton 1962.8 1963.6 mfh
Pence M L Jr MSG 111-W 34 Tidball 1958.5 1960.1 usacc
Pennington R R SSG 114-E 24 Harrison 1926 1927 '27cd
Pennington R R MSG 31-N 40 Hampton 1940 1942 '40-41PhBks
Pennington R R CWO 191-N 4 Pratt 1943.6 1945.4 '43-44PhBks
Pennington R R TSG 110-W 38 Tidball 1937 1939 '37-39cds
Penny R SP6 155-N 185 Bernard 1974.5 1974.7 mfh
Perdue G D SSG 115-E 20 Harrison 1970.9 1970.11 mfh
Perez D D SGM 196-S 9 Pratt 1982.8 1983.2 mfh
Perkins D G E-6 156-N 181 Bernard 1968.12 1971.4 mfh
Perkins L SP5 167-A 7 Patch 1979.1 1980.6 mfh
Peters W J H CSM 64 71 Fenwick 1983.8 1987.7 mfh
Peterson A M MSG 155-N 185 Bernard 1957.5 1958.11 usacc
Peterson D SSG 167-A 7 Patch 1982.3 1984.5 mfh
Petrey F D SFC 151-E 10 Patch 1967.1 1967.8 mfh
Phillingane J SSG 149-S 9 Moat Walk 1978.9 1979.3 mfh
Phillips J L SFC 137-E 23 Hatch 1950.10 1950.11 mfh
Phillips J L SFC 114-W 22 Harrison 1950.11 1951.5 usacc
Phillips A SFC 191-N 4 Pratt 1978.4 1982.1 mfh
Phillips A Jr E-6 149-S 9 Moat Walk 1974.7 1977.3 mfh
Picard T W E-9 186-S 17 Murray 1968.10 1970.3 mfh
Pickard C L SP5 109-N 3 Frank Lane 1974.12 1977.6 mfh
Pierce H E CWO 188-S 25 Murray 1942.6 1950.3 '43-45PhBk usacc
Pierce H E MSG 188-S 25 Murray 1934 1939 Pugh
Pierce H E SSG 156-S 179 Bernard 1939 1941 '40-41PhBks
Pierce J SFC 188-S 25 Murray 1977.12 1979.11 mfh
Pierce J SSG 152-E 14 Patch 1975.10 1977.12 mfh
Pierson F SGT 150-S 13 Moat Walk 1916 1917 '17cd
Pihokken S A MSG 109-S 1 Frank Lane 1957.8 1959.11 usacc
Pike J T MSG 115-W 18 Harrison 1945.11 1947.7 usacc
Placzkouski T J SP7 148-S 7 Moat Walk 1959.11 1961.3 usacc
Plumley B E MSG 150-N 15 Moat Walk 1954.9 1955.5 usacc
Plummer E L E-9 191-N 4 Pratt 1971.6 1977.8 mfh
Plummer E W MSG 26-E 31 Tidball 1958.9 1962.10 mfh
Poe H K SSG 72-W 21 Harrison 1968.7 1968.10 usacc
Pogan L S SSG 149-S 9 Moat Walk 1942.6 1944.9 '43PhBk
Polk C E SP4 136-N 17 Hatch 1963.8 1963.9 mfh
Polkingham M S MSG 137-E 23 Hatch 1932 1939 '33-37cd '39PhBk
Pool R V CWO 61-N 45 Ingalls 1961.10 1963.8 mfh
Poole W R Jr E-9 193-N 12 Pratt 1964.11 1966.4 mfh
Pope D K SP4 113-W 26 Tidball 1986.12 1987.10 mfh
Porta R J E-7 150-S 13 Moat Walk 1969.1 1970.1 mfh
Porter G I MSG 110-E 40 Tidball 1948.10 1949.8 usacc
Posey R L E-5 114-E 24 Harrison 1970.9 1971.12 mfh

Poston W B SFC 72-W 21 Harrison 1965.10 1968.3 usacc
Potter R MSG 131-W 20 Tidball 1943.6 1944.10 '43PhBk
Potter R MSG 131-E 18 Tidball 1955.1 1955.3 usacc
Potter R MSG 149-S 9 Moat Walk 1956.3 1957.1 usacc
Potter R MSG 112-E 32 Tidball 1944.10 1945 '45PhBk
Potter J R SGM 111-E 36 Tidball 1907 ? '08cd
Potter R MSG 186-S 17 Murray 1946.9 1948.10 usacc
Potter R MSG 187-S 21 Murray 1955.3 1955.8 usacc
Potts J O MSG 137-E 23 Hatch 1966.6 1966.9 usacc
Potts J O MSG 154-N 15 Murray 1966.9 1968.2 mfh
Powell J H E-7 140-N 19 Moat Walk 1967.2 1968.1 mfh
Powell G W SFC 188-N 27 Murray 1963.4 1965.5 mfh
Powell W H SFC 191-S 2 Pratt 1952.6 1984.4 mfh
Powers F W MSG 196-N 11 Pratt 1952.9 1953.3 usacc
Prall R M E-6 113-E 28 Tidball 1968.10 1970.4 mfh
Price P H Mr 111-W 34 Tidball 1949.8 1951.11 usacc
Price D SSG 7 Big Bethel 1976.12 1978.8 mfh
Price R SFC 61-N 45 Ingalls 1970.5 1971.8 mfh
Pride H E 1LT 153-N 13 Hatch 1917 1918 '19cd
Proctor J C SGT 130-S 22 Tidball 1984.9 1985.8 mfh
Propst A W MSG 140-S 17 Moat Walk 1965.8 1966.1 mfh
Prosise S M E-8 155-N 185 Bernard 1965.9 1966.5 mfh
Pross L MSG 154-N 15 Murray 1946.10 1948.5 usacc
Pryor R F SP3 137-E 23 Hatch 1956.1 1957.2 usacc
Puckett J E E-8 154-S 13 Murray 1964.11 1965.5 mfh
Pugh R O WO 194-N 3 Pratt 1937.5 1939 '37-39cds Pugh
Pugh I E MSG 131-W 20 Tidball 1956.12 1958.4 usacc
Pugh R O MSG 149-S 9 Moat Walk 1933 1937.5 '33cd Pugh
Pugh I E MSG 153-S 15 Hatch 1953.2 1953.4 usacc
Purser J E SSG 112-E 32 Tidball 1964.7 1964.11 mfh
Purser J E SSG 72-E 23 Harrison 1962.7 1962.8 mfh
Putney J W SFC 72-W 21 Harrison 1953.2 1953.3 usacc
Puu D A E-7 149-S 9 Moat Walk 1967.7 1969.7 mfh
Pyatt M D CPT 30-N 36 Hampton 1984.6 1985.5 mfh
Quarles O R MSG 112-E 32 Tidball 1948.12 1950.6 usacc
Queen J 1SG 195-S 5 Pratt 1980.7 1982.6 mfh
Quigley H P WOJG 137-E 23 Hatch 1942.8 1944.6 '43PhBk
Quist L E CWO 31-N 40 Hampton 1950.4 1953.9 usacc
Racicot R P CWO 25-W 33 Tidball 1948.9 1951.10 usacc
Radimak J M E-3 72-W 21 Harrison 1969.12 1970.12 mfh
Radley H F SGM 187-S 21 Murray 1968.1 1969.3 mfh
Ragsdale P W MSG 192-N 8 Pratt 1971.3 1973.6 mfh
Ralph M C SGT 114-W 22 Harrison 1953.4 1953.8 usacc
Ramer R S SGM 26-W 29 Tidball 1984.8 1986.2 mfh
Randolph R C SGM 31-N 40 Hampton 1965.10 1966.8 mfh
Randolph J W Jr MSG 115-E 20 Harrison 1958.3 1961.4 usacc
Randolph J W Jr MSG 136-N 17 Hatch 1958.1 1958.3 usacc
Rankin D D SFC 113-W 26 Tidball 1960.4 1962.4 mfh
Rankin D D MSG 130-S 22 Tidball 1965.3 1967.6 mfh
Rapetti A J MSG 187-S 21 Murray 1951.3 1952.4 usacc
Rapetti A J MSG 136-N 17 Hatch 1950.5 1951.3 usacc
Rasmussen C SGT 130-S 22 Tidball 1912 1913 '13cd
Ratchford P ? 195-S 5 Pratt 1978.7 1980.2 mfh

Ratliff R G SFC 188-S 25 Murray 1974.8 1977.12 mfh
Ray J F Mr 61-S 43 Ingalls 1943.11 1945.4 '43-45PhBks
Ray W J MSG 194-S 1 Pratt 1947.9 1948.1 usacc
Raynor J S SFC 113-W 26 Tidball 1963.5 1965.2 mfh
Rea H E MSG 188-N 27 Murray 1960.6 1962.2 mfh
Rea J MSG 196-S 9 Pratt 1983.2 1987.5 mfh
Rea H E MSG 132-E 15 Tidball 1959.2 1960.6 usacc
Ream A F MSG 112-W 30 Tidball 1946.12 1949.10 usacc
Reardon J E TSG 72-E 23 Harrison 1926 1933 '27-33cds
Reaux R J E-7 150-N 15 Moat Walk 1967.6 1968.6 mfh
Redden J L SP5 136-E 19 Hatch 1968.4 1969.8 usacc
Reddick W E MSG 113-E 28 Tidball 1949.8 1950.1 usacc
Reeb V S MSG 112-W 30 Tidball 1955.2 1955.10 usacc
Reeb V S MSG 109-S 1 Frank Lane 1955.10 1956.10 usacc
Reece W SFC 192-N 8 Pratt 1978.5 1980.2 mfh
Reed J SP5 148-N 5 Moat Walk 1980.2 1981.8 mfh
Reedy L E CWO 193-N 12 Pratt 1947.11 1949.1 usacc
Reeves J R MSG 151-E 10 Patch 1952.7 1953.1 usacc
Reid C W SGT 155-S 183 Bernard 1951.6 1952.12 usacc
Renew K SGT 130-S 22 Tidball 1978.12 1980.1 mfh
Renish L Mr 114-W 22 Harrison 1914 1916 '14-16PhBks
Restivo L S SP5 151-W 8 Patch 1968.1 1968.5 mfh
Reuschlein J W CWO 25-W 33 Tidball 1945.9 1947.7 usacc
Revis S SP4 152-E 14 Patch 1978.9 1979.7 mfh
Reymonds B SFC 115-W 18 Harrison 1972.3 1973.5 mfh
Reynolds E R E-7 112-W 30 Tidball 1968.11 1971.11 mfh
Rhodes R R SP4 112-E 32 Tidball 1975.11 1976.1 mfh
Rhodes R W SP4 113-W 26 Tidball 1985.10 1986.11 mfh
Rhyne L V MSG 192-N 8 Pratt 1946.10 1952.11 usacc
Rice J F CSM 60 67 Fenwick 1986.9 1987.? mfh
Rice M F CSM 79-N 95 Ingalls 1986.7 1987.3 mfh
Richards K SP6 151-W 8 Patch 1978.8 1980.3 mfh
Richards P MSG 195-S 5 Pratt 1980.3 1982.6 mfh
Richards K P SP6 152-W 12 Patch 1974.5 1975.5 mfh
Richardson J T MSG 188-N 27 Murray 1939 1946 '39cd 40-45PhBks
Richardson H C SFC 148-N 5 Moat Walk 1962.8 1963.8 mfh
Richmond E W 1SG 193-S 10 Pratt 1939 1940 '39cd
Richmond E W 1SG 151-E 10 Patch 1936 1937 '37cd
Richmond E W 1SG 193-N 12 Pratt 1940 1941 '40-41PhBks
Ricketson M A MSG 192-N 8 Pratt 1945.6 1946.10 AN306
Ricketson M A MSG 131-W 20 Tidball 1944.10 1945.6 '44-45PhBks
Rideout D J SP5 136-E 19 Hatch 1975.9 ? mfh
Ridgeway J L E-9 26-W 29 Tidball 1970.2 1973.6 mfh
Rimlinger J H E-6 115-W 18 Harrison 1970.12 1972.2 mfh
Rimmer O H Jr SFC 156-S 179 Bernard 1965.1 1966.3 mfh
Rimmer O H Jr E-6 153-S 15 Hatch 1966.3 1967.1 mfh
Ringer V P E-7 151-W 8 Patch 1971.5 1973.6 mfh
Rishell E L SFC 193-N 12 Pratt 1983.10 1985.6 mfh
Ritter J A SGT 132-W 13 Tidball 1950.4 1952.9 usacc
Ritz H E MSG 187-S 21 Murray 1946.9 1951.1 usacc
Robas F W CWO 30-S 34 Hampton 1943.10 1946.9 '43-45PhBk AN306
Robb R SP5 114-W 22 Harrison 1977.9 1981.1 mfh
Robbins W D MSG 109-S 1 Frank Lane 1944.11 1946.11 '44-45PhBks

Roberge J A SSG 153-N 13 Hatch 1964.2 1968.7 usacc
Roberson J H MSG 187-S 21 Murray 1952.11 1953.5 usacc
Roberson J H MSG 140-S 17 Moat Walk 1952.8 1952.11 usacc
Roberson L B SGT 112-E 32 Tidball 1907 ? '08cd
Roberts E L SFC 49 49 Bernard 1952.5 1952.5 usacc
Roberts C SFC 35 W-1 4 Reeder Cir 1985.8 1987.10 mfh
Roberts R R E-9 26-E 31 Tidball 1969.2 1970.5 mfh
Roberts A H E-6 153-S 15 Hatch 1965.10 1966.3 mfh
Roberts J W TSG 155-N 185 Bernard 1945.2 1946.11 '45PhBk
Robertson H L WOJG 194-N 3 Pratt 1944.11 1946.1 '44-45PhBks
Robinson C C MSG 195-S 5 Pratt 1956.12 1958.7 usacc
Robinson L N SFC 154-N 15 Murray 1963.1 1965.10 mfh
Robinson J E WO 26-W 29 Tidball 1934 1937 '34-37cds
Robinson J E WO 111-E 36 Tidball 1933 1934 Pugh
Rochette E P MSG 113-E 28 Tidball 1946.10 1947.6 usacc
Rocker B B SFC 196-N 11 Pratt 1980.11 1981.8 mfh
Rodriguez C SGT 140-N 19 Moat Walk 1986.2 1986.9 mfh
Rodwell J J CWO 196-S 9 Pratt 1947.5 1951.2 usacc
Roger C D MSG 132-W 13 Tidball 1954.3 1954.5 usacc
Rogers R E L SGT 156-N 181 Bernard 1915 1916 '16cd
Rogers H C Mr 191-S 2 Pratt 1941.5 1944.6 '43PhBk
Rogers I W SGM 196-N 11 Pratt 1965.12 1966.10 mfh
Rohde A H E-6 150-S 13 Moat Walk 1966.1 1967.10 mfh
Rohrbaugh R H WO 186-N 19 Murray 1931 1934 '31-33cds
Rollins S SP5 112-E 32 Tidball 1977.11 1980.4 mfh
Romeo J F SFC 113-W 26 Tidball 1951.7 1952.6 usacc
Romeo V G SFC 72-E 23 Harrison 1952.6 1952.12 usacc
Ronning J H SP4 151-E 10 Patch 1984.12 1985.11 mfh
Rosebush K A SP5 130-N 24 Tidball 1975.5 1975.11 mfh
Ross A SGT 140-N 19 Moat Walk 1918 1919 '19cd
Ross W L SSG 149-N 11 Moat Walk 1970.12 1974.5 mfh
Roswold R E SFC 137-E 23 Hatch 1949.4 1950.9 usacc
Rothauser H MSG 132-E 15 Tidball 1948.7 1949.7 usacc
Rowe N A MSG 113-W 26 Tidball 1959.8 1960.3 usacc
Rowe N A SGM 26-W 29 Tidball 1960.4 1963.8 mfh
Rowe J L SP6 132-W 13 Tidball 1974.2 1976.7 mfh
Rozier D SFC 186-S 17 Murray 1981.6 1982.6 mfh
Rudisill C F SFC 152-E 14 Patch 1970.11 1972.6 mfh
Ruffin J R SFC 186-N 19 Murray 1963.5 1964.12 mfh
Ruffin J R SFC 153-N 13 Hatch 1962.8 1963.5 usacc
Ruleford J A SFC 25-W 33 Tidball 1973.12 1975.12 mfh
Ryan H B MSG 186-N 19 Murray 1962.12 1963.4 mfh
Saberhagen H A SSG 152-E 14 Patch 1936 1939 '37cd
Saberhagen H A TSG 152-W 12 Patch 1939 1941 '40-41PhBks
Sackerman G W SFC 72-E 23 Harrison 1962.8 1965.5 mfh
Sagraves J H E-7 109-N 3 Frank Lane 1963.3 1963.12 mfh
Sahms R E MSG 35 W-2 2 Reeder Cir 1981.6 1982.5 mfh
Sahwhan F L MSG 193-S 10 Pratt 1961.11 1962.11 mfh
Salazar P SSG 149-N 11 Moat Walk 1967.10 1968.8 mfh
Salazar P SFC 115-E 20 Harrison 1966.5 1967.3 mfh
Salazar P SFC 148-N 5 Moat Walk 1969.12 1971.5 mfh
Sample G W SSG 131-W 20 Tidball 1984.9 1987.2 mfh
Sampson C Jr SFC 192-N 8 Pratt 1973.6 1978.4 mfh

Sansale B J SGT 150-S 13 Moat Walk 1983.5 1986.10 mfh
Santos C SSG 109-N 3 Frank Lane 1980.7 1983.4 mfh
Sapp S E SGM 187-S 21 Murray 1973.3 1975.7 mfh
Sapp S E MSG 152-E 14 Patch 1968.9 1970.10 mfh
Sather A L SSG 114-W 22 Harrison 1966.1 1966.9 mfh
Satterfield A C SP5 154-S 13 Murray 1974.11 1975.8 mfh
Saunders C W MSG 115-W 18 Harrison 1948.2 1949.5 usacc
Savage G H WO 153-N 13 Hatch 1947.7 1948.1 usacc
Savoie X 1SG 71-W 17 Harrison 1943 1944 '44PhBk
Sawyer W D E-7 109-N 3 Frank Lane 1970.4 1973.7 mfh
Schabbehar R SSG 112-W 30 Tidball 1972.11 1973.12 mfh
Schaefer T L SSG 110-W 38 Tidball 1967.4 1967.8 mfh
Schafer D SSG 90 21 Moat Walk 1976.3 1977.11 mfh
Schafer D SSG 90 21 Moat Walk 1976.3 1977.11 mfh
Schafer D H SP5 137-W 21 Hatch 1972.9 ? mfh
Schaller D G SP7 110-W 38 Tidball 1959.12 1962.10 mfh
Schaller D G SP7 187-N 23 Murray 1962.10 1964.4 mfh
Schifer G R MSG 154-S 13 Murray 1946.9 1948.6 usacc
Schlechte A W CWO 196-S 9 Pratt 1942.7 1947.5 usacc
Schmidt G MSG 130-N 24 Tidball 1928 1931.6 '29cd
Schmitt G A SGM 186-N 19 Murray 1964.12 1966.6 mfh
Schultens J MSG 196-S 9 Pratt 1936 1937 '37cd
Schultens J SSG 132-E 15 Tidball 1933 1934 '33cd
Schultens J SGT 131-E 18 Tidball 1926 1927 '27cd
Schurr SGT 114-W 22 Harrison 1912 1914 '13-14cds
Schwarz C MSG 149-S 9 Moat Walk 1948.12 1951.6 usacc
Scobee M SFC 193-S 10 Pratt 1981.7 1983.9 mfh
Scobee L E SFC 195-N 7 Pratt 1963.6 1963.12 mfh
Scott M L E-7 149-S 9 Moat Walk 1960.10 1963.3 mfh
Scott G A Mr 137-W 21 Hatch 191 1914 '13-14cds
Scott M L SFC 130-S 22 Tidball 1964.8 1965.3 mfh
Scriven C A SGT 90 21 Moat Walk 1981.5 1982.2 mfh
Scriven R L 1LT 113-W 26 Tidball 1918 1919 '19cd
Scriven C A SGT 90 21 Moat Walk 1981.5 1982.2 mfh
Scully R E SP5 155-N 185 Bernard 1970.6 1971.7 mfh
Searle-Spratt G E 1SG 188-N 27 Murray 1971.8 1975.8 mfh
Sedlock A J SSG 154-N 15 Murray 1942.6 1943.11 '43PhBk
Sedlock A J SSG 137-E 23 Hatch 1944.6 1945.12 '44-45PhBks
Seitler K J 1SG 188-S 25 Murray 1939 1942.6 '39cd '40-41PhBks
Self R SFC 191-N 4 Pratt 1977.9 1978.4 mfh
Sellars B A SP4 156-N 181 Bernard 1986.3 1987.10 mfh
Senn N H SSG 109-N 3 Frank Lane 1940 1942 '40-41PhBks
Servin O CWO 26-W 29 Tidball 1946.9 1949.6 usacc
Sessman W G SGT 155-S 183 Bernard 1915 1916 '16cd
Seymour L R SSG 150-S 13 Moat Walk 1967.11 1969.1 mfh
Shaffer P K MSG 188-N 27 Murray 1968.11 1969.8 mfh
Shaffer E L SSG 156-N 181 Bernard 1968.11 1968.12 mfh
Shambley G W SFC 156-S 179 Bernard 1950.5 1950.9 usacc
Shanhan F L MSG 156-N 181 Bernard 1959.9 1961.12 usacc
Shank V E SSG 130-S 22 Tidball 1930 1933 '33cd
Shannon G C MSG 193-S 10 Pratt 1962.12 1964.1 mfh
Shannon T E MSG 137-E 23 Hatch 1954.10 1955.4 usacc
Sharer J A MSG 154-N 15 Murray 1948.11 1949.12 usacc

Shaw H W SSG 136-N 17 Hatch 1934 1937 '37cd
Shawl C L SFC 114-W 22 Harrison 1963.4 1963.10 mfh
Shawl C L MSG 112-E 32 Tidball 1964.11 1965.7 mfh
Shawl C L MSG 193-S 10 Pratt 1965.7 1968.12 mfh
Sheetz K SGM 35-W-1 4 Reeder Cir 1983.3 1985.8 mfh
Shelton W F SGT 150-N 15 Moat Walk 1952.4 1953.3 usacc
Shelton T SP4 153-N 13 Hatch 1978.2 1983.8 mfh
Shepard J M SFC 186-S 17 Murray 1985.12 1987.5 mfh
Shepard J ? 113-E 28 Tidball 1980.2 1981.4 mfh
Shepherd D SSG 167-A 7 Patch 1980.6 1982.3 mfh
Shepherd W L MSG 35-E-1 8 Reeder Cir 1985.6 1986.11 mfh
Sheppard L C SP5 61-N 45 Ingalls 1972.4 1974.5 mfh
Sherman E P MSG 140-S 17 Moat Walk 1950.6 1951.6 usacc
Sherman E P MSG 136-E 19 Hatch 1950.5 1950.6 usacc
Sherman E P MSG 194-S 1 Pratt 1951.6 1951.11 usacc
Sherman I J Jr E-7 155-N 185 Bernard 1964.4 1964.10 mfh
Shillingburg C SGT 155-S 183 Bernard 1978.1 1978.5 mfh
Shine T B WO 150-S 13 Moat Walk 1928 1931 '29cd
Shingleton J D SP6 155-S 183 Bernard 1974.2 1976.8 mfh
Shipley R SP5 167-B 9 Patch 1980.3 1980.7 mfh
Shirk J D MSG 187-S 21 Murray 1939 1941 '39cd '40PhBk
Shoemaker J K E-7 140-N 19 Moat Walk 1962.10 1967.2 mfh
Short SFC 155-N 185 Bernard 1951.1 1952.2 usacc
Showalter E R Jr SFC 110-E 40 Tidball 1962.4 1963.4 mfh
Shrenk W TSG 155-S 183 Bernard 1942 1944 '43PhBk
Shrewsbury R L SFC 113-E 28 Tidball 1983.7 1985.6 mfh
Shriver R J SGT 130-N 24 Tidball 1982.7 1983.7 mfh
Shropshire R A SSG 136-N 17 Hatch 1928 1929 '29cd
Shufelt R J MSG 155-N 185 Bernard 1956.5 1957.4 usacc
Shupe J W SGT 72-E 23 Harrison 1953.7 1954.5 usacc
Sifuents C L SFC 114-E 24 Harrison 1960.6 1963.9 mfh
Simank L W SGT 137-E 23 Hatch 1964.9 1965.5 usacc
Simmons A B SGT 71-E 19 Harrison 1953.1 1954.10 usacc
Simmons A B MSG 136-E 19 Hatch 1952.11 1953.1 usacc
Simmons R F SFC 49 49 Bernard 1950.6 1951.6 usacc
Simmons W H SGT 152-W 12 Patch 1972.12 1974.1 mfh
Simpkins W H E-7 193-N 12 Pratt 1973.9 1980.8 mfh
Simpson B L 1SG 30-N 36 Hampton 1937 1942.6 '37-39cd '40-41PhB
Simpson B L CPT 30-S 34 Hampton 1942.6 1943.10 '43PhBk AN306
Simpson B L 1SG 131-E 18 Tidball 1933 1937 Pugh
Simpson F A SFC 193-S 10 Pratt 1983.9 1985.7 mfh
Singer G E SFC 71-W 17 Harrison 1962.2 1963.12 mfh
Singer J SP6 150-S 13 Moat Walk 1976.9 1980.8 mfh
Skaggs F SSG 140-N 19 Moat Walk 1968.1 1968.5 mfh
Skeen W L WOJG 25-W 33 Tidball 1945.12 1946.9 '45PhBk
Skelton C R Jr SFC 148-N 5 Moat Walk 1966.5 1966.8 mfh
Skinner C MSG 130-S 22 Tidball 1948.11 1949.3 usacc
Skinner C A MSG 195-N 7 Pratt 1946.10 1953.4 usacc
Sliwoski J J SP5 136-E 19 Hatch 1959.2 1959.10 usacc
Smith D F SSG 153-S 15 Hatch 1944.6 1945.11 '44-45PhBks
Smith C L SP5 113-W 26 Tidball 1972.6 1972.8 mfh
Smith A C SSG 71-W 17 Harrison 1944 1945 '45PhBk
Smith O C MSG 151-E 10 Patch 1956.3 1956.4 usacc

Smith W W MSG 90 21 Moat Walk 1928 1929 '29cd
Smith A E-7 151-E 10 Patch 1969.6 1970.6 mfh
Smith J V CWO 26-E 31 Tidball 1946.9 1948.11 usacc
Smith A L 1SG 112-W 30 Tidball 1939 1940 '40PhBk
Smith G SGT 5 Big Bethel 1979.5 1979.8 mfh
Smith G SSG 131-E 18 Tidball 1946.9 1948.9 usacc
Smith W MSG 194-N 3 Pratt 1961.6 1963.3 mfh
Smith E D SSG 151-E 10 Patch 1976.7 1977.5 mfh
Smith J SGT 130-N 24 Tidball 1980.12 1982.6 mfh
Smith R SP5 130-N 24 Tidball 1976.10 1978.3 mfh
Smith K SFC 26-W 29 Tidball 1979.10 1982.5 mfh
Smith C F SGT 155-N 185 Bernard 1915 1916 '16cd
Smith H H 1LT 152-W 12 Patch 1918 1919 '19cd
Smith W M MSG 31-S 38 Hampton 1976.12 1983.7 mfh
Smith R L TSG 151-W 8 Patch 1936 1937 '37cd
Smith A W MSG 109-S 1 Frank Lane 1959.12 1961.7 usacc
Smith M J MSG 115-E 20 Harrison 1956.5 1957.1 usacc
Smith J W E-7 115-W 18 Harrison 1968.12 1970.12 mfh
Smith W E MSG 71-E 19 Harrison 1950.6 1952.7 usacc
Smith G E SFC 155-N 185 Bernard 1966.5 1967.12 mfh
Smith A L SP5 136-N 17 Hatch 1958.9 1958.12 usacc
Smith T SP4 114-W 22 Harrison 1982.9 1983.4 mfh
Smitherman SFC 71-W 17 Harrison 1950.2 1952.1 usacc
Smith H Jr SP5 152-W 12 Patch 1975.5 1975.10 mfh
Snead L E MSG 188-S 25 Murray 1967.7 1968.6 mfh
Snowden J C SFC 195-S 5 Pratt 1958.7 1960.6 usacc
Snyder J SGT 155-S 183 Bernard 1978.5 1980.7 mfh
Snyder K MSG 109-N 3 Frank Lane 1946.12 1947.9 usacc
Snyder J R SSG 132-E 15 Tidball 1982.1 1983.3 mfh
Snyder F J SGM 196-S 9 Pratt 1968.7 1972.4 mfh
Snyder K R TSG 151-W 8 Patch 1938 1940 '39cd '40PhBk
Snyder C E Jr MSG 192-S 6 Pratt 1953.1 1954.10 usacc
Solmiren S SP6 61-N 45 Ingalls 1968.8 1970.4 mfh
Soto L L SGT 130-S 22 Tidball 1982.9 1983.11 mfh
Sovia R E MSG 154-N 15 Murray 1953.2 1953.3 usacc
Sovia R E MSG 196-N 11 Pratt 1953.3 1953.11 usacc
Spackman F T TSG 151-W 8 Patch 1945.1 1946.9 '45PhBk
Spain C A SGM 25-E 35 Tidball 1963.3 1966.6 mfh
Spangler G ? 30-N 36 Hampton 1978.4 1979.3 mfh
Spears J C SGT 110-W 38 Tidball 1982.7 1984.3 mfh
Spencer L E ? 151-W 8 Patch 1916 1917 '17cd
Spencer S D SP5 113-E 28 Tidball 1968.9 1968.10 mfh
Spencer L SSG 109-S 1 Frank Lane 1977.3 1981.2 mfh
Spencer H L SSG 156-N 181 Bernard 1940 ? '40PhBk
Sperl F SSG 131-W 20 Tidball 1940 1941 '40-41PhBks
Spina N SFC 110-E 40 Tidball 1952.4 1953.2 usacc
Spooner W A SP5 150-S 13 Moat Walk 1973.9 1976.9 mfh
Spork J W SGT 72-W 21 Harrison 1951.10 1952.4 usacc
Spradlen D J SFC 114-E 24 Harrison 1952.10 1952.12 usacc
Sprague W R SGM 151-E 10 Patch 1913 1916 '13-16cds
Sprague W R SGM 140-N 19 Moat Walk 1916 1918 '17cd
Sprague W R SGT 114-W 22 Harrison 1918 1920 AN306
Sprinkle J K SFC 109-N 3 Frank Lane 1950.12 1952.12 usacc

Sprinkle J K MSG 140-S 17 Moat Walk 1952.12 1955.12 usacc
Sprinkle J K MSG 132-W 13 Tidball 1956.2 1963.4 mfh
Spruill C B E-5 33 67 Fenwick 1967.7 1970.7 usacc
St Amand A P MSG 25-W 33 Tidball 1955.9 1958.8 usacc
St Amand A P MSG 148-N 5 Moat Walk 1955.8 1955.9 usacc
St Sauver M SP4 140-N 19 Moat Walk 1978.10 1980.6 mfh
Stacey T Mr 186-N 19 Murray 1943 1944 '43-44PhBks
Staff F B SSG 151-E 10 Patch 1982.9 1984.12 mfh
Stahl W R SFC 187-N 23 Murray 1978.7 1980.8 mfh
Stainbrook N L E-8 194-S 1 Pratt 1969.9 1972.11 mfh
Stainbrook N L SGM 187-S 21 Murray 1975.8 1980.8 mfh
Stallings M O CWO 196-N 11 Pratt 1938 1946 '39cd 40-45PhBk
Stambaugh D M SP5 140-S 17 Moat Walk 1973.7 1974.9 mfh
Stanford G E Jr MSG 31-N 40 Hampton 1958.9 1959.5 usacc
Stanley W J SFC 156-N 181 Bernard 1949.8 1949.11 usacc
Stanley C M TSG 61-S 43 Ingalls 1939 1940.9 '40-41PhBks
Starkey J L SGT 72-W 21 Harrison 1912 1914 '13-14PhBks
Staszcuk S R SFC 193-N 12 Pratt 1985.6 1987.2 mfh
Steele R L MSG 132-E 15 Tidball 1965.9 1965.9 mfh
Steele C M TSG 154-S 13 Murray 1940 1941 '40-41PhBks
Steffey J F SSG 130-S 22 Tidball 1926 1929 '27-29cds
Steig T SFC 194-S 1 Pratt 1983.3 1985.5 mfh
Stein E N E-8 26-W 29 Tidball 1968.2 1970.1 mfh
Stelle R L MSG 191-N 4 Pratt 1965.9 1966.6 mfh
Stern SGT 113-E 28 Tidball 1935 1937 Pugh
Stevens W R MSG 130-N 24 Tidball 1954.2 1954.8 usacc
Stevens W H MSG 115-E 20 Harrison 1928 1929 '29cd
Stevens R D MSG 35 E-1 6 Reeder Cir 1986.3 1986.7 mfh
Stevenson E W MSG 115-E 20 Harrison 1961.5 1962.6 mfh
Stevenson E M SP5 110-W 38 Tidball 1972.10 1975.8 mfh
Stiber A C MSG 111-W 34 Tidball 1960.2 1962.10 mfh
Stiles J G SGM 191-S 2 Pratt 1962.6 1967.2 mfh
Stirni J MSG 114-W 22 Harrison 1928 1930 '29cd
Stites T SFC 195-N 7 Pratt 1979.9 1980.4 mfh
Stocks C M MSG 130-S 22 Tidball 1956.4 1958.4 usacc
Stogsdill C E SSG 71-W 17 Harrison 1966.9 1967.3 mfh
Stogsdill C E SSG 115-E 20 Harrison 1967.3 1969.1 mfh
Stone G P SGM 113-E 28 Tidball 1917 1919 '18-19cds
Stone G P MGnr 113-W 26 Tidball 1916 1917 '17cd
Stone G P MGnr 113-W 26 Tidball 1912 1914 '13-14cds
Stone J B SP6 72-W 21 Harrison 1968.4 1968.7 usacc
Stonehill R W MSG 114-W 22 Harrison 1942 1943 '43PhBk
Storms K A SGM 192-S 6 Pratt 1961.4 1963.2 mfh
Storms K A MSG 150-S 13 Moat Walk 1961.1 1961.4 usacc
Stotler H E WOJG 152-E 14 Patch 1943.5 1946.11 '44-45PhBks
Stott P CWO 196-N 11 Pratt 1946.7 1947.10 usacc
Stott P A CWO 156-N 181 Bernard 1934 1944 '43PhBk
Stouffer H SFC 194-S 1 Pratt 1981.4 1982.4 mfh
Strake R A SFC 148-S 7 Moat Walk 1971.10 1972.8 mfh
Streagle M SGT 132-E 15 Tidball 1981.5 1981.12 mfh
Strickland J L E-7 148-S 7 Moat Walk 1969.9 1971.7 mfh
Strickland J L SFC 130-N 24 Tidball 1967.10 1968.6 mfh
Strickland L G E-6 132-E 15 Tidball 1969.5 1969.10 mfh

Strong R L MSG 193-N 12 Pratt 1962.10 1963.1 mfh
Strong R L E-8 140-N 19 Moat Walk 1962.2 1962.10 mfh
Stroup D F TSG 114-E 24 Harrison 1939 1940 '40PhBk
Strunk H C J MSG 187-N 23 Murray 1974.12 1978.6 mfh
Struth J F MSG 151-W 8 Patch 1946.9 1951.2 usacc
Stultz B R SFC 154-S 13 Murray 1952.3 1952.10 usacc
Sturdy K C SGM 186-S 17 Murray 1965.9 1966.4 mfh
Styers C MSG 113-E 28 Tidball 1947.7 1948.4 usacc
Suchecki A E SP5 115-W 18 Harrison 1964.4 1965.9 mfh
Sudduth R SGT 109-N 3 Frank Lane 1983.4 1985.3 mfh
Suggs W E SFC 110-E 40 Tidball 1968.11 1969.10 mfh
Sullivan G SP5 131-E 18 Tidball 1976.9 1978.4 mfh
Sullivan F J MSG 193-N 12 Pratt 1963.9 1964.8 mfh
Sullivan W J SGM 25-E 35 Tidball 1966.8 1969.11 mfh
Sullivan F J MSG 148-N 5 Moat Walk 1963.8 1963.9 mfh
Sulzberger R F TSG 193-S 10 Pratt 1940 1941 '40PhBk
Sumpter T SFC 25-W 33 Tidball 1977.8 1978.5 mfh
Sumrall J G MSG 115-E 20 Harrison 1962.6 1962.9 mfh
Sumrall J G MSG 192-N 8 Pratt 1962.9 1963.5 mfh
Sundberg W J MSG 113-E 28 Tidball 1943 1944 '43-44PhBks
Sundstrom G E SP5 153-N 13 Hatch 1974.9 1976.7 mfh
Suter J E MSG 113-W 26 Tidball 1955.1 1955.7 usacc
Sutton T K SP5 148-N 5 Moat Walk 1983.12 1986.2 mfh
Sutton C B SFC 110-W 38 Tidball 1962.12 1965.8 mfh
Swagger R L E-7 111-W 34 Tidball 1966.4 1967.6 mfh
Swanson R A E-6 154-S 13 Murray 1965.5 1966.1 mfh
Swanson E L SSG 115-W 18 Harrison 1965.9 1967.9 mfh
Sweeney J SFC 72-E 23 Harrison 1960.4 1962.6 mfh
Sweet R SSG 110-W 38 Tidball 1976.8 1977.1 mfh
Swift N T E-8 194-S 1 Pratt 1973.1 1975.6 mfh
Swinart R D SP5 130-S 22 Tidball 1972.9 1973.9 mfh
Szymczak J SSG 150-N 15 Moat Walk 1983.11 1986.6 mfh
Talley W CSM 60 67 Fenwick 1979.1 1980.10 mfh
Talovich M MSG 196-N 11 Pratt 1951.5 1952.9 usacc
Talovich M MSG 110-W 38 Tidball 1950.4 1951.5 usacc
Tarver A S SFC 187-S 21 Murray 1953.7 1953.11 usacc
Tate R R SFC 25-E 35 Tidball 1976.7 1980.2 mfh
Tate G D SGT 111-W 34 Tidball 1985.9 1986.7 mfh
Tatti J SGM 31-N 40 Hampton 1970.1 1970.9 mfh
Taylor D SGT 149-S 9 Moat Walk 1979.3 1980.3 mfh
Taylor R E E-5 71-E 19 Harrison 1966.12 1969.5 mfh
Taylor R MSG 25-W 33 Tidball 1978.5 1982.4 mfh
Taylor C R SFC 140-N 19 Moat Walk 1950.2 1950.10 usacc
Teffer J E MSG 188-S 25 Murray 1952.11 1955.4 usacc
Test C F SSG 111-E 36 Tidball 1937.6 1942.12 '37-41PhBks
Teubner C E SSG 113-W 26 Tidball 1939 1940 '40-41PhBks
Teubner C E SSG 71-E 19 Harrison 1939 1940 '40PhBk
Theis W F ? 72-E 23 Harrison 1972.6 1973.7 mfh
Thoburn J E SGM 31-N 40 Hampton 1966.8 1967.3 mfh
Thomas R A SGM 191-N 4 Pratt 1966.6 1967.12 mfh
Thomas D E SP4 150-S 13 Moat Walk 1982.9 1983.5 mfh
Thomas J I MSG 110-E 40 Tidball 1963.8 1963.11 mfh
Thomas J I MSG 151-E 10 Patch 1958.3 1959.2 usacc

Thomas E SP4 154-S 13 Murray 1979.8 1980.2 mfh
Thomas J I MSG 25-W 33 Tidball 1960.2 1960.6 usacc
Thomas L SSG 132-E 15 Tidball 1978.2 1978.11 mfh
Thomas J H H SSG 111-W 34 Tidball 1931 1932 Thomas Farley
Thomas J I SGM 194-S 1 Pratt 1963.11 1966.2 mfh
Thomas E SSG 132-W 13 Tidball 1981.11 1985.6 mfh
Thomas E ? 6 Big Bethel 1977.6 1980.1 mfh
Thomas T D SGT 110-W 38 Tidball 1985.10 1987.5 mfh
Thompson G SSG 115-E 20 Harrison 1936 1937 '37cd
Thompson C L SFC 109-N 3 Frank Lane 1958.8 1960.5 usacc
Thompson W W E-8 115-W 18 Harrison 1968.7 1968.12 mfh
Tiedemann F L SGM 30-S 34 Hampton 1970.3 1974.6 mfh
Tiedemann F L SGM 30-S 34 Hampton 1967.6 1968.11 mfh
Timmerman W F E-7 151-W 8 Patch 1962.5 1966.9 mfh
Timmons C S SGT 114-W 22 Harrison 1916 1917 '17cd
Tinder E P SFC 136-E 19 Hatch 1966.9 1967.3 usacc
Tinder E P E-7 61-N 45 Ingalls 1967.3 1968.7 mfh
Tippins SFC 192-S 6 Pratt 1976.9 1977.11 mfh
Tipton W P BMC 30-N 36 Hampton 1953.9 1955.5 USN usacc
Tobin E A SGT 136-E 19 Hatch 1951.10 1952.6 usacc
Todd J C MSG 186-S 17 Murray 1940 1943 '40-41PhBks
Todd J C MSG 131-E 18 Tidball 1937 1938 '37cd
Todd E A 1SG 110-W 38 Tidball 1939 1940 '40PhBk
Todd H P MSG 187-N 23 Murray 1950.3 1952.12 usacc
Todd H P MSG 72-W 21 Harrison 1948.10 1950.3 usacc
Todd W R MSG 156-N 181 Bernard 1954.6 1954.9 usacc
Tollison D J SFC 151-W 8 Patch 1958.2 1958.6 usacc
Tolppi C E MSG 109-S 1 Frank Lane 1952.12 1953.3 usacc
Toth W J SSG 130-N 24 Tidball 1944.10 1946.10 '44-45PhBks
Towers F W MSG 148-N 5 Moat Walk 1952.9 1952.9 usacc
Townsend W R SFC 112-W 30 Tidball 1951.10 1952.8 usacc
Trapp R W SFC 152-W 12 Patch 1969.2 1969.7 mfh
Tredway A L MSG 25-W 33 Tidball 1958.8 1960.1 usacc
Trigg R E CWO 26-E 31 Tidball 1948.11 1951.8 usacc
Troy W SGT 154-S 13 Murray 1979.4 1979.8 mfh
Trudo D R SP5 109-S 1 Frank Lane 1974.1 1976.6 mfh
Turner M L SSG 114-W 22 Harrison 1965.6 1965.12 mfh
Turner B J SP5 167-A 7 Patch 1973.3 1973.9 mfh
Turner J B SGT 71-E 19 Harrison 1915 1916 '16cd
Turner G MSG 192-S 6 Pratt 1971.10 1974.3 mfh
Turner E W MSG 193-S 10 Pratt 1956.1 1958.2 usacc
Turner E S TSG 195-S 5 Pratt 1934 1938 Hricinak
Tursini N J SFC 113-E 28 Tidball 1950.11 1952.4 usacc
Twyman J H 1SG 109-S 1 Frank Lane 1909 1910 Twyman
Tyler C R TSG 72-W 21 Harrison 1940 1941 '40-41PhBks
Tyler J B ? 154-N 15 Murray 1915 1916 '15cd
Tyrell W J 1SG 30-S 34 Hampton 1953.2 1962.5 mfh
Uebelhoer E F MSG 148-S 7 Moat Walk 1967.7 1968.5 mfh
Umana R MSG 192-N 8 Pratt 1956.1 1962.7 mfh
Valerlaus J H ? 71-E 19 Harrison 1912 1913 '13cd
Valles R MSG 149-S 9 Moat Walk 1958.8 1960.10 usacc
Valles J R SGM 194-N 3 Pratt 1965.3 1970.3 mfh
Van Arsdale R H ? 149-N 11 Moat Walk 1965.10 1965.12 mfh

Van Vranken J J SFC 192-N 8 Pratt 1981.12 1985.10 mfh
Van Winkle L W SSG 148-N 5 Moat Walk 1974.4 1977.5 mfh
Vandergriff R MSG 111-W 34 Tidball 1949.6 1949.8 usacc
Vanderkieft J L E-5 71-W 17 Harrison 1968.7 1969.6 mfh
Vannest D SGT 109-N 3 Frank Lane 1977.6 1979.7 mfh
Vanover J SSG 61-N 45 Ingalls 1971.9 1972.1 mfh
Vargo J SGT 149-N 11 Moat Walk 1952.12 1954.9 usacc
Vargo J SFC 71-W 17 Harrison 1952.11 1952.12 usacc
Varns E MSG 132-E 15 Tidball 1960.6 1961.7 usacc
Vasquez-Ortiz A M SP6 149-S 9 Moat Walk 1966.5 1967.6 mfh
Veatch W R SSG 115-W 18 Harrison 1937 1939 '37-39cds
Veld E D SSG 109-S 1 Frank Lane 1968.7 1969.1 mfh
Vellon W K MSG 193-S 10 Pratt 1964.1 1965.6 mfh
Vellon W K MSG 152-E 14 Patch 1962.3 1964.1 mfh
Venable J A SGM 26-W 29 Tidball 1964.10 1965.7 mfh
Veneri V F SP5 148-S 7 Moat Walk 1981.1 1982.9 mfh
Ventura C SGT 71-W 17 Harrison 1952.12 1953.12 usacc
VEQ 61-S 43 Ingalls 1974.12 ? Perry House VEQ
Vera F SFC 156-N 181 Bernard 1973.2 1976.11 mfh
Veraldo D J E-6 71-W 17 Harrison 1970.4 1972.8 mfh
Verdonck E P SFC 137-E 23 Hatch 1953.1 1954.10 usacc
Verniel J MSG 114-W 22 Harrison 1946.11 1949.7 usacc
Vernon J WO 186-S 17 Murray 1931 1935 '31-33cds
Versouza B R SP6 115-W 18 Harrison 1973.6 1974.2 mfh
Vest J E SGT 136-E 19 Hatch 1955.8 1957.9 usacc
Vincent O E SGT 109-N 3 Frank Lane 1953.3 1954.8 usacc
Vitrikas H CWO 31-S 38 Hampton 1949.2 1952.9 usacc
Vitt W Band 3-F Casemate 1918.4 ? AN306
Vivian H W MSG 151-E 10 Patch 1956.6 1957.9 usacc
Vogel C MSG 30-N 36 Hampton 1979.3 1984.6 mfh
VonBlumenthal A CWO 30-N 36 Hampton 1944.10 1946.10 44-45PhBk
    AN306
Vuckovich T SFC 192-S 6 Pratt 1977.12 1978.7 mfh
Waddell J C MSG 193-S 10 Pratt 1937 1939 '37-39cd Pugh
Waddell J C MSG 194-S 1 Pratt 1941.7 1947.9 usacc
Wagner MSG 35 W-2 2 Reeder Cir 1980.6 1981.6 mfh
Walden D L SFC 112-E 32 Tidball 1963.6 1964.7 mfh
Walker J R SGT 131-W 20 Tidball 1952.5 1952.12 usacc
Walker N R MSG 25-E 35 Tidball 1956.12 1957.9 usacc
Walker SP5 131-W 20 Tidball 1970.5 1973.7 mfh
Walker L P SP6 71-E 19 Harrison 1963.3 1964.5 mfh
Walker M SP5 136-E 19 Hatch 1974.5 1974.10 mfh
Walker D F CWO 25-W 33 Tidball 1947.7 1948.8 usacc
Walker W H MSG 31-N 40 Hampton 1970.10 1971.9 mfh
Walker M SGT 150-N 15 Moat Walk 1974.10 1975.12 mfh
Wall J A SSG 111-W 34 Tidball 1943 1945 '45PhBk
Wallace S SSG 131-W 20 Tidball 1975.1 1976.8 mfh
Wallace P R SFC 154-S 13 Murray 1966.3 1969.3 mfh
Walton W SFC 131-E 18 Tidball 1951.6 1954.12 usacc
Walton W T MSG 132-E 15 Tidball 1956.2 1958.5 usacc
Walton W SP1 140-N 19 Moat Walk 1956.4 1957.3 usacc
Walton M H SP5 140-S 17 Moat Walk 1974.10 1975.8 mfh
Walton J SGT 149-S 9 Moat Walk 1981.4 1983.3 mfh

Walton W SFC 156-N 181 Bernard 1959.5 1959.9 usacc
Walton R E-8 193-S 10 Pratt 1969.1 1969.5 mfh
Waltz C O MSG 109-N 3 Frank Lane 1965.10 1967.5 mfh
Wambold SP6 4 Big Bethel 1976.8 1977.6 mfh
Ward D SGT 130-N 24 Tidball 1978.3 1980.11 mfh
Ward B B Jr SFC 114-W 22 Harrison 1961.3 1961.8 usacc
Washburn C W SFC 113-E 28 Tidball 1954.2 1957.1 usacc
Washington P C MSG 72-E 23 Harrison 1955.9 1956.3 usacc
Wasilewski J J SFC 153-S 15 Hatch 1953.4 1955.10 usacc
Wasner H W MSG 191-N 4 Pratt 1939 1940 '40PhBk
Waters C T MSG 196-N 11 Pratt 1936 1937 '37cd
Waters K SSG 150-N 15 Moat Walk 1980.6 1983.11 mfh
Waters C T MSG 150-S 13 Moat Walk 1933 1934 Pugh
Waters D H Jr E-6 132-W 13 Tidball 1968.5 1968.12 mfh
Watkins M G SP3 136-E 19 Hatch 1958.7 1959.1 mfh
Watson W L SP5 130-S 22 Tidball 1974.1 1976.1 mfh
Watson P SFC 187-S 21 Murray 1980.8 1984.6 mfh
Watters D SFC 191-S 2 Pratt 1978.8 1979.8 mfh
Watts J F SFC 137-W 21 Hatch 1951.5 1951.12 usacc
Weatherford J H MSG 110-E 40 Tidball 1966.7 1966.9 mfh
Weaver J T E-7 113-E 28 Tidball 1970.5 1971.2 mfh
Webb A P SP4 109-N 3 Frank Lane 1985.12 1986.9 mfh
Webb N SP5 155-S 183 Bernard 1973.11 1973.12 usacc
Webber H J SGT 154-N 15 Murray 1914 1915 '14PhBk
Webber P CWO 30-N 36 Hampton 1948.8 1953.6 usacc
Wehlert W N MSG 136-N 17 Hatch 1942.8 1944.9 '43PhBk
Weiscops L MSG 130-S 22 Tidball 1949.3 1951.10 usacc
Welcome L C SP6 114-W 22 Harrison 1972.1 1973.10 mfh
Welker D M TSG 193-N 12 Pratt 1937 1939 '39PhBk
Welsh W R SP5 90 21 Moat Walk 1973.6 1973.7 mfh
Wencl J G SP4 152-E 14 Patch 1983.12 1984.10 mfh
Wertzberger J C MSG 153-N 13 Hatch 1961.2 1962.8 usacc
Wescoe W P MSG 136-E 19 Hatch 1945.10 1946.12 usacc
Wescott R L SSG 136-E 19 Hatch 1938.8 1942.6 '40-41PhBks
West I SSG 150-S 13 Moat Walk 1980.8 1982.1 mfh
West E G SGT 112-W 30 Tidball 1912 1914 '13-14cds
West H A E-5 71-E 19 Harrison 1966.1 1966.6 mfh
Westfall F S SGM 186-N 19 Murray 1967.6 1968.9 mfh
Weston J W Jr SGM 31-S 38 Hampton 1966.3 1967.6 mfh
Weston J W Jr SGM 154-S 13 Murray 1966.1 1966.3 mfh
Whaley R SP5 113-W 26 Tidball 1977.9 1978.3 mfh
Wharton E B SGM 110-E 40 Tidball 1914 1915 '14cd
Wheeler R H MSG 156-N 181 Bernard 1947.1 1948.4 usacc
Wheeler T MSG 196-N 11 Pratt 1975.8 1978.5 mfh
Wheeler T W MSG 196-N 11 Pratt 1975.8 ? mfh
Whelan J P MSG 110-W 38 Tidball 1953.8 1955.10 usacc
Wherrett W Z MSG 90 21 Moat Walk 1931.2 1937.9 '31-37cds
Whichard W K SSG 71-W 17 Harrison 1938 1941 '38-41PhBks
Whitaker J D SGT 137-E 23 Hatch 1961.7 1964.6 usacc
White M SSG 152-E 14 Patch 1979.7 1983.11 mfh
White E L E-8 111-W 34 Tidball 1970.9 1972.1 mfh
White L SP5 7 Big Bethel 1982.8 1984.4 mfh
White A J SP7 151-W 8 Patch 1960.1 1962.5 mfh

White J P SSG 156-N 181 Bernard 1967.3 1968.10 mfh
Whitehead J E SSG 136-E 19 Hatch 1926 1929 '27-29cds
Whitehead W S MSG 131-W 20 Tidball 1965.7 1965.9 mfh
Whitman G S SGM 110-E 40 Tidball 1915 1917 '16-17cds
Whitney O SGT 110-E 40 Tidball 1977.7 1981.1 mfh
Whittleman R J MSG 136-E 19 Hatch 1952.8 1952.10 usacc
Whittleman R J MSG 152-E 14 Patch 1952.10 1953.12 usacc
Whybark G W MGnr 136-N 17 Hatch 1916 1917 '17cd
Whybark G W MGnr 72-W 21 Harrison 1914 1916 '14-16cds
Wickham F M SGM 151-E 10 Patch 1964.12 1965.3 mfh
Widincamp J S CWO 30-S 34 Hampton 1947.5 1947.10 usacc
Wiencek V MSG 192-S 6 Pratt 1950.2 1952.7 usacc
Wiggins E J SGT 137-E 23 Hatch 1951.5 1951.8 usacc
Wightman B C SGT 167-B 9 Patch 1986.3 1988.3 mfh
Wilbur R E MSG 187-S 21 Murray 1966.5 1967.12 mfh
Wilder J B MSG 110-W 38 Tidball 1965.8 1967.3 mfh
Wilder J B SGM 191-S 2 Pratt 1967.3 1968.8 mfh
Wiley T R 1SG 155-N 185 Bernard 1936 1939 '37cd
Wiley T R 1SG 25-W 33 Tidball 1939 1940 '39PhBk
Wilkerson T B MSG 149-S 9 Moat Walk 1953.4 1955.2 usacc
Wilkes A A SP5 167-B 9 Patch 1973.3 1977.1 mfh
Willette F L SGM 195-N 7 Pratt 1968.7 1969.8 mfh
Williams C H MSG 155-N 185 Bernard 1958.11 1959.8 usacc
Williams S F 1LT 149-S 9 Moat Walk 1916 1919 '16-19cds
Williams R E E-6 114-W 22 Harrison 1970.8 1971.12 mfh
Williams C SP4 130-S 22 Tidball 1980.12 1982.9 mfh
Williams B H MSG 72-E 23 Harrison 1954.12 1955.3 usacc
Williams R R SSG 71-E 19 Harrison 1940 1941 '40-41PhBks
Williams W E-7 90 21 Moat Walk 1971.6 1972.10 mfh
Williams G R MSG 109-S 1 Frank Lane 1950.12 1952.6 usacc
Williams T L SFC 110-E 40 Tidball 1969.10 1973.12 mfh
Williams E D SFC 156-S 179 Bernard 1950.10 1951.8 usacc
Williams C H MSG 191-S 2 Pratt 1959.8 1960.11 usacc
Williams T Jr SP5 137-W 21 Hatch 1971.11 1972.2 mfh
Williams T Jr SP5 111-E 36 Tidball 1972.2 1973.10 mfh
Williams H T Jr SSG 148-N 5 Moat Walk 1967.12 1969.12 mfh
Willians M E MSG 155-N 185 Bernard 1947.10 1949.6 usacc
Willis J K MSG 191-S 2 Pratt 1951.4 1956.11 usacc
Willis J K MSG 195-N 7 Pratt 1958.4 1961.3 usacc
Willis J K MSG 110-W 38 Tidball 1956.2 1958.4 usacc
Willis J K MSG 155-S 183 Bernard 1950.5 1951.4 usacc
Willoughby B SP5 156-S 179 Bernard 1978.7 1980.5 mfh
Wilson J L MSG 132-E 15 Tidball 1962.8 1964.5 mfh
Wilson SGT 148-S 7 Moat Walk 1973.6 1973.10 mfh
Wilson S SGT 150-N 15 Moat Walk 1978.5 1979.19 mfh
Wilson C G SGT 112-W 30 Tidball 1907 ? '08cd
Wilson R SGM 195-N 7 Pratt 1972.7 1973.6 mfh
Wilson J A ? 151-W 8 Patch 1912 1914 '13-14cds
Wilson S 1SG 149-N 11 Moat Walk 1940 1942.6 '40-41PhBks
Wilson J L MSG 187-N 23 Murray 1964.5 1966.4 mfh
Wilson C L 1SG 109-S 1 Frank Lane 1946.12 1950.8 usacc
Wilson J P MSG 194-N 3 Pratt 1949.11 1952.6 usacc
Wilson C L 1SG 156-N 181 Bernard 1946.9 1946.12 usacc

Wilson G E-5 72-W 21 Harrison 1971.10 1972.7 mfh
Wilson K G SP6 130-N 24 Tidball 1974.12 1975.5 mfh
Wilson R B SFC 148-N 5 Moat Walk 1949.2 1950.10 usacc
Wilson J P MSG 132-E 15 Tidball 1949.8 1949.11 usacc
Wilson R E MGnr 150-S 13 Moat Walk 1912 1914 '13-14cds
Wilson D R E-5 153-S 15 Hatch 1964.3 1964.3 mfh
Wilsson T SP5 167-B 9 Patch 1977.1 1980.3 mfh
Wilt R Mr 151-E 10 Patch 1960.4 1963.5 mfh
Wimberley J G MSG 155-N 185 Bernard 1964.12 1965.8 mfh
Winfield W MSG 152-E 14 Patch 1953.12 1958.1 usacc
Winfield W MSG 151-W 8 Patch 1958.6 1959.12 usacc
Wingo C SSG 111-W 34 Tidball 1980.3 1982.9 mfh
Wintermute H C TSG 140-N 19 Moat Walk 1940 1941 '40-41PhBks
Wintermute H C SSG 130-S 22 Tidball 1938 1939 '39PhBk
Winters L M CWO 25-E 35 Tidball 1946.9 1949.8 usacc
Wirt H G BM2 33 67 Fenwick 1964.6 1967.7 usacc
Wise R G WO1 31-N 40 Hampton 1982.6 1982.8 mfh
Wise I Clerk 49 49 Bernard 1903.9 1912 d-616
Wojoik J D SP5 167-A 7 Patch 1973.10 1976.4 mfh
Wolfangle H H Mr 130-S 22 Tidball 1918.4 1919.? '19cd
Wolfe O K CWO 193-N 12 Pratt 1946.9 1947.11 usacc
Wolford F E SP4 137-W 21 Hatch 1958.8 1959.7 usacc
Wood J W SP4 137-W 21 Hatch 1959.10 1960.3 usacc
Wood R H CWO 30-S 34 Hampton 1947.10 1950.2 usacc
Wood J SGT 130-S 22 Tidball 1980.1 1980.12 mfh
Wood W H WOJG 192-N 8 Pratt 1943.11 1945.6 '43-45PhBks
Woodbury M W SGT 137-E 23 Hatch 1965.6 1966.4 usacc
Woodbury M W SSG 90 21 Moat Walk 1966.4 1966.9 mfh
Woodland P S CWO 193-S 10 Pratt 1943.11 1946.9 '43-45PhBks
Woods G W SSG 149-N 11 Moat Walk 1982.8 1986.6 mfh
Woods T H SFC 154-S 13 Murray 1952.10 1953.1 usacc
Woofter J R SFC 131-E 18 Tidball 1962.10 1966.6 mfh
Woolard J H SFC 152-W 12 Patch 1969.7 1970.2 mfh
Wooldridge W F TSG 113-E 28 Tidball 1932 1935 Wooldridge
Wooldridge W F MSG 186-N 19 Murray 1935 1941 '37cd '40PhBk
Wooldridge W F SGT 137-E 23 Hatch 1925 1930 Wooldridge
Worfred J H CPT 154-S 13 Murray 1912.6 1920.9 '13-20cd S&F
ENGR
Workman D SFC 30-S 34 Hampton 1977.8 1978.4 mfh
Worley J MSG 186-S 17 Murray 1977.7 1979.2 mfh
Worrell E P 1LT 152-W 12 Patch 1918 1919 '19cd
Wratchford C E SGT 154-N 15 Murray 1953.4 1954.8 usacc
Wren H CSM 64 71 Fenwick 1978.3 1980.8 mfh
Wren T CSM 30-N 36 Hampton 1977.6 1978.3 mfh
Wright R S MSG 113-E 28 Tidball 1948.10 1949.7 usacc
Wright E P 2LT 112-W 30 Tidball 1918.4 1919.1 '19cd rms?
Wright D E MSG 90 21 Moat Walk 1957.9 1958.7 usacc
Wright J E MSG 193-N 12 Pratt 1982.9 1983.9 mfh
Wunder A MSG 149-N 11 Moat Walk 1949.1 1950.1 usacc
Wunder J H III MSG 187-N 23 Murray 1966.4 1967.2 mfh
Wunder J H III MSG 152-E 14 Patch 1965.6 1966.4 mfh
Yanez E E E-8 186-N 19 Murray 1969.6 1971.7 mfh
Yankwitt R E-8 156-S 179 Bernard 1971.11 1972.10 mfh

Yassel L S ? 112-E 32 Tidball 1912 1917 '12-17cds
Yeatman A A Clerk 71-E 19 Harrison 1900 1906 '00-06cds
York V D Sr E-7 150-N 15 Moat Walk 1969.11 1970.11 mfh
Young R A MSG 187-S 21 Murray 1955.8 1962.3 mfh
Young D A SP5 132-E 15 Tidball 1973.6 1976.3 mfh
Young R A MSG 110-E 40 Tidball 1954.1 1955.8 usacc
Zabel E ? 136-E 19 Hatch 1916 1917 '17cd
Zedicher P G SP5 113-E 28 Tidball 1975.3 1976.9 mfh
Zeiders CWO 196-N 11 Pratt 1949.4 1951.5 usacc
Zephir W SGM 110-E 40 Tidball 1907 1914 '07-13cds
Zerlett A 1LT 132-E 15 Tidball 1918 1919 '19cd
Ziegenhagen H SGM 31-S 38 Hampton 1970.7 1973.3 mfh
Ziegler F D SSG 156-S 179 Bernard 1967.3 1968.4 mfh
Zimmerman E A CSM 25-W 33 Tidball 1961.10 1964.8 mfh
Zimmerman E A CMSGT 109-S 1 Frank Lane 1961.8 1961.10 usacc
Zindel L C SSG 137-W 21 Hatch 1940 1941 '40-41PhBks
Zindel L C CWO 31-N 40 Hampton 1945.1 1946.9 '45PhBk
Zindel L C CWO 155-N 185 Bernard 1942.6 1945.1 '43-44PhBks

Abbott E G CPT 127-E 147 Bernard 1909.7 1912.12 cds Arthur +
Abernethy R S CPT 121-W 41 Fenwick 1907.6 1909.9 Ret BG '08-09cd
Abernethy R S COL 118 29 Fenwick 1925.5 1928.8 Ret BG Hartel
Abrams W L LTC 34-S-1 96 Ingalls 1948.2 1950.4 usacc
Abrams W L LTC 17-E-2 47-B Bernard 1947.9 1948.2 usacc
Acheson H H? MAJ 143-N-2 35-D Ingalls 1931.6 1932.6 Phillips '31cd
Acheson H M? LTC 54-S-2 134 Ingalls 1932.6 1936.6 Devens Hopkin
Adams A J MG 101-N 57 Ingalls 1966.6 1966.7 mfh
Adams W G MAJ 54-S-1 136 Ingalls 1982.7 1984.6 mfh
Adams W CPT 50-E 129 Bernard 1879.7 1879.9 ORD
Adams N L CPT 45-E-1 114 Ingalls 1932.8 1933.7 '33cd
Adams S J COL 144-N-2 41-D Ingalls 1947.6 1949.5 '47PhBk usacc
Adams W CPT 50-E 129 Bernard 1882.6 1883.1 ORD
Adams G N 1LT 79-N 95 Ingalls 1937.8 1938.6 Descheneaux
Adams A W MAJ 126-N 165 Bernard 1944.6 1946.1 Ret BG PhBk
Adams J W COL 19 18 Bernard 1981.6 1984.6 mfh
Adams R H COL 51-N-2 124 Ingalls 1958.7 1958.9 Ret MG usacc
Adams G N 1LT 52-E-2 126 Ingalls 1938.6 1939.7 Descheneaux
Adams R E COL 143-N-2 35-D Ingalls 1964.10 1965.10 Ret MG mfh
Adams A J MG 93 75 Ingalls 1966.7 1967.3 mfh
Adams R H COL 62-S 30 Ruckman 1958.9 1959.8 Ret MG usacc
Adams H L Jr LTC 51-N-2 124 Ingalls 1970.11 1972.5 mfh
Addison T MAJ 52-W-1 130 Ingalls 1977.6 1979.11 mfh
Adkins A E COL 146 146 Engr Ln 1974.9 1976.4 mfh
Adlington W S COL 3-S 167 Bernard 1950.3 1953.8 usacc
Adsit J M COL 19 18 Bernard 1980.7 1981.6 mfh
Aerni F J COL 45-W-2 110 Ingalls 1966.8 1966.8 mfh
Ahern M LTC 18-E-1 37-A Bernard 1980.6 19826 mfh
Ahnfeldt A L COL 51-S-2 118 Ingalls 1953.9 1953.9 usacc
Aigeltinger G B 1LT 67-S 34 Ingalls 1918 1919 BOQ WWI '19cd
Ainsworth C H CPT 143-N-2 35-D Ingalls 1925.7 1929.7 Hartel Winton
Akam G R MAJ 144-S-1 41-A Ingalls 1972.7 1974.12 mfh
Akerman W S CPT 45-W-2 110 Ingalls 1943.2 1946.9 '43-45PhBks
Akers F MAJ 16-E 53 Bernard 1976.7 1977.7 mfh
Albritton J D LTC 54-N-2 140 Ingalls 1972.8 1974.4 mfh
Alcala R H COL 128-W 107 Bernard 1985.7 1987.6 mfh
Alden J LTC 54-S-1 136 Ingalls 1980.6 1982.7 mfh
Alderdyce J C LTC 102-S 59 Ingalls 1943.1 1944.10 PhBk
Alexander M S COL 51-N-1 122 Ingalls 1964.7 1967.6 mfh
Alexander D S 1LT 34-N-1 98 Ingalls 1937.7 1938.8 Steele '37PhDk
Alexander W S CPT 66-N 40 Ingalls 1891.6 1901.8 Librarian
Alexander W COL 54-S-1 136 Ingalls 1946.5 1948.10 usacc

Alfrey J 1LT 44-N-2 108 Ingalls 1940.6 1941.6 Walter PhBk
Alfrey J 1LT 17-W-1 41-A Bernard 1939.7 1940.6 PhBk rms
Alger J D LTC 3-S 167 Bernard 1948.7 1949.9 Ret LTG usacc
Aliotta M F LTC 43-W-2 1 Reeder 1963.7 1965.4 mfh
Allen T H COL 43-W-1 3 Reeder 1949.8 1950.9 usacc
Allen C C W COL 143-S-1 35-A Ingalls 1946.9 1949.4 usacc
Allen R R BG 120 37 Fenwick 1947.10 1948.4 Ret MG usacc
Allen R R BG 121-W 41 Fenwick 1947.10 1947.10 Ret MG usacc
Alley C R CPT 143-S-2 35-C Ingalls 1914.6 1915.12 '16cd
Allison R E CPT 31-N 40 Hampton 1986.6 1986.12 mfh
Alloway C H LTC 17-E-2 47-B Bernard 1966.11 1968.11 mfh
Allport G H LTC 143-N-2 35-D Ingalls 1986.6 1987.6 mfh
Almes E LTC 51-N-2 124 Ingalls 1981.7 1983.8 mfh
Aloe R C COL 50-E 129 Bernard 1951.8 1954.6 Ret BG usacc
Alsheimer R H COL 126-S 165 Bernard 1984.8 1985.6 mfh
Ammons B T COL 3-N 169 Bernard 1952.9 1955.5 usacc
Anderson K S 1LT 18-E-2 37-B Bernard 1944.10 1946.10 PhBks
Anderson J B COL 125 73 Ingalls 1940.11 1943.12 PhBk
Anderson G LTC 61-S 43 Ingalls 1940.9 1943.11 Anderson S&F
Anderson S W MAJ 68-S 81 Ingalls 1939.6 1943.9 Anderson
Anderson P E MAJ 44-S-2 102 Ingalls 1970.8 1973.1 mfh
Anderson J M MAJ 17-W-1 41-A Bernard 1974.9 1976.1 mfh
Anderson T E COL 67-N 36 Ingalls 1973.9 1975.11 mfh
Anderson R F 1LT 69-N 87 Ingalls 1910.9 1911.9 '11cd
Anderson S MAJ 17-E-1 47-A Bernard 1976.8 1977.8 mfh
Anderson G P MAJ 63-N 24 Ruckman 1929.8 1930.7 Bennett
Anderson S W CPT 52-W-2 132 Ingalls 1931.9 1932.6 Anderson
Anderson G L 1LT 63-N 24 Ruckman 1890.11 1891.1 c-27
Anderson G A M COL 70-N 91 Ingalls 1947.8 1948.6 usacc
Anderson P LTC 43-W-1 3 Reeder 1977.7 1978.9 mfh
Anderson R L 1LT 18-W-1 29-A Bernard 1935.7 1936.6 Anderson
Anderson J B LTC 102-N 61 Ingalls 1938.7 1940.11 PhBk Anderson
Anderson J B LTC 50-E 129 Bernard 1937.6 1938.7 '37cd
Anderson G 1LT 51-N-2 124 Ingalls 1934.9 1935.6 Anderson
Anderson E G COL 102-S 59 Ingalls 1985.12 1987.12 mfh
Anderson P LTC 79-N 95 Ingalls 1978.9 1979.8 mfh
Andrae H H COL 123-W 2 Ruckman 1957.2 1960.9 usacc
Andrew J D CPT 67-S 34 Ingalls 1958.7 1958.7 USN usacc
Andrew J D CPT 144-S-1 41-A Ingalls 1958.7 1958.9 usacc
Andrews A A CPT 45-E-1 114 Ingalls 1941.2 1943.12 Splain '43PhBk
Andrews D A LTC 54-N-1 138 Ingalls 1968.7 1969.8 mfh
Andrews T H BG 121-E 43 Fenwick 1968.9 1971.10 mfh
Andrews Z LTC 17-E-1 47-A Bernard 1980.7 1987.7 mfh
Andrews T H BG 146 146 Engr Ln 1968.7 1968.9 mfh
Andrews A C MAJ 43-W-1 3 Reeder 1943.6 1944.6 PhBk
Andrick E L COL 34-S-2 94 Ingalls 1956.10 1958.9 usacc
Andruss M P 1LT 18-E-2 37-B Bernard 1908.9 1909.9 '09cd
Andry G R 2LT 17-W-1 41-A Bernard 1943.6 1943.12 Splain '43PhBk
Andry G R 1LT 54-S-2 134 Ingalls 1944 1945 44-45PhBk Toley
Ansart F CPT 18-E-2 37-B Bernard 1824.4 1826.3 '25rq rms?
Apple G M 1LT 68-S 81 Ingalls 1905.9 1906.9 '06cd b-26
Applehans R B LTC 45-W-1 112 Ingalls 1984.7 1986.10 mfh
Applewhite P P 1LT 16-E 53 Bernard 1920 1921 CAS'21

Applin F D MAJ 102-N 61 Ingalls 1918 1919 BOQ WWI '19cd
Argo R W CPT 45-E-2 116 Ingalls 1931.8 1932.7 RetMG deCamp32
Argo R W CPT 66-N 40 Ingalls 1925.6 1926.6 Ret MG '25cd
Argo R W MAJ 79-S 93 Ingalls 1935.6 1936.6 Ret MG JHC +
Armistead C 1LT 66-N 40 Ingalls 1901.9 1902.9 BOQ? '02cd
Armistead W K BG 1 151 Bernard 1834.8 1836.11 CG NA w Arthur
Armstrong D CPT 55 42 Ingalls 1917.1 1917.5 Ret BG Armstrong
Armstrong M G CPT 158 32 Ingalls 1930.9 1931.6 Armstrong
Armstrong D MAJ 121-E 43 Fenwick 1917.6 1918.5 Ret BG Armstrong
Armstrong J R CPT 3-S 167 Bernard 1944.11 1946.6 PhBk
Armstrong M G CPT 16-W 51 Bernard 1921 1923 Armstrong
Armstrong D P COL 128-E 109 Bernard 1946.8 1946.12 usacc
Armstrong C H Jr LTC 43-W-2 1 Reeder 1967.5 1968.1 mfh
Arnold A V MG 141 53 Fenwick 1946.11 1948.5 usacc
Arnold A C 1LT 15-S 36 Ruckman 1919.12 1920.6 '20cd
Arthur R 1LT 144-N-2 41-D Ingalls 1911.9 1913.12 '12-14cds
Arthur R MAJ 93 75 Ingalls 1925.6 1928.8 Arthur PhBk
Arthur R 1LT 129-S 101 Ingalls 1913.12 1915.4 PhBk
Ash W M CPT 50-W 121 Bernard 1941 1942 Haldeman
Ash H L BG 128-W 107 Bernard 1966.4 1967.12 mfh
Ashbridge D M 1LT 67-S 34 Ingalls 1913.12 1914.12 CAS'14 PhBk
Ashbridge D M MAJ 124-S 67 Ingalls 1921.9 1922.6 '22FOcs
Ashworth T D COL 69-N 87 Ingalls 1961.7 1964.6 mfh
Atanasoff O V DR 126-S 163 Bernard 1948.11 1950.8 MedC usacc
Atkinson C E MAJ 67-N 36 Ingalls 1938.6 1940.8 PhBk
Atkinson C E LTC 102-S 59 Ingalls 1940.8 1941.9 Dennen
Atwood F J 1LT 17-W-1 41-A Bernard 1920.9 1921.7 '21BtryOCs
Aurand H S CPT 67-N 36 Ingalls 1919.4 1920.1 Ret LTG Aurand
Aurand H S 1LT 17-E-2 47-B Bernard 1916.8 1916.10 Ret LTG Aurand
Aurentz F W MAJ 17-W-2 41-B Bernard 1984.1 1986.7 mfh
Ausmus D CPT 15-S 36 Ruckman 1926.8 1927.8 '27BtryOCs
Austin F L LTC 35-W-1 4 Reeder 1947.10 1948.8 usacc
Austin T C CPT 102-N 61 Ingalls 1915.8 1916.8 JHC
Austin T C CPT 124-N 69 Ingalls 1916.8 1917.6 '17cd
Austin O W BM1 33 CGH 67 Fenwick 1961.7 1964.6 usacc
Avery H G 1LT 18-W-2 29-B Bernard 1944 1945 '44 PhBk
Avery R L 1LT 18-E-1 37-A Bernard 1911.9 1912.12 CAS'12 '13-14cd
Awtrey J G MAJ 143-S-1 35-A Ingalls 1981.12 1984.4 mfh
Axelrod P J 1LT 167 A 7 Patch Road 1966.2 1966.8 mfh
Axelson O A 1LT 67-S 34 Ingalls 1918 1919 BOQ WWI '19cd
Axelson O A COL 33-E-1 61 Fenwick 1950.7 1951.11 usacc
Axtater K S LTC 102-N 61 Ingalls 1941 1942 InstrCAS
Axtell E N LTC 33-E-2 63 Fenwick 1961.3 1962.8 mfh
Ayers L G 1LT 71-E 19 Harrison 1918.12 1919.12 '19cd rms?
Ayres T D BG 121-E 43 Fenwick 1974.7 1975.7 Ret LTG mfh
Babbit L MAJ 93 75 Ingalls 1882.6 1887.11 Arthur
Babbitt L MAJ 50-E 129 Bernard 1879.9 1882.6 Ord Arsenal
Babcock F MAJ 101-N 57 Ingalls 1926.8 1927.8 '17AdvCs
Bacci J J COL 66-S 38 Ingalls 1973.8 1976.6 mfh
Badens CPT 18-W-1 29A Bernard 1826.9 1828.3 d-684
Baege L Clerk 61-N 45 Ingalls 1900 1912 QMC
Baetcke B G COL 45-E-1 114 Ingalls 1951.8 1952.1 Ret GEN usacc
Baetcke B G COL 62-N 28 Ruckman 1952.1 1954.6 Ret GEN usacc

Baetcke B G COL 128-E 109 Bernard 1957.7 1961.1 usacc
Bagby R G CPT 146 146 Engr Ln 1971.7 1973.6 USN mfh
Bagg H A LTC 124-S 67 Ingalls 1918.9 1919.6 Arthur
Bagley LT 35-E-1 6 Reeder 1942 1943 Chaplain Ellis
Bagnal C W LTG 120 37 Fenwick 1983.9 1985.6 mfh
Bahnsen J C Jr COL 126-S 165 Bernard 1976.8 1977.7 mfh
Bahnsen J C Jr LTC 43-E-2 7 Reeder 1975.8 1976.8 mfh
Bailey D J CPT 35-E-2 8 Reeder 1934.7 1935.8 Ward deCamp
Bailey D W COL 128-W 107 Bernard 1948.9 1950.9 usacc
Bailey C J MAJ 14 32 Ruckman 1906.5 1907.9 Ret MG Shull
Bailey H L LTC 158 32 Ingalls 1933.6 1934.6 '33cd
Bailey G G MAJ 34-N-1 98 Ingalls 1973.9 1975.7 mfh
Bainbridge C A COL 66-N 40 Ingalls 1974.3 1974.8 Chaplain mfh
Bainbridge CPT 18-W-1 29-A Bernard 1842.7 1846.6 '44-46rq d-686
Baird R MAJ 51-S-1 120 Ingalls 1981.4 1984.5 mfh
Baird C W LTC 101-S 55 Ingalls 1929.8 1931.9 Kean Warren
Baird L C CPT 55 42 Ingalls 1931.6 1934.10 deCamp '33cd
Baker W C 1LT 63-S 26 Ruckman 1909.9 1911.9 Ret MG '11cd
Baker R K LTC 54-S-1 136 Ingalls 1986.8 1987.6 mfh
Baker R C COL 69-S 85 Ingalls 1960.8 1963.7 Ret MG QMC mfh
Baker R C COL 33-E-2 63 Fenwick 1959.2 1960.8 Ret MG usacc
Baker E E COL 54-N-2 140 Ingalls 1959.6 1962.2 usacc
Baker D COL 50-E 129 Bernard 1980.7 1982.2 mfh
Baker J COL 18-E-2 37-B Bernard 1969.10 1970.5 mfh
Baker W C CPT 101-S 55 Ingalls 1912.12 1916.12 Ret MG PhBk
Baker R L CPT 17-W-1 41-A Bernard 1824.6 1828.4 '26rq ORD
Baker J MAJ 17-W-1 41-A Bernard 1978.8 1981.2 mfh
Ball H P COL 126-S 163 Bernard 1973.7 1974.6 mfh
Balogh Z MAJ 143-S-1 35-A Ingalls 1977.1 1978.6 mfh
Baltzer N W COL 70-S 89 Ingalls 1954.10 1957.6 usacc
Baltzer N W COL 143-S-1 35-A Ingalls 1952.2 1954.10 usacc
Baltzer N W COL 44-N-2 108 Ingalls 1959.10 1959.12 usacc
Baltzer N W COL 101-S 55 Ingalls 1959.12 1964.12 mfh
Bambace F S COL 52-E-1 128 Ingalls 1952.8 1952.12 usacc
Bambace F S COL 16-W 51 Bernard 1952.12 1953.3 usacc
Bane J C COL 44-N-2 108 Ingalls 1954.8 1957.8 usacc
Bankhead J BG 1 151 Bernard 1848.10 1853.11 CG w
Bankhead M J MAJ 55 42 Ingalls 1942.31 1944.12 PhBk
Banks J M 2LT 18-W-2 29-B Bernard 1940.5 1940.9 '40PhBk
Barber E 1LT 51-N-2 124 Ingalls 1936.6 1937.6 '37cd
Barber E CPT 15-N 34 Ruckman 1936.7 1937.8 Ret BG Barber
Barber E 1LT 51-N-2 124 Ingalls 1933.8 1934.8 Ret BG Son
Barber J T LTC 50 A 125 Bernard 1945 1946 Moorman
Barber J T 1LT 51-N-1 122 Ingalls 1935.9 1938.8 Starr Pohl
Barberis C V COL 144-N-1 41-B Ingalls 1958.7 1962.7 mfh
Barber H A Jr COL 102-N 61 Ingalls 1948.1 1950.1 Ret BG usacc
Barbour T E P LTC 17-W-2 41-B Bernard 1953.11 1954.3 usacc
Barco E T LTC 18-E-1 37-A Bernard 1948.9 1948.10 usacc
Bardsley G H 1LT 66-N 40 Ingalls 1926.6 1927.8 '27cd
Baresel K G CPT 34-S-2 94 Ingalls 1943.9 1946.6 43-45 PhBks
Bare W E Jr COL 63-S 26 Ruckman 1953.11 1956.8 usacc
Barickman R J LTC 44-S-1 104 Ingalls 1964.7 1965.8 mfh
Barkalow R G COL 50-E 129 Bernard 1948.7 1951.8 Ret BG usacc

Barker W L 1LT 34-S-2 94 Ingalls 1931.8 1932.8 Lewis J T
Barker W L CPT 66-S 38 Ingalls 1937.7 1937.8 '37cd
Barker W L CPT 63-N 24 Ruckman 1937.9 1938.6 Lewis J T
Barker B Jr CPT 35-W-2 2 Reeder 1978.6 1980.5 mfh
Barkley A W 1LT 18-W-1 29-A Bernard 1911.9 1912.9 NAdoc 334447
Barksdale G E CPT 15-S 36 Ruckman 1919 '19cd
Barksdale B M LTC 18-W-1 29-A Bernard 1953.11 1956.10 usacc
Barlow D COL 79-S 93 Ingalls 1979.7 1983.6 mfh
Barlow E F 1LT 79-S 93 Ingalls 1914.12 1915.12 '15cd
Barlow K COL 123-E 4 Ruckman 1979.7 1981.7 mfh
Barnes H C CPT 68-S 81 Ingalls 1911.9 1912.12 Ret BG '12cd
Barnes H C 1LT 63-N 24 Ruckman 1905.9 1906.9 Ret BG BOQ '06cd
Barnes M A LTC 17-E-1 47-A Bernard 1969.8 1970.6 mfh
Barnes H C CPT 128-W 107 Bernard 1912.12 1913.12 Ret BG '13cd
Barnes J P COL 18-E-1 37-A Bernard 1967.6 1969.7 mfh
Barnes H C COL 120 37 Fenwick 1918.12 1919.10 Ret BG '18cd
Barnes J E MAJ 44-N-1 106 Ingalls 1968.2 1969.7 mfh
Barnes V B COL 143-N-1 35-B Ingalls 1946.1 1947.8 usacc
Barnes J P COL 102-N 61 Ingalls 1969.7 1970.4 mfh
Barnes H C 1LT 17-E-1 47-A Bernard 1904.9 1905.9 Ret BG CAS'05
Baron A S 1LT 33-W-1 59 Fenwick 1935.7 1936.8 Shepherd
Barr R S CPT 143-S-1 35-A Ingalls 1919 '19cd rms?
Barr D B MG 142 51 Fenwick 1945.9 1946.9 Hyssong
Barragan M B 1LT 67-S 34 Ingalls 1918 1919 BOQ WWI '19cd
Barrand K W LTC 33-E-1 61 Fenwick 1973.2 1974.1 mfh
Barratt T H COL 52-E-1 128 Ingalls 1961.3 1961.10 usacc
Barratt T H COL 64 71 Fenwick 1961.10 1964.1 mfh
Barrett R E CPT 51-S-2 118 Ingalls 1942 1943 '43PhBk
Barrett LT 17-E-2 47-B Bernard 1890 1892 c-25
Barrett R T CPT 63-S 26 Ruckman 1932.8 1933.7 '33cd
Barrette J D MAJ 93 75 Ingalls 1905 1906 Ret BG '06cd
Barrette J D CPT 65-S 46 Ingalls 1902 Ret BG S&F c-46
Barrows E R CPT 35-W-1 4 Reeder 1930.12 1931.7 '31cd
Barry W F MG 1 151 Bernard 1867.11 1877.3 CG w
Barry T W Rev 15-S 36 Ruckman 1901.6 1905.9 Chaplain '02cd
Bartholet J C COL 44-N-1 106 Ingalls 1961.1 1963.12 mfh
Bartlett L W CPT 69-N 87 Ingalls 1933.9 1938.8 Bartlett
Bartlett L W 1LT 35-E-1 6 Reeder 1932.8 1933.9 Bartlett
Bartlett L 1LT 79-N 95 Ingalls 1907.9 1908.9 '09cd
Bartlett J R CPT 15-N 34 Ruckman 1929.11 1930.6 Bartlett
Bartlett G T CPT 3-S 167 Bernard 1902.7 1906.5 S&F c-46 b-21
Bartok L J MAJ 31-S 38 Hampton 1983.7 1985.6 mfh
Barton J E COL 66-S 38 Ingalls 1967.1 1970.8 mfh
Barton R CPT 143-N-2 35-D Ingalls 1941.8 1941.8 Tolley
Barton R L CPT 143-N-2 35-D Ingalls 1945.1 1946.9 '45PhBk
Bass R L LTC 35-E-1 6 Reeder 1974.8 1976.12 mfh
Bass R L COL 124-S 67 Ingalls 1976.11 1978.8 mfh
Batchelor V W COL 126-S 163 Bernard 1947.11 1948.10 usacc
Bates J C CPT 45-E-2 116 Ingalls 1932.8 1933.6 Gower
Bates R H LTC 34-N-2 100 Ingalls 1949.2 1949.4 usacc
Bates R E COL 63-N 24 Ruckman 1971.7 1972.4 mfh
Bathurst R M BG 157 101 Bernard 1946.12 1949.7 usacc
Batte J H BG 70-S 89 Ingalls 1969.1 1969.2 mfh

Batte J H BG 93 75 Ingalls 1969.2 1970.7 mfh
Battery R T II COL 63-S 26 Ruckman 1951.4 1951.5 usacc
Battle M S 1LT 65-S 46 Ingalls 1908.6 1909.8 S&F Arthur
Battle M S CPT 50-E 129 Bernard 1916.12 1917.12 '16cd
Battle M S LTC 93 75 Ingalls 1920.11 1921.8 S&F '21FOcs
Battle M S 2LT 69-N 87 Ingalls 1902.5 1902.9 BOQ? c-46
Bauer M H LTC 34-S-1 96 Ingalls 1963.7 1963.12 mfh
Bauman J W MAJ 70-S 89 Ingalls 1923.6 1925.6 MedC Hartel
Bautz E Jr MG 142 51 Fenwick 1971.1 1973.7 mfh
Bayless H K COL 144-N-1 41-B Ingalls 1956.9 1957.11 usacc
Bayley C C 1LT 16-W 51 Bernard 1944.9 1946.6 PhBk
Baylor T G COL 50-E 129 Bernard 1867.11 1876.6 ORD
Bayne R H COL 124-N 69 Ingalls 1954.8 1956.9 usacc
Bazley Dr 17-E-1 47-A Bernard 1886 MedC c-14
Beach G C 1LT 124-N 69 Ingalls 1915.12 1916.6 '17cd
Beall J A Jr COL 69-S 85 Ingalls 1957.7 1960.0 Ret MG usacc
Beard W N COL 50-E 129 Bernard 1962.7 1966.7 mfh
Beasley R W BG 158 32 Ingalls 1949.3 1952.10 usacc
Becton J LTG 120 37 Fenwick 1981.7 1983.8 mfh
Beddow J H COL 17-W-1 41-A Bernard 1964.7 1964.9 mfh
Beddow J H COL 62-N 28 Ruckman 1964.9 1966.7 mfh
Beere D C LTC 50-A 125 Bernard 1949.11 1951.8 usacc
Begland R MAJ 34-S-2 94 Ingalls 1979.5 1980.8 mfh
Begland R LTC 51-N-2 124 Ingalls 1983.8 1986.5 mfh
Behr F J COL 50-E 129 Bernard 1917.12 1918.11 '17cd
Behr F J CPT 143-S-2 35-C Ingalls 1910.8 1913.4 '11-12cd
Behr F J LTC 127-E 147 Bernard 1921.9 1922.8 '22FOcs Arthur
Behr F J LTC 121-W 41 Fenwick 1926.6 1928.7 Bennett
Bell J D COL 54-N-1 138 Ingalls 1955.2 1955.12 usacc
Bell W R 1LT 18-E-1 37-A Bernard 1912.12 1913.12 CAS'12 '13cd
Bell W H LT 17-W-1 41-A Bernard 1828.4 1830 '29rq CAS'30
Bellican C P COL 66-N 40 Ingalls 1953.7 1954.10 usacc
Bellican C P COL 43-W-2 1 Reeder 1952.7 1953.7 usacc
Belt R L COL 63-S 26 Ruckman 1965.9 1970.7 mfh
Belt R L COL 54-S-2 134 Ingalls 1965.6 1965.8 mfh
Bembry T J Jr LTC 52-W-2 132 Ingalls 1968.4 1968.9 usacc
Bender L B MAJ 70-N 91 Ingalls 1920.8 1921.8 Broudy
Bender L B 1LT 62-S 30 Ruckman 1915.12 1916.12 Brown Payne
Bender A H CPT 45-E-2 116 Ingalls 1934.9 1936.6 Ret BG Bender
Bender A H 1LT 45-W-2 110 Ingalls 1933.7 1934.8 Ret BG Bender
Bender A H CPT 143-S-2 35-C Ingalls 1939.6 1941.6 Ret BG Bender
Bender L B 1LT 79-N 95 Ingalls 1916.12 1917.12 '17cd
Benitez E M MAJ 127-W 145 Bernard 1937.6 1938.6 Cramer
Benjamin S N Rank unk 18 Bernard 1869.8 1875.4 S&F c-27
Bennett R J COL 44-S-1 104 Ingalls 1960.8 1962.7 mfh
Bennett J LTC 67-N 36 Ingalls 1978.6 1980.1 mfh
Bennett W LTC 33-E-2 63 Fenwick 1962.8 1965.6 mfh
Bennett R K LTC 123-W 2 Ruckman 1942.7 1946.4 '43-45PhBks
Bennett E E COL 118 29 Fenwick 1938.12 1940.10 Bennett
Bennett E E MAJ 14 32 Ruckman 1925.6 1926.10 Bennett
Bennett E E MAJ 124-N 69 Ingalls 1917.8 1918.8 Bennett
Bennett E E MAJ 121-E 43 Fenwick 1926.10 1930.10 Bennett
Bennett E E 1LT 64-S 22 Ruckman 1913.12 1914.12 PhBk

Bennett I L CPT 14 32 Ruckman 1930.7 1933.1 Ret MG Chap
Bennett E E 2LT 1 151 Bernard 1907.0 1910.0 Bennett
Bennis J LTC 44-S-1 104 Ingalls 1977.6 1978.7 mfh
Bennis J M MAJ 52-E-1 128 Ingalls 1973.10 1976.2 mfh
Bennis J LTC 65-S 45 Ingalls 1978.8 1979.6 mfh
Benson J S COL 144-S-1 41-A Ingalls 1958.10 1962.6 mfh
Bentley W R COL 68-N 83 Ingalls 1974.2 1974.8 mfh
Benz H J CPT 70-S 89 Ingalls 1933.7 1936.7 '33cd
Benz H T LTC 43-E-1 5 Reeder 1941.5 1942.2 Benz
Benz H T 2LT 16-W 51 Bernard 1927 1928 Benz
Bergeron D M LTC 143-S-2 35-C Ingalls 1983.4 1986.6 mfh
Bergman J T LTC 33-W-2 57 Fenwick 1967.3 1968.8 mfh
Berkhimer W C LTC 62-S 30 Ruckman 1905.9 1906.9 '06cd
Berliner S 1LT 35-W-1 4 Reeder 1931.7 1932.7 '31cd
Bermingham P F COL 18-W-1 29-A Bernard 1967.10 1968.4 mfh
Bermingham P F COL 128-E 109 Bernard 1968.4 1970.12 mfh
Bernard L W COL 126-S 163 Bernard 1960.8 1963.8 mfh
Bernard J S Jr CPT 43-W-1 3 Reeder 1944.6 1945.8 Dentist PhBk
Berrios L MAJ 33-W-2 57 Fenwick 1979.1 1980.11 mfh
Berry C L CPT 18-W-2 29-B Bernard 1923.6 1925.6 '23cd
Berry J A COL 143-N-2 35-D Ingalls 1946.9 1948.4 Ret BG usacc
Berry L C COL 124-S 67 Ingalls 1946.4 1947.4 usacc
Berry J A 1LT 15-N 34 Ruckman 1908.9 1909.9 Ret MG '09cd
Berry M MAJ 68-S 81 Ingalls 1929.6 1931.8 MedC Coates
Berry W Mrs. 19 18 Bernard 1918 1919 Officers' Mess
Berry C L CPT 63-S 26 Ruckman 1922.7 1923.6 '23BtryOcs
Berry C L CPT 62-S 30 Ruckman 1934.8 1935.7 '34AdvCs
Berry W MSG 33-E-2 63 Fenwick 1978.8 1979.3 mfh
Berry L P CPT 16-E 53 Ingalls 1942.4 1943.2 Berry
Berry L P MAJ 67-N 36 Ingalls 1943.2 1946.2 PhBk
Berst R D 1LT 102-N 61 Ingalls 1918 1919 BOQ WWI '19cd
Bertram E H COL 66-S 38 Ingalls 1970.9 1973.6 mfh
Bertram E H COL 35-W-1 4 Reeder 1970.7 1970.9 mfh
Besse W E LTC 44-S-2 102 Ingalls 1952.8 1954.8 usacc
Best C L MAJ 93 75 Ingalls 1902 1903 c-466 '21ArtyBd
Best G H MAJ 54-N-1 138 Ingalls 1941.10 1943.7 Best
Best J C MAJ 19 18 Bernard 1901.9 1902.9 '02cd Died
Best G H MAJ 123-E 4 Ruckman 1943.10 1946.5 Best PhBks
Bettis J SGM 35-W-2 2 Reeder 1982.5 1986.1 mfh
Bettison W R MAJ 129-S 101 Ingalls 1917.6 1918.6 S&F Cary
Bettison W R CPT 15-N 34 Ruckman 1909.9 1910.9 CAS'10
Bettison W R 1LT 63-N 24 Ruckman 1908.9 1909.9 '09cd
Betts A W LTC 34-N-1 98 Ingalls 1948.7 1949.1 Ret LTG usacc
Bewley W M MAJ 45-W-1 112 Ingalls 1982.9 1984.7 mfh
Beyer D J COL 102-N 61 Ingalls 1986.1 1987.6 mfh
Bibby L N CPT 69-S 85 Ingalls 1951.4 1952.6 USN usacc
Biddle D MAJ 34-N-1 98 Ingalls 1976.7 1980.2 mfh
Biehl P F CPT 52-W-1 130 Ingalls 1931.9 1932.6 Biehl
Biehl P F CPT 65-N 48 Ingalls 1923.7 1925.6 Biehl
Biehl P F CPT 63-N 24 Ruckman 1925.7 1926.7 Biehl
Bienvenu T S LTC 147 147 Engr Ln 1950.6 1952.9 usacc
Bierck W MAJ 16-E 53 Bernard 1948.12 1950.10 usacc
Big B COL 79-N 95 Ingalls 1969.7 1969.9 mfh

Big B COL 103-S 63 Ingalls 1969.9 1976.1 mfh w
Biggar W R CPT 51-S-2 118 Ingalls 1944 1945 '44-45PhBks
Biggerstaff W H COL 143-N-1 35-B Ingalls 1952.8 1953.8 usacc
Bingham S V Jr COL 144-S-1 41-A Ingalls 1946.9 1949.4 usacc PhBks
Binkley H L LTC 54-N-1 138 Ingalls 1948.11 1949.2 usacc
Bird M B 1LT 17-W-2 41-B Bernard 1944.1 1946.1 PhBks
Birdsall J N 2LT 16-E 53 Bernard 1912.1 1912.4 '12cd
Bishop P P COL 142 51 Fenwick 1930.9 1934.6 Ret MG JHC +
Bishop P P 1LT 63-N 24 Ruckman 1901.9 1902 Ret MG S&F '02cd
Bissell E B LTC 54-S-2 134 Ingalls 1957.1 1959.1 usacc
Bittrich L LTC 51-S-2 118 Ingalls 1981.6 1982.8 mfh
Bixby H O 1LT 17-W-2 41-B Bernard 1922.6 1924.7 Cary '23cd
Bjostad L COL 129-S 101 Ingalls 1978.2 1978.6 mfh
Black C S COL 18-E-2 37-B Bernard 1967.9 1969.6 mfh
Blacker K K COL 52-E-1 128 Ingalls 1960.7 1961.3 usacc
Blacker K K COL 66-N 40 Ingalls 1961.3 1962.2 mfh
Blackmore P C 2LT 16-E 53 Bernard 1912.4 1912.12 '12cd
Blackshear E CPT 15-S 36 Ruckman 1928.8 1930.8 MedC '29cd
Blackshear E CPT 19 18 Bernard 1926.6 1927.9 Hartel
Blackwell H H COL 103-N 65 Ingalls 1943.8 1944.8 PhBk
Blackwell H H COL 121-W 41 Fenwick 1944.8 1946.8 PhBk
Blackwell H H CPT 1 151 Bernard 1925 1926.5 '25cd
Blackwell H H CPT 67-S 34 Ingalls 1926.5 1931.6 Crowell
Blair W A COL 64 71 Fenwick 1971.7 1973.6 mfh
Blair J S COL 101-S 55 Ingalls 1958.9 1959.11 usacc
Blair B B CPT 19 18 Bernard 1927.9 1929.7 Hesketh
Blake D C LTC 34-S-1 96 Ingalls 1954.3 1956.8 usacc
Blakelock D H COL 121-E 43 Fenwick 1948.9 1949.7 Ret MG usacc
Blakelock D H COL 101-S 55 Ingalls 1947.10 1948.9 Ret MG usacc
Blanck H R 2LT 17-E-1 47-A Bernard 1940.9 1942 PhBks
Blandford W O COL 14 32 Ruckman 1955.10 1956.12 Ret BG usacc
Blandford W O COL 52-W-1 130 Ingalls 1955.8 1955.10 Ret BG usacc
Blanks H CPT 167 B 9 Patch Road 1969.10 1970.2 mfh
Blascak D W COL 68-N 83 Ingalls 1985.7 1985.? mfh
Blesse H S COL 103-N 65 Ingalls 1949.10 1951.9 usacc
Blesse H S COL 35-W-2 2 Reeder 1949.7 1949.10 usacc
Blesse F A LTC 124-N 69 Ingalls 1946.9 1950.1 Ret BG usacc
Block E H CPT 66-N 40 Ingalls 1922.7 1924.6 '23cd
Block E H CPT 144-S-2 41-C Ingalls 1924.6 1926.7 Holmes '25cd QMC
Blocker J S COL 34-N-1 98 Ingalls 1955.9 1957.9 Ret BG usacc
Blocker J S COL 67-S 34 Ingalls 1957.8 1958.7 Ret BG usacc
Blohm R W Jr MAJ 35-E-2 8 Reeder 1955.10 1957.3 usacc
Blohm R W Jr LTC 35-E-1 6 Reeder 1957.3 1957.10 usacc
Blood K T MAJ 129-N 103 Ingalls 1931.7 1933.6 Ret MG Blood
Blood K T MAJ 126-S 163 Bernard 1924.9 1925.8 Ret MG Blood
Blood K T LTC 101-S 55 Ingalls 1933.7 1935.8 Ret MG Blood
Blount J B MG 142 51 Fenwick 1979.7 1983.6 mfh
Bluhm J L LTC 52-E-1 128 Ingalls 1968.6 1973.6 mfh
Boatwright W P 1LT 144-S-1 41-A Ingalls 1913.12 1914.12 Ret BG '14PhBk
Boatwright W P CPT 127-W 145 Bernard 1915.6 1916.6 Ret BG '17cd
Boatwright W P CPT 14 32 Ruckman 1916 1917 Ret BG
Bobo P O CPT 43-W-1 3 Reeder 1945.8 1946.8 PhBk
Bodel J K LTC 128-E 109 Bernard 1935.8 1941.4 Chaplain PhBk

Bodey E R COL 54-S-2 134 Ingalls 1953.2 1953.10 usacc
Bodey E R COL 101-S 55 Ingalls 1953.10 1954.12 usacc
Bodine D R LTC 52-W-2 132 Ingalls 1948.10 1950.4 usacc
Body R MAJ 50-E 129 Bernard 1944.6 1946.7 PhBk
Body R MAJ 33-E-2 63 Fenwick 1942.3 1944.6 Walter PhBks
Boers W A MAJ 128-E 109 Bernard 1944.3 1945.10 PhBk
Bogart F A 1LT 52-E-2 126 Ingalls 1936.6 1937.7 Ret LTG AF
Bogart F A 1LT 43-W-2 1 Reeder 1937.7 1938.6 Bogart
Boling D L COL 50-E 129 Bernard 1976.8 1980.7 mfh
Boller Q D COL 52-W-1 130 Ingalls 1966.2 1968.6 mfh
Bolte C L MG 142 51 Fenwick 1946.9 1948.7 Ret GEN usacc
Bolte D E COL 129-N 103 Ingalls 1972.8 1974.7 mfh
Bolton V W COL 65-S 46 Ingalls 1973.7 1975.6 mfh
Bolton MAJ 17-E-1 47-A Bernard 1844.10 '44rq d-686
Bolton R CPT 129-S 101 Ingalls 1947.10 1949.6 USN usacc
Bomar E C CPT 66-N 40 Ingalls 1924.7 1925.6 S&F
Bond O J CPT 79-S 93 Ingalls 1923.2 1927.7 '23-27cd
Bondshu L T LTC 17-W-2 41-B Bernard 1950.10 1953.10 usacc
Bondshu L T LTC 17-W-1 41-A Bernard 1953.10 1955.2 usacc
Bone G A COL 33-E-2 63 Fenwick 1967.8 1968.4 mfh
Booth L D 1LT 3-N 169 Bernard 1915.12 1916.12 Cochran
Booth L B CPT 65-S 46 Ingalls 1917 '17cd
Booth R A MG 157 101 Bernard 1958.7 1959.10 usacc
Booth B N 1LT 66-S 38 Ingalls 1916.12 1917.6 Ford
Booth B N MAJ 124-S 67 Ingalls 1922.6 1923.6 '23AdvCs '23cd
Booth R H COL 79-N 95 Ingalls 1947.1 1948.12 usacc
Booth B N MAJ 101-S 55 Ingalls 1931.9 1933.1 deCamp
Booth R H COL 93 75 Ingalls 1948.12 1949.8 usacc
Boots F W CWO 147 147 Engr Ln 1963.2 1965.6 mfh
Borden N E LTC 126-N 165 Bernard 1942.4 1944.6 Borden
Borden H I 1LT 17-W-2 41-B Bernard 1926.7 1927.7 '27BtryOCs
Borgman G J 1LT 17-E-1 47-A Bernard 1943 1946 '43-45PhBks
Bostancic J F MAJ 34-S-2 94 Ingalls 1974.11 1978.5 mfh
Bothwell L D COL 68-N 83 Ingalls 1958.7 1959.7 usacc
Bothwell L D COL 18-E-2 37-B Bernard 1958.4 1958.7 usacc
Bottoms S F CPT 14 32 Ruckman 1910.0 1912.9 '11cd
Bourgault B LTC 45-W-1 112 Ingalls 1977.8 1980.6 mfh
Bovee B W 1LT 167 A 7 Patch Road 1958.10 1960.8 usacc
Bowen D C 1LT 18-E-2 37-B Bernard 1915.12 1916.8 CAS'16
Bowen W S MAJ 143-S-1 35-A Ingalls 1920.11 1923.8 JHC '23cd
Bowen W S COL 120 37 Fenwick 1939.6 1942.6 PhBk
Bowen J W LTG 141 53 Fenwick 1963.10 1964.3 mfh
Bowering B CPT 68-N 83 Ingalls 1922.10 1923.8 '23cd
Bowers V L BG 157 101 Bernard 1968.4 1969.3 mfh
Bowers B T MAJ 54-S-1 136 Ingalls 1939.7 1940.6 '39cd
Bowler L J CPT 50-W 121 Bernard 1931.6 1933.6 '31-33cd
Bowman C A 1LT 102-N 61 Ingalls 1918 1919 BOQ WWI '19cd
Bowman O D 1LT 17-E-1 47-A Bernard 1923.6 1925.6 Higgins
Bowman F O BG 121-W 41 Fenwick 1946.8 1947.10 Ret MG usacc
Boyce R C MAJ 143-N-1 35-B Ingalls 1942.4 1944.2 '43 PhBk
Doyd II R CPT 63 N 24 Ruckman 1939.9 1940.6 Boyd
Boyd L R MAJ 69-S 85 Ingalls 1931.7 1932.7 Ret BG INF
Boyd L R MAJ 143-N-1 35-B Ingalls 1930.6 1931.7 '31cd

Boyd R K LTC 35-E-1 6 Reeder 1950.1 1951.8 usacc
Boyd L R MAJ 144-S-1 41-A Ingalls 1932.7 1934.8 INF '33cd
Boyd W T Jr 1LT 3-N 169 Bernard 1917 '17cd
Boyer H LTC 17-W-1 41-A Bernard 1970.9 1973.6 mfh
Boykin R P CPT 79-S 93 Ingalls 1934.6 1935.6 JHC Bartlett
Boykin R H CPT 79-N 95 Ingalls 1919.6 1920.8 '20cd
Boyle A J COL 35-W-1 4 Reeder 1957.7 1957.7 Ret LTG usacc
Boyle A J COL 70-S 89 Ingalls 1957.7 1959.7 Ret LTG usacc
Boyle C L COL 128-E 109 Bernard 1951.7 1954.6 usacc
Boyle C L COL 63-N 24 Ruckman 1951.3 1951.7 usacc
Boyle R D MG 141 53 Fenwick 1981.9 1982.6 mfh
Boys R C 1LT 45-W-1 112 Ingalls 1940.6 1941.6 '40-41PhBk
Bradbury S H CPT 102-N 61 Ingalls 1918 1919 BOQ WWI '19cd
Bradford W B BG 157 101 Bernard 1949.8 1951.8 usacc
Bradford W B BG 3-N 169 Bernard 1949.6 1949.8 usacc
Bradford L L CPT 15-N 34 Ruckman 1935.6 1936.7 '36Sojourner
Bradford W B BG 120 37 Fenwick 1951.8 1952.5 usacc
Bradin J COL 16-W 53 Bernard 1977.7 1980.6 mfh
Bradshaw A Jr CPT 14 32 Ruckman 1921.7 1923.6 Ret MG Bradshaw
Brady R D CPT 44-N-1 106 Ingalls 1943.6 1946.6 '43-45 PhBks
Braly W C CPT 50-W 121 Bernard 1930.9 1931.6 Braly
Bramble P H COL 54-S-1 136 Ingalls 1964.2 1965.7 mfh
Bramblet W COL 126-S 165 Bernard 1977.7 1979.8 mfh
Bramblet W COL 93 75 Ingalls 1979.8 1982.6 mfh
Brashears B F BG 158 32 Ingalls 1985.7 1988.1 mfh
Braude M A COL 101-N 57 Ingalls 1955.8 1958.8 usacc
Braude M A COL 34-N-1 98 Ingalls 1955.7 1955.8 usacc
Bray N C LTC 33-E-2 63 Fenwick 1969.11 1970.8 mfh
Breaks R W COL 16-W 51 Bernard 1958.6 1961.7 usacc
Breckenridge A K COL 129-S 101 Ingalls 1963.7 1964.1 mfh
Breen C COL 54-N-2 140 Ingalls 1966.8 1968.8 mfh
Brennan J M MAJ 33-E-2 63 Fenwick 1984.6 1987.12 mfh
Brett W R COL 123-W 2 Ruckman 1975.8 1979.11 mfh
Brey W J CPT 63-N 24 Ruckman 1930.7 1931.6 '31cd
Brey W J CPT 51-S-1 120 Ingalls 1931.7 1932.7 Brey deCamp
Brice C S CPT 125 73 Ingalls 1918.8 1919.2 WWI BOQ? '19cd
Bridenstine W A COL 66-N 40 Ingalls 1969.6 1972.4 mfh
Briggs B G LTC 17-E-2 47-B Bernard 1972.8 1974.8 mfh
Briggs K M CPT 62-S 30 Ruckman 1940.6 1943.1 PhBk
Briggs D V MAJ 79-N 95 Ingalls 1944 1945 PhBks
Briggs C F COL 123-E 4 Ruckman 1975.10 1977.6 mfh
Brigham C E 1LT 64-N 20 Ruckman 1909 Ret MG '09cd
Brigham C E CPT 103-S 63 Ingalls 1914.1 1917.5 Ret MG S&F PhBk
Brinton L C Jr CPT 69-N 87 Ingalls 1911.9 1912.6 CAS'12
Britt A COL 15-S 36 Ruckman 1978.6 1980.6 mfh
Brittain F W CPT 147 147 Engr Ln 1976.11 1979.9 mfh
Britton G R LTC 17-E-2 47-B Bernard 1953.8 1954.9 usacc
Brockmyer J J COL 123-E 4 Ruckman 1972.2 1972.9 mfh
Broderick E S COL 15-S 36 Ruckman 1985.2 1987.7 mfh
Brody W MAJ 144-N-1 41-B Ingalls 1944 1945 '45PhBk
Brogan W T COL 44-S-2 102 Ingalls 1959.10 1961.6 usacc
Brokow C 1LT 70-S 89 Ingalls 1918 1919 BOQ WWI '19cd
Bromley C J COL 129-N 103 Ingalls 1950.11 1952.4 usacc

Brooke P CPT 65-N 48 Ingalls 1905.9 1906.9 '06cd
Brooke G M 1LT 79-S 95 Ingalls 1905.9 1906.9 '06cd b-26
Brooks J A 2LT 18-W-2 29-B Bernard 1915.4 1915.9 Brooks
Broom T A COL 33-W-1 59 Fenwick 1950.6 1952.9 Ret BG usacc
Brosseau H CPT 30-B 36 Hampton 1982.5 1984.6 mfh
Broudy H COL 33-E-1 61 Fenwick 1967.7 1969.12 mfh
Brown T T BG 125 73 Ingalls 1963.8 1964.7 mfh
Brown E 1LT 15-N 34 Ruckman 1912.12 1913.12 '13cd
Brown W D COL 103-N 65 Ingalls 1975.9 1977.7 mfh
Brown G C COL 19 18 Bernard 1984.7 1986.10 mfh
Brown J D MAJ 126-N 165 Bernard 1920.3 1921.9 '20cd
Brown C E COL 68-N 83 Ingalls 1956.11 1958.7 usacc
Brown R H COL 19 18 Bernard 1953.8 1954.6 Ret BG usacc
Brown J W E-8 61-N 45 Ingalls 1967.3 1967.3 mfh
Brown H C COL 43-W-1 3 Reeder 1964.8 1965.10 mfh
Brown C P BG 118 29 Fenwick 1965.6 1966.7 mfh
Brown J D CPT 18-W-1 29-A Bernard 1919.1 1919.3 '19cd
Brown J D MAJ 127-E 147 Bernard 1932.7 1933.6 '33cd
Brown R D CPT 69-N 87 Ingalls 1920.8 1921.8 Brown
Brown A E LTC 124-N 69 Ingalls 1940.3 1942.4 DC Brown PhBk
Brown T T BG 45-E-2 116 Ingalls 1963.7 1963.8 mfh
Brown J G C COL 33-W-2 57 Fenwick 1968.11 1970.8 mfh
Brown J D CPT 65-N 48 Ingalls 1926.7 1927.7 Ely
Brown R H COL 79-N 95 Ingalls 1952.7 1953.8 Ret BG usacc
Brown H C COL 143-S-2 35-C Ingalls 1965.10 1965.12 mfh
Brown L W COL 143-S-1 35-A Ingalls 1969.6 1972.12 mfh
Brown H C COL 51-S-2 118 Ingalls 1965.12 1967.1 mfh
Brown C E COL 34-S-1 96 Ingalls 1956.9 1956.11 usacc
Brown L W COL 35-W-1 4 Reeder 1969.2 1969.6 mfh
Brown J D 1LT 63-N 24 Ruckman 1916.12 1917.6 Ford
Brown D E COL 128-W 107 Bernard 1974.8 1977.8 mfh
Brown R COL 65-S 46 Ingalls 1980.11 1984.6 mfh
Brown H MAJ 17-E-2 47-B Bernard 1844.10 '44rq d-686
Brown F MG 125 73 Ingalls 1981.8 1983.1 mfh
Brown W D COL 101-N 57 Ingalls 1946.8 1947.2 usacc
Browne H C 2LT 16-W 51 Bernard 1911 1912 BOQ? '11cd
Brownfield P H COL 54-N-2 140 Ingalls 1962.12 1963.9 mfh
Brownlee L H CPT 144-N-1 41-B Ingalls 1939.6 1940.8 PhBks
Brownlee R L LTC 18-W-1 29-A Bernard 1973.6 1975.7 mfh
Brown M Jr MAJ 51-S-1 120 Ingalls 1974.6 1977.9 mfh
Brown L C Jr MAJ 144-N-1 41-B Ingalls 1981.1 1983.7 mfh
Brown S G Jr COL 144-S-2 41-C Ingalls 1951.6 1952.6 usacc
Brown H M Jr COL 144-N-2 41-D Ingalls 1963.10 1966.8 Ret BG mfh
Broyles H E LTC 18-E-2 37-B Bernard 1946.10 1948.7 usacc
Bruce C O COL 33-W-2 57 Fenwick 1946.8 1948.9 usacc
Brusher H A CPT 54-N-1 138 Ingalls 1935.7 1937.7 Ellsworth +
Brushie L MAJ 143-S-1 35-A Ingalls 1978.7 1981.12 mfh
Bryant A H 1LT 64-S 22 Ruckman 1909 '09cd
Bryde W J COL 33-E-1 61 Fenwick 1958.8 1960.2 usacc
Buchanan D H LTC 35-E-1 6 Reeder 1949.8 1950.1 usacc
Buchanan D H MG 141 53 Fenwick 1961.11 1962.12 mfh
Buchanan T W COL 103-N 65 Ingalls 1972.10 1975.8 mfh
Buchanan D H LTC 69-S 85 Ingalls 1950.1 1950.9 usacc

Bucher O B CPT 15-N 34 Ruckman 1924.6 1926.6 Ret BG '25cd
Bucher O B CPT 51-N-1 122 Ingalls 1931.8 1932.7 Ret BG decamp +
Bucher O B MAJ 126-N 165 Bernard 1935.7 1937.7 Ret BG Unger +
Bucher O B CPT 50-E 129 Bernard 1918.12 1919.6 Ret BG '19cd
Bucher O B CPT 144-N-2 41-D Ingalls 1919.6 1920.3 Ret BG Unger
Buck L N COL 45-E-1 114 Ingalls 1947.6 1948.11 usacc
Buck F L 1LT 18-W-1 29-A Bernard 1903 1904 b-21
Buck F L CPT 123-E 4 Ruckman 1912.12 1913.12 CAS'13 '13cd
Buck F L LTC 124-N 69 Ingalls 1920.7 1921.6 '22FOcs
Buckingham N A MAJ 144-N-1 41-B Ingalls 1964.7 1966.9 mfh
Buckles R C LTC 17-W-1 41-A Bernard 1956.1 1959.1 usacc
Budge V M COL 34-N-2 100 Ingalls 1955.7 1958.6 usacc
Buechler T E COL 126-N 165 Bernard 1951.2 1953.8 Ret BG usacc
Bukey N J MAJ 65-S 46 Ingalls 1941.4 1942.4 Bukey
Buldain L P COL 18-W-1 29-A Bernard 1968.4 1969.7 mfh
Bullard A L 1LT 17-E-2 47-B Bernard 1923.9 1924.6 Higgins
Bullene L B 1LT 17-W-1 41-A Bernard 1922.7 1923.7 Cary '23cd
Bullene L B 1LT 35-E-1 6 Reeder 1930.12 1931.7 deCamp
Bullock S E COL 44-S-2 102 Ingalls 1946.8 1948.7 usacc
Bultman H F E CPT 35-E-2 8 Reeder 1930.12 1931.6 '31cd
Bultman H F E CPT 79-S 93 Ingalls 1929.6 1930.12 Widow Warren
Bultman H F E CPT 14 32 Ruckman 1928.6 1929.6 '29cd
Bundy C W MAJ 70-S 89 Ingalls 1929.6 1931.6 Kinnard +
Bundy C W MAJ 101-N 57 Ingalls 1931.6 1933.6 KIA 1941
Bundy C W MAJ 126-N 165 Bernard 1921.9 1925.6 Daughter '23cd
Bunker C G CPT 50-W 121 Bernard 1909.6 1912.12 '11-12cd
Bunker C G LTC 144-N-1 41-B Ingalls 1920.9 1921.6 '21FOcs
Bunn H W 1LT 17-E-1 47-A Bernard 1909.9 1910.9 CAS'10
Bunshaw R H COL 52-W-1 130 Ingalls 1950.10 1953.7 usacc
Bunshaw R H COL 101-S 55 Ingalls 1967.8 1968.6 mfh
Bunshaw R H COL 34-S-1 96 Ingalls 1967.6 1967.8 mfh
Burch G C COL 123-W 2 Ruckman 1972.3 1974.7 mfh
Burdeshaw W B COL 124-N 69 Ingalls 1974.3 1975.9 Ret BG mfh
Burdeshaw W B BG 125 73 Ingalls 1975.9 1977.7 Ret BG mfh
Burdge J M Jr COL 54-N-2 140 Ingalls 1950.9 1953.9 usacc
Burdick H D 2LT 16-W 51 Bernard 1912 1913 '12cd BOQ
Burdick H D MAJ 102-N 61 Ingalls 1935.6 1936.6 '36Sojourner
Burgess D COL 70-S 89 Ingalls 1982.2 1984.7 mfh
Burgess G R CPT 79-S 93 Ingalls 1938.8 1939.6 PhBk
Burke M LTC 1 151 Bernard 1857.4 1857.5 Arthur
Burke W J CPT 62-N 28 Ruckman 1928.8 1929.6 '29cd
Burnell N A CPT 44-S-1 104 Ingalls 1934.6 1938.6 Ret MG Burnell
Burnell N A 1LT 44-S-2 102 Ingalls 1932.8 1934.6 Ret MB Burnell
Burnell N A 1LT 17-E-2 47-B Bernard 1930.5 1931.9 Ret MG Burnel
Burnett J R 2LT 18-W-2 29-B Bernard 1929.8 1932.6 Burnett '31cd
Burns G T COL 127-E 147 Bernard 1973.7 1977.9 mfh
Burns S E COL 34-N-1 98 Ingalls 1957.11 1960.4 usacc
Burt C C LTC 103-S 63 Ingalls 1921.8 1922.6 '22FOcs
Burt W H 1LT 65-S 46 Ingalls 1903.9 1904.9 CAS'04
Burt C C 2LT 63-N 24 Ruckman 1905.9 1906.9 BOQ '06cd b-26
Burton E Y COL 63-N 24 Ruckman 1961.10 1964.6 mfh
Burton A W CPT 62-S 30 Ruckman 1924.4 1925.5 Higgins
Bush J K COL 70-N 91 Ingalls 1946.9 1947.6 usacc

Bush F D LTC 54-N-1 138 Ingalls 1969.11 1972.1 mfh
Bushyaeger W E MAJ 68-S 81 Ingalls 1943.9 1945.11 Bushyaeger
Bushyaeger W E CPT 45-W-2 110 Ingalls 1941.10 1942.2 Bushyeager
Butler H L 1LT 69-N 87 Ingalls 1902.9 1903.9 c-46
Butler H L 1LT 17-E-2 47-B Bernard 1906.9 1907.9 CAS'07
Butler B F MG 1 151 Bernard 1861.5 1861.8 CG w
Butler G E COL 102-S 59 Ingalls 1946.9 1947.4 usacc
Butler B F MG 1 151 Bernard 1863.11 1864.5 CG w
Butler J D 1LT 17-W-1 41-A Bernard 1945.1 1946.10 '45PhBk
Butler H L LTC 1 151 Bernard 1921 1923 '23cd
Butterfield T E MAJ 125 73 Ingalls 1917.8 1918.8 WWI BOQ '19cd
Buttgenbach W J CPT 143-S-2 35-C Ingalls 1915.12 1916.12 '17cd
Button P S CPT 144-N-2 41-D Ingalls 1941 1942 AN306
Butts W LTC 66-S 38 Ingalls 1979.3 1980.9 mfh
Buyers A S MAJ 126-S 163 Bernard 1922.9 1923.8 S&F Chapel +
Buynoski A S COL 67-N 36 Ingalls 1959.7 1963.6 mfh
Byam L T LTC 18-E-1 37-B Bernard 1980.8 1981.6 mfh
Byam L T MAJ 144-N-2 41-D Ingalls 1974.9 1977.10 mfh
Byers J W COL 54-N-1 138 Ingalls 1950.7 1953.6 usacc
Byon J B DR 64 71 Fenwick 1952.2 1956.4 usacc MedC
Byrd L MAJ 52-W-1 130 Ingalls 1985.1 1985.7 mfh
Byrd W H COL 54-S-2 134 Ingalls 1960.8 1964.6 Ar Avia mfh
Byrnes W P Rev 7 Frank Lane 1940 1941 '40-41PhBk Priest
Cabler J MAJ 17-W-2 41-B Bernard 1981.4 1983.12 mfh
Cairns B S BG 157 101 Bernard 1956.1 1957.1 Ret MG usacc
Caldwell A LTC 3-S 167 Bernard 1941.5 1944.8 PhBk
Caleb J H CPT 17-E-1 47A Bernard 1875.5 1881.5 S&F
Callagy T A COL 15-N 34 Ruckman 1971.4 1973.8 mfh
Callahan A III CPT 54-N-2 140 Ingalls 1944 1945 PhBks
Callan R E BG 119 33 Fenwick 1924.12 1929.6 Ret MG Hartel
Callan R E MAJ 93 75 Ingalls 1913.7 1916.12 Ret MG Hall
Callanan E F COL 65-N 48 Ingalls 1972.8 1973.6 mfh
Callaway J W COL 124-N 69 Ingalls 1966.3 1968.1 mfh
Callaway J W COL 143-N-2 35-D Ingalls 1965.10 1966.3 mfh
Call L W Jr 2LT 16-W 51 Bernard 1927 1928 Pohl BOQ
Calverase F LTC 51-S-1 120 Ingalls 1980.12 1981.4 mfh
Calvert C W COL 33-E-1 61 Fenwick 1960.10 1962.7 mfh
Calvin H L 1LT 3-N 169 Bernard 1926.6 1927.6 '27cd
Camm F A LTG 141 53 Fenwick 1975.9 1977.8 mfh
Camp R E LTC 43-E-2 7 Reeder 1973.8 1974.6 mfh
Campbell R N 1LT 17-W-1 41-A Bernard 1913.12 1914.12 CAS'14 PhBk
Campbell W R LTC 43-W-2 1 Reeder 1953.8 1954.9 usacc
Campbell R J LTC 51-N-1 122 Ingalls 1941.8 1944.3 Campbell PhBk
Campbell D M COL 63-S 26 Ruckman 1984.7 1987.8 mfh
Campbell R J LTC 128-W 107 Bernard 1944.3 1945.7 PhBk Campbell
Campbell J T MAJ 66-S 38 Ingalls 1928.8 1929.7 '29cd
Campbell R J COL 62-S 30 Ruckman 1945.7 1945.10 Campbell
Campbell CPT 19 18 Bernard 1882.5 1888.1 S&F c-14 d-691
Campbell J T CPT 143-N-1 35-B Ingalls 1931.7 1932.8 Detwiler
Campbell A B CPT 17-E-2 47-B Bernard 1919.6 1922.6 '19cd
Campbell J T MAJ 66-S 38 Ingalls 1933.9 1935.6 Payne Wolfe
Campbell A G 1LT 17-E-2 47-B Bernard 1911.12 1912.12 '12cd
Campbell J B MAJ 50-W 121 Bernard 1868.10 1870.10 c-27 Arsenal

Campbell A H CPT 18-W-1 29-A Bernard 1920.9 1921.6 '21BtryOcs
Canfield E Jr CPT 69-S 85 Ingalls 1909.9 1910.9 CAS'10
Cannon A MG 1 151 Bernard 1982.5 1983.8 mfh
Cannon F 1LT 143-N-2 35-D Ingalls 1917.6 1918.4 '17cd
Cannon J A COL 55 42 Ingalls 1954.6 1958.8 usacc
Capers T S COL 3-S 167 Bernard 1967.1 1968.9 mfh
Capers T S COL 45-W-2 110 Ingalls 1966.9 1967.1 mfh
Caperton J N MAJ 129-S 101 Ingalls 1933.7 1935.7 JHC
Caperton J N MAJ 35-W-2 2 Reeder 1931.7 1933.7 Davis deCamp
Caperton J N MAJ 129-N 103 Ingalls 1930.6 1931.7 '31cd
Caple D F COL 54-N-1 138 Ingalls 1965.4 1967.5 mfh
Carah K J LTC 17-E-1 47-A Bernard 1970.7 1972.1 mfh
Cardwell S C 1LT 19 18 Bernard 1910.9 1911.9 '11cd
Cardwell S C 1LT 69-N 87 Ingalls 1909.9 1910.9 CAS'10
Carew W L COL 67-S 34 Ingalls 1986.8 1987.8 mfh
Carey G R 2LT 17-E-1 47-A Bernard 1834,7 1935.6 Carey
Cargill J N MAJ 43-E-1 5 Reeder 1942.2 1944.6 PhBk AN306
Carlisle W A 1LT 15-N 34 Ruckman 1920 1922.9 Williams +
Carlson V P LTC 18-E-2 37-B Bernard 1954.8 1955.6 usacc
Carlson L G COL 51-N-2 124 Ingalls 1963.8 1964.8 mfh
Carlson L G COL 63-N 24 Ruckman 1964.8 1966.1 mfh
Carlson W R CPT 16-E 53 Bernard 1929 '19cd
Carlson J W COL 54-N-2 140 Ingalls 1956.5 1959.5 usacc
Carlson D CPT 147 147 Engr Ln 1979.10 1983.9 mfh
Carmichael R L 1LT 69-S 85 Ingalls 1900.9 1901.9 Ret MG CAS'01
Carmichael R L Jr COL 14 32 Ruckman 1952.7 1955.4 usacc
Carmichael P L Jr COL 44-N-2 108 Ingalls 1952.7 1952.7 usacc
Carnes N D COL 143-S-2 35-C Ingalls 1957.2 1960.8 usacc
Carney T P MAJ 17-E-2 47-B Bernard 1975.9 1977.7 mfh
Carney H M MAJ 54-N-2 140 Ingalls 1983.5 1984.2 mfh
Carpenter E COL 120 37 Fenwick 1924.6 1927.6 Hartel +
Carpenter G R COL 69-S 85 Ingalls 1950.9 1951.3 usacc
Carpenter W T 1LT 144-S-1 41-A Ingalls 1911.9 1912.9 CAS'12 '12cd
Carpenter E CPT 62-S 30 Ruckman 1902.9 1903.9 CAS'02
Carpenter L L COL 143-S-2 35-C Ingalls 1950.3 1953.3 usacc
Carpenter W T MAJ 128-E 109 Bernard 1921.9 1922.8 '20FOcs
Carpenter G R COL 125 73 Ingalls 1951.3 1953.6 usacc
Carr D J LTC 50-A 125 Bernard 1984.8 1985.8 mfh
Carretson R B COL 19 18 Bernard 1954.8 1956.4 usacc
Carrington G D MAJ 127-E 147 Bernard 1931.7 1932.7 deCamp
Carrington G D 2LT 50-W 121 Bernard 1917.1 1917.4 WWI BOQ Purdie
Carroll L S LTC 51-S-1 120 Ingalls 1948.9 1949.9 usacc
Carroll F L LTC 18-E-2 37-B Bernard 1959.7 1960.6 usacc
Carroll J H Jr COL 128-E 109 Bernard 1971.8 1975.9 mfh
Carson M COL 3-S 167 Bernard 1949.9 1950.2 usacc
Carson M COL 15-S 36 Ruckman 1950.2 1951.6 usacc
Carson C C CPT 63-N 24 Ruckman 1915.12 1916.12 Cochran
Carswell R M CPT 63-S 26 Ruckman 1921.8 1922.7 '22BtryOCs
Carswell R M MAJ 67-S 34 Ingalls 1931.6 1932.6 deCamp
Carter C C CPT 128-E 109 Bernard 1912.12 1914.12 PhBk
Carter C C CPT 123-W 2 Ruckman 1909.7 1911.5 '11cd
Carter J H COL 3-N 169 Bernard 1968.2 1971.6 mfh
Carter M S 1LT 54-N-1 138 Ingalls 1939.8 1940.6 Ret LTG PhBk

Carter W F MAJ 125 73 Ingalls 1909.9 1911.8 MedC '09cd
Carter W F CPT 101-S 55 Ingalls 1907.9 1909.9 MedC '07-09cd
Carter C C CPT 67-S 34 Ingalls 1903.9 1905.10 '06cd
Carter W G III MAJ 33-W-1 59 Fenwick 1975.6 1977.5 mfh
Carver R K COL 54-S-1 136 Ingalls 1960.7 1962.8 mfh
Carver R K LTC 54-S-2 134 Ingalls 1959.11 1960.7 usacc
Cary M G 1LT 17-E-1 47-A Bernard 1922.6 1923.6 Cary '23cd
Case H CPT 144-S-1 41-A Ingalls 1927.9 1931.7 Ret BG Case '29cd
Casey S LTC 1 151 Bernard 1855.6 1855.7 w
Cash J H II COL 50-E 129 Bernard 1954.6 1955.12 Ret BG usacc
Cassard H D CPT 18-W-2 29-B Bernard 1928.8 1929.8 '29cd
Cassard H D 1LT 18-W-2 29-B Bernard 1925.6 1926.8 Starr '25cd
Cassidy R F COL 65-N 48 Ingalls 1961.4 1962.7 MedC mfh
Cassidy G O MAJ 144-N-2 41-D Ingalls 1982.8 1985.8 mfh
Cassidy P F COL 70-S 89 Ingalls 1959.8 1961.8 Ret LTG usacc
Castrale J LTC 18-E-2 37-B Bernard 1966.2 1967.1 mfh
Cather L W COL 63-N 24 Ruckman 1953.10 1954.9 usacc
Caughey J H MG 142 51 Fenwick 1964.4 1964.8 mfh
Caughey J H MG 1 151 Bernard 1964.8 1965.9 mfh
Cavanaugh C MAJ 30-A 34 Hampton 1981.6 1983.11 mfh
Cavness W D COL 51-S-2 118 Ingalls 1959.5 1961.8 usacc
Cento D J LTC 52-W-2 132 Ingalls 1970.12 1971.12 usacc
Chace E N CPT 34-S-1 96 Ingalls 1938.8 1940.6 OPC PhBk
Chalgren E Jr COL 143-N-1 35-B Ingalls 1966.5 1966.6 mfh
Chalgren E Jr COL 103-S 63 Ingalls 1966.6 1968.7 mfh
Chamberlain E W CPT 62-S 30 Ruckman 1937.6 1939.5 Ret BG Son
Chamberlain LT 17-E-2 47-B Bernard 1886 1890 c-25
Chamberlain E W 1LT 35-W-1 4 Reeder 1936.6 1937.6 Ret BG
Chamberlain E W 1LT 52-W-1 130 Ingalls 1935.9 1936.6 Chamberlain
Chamberlaine W BG 119 33 Fenwick 1919.1 1919.9 Ret BG Arthur
Chamberlaine W MAJ 118 29 Fenwick 1911.9 1913.7 Ret BG Arthur
Chamberlain F R Jr 1LT 35-W-2 2 Reeder 1933.9 1934.5 '33cd
Chamberlain F R Jr MAJ 62-N 28 Ruckman 1938.8 1940.6 Chamberlain
Chamberlain F R Jr CPT 52-W-1 130 Ingalls 1936.6 1937.8 '37cd deCamp
Chamberlain F R Jr MAJ 129-N 103 Ingalls 1940.6 1940.11 PhBk +
Chamberlain F R Jr CPT 1 151 Bernard 1934.5 1935 deCamp
Chamberlin S J LTC 65-S 46 Ingalls 1937.6 1939.8 INF Ret MG Faye
Chambers L B 1LT 66-N 40 Ingalls 1914.12 1915.12 '16cd
Chambers W H 1LT 79-N 95 Ingalls 1902.9 1905.9 b-19 '02cd DC
Chandler N P LTC 44-S-2 102 Ingalls 1967.10 1970.5 mfh
Channon J A LTC 43-W-2 1 Reeder 1946.9 1947.1 usacc
Chapin W M MAJ 128-E 109 Bernard 1929.9 1930.6 Ret BG AdvCs
Chapin W M CPT 50-W 121 Bernard 1922.6 1923.9 Ret BG '23cd
Chapin C H MAJ 55 42 Ingalls 1917.9 1918.11 Widow
Chaplin R T CPT 50-W 121 Bernard 1928.6 1929.9 Chaplin
Chapman J R COL 63-N 24 Ruckman 1968.6 1969.7 mfh
Chapman C A 1LT 17-E-1 47-A Bernard 1914.12 1915.12 '15cd
Chapman J R COL 52-E-1 128 Ingalls 1968.4 1968.6 mfh
Chapman T H CPT 51-N-2 124 Ingalls 1937.9 1938.6 Cochran
Chapman G C COL 129-S 101 Ingalls 1957.8 1961.3 usacc
Chapman E A 1LT 17-E-2 47-D Bernard 1937.8 1938.6 Ret MG Chapman
Chapman G C COL 3-S 167 Bernard 1957.7 1957.8 usacc
Chappuis S A COL 34-N-2 100 Ingalls 1946.9 1948.3 Ret BG usacc

Chappuis S A MG 121-E 43 Fenwick 1964.11 1967.2 Ret BG mfh
Chappuis S A BG 127-E 147 Bernard 1964.8 1964.11 Ret BG mfh
Charlton G F COL 54-S-1 136 Ingalls 1969.12 1970.9 mfh
Charlton G F COL 123-W 2 Ruckman 1970.9 1972.1 mfh
Charlton G F LTC 44-N-1 106 Ingalls 1964.1 1965.8 mfh
Charrney CPT 67-S 34 Ingalls 1918 1919 BOQ WWI '19cd
Chase T M MAJ 63-N 24 Ruckman 1921.6 1922.6 CAS'22
Cheek L B Jr COL 15-N 34 Ruckman 1968.11 1971.4 mfh
Cheek L B Jr COL 52-W-2 132 Ingalls 1968.9 1968.11 usacc
Chesledon A C CPT 65-N 48 Ingalls 1921.9 1922.6 CAS'22
Chesney R M COL 101-S 55 Ingalls 1985.8 1986.1 mfh
Chester J CPT 16-W 51 Bernard 1882.5 1885.6 c-14 c-27
Chester G A CPT 51-S-2 118 Ingalls 1936.8 1940.8 Chester + PhBk
Chicago F J MAJ 33-W-2 57 Fenwick 1986.6 1987.6 mfh
Christenson D P COL 70-N 91 Ingalls 1956.8 1957.9 usacc
Christian F L CPT 54-S-2 134 Ingalls 1931.6 1932.6 '31cd
Christian F L COL 1 151 Bernard 1942.9 1944.2 Christian
Christian F L MAJ 67-S 34 Ingalls 1932.6 1936.6 Cochran Blood
Christian E H MAJ 15-N 34 Ruckman 1942 1943 Christian
Christian F L CPT 15-N 34 Ruckman 1930.9 1931.6 Christian
Christian F L LTC 124-S 67 Ingalls 1940.11 1942.9 Christian
Church B CW4 54-N-2 140 Ingalls 1979.12 1983.5 mfh
Church J H BG 142 51 Fenwick 1948.9 1949.9 usacc
Church J H BG 125 73 Ingalls 1948.2 1948.9 usacc
Ciccolella R G BG 66-N 40 Ingalls 1962.2 1964.1 Ret MG mfh
Ciccolella R G COL 51-S-2 118 Ingalls 1962.2 1962.2 Ret MG mfh
Ciccotelli D R CWO 167 B 9 Patch Road 1955.11 1959.2 usacc
Cipraino C R COL 146 146 Engr Ln 1976.5 1978.6 mfh
Clark F S MAJ 129-N 103 Ingalls 1919.5 1924.7 Ret BG '20-23cd
Clark S T MAJ 18-W-1 19-A Bernard 1983.7 1986.10 mfh
Clark F S LTC 126-S 163 Bernard 1935.8 1936.11 Ret BG Clark
Clark F S LTC 126-S 163 Bernard 1937.6 1938.6 Ret BG Clark
Clark F S 2LT 1 151 Bernard 1909.0 1910.0 Ret BG Clark
Clark W J Mr 33 CGH 67 Fenwick 1949.10 1957.10 usacc
Clark C A 1LT 66-N 40 Ingalls 1909.9 1910.9 CAS'10
Clark T A 1LT 55 42 Ingalls 1910.9 1911.9 '11cd
Clark F S BG 141 53 Fenwick 1940.10 1942.1 Ret BG Clark
Clark R CPT 43-W-2 1 Reeder 1979.7 1981.6 mfh
Clark H T 1LT 65-N 48 Ingalls 1913.12 1914.12 PhBk
Clark W L 1LT 64-S 22 Ruckman 1914.12 1915.12 '16cd
Clark T A 1LT 144-N-1 41-B Ingalls 1911.9 1912.6 CAS'12 '12cd
Clark CPT 18-W-2 29-B Bernard 1844.10 '44rq d-686
Clark T A 1LT 143-S-2 35-C Ingalls 1913.6 1914.6 '13cd '14PhBk
Clark M W GEN 119 33 Fenwick 1949.9 1952.6 usacc
Clarke F P BG 125 73 Ingalls 1973.8 1975.7 mfh
Clarke B C GEN 119 33 Fenwick 1958.7 1960.10 Ret GEN usacc
Clarke B C BG 125 73 Ingalls 1946.8 1948.1 Ret GEN usacc
Clarke C W Jr BG 127-W 145 Bernard 1970.12 1973.2 mfh
Clark P Jr COL 62-S 30 Ruckman 1953.8 1954.8 usacc
Clark W J Jr MAJ 147 147 Engr Ln 1955.8 1957.1 usacc
Clark P Jr COL 126-S 163 Bernard 1954.8 1960.8 usacc
Clark P Jr LTC 17-W-2 41-B Bernard 1946.1 1947.1 usacc
Clay C L LTC 70-S 89 Ingalls 1944 1945 '45 PhBk

Clay C L LTC 17-W-1 41-A Bernard 1952.1 1953.7 usacc
Clayman D C BG 158 32 Ingalls 1963.8 1965.6 mfh
Clayton C C COL 34-N-2 100 Ingalls 1969.12 1970.1 mfh
Clayton C C COL 3-S 167 Bernard 1970.1 1971.7 mfh
Cleary T J Jr COL 50-W 121 Bernard 1966.2 1967.7 mfh
Cleary T J Jr COL 43-E-2 7 Reeder 1965.2 1966.2 mfh
Cleland J M CPT 18-W-1 29-A Bernard 1942 1943 PhBk
Clement A W LTC 52-W-2 132 Ingalls 1943 1945 Wiley PhBks
Cleveland A C CPT 62-N 28 Ruckman 1923.8 1924.7 Higgins
Clinger C LTC 33-E-2 63 Fenwick 1981.7 1984.6 mfh
Cloke H E COL 120 37 Fenwick 1932.8 1935.7 Cochran +
Cloke H E COL 144-S-1 41-A Ingalls 1931.7 1932.4 '31cd
Cloke H E COL 141 53 Fenwick 1923 1924 Chapel JHC
Cloke H E COL 119 33 Fenwick 1932.4 1932.8 Cochran +
Coakley R J COL 129-N 103 Ingalls 1969.6 1970.11 mfh
Coates C E COL 65-S 46 Ingalls 1975.8 1978.6 mfh
Coates C E LTC 35-W-2 2 Reeder 1966.11 1967.7 mfh
Coates E A Jr MAJ 93 75 Ingalls 1931.8 1936.4 MedC Coates
Coates E A Jr MAJ 126-N 165 Bernard 1931.7 1931.8 MedC Coates
Coats W L LTC 51-S-1 120 Ingalls 1972.6 1974.5 mfh
Cocheu G W 1LT 129-S 101 Ingalls 1909.9 1910.9 CAS'10 '11cd
Cocheu G W LTC 141 53 Fenwick 1927 1928 '27cd
Cocheu G W 1LT 18-E-2 37-B Bernard 1906.9 1907.9 CAS'07
Cochran J H MAJ 103-S 63 Ingalls 1933.7 1936.8 Tilton JHC
Cochran J H MAJ 143-N-2 35-D Ingalls 1920.9 1922.7 JHC
Cochran A M LTC 44-S-2 102 Ingalls 1948.8 1950.8 usacc
Cochran C C CWO 167 A 7 Patch Road 1960.8 1962.11 mfh
Cochran H W MAJ 50-E 129 Bernard 1932.9 1936.5 Cochran
Cochran H W CPT 35-E-1 6 Reeder 1931.7 1932.8 Cochran
Cochran H W CPT 14 32 Ruckman 1924.9 1925.6 Cochran
Cochran H M III CPT 62-S 30 Ruckman 1932.8 1933.7 Bennett
Cochran H M III CPT 64-N 20 Ruckman 1930.6 1931.7 '31cd
Cochran H M III MAJ 70-S 89 Ingalls 1937.7 1938.6 '37cd
Cochran H M III MAJ 129-N 103 Ingalls 1938.6 1940.6 PhBk
Cocke J G COL 33-E-2 63 Fenwick 1949.8 1950.8 usacc
Cocke J G COL 127-W 145 Bernard 1958.7 1961.6 usacc
Cockill M COL 68-N 83 Ingalls 1980.8 1983.6 mfh
Cocroft R B COL 141 53 Fenwick 1939.8 1940.10 PhBk
Cocroft R B 1LT 17-E-1 47-A Bernard 1915.12 1916.12 CAS'16
Cocroft R B COL 121-W 41 Fenwick 1938.? 1939.8 PhBk
Coe F W CPT 62-S 30 Ruckman 1907.9 1909.10 '08-09cd
Coe F W MAJ 118 29 Fenwick 1909.11 1911.8 w
Coe J P Jr COL 50-W 121 Bernard 1969.8 1970.5 mfh
Coffey C F COL 54-N-1 138 Ingalls 1964.9 1965.4 mfh
Coffey C F COL 103-N 65 Ingalls 1965.4 1966.6 mfh
Coffin J S Mr 33 CGH 67 Fenwick 1875 'Til death Carpenter Granddaughter
Cogswell J K 1LT 50-E 129 Bernard 1919.6 1919.10 '19cd
Cohen J CPT 18-E-2 37-B Bernard 1943.3 1944.10 '43 PhBk
Coker S Y COL 126-S 163 Bernard 1965.8 1966.8 mfh
Colburn E COL 126-N 165 Bernard 1987.9 1983.7 mfh
Colby T L LTC 128 E 109 Bernard 1925.8 1927.8 MedC Putney
Cole P W COL 101-N 57 Ingalls 1941.7 1942.1 Cole
Cole D? M MAJ 143-N-2 35-D Ingalls 1929.8 1930.6 '30 AdvCs

Cole W E COL 118 29 Fenwick 1928.8 1930.8 Ret MG '29cd
Cole W E CPT 123-E 4 Ruckman 1910.9 1912.12 Ret MG CAS'11
Cole J? M CPT 64-N 20 Ruckman 1925 '25cd
Cole W LTC 143-N-1 35-B Ingalls 1977.9 1981.8 mfh
Cole W E COL 119 33 Fenwick 1920.9 1920.11 Ret MG w
Coleman B R 1LT 18-E-1 37-A Bernard 1916.12 1917.12 CAS'17 Ford
Coleman L CPT 127-W 145 Bernard 1912.7 1913.12 '13cd
Coleman L CPT 127-E 147 Bernard 1913.12 1914.12 PhBk
Colenso-Jones G M B LTC 34-S-2 94 Ingalls 1969.3 1970.6 mfh
Colladay E B MAJ 102-S 59 Ingalls 1928.7 1929.8 Ret BG Colladay
Colladay E B 2LT 17-W-2 41-B Bernard 1914.12 1915.9 Ret BG '15cd
Colley H G 1LT 17-E-1 47-A Bernard 1911.9 1912.9 NAdoc 335547
Collier J H BG 121-E 43 Fenwick 1951.9 1952.8 Ret LTG usacc
Collier SNCB 33 CGH 67 Fenwick 1957.10 1961.7 usacc USN
Collins R W CPT 69-N 87 Ingalls 1908.9 1909.9 '09cd
Collins G R COL 51-N-1 122 Ingalls 1967.6 1969.7 mfh
Collins C E MAJ 34-N-2 100 Ingalls 1972.9 1974.8 mfh
Collins F W COL 44-N-1 106 Ingalls 1960.4 1960.12 Ret BG usacc
Collins O G CPT 66-N 40 Ingalls 1911.9 1912.9 CAS'12 '12cd
Collins W R BG 121-W 41 Fenwick 1961.7 1964.1 mfh
Collins F W COL 79-N 95 Ingalls 1960.12 1963.5 Ret BG mfh
Colonna A F CPT 1 151 Bernard 1945.7 1946.6 Tilton
Colton R B MAJ 143-S-2 35-C Ingalls 1922.7 1923.12 Ret MG Colton
Colwell R C LTC 18-E-1 37-A Bernard 1970.1 1970.10 mfh
Comstock H E COL 158 32 Ingalls 1931.6 1933.6 deCamp JHC
Congden N A 2LT 17-W-1 41-A Bernard 1933.9 1935.9 Congden '33cd
Congdon N A 1LT 43-W-1 3 Reeder 1937.8 1938.10 Congdon
Congdon N A 2LT 63-N 24 Ruckman 1931.1 1932.3 Congdon
Conk R H COL 65-S 46 Ingalls 1957.4 1959.8 usacc
Conklin A S CPT 128-W 107 Bernard 1911.8 1912.12 '12cd
Conklin A S CPT 62-S 30 Ruckman 1889 1890 Gifford +
Conklin A S COL 120 37 Fenwick 1927.6 1928.6 '27cd
Conklin A S CPT 55 42 Ingalls 1907.9 1910.9 S&F Arthur
Conklin A S LT 64-N 20 Ruckman 1888 1889 c-25
Conley S G BG 123-W 2 Ruckman 1952.8 1952.9 Ret BG usacc
Conley S G BG 157 101 Bernard 1953.7 1955.11 Ret BG usacc
Conley S G BG 127-E 147 Bernard 1952.9 1953.7 Ret BG usacc
Conley S G COL 102-N 61 Ingalls 1946.9 1948.1 Ret BG usacc
Conlin C A 1LT 18-W-1 29-A Bernard 1940.6 1941 PhBk
Conn J L MAJ 43-W-2 1 Reeder 1971.11 1973.7 mfh
Conn J L COL 63-N 24 Ruckman 1973.8 1986.5 mfh
Connell R M BG 128-W 107 Bernard 1973.8 1974.8 Ret BG mfh
Connell R M CPT 19 18 Bernard 1921.9 1922.6 Ret BG CAS'22
Conner J A 61-S 43 Ingalls 1906 1908 QM Clk '08PhBk
Connerat W H COL 63-S 26 Ruckman 1961.11 1962.10 mfh
Connolly J C COL 68-N 83 Ingalls 1983.6 1985.7 mfh
Connolly H A COL 69-S 85 Ingalls 1957.3 1957.6 usacc
Connolly H A COL 52-E-1 128 Ingalls 1957.2 1957.3 usacc
Conroy R 1LT 156-N 181 Bernard 1919 '19cd rms?
Cook R L COL 65-N 48 Ingalls 1951.10 1953.5 Ret BG usacc
Cook R L COL 44-N-2 108 Ingalls 1950.7 1951.10 Ret BG usacc
Cook M R LTC 17-E-2 47-B Bernard 1985.7 1985.9 mfh
Cook T C MAJ 126-S 163 Bernard 1921.9 1922.6 '22FOcs

Cook H COL 157 101 Bernard 1977.10 1979.8 mfh
Cook L COL 67-S 34 Ingalls 1979.3 1980.9 mfh
Cook T C LTC 102-S 59 Ingalls 1929.8 1933.8 deCamp Blood
Cook T C 1LT 15-S 36 Ruckman 1915.12 1916.12 CAS'16
Cook F N CPT 70-N 91 Ingalls 1905.9 1906.9 b-26
Cooke T W COL 45-W-1 112 Ingalls 1954.9 1954.10 usacc
Cooke F N CPT 18-W-2 29-B Bernard 1911.9 1912.12 CAS'12 '12cd b-26
Cooke V R MAJ 65-N 48 Ingalls 1942.7 1944.6 PhBk
Cooke T W COL 50-W 121 Bernard 1954.10 1958.9 usacc
Cool H M 1LT 156-N 181 Bernard 1919 '19cd rms?
Coolen E A LTC 68-N 83 Ingalls 1961.8 1962.8 mfh
Cooper A J 1LT 52-E-2 126 Ingalls 1939.7 1940.7 PhBk Rumsey
Cooper D COL 45-W-1 112 Ingalls 1964.10 1965.6 mfh
Cooper H P 1LT 54-N-2 140 Ingalls 1936.8 1937.8 '37cd
Cooper A J MAJ 128-W 107 Bernard 1923.8 1924.8 S&F
Cooper A J Jr 1LT 17-W-1 41-A Bernard 1938.9 1939.7 CAS'39
Cooper H B Jr 1LT 44-N-2 108 Ingalls 1939.6 1940.6 '39cd
Copthorne W A MAJ 66-N 40 Ingalls 1921.8 1922.7 '22BtryOCs
Corbin C L 1LT 143-N-2 35-D Ingalls 1911.9 1912.9 CAS'12 12cd
Corbin C L 1LT 14 32 Ruckman 1912.9 1913.12 '13cd
Corbin F P Jr 1LT 45-W-2 110 Ingalls 1936.6 1937.7 Ret BG Corbin
Corbin F P Jr 1LT 45-E-1 114 Ingalls 1937.7 1939.6 Ret BG
Corbitt T R MAJ 18-E-1 37-A Bernard 1894.8 1987.8 mfh
Corbusier DR 68-S 81 Ingalls 1895 b-12
Corcoran E F COL 62-S 30 Ruckman 1974.9 1977.8 mfh
Cordell B E 1LT 69-N 87 Ingalls 1931.6 1932.8 '31cd
Cordell B E 1LT 16-W 51 Bernard 1927 1928 Tasker
Cordell B E COL 129-N 103 Ingalls 1947.7 1948.10 usacc
Cordell B E 1LT 45-W-2 110 Ingalls 1934.8 1935.7 Shaw
Corey R R COL 44-S-1 104 Ingalls 1962.8 1964.6 mfh
Corlett C R MAJ 129-S 101 Ingalls 1925.6 1927.6 Ret MG INF '26cd
Corley J T COL 15-S 36 Ruckman 1951.6 1953.8 Ret BG usacc
Corns J H MG 125 73 Ingalls 1985.6 1986.10 mfh
Corput R V D 1LT 79-S 93 Ingalls 1903.9 1904.9 CAS'04
Cory I W COL 143-N-2 35-D Ingalls 1951.8 1954.6 usacc
Costello N A COL 14 32 Ruckman 1950.3 1952.6 Ret MG usacc
Costello N A COL 54-N-2 140 Ingalls 1949.7 1950.3 Ret MG usacc
Cotter C E MAJ 144-S-2 41-C Ingalls 1930.7 1931.3 Smith Widow
Cotter C E MAJ 123-W 2 Ruckman 1934.8 1937.3 Daughter
Cotter C E MAJ 34-N-1 98 Ingalls 1933.6 1934.8 Widow
Cotton B 1LT 79-N 95 Ingalls 1906.9 1907.9 CAS'07
Cottrell J F 1LT 15-N 34 Ruckman 1915.12 1916.12 CAS'16
Cottrell J F LTC 101-S 55 Ingalls 1935.8 1939.12 Cottrell
Cottrell J F LTC 128-E 109 Bernard 1934.9 1935.8 Cottrell
Couch R B COL 54-S-2 134 Ingalls 1968.7 1969.5 mfh
Couch G R LTC 18-E-1 37-A Bernard 1957.4 1959.9 usacc
Coughlin J G COL 144-N-2 41-D Ingalls 1952.8 1954.6 usacc
Coughlin J G COL 50-E 129 Bernard 1954.6 1954.8 usacc
Council R L MAJ 17-E-1 47-A Bernard 1973.7 1974.7 mfh
Counihan T J COL 63-N 24 Ruckman 1956.6 1958.8 usacc
Courtney J CPT 3-S 167 Bernard 1917.12 1919.1 S&F Arthur
Courtney J CPT 148-S 7 Moat Walk 1919.1 1920 '19-20cd AN306
Cousland W C BG 1 151 Bernard 1980.11 1982.5 mfh

Covault M L COL 66-N 40 Ingalls 1986.11 1987.7 mfh
Coverdale C E LTC 44-N-1 106 Ingalls 1984.6 1986.5 mfh
Covington W A CPT 79-S 93 Ingalls 1909.9 1910.9 CAS'10
Covington B III COL 123-W 2 Ruckman 1986.2 mfh
Coward J M CPT 3-N 169 Bernard 1907 1910.9 '08-09cd
Coward J M CPT 102-N 61 Ingalls 1916.8 1917.12 '16-17cd
Coward J M CPT 103-S 63 Ingalls 1910.9 1911.9 CAS'10 '11-12cd
Cowen E G CPT 70-N 91 Ingalls 1928.8 1929.7 '29cd
Cowles D H COL 33-W-1 59 Fenwick 1964.7 1965.6 mfh
Cox R F MAJ 62-N 28 Ruckman 1931.1 1931.8 Ret BG Bennett
Cox R F COL 121-E 43 Fenwick 1936.5 1940.5 Ret BG PhBk
Cox R F 1LT 144-S-1 41-A Ingalls 1915.1 1915.10 Ret BG Cox
Cozantis E A COL 70-S 89 Ingalls 1986.5 1987.7 mfh
Crabill E B COL 33-E-1 61 Fenwick 1951.12 1951.12 usacc
Crabill E B COL 19 18 Bernard 1951.12 1953.8 usacc
Craft J C SM 64 71 Fenwick 1980.8 1983.7 mfh
Craig D E COL 69-S 85 Ingalls 1963.9 1965.11 mfh
Craig F S 1LT 3-N 169 Bernard 1920.8 1922.8 Taliaferro MedC
Craig M Jr COL 67-N 36 Ingalls 1950.12 1952.5 usacc
Craig M Jr COL 144-S-2 41-C Ingalls 1950.9 1950.12 usacc
Crain J K 1LT 18-W-2 29-B Bernard 1902 micro 617
Crain J K CPT 123-E 4 Ruckman 1914.12 1917.7 Ret MG JHC '16-17cd
Crain J K 1LT 18-E-2 37-B Bernard 1910.9 1911.9 Ret MG '11cd
Cralle M S COL 35-W-1 4 Reeder 1946.9 1947.10 usacc
Cralle M S Jr MAJ 44-N-1 106 Ingalls 1969.7 1973.7 mfh
Cramer R G LTC 143-N-2 35-D Ingalls 1966.3 1967.8 mfh
Cramer R V LTC 102-N 61 Ingalls 1934.6 1935.6 Cramer
Cramer R V MAJ 123-W 2 Ruckman 1925.9 1926.7 Cramer
Cramer R V LTC 103-S 63 Ingalls 1936.8 1938.6 Cramer PhBk
Cramer R V MAJ 50-E 129 Bernard 1922.9 1925.9 Cramer
Crandall R G LTC 17-W-1 41-A Bernard 1947.8 1948.5 usacc
Crandall H W COL 70-S 89 Ingalls 1946.9 1947.11 usacc
Crane I B COL 1 151 Bernard 1853.11 1855.6 CG Arthur
Crane F A CPT 17-W-1 41-A Bernard 1928.7 1930.12 '29cd
Crane F A MAJ 33-W-1 59 Fenwick 1930.12 1932.6 Dentist '31cd
Cranford T G Jr 1LT 18-W-1 29-A Bernard 1927.7 1928.7 Goff
Cravens R K 1LT 69-S 85 Ingalls 1904.9 1905.9 CAS'05
Crawford L C 1LT 62-S 30 Ruckman 1910.9 1912.9 '11cd
Crawford L S LTC 34-S-1 96 Ingalls 1963.12 1966.10 mfh
Crawford J L COL 128-W 107 Bernard 1953.8 1958.6 Ret BG usacc
Crawford G H 1LT 34-N-1 98 Ingalls 1938.8 1939.7 '39 cd
Crawford A M 1LT 149-N 11 Moat Walk 1917.6 1919.4 S&F Arthur '19cd
Crawford L C 1LT 17-E-1 47-A Bernard 1908.9 1909.9 '09cd
Crawford J B MAJ 143-N-1 35-B Ingalls 1924.8 1925.7 Ret BG '25AdvCs
Crawford J B COL 44-N-2 108 Ingalls 1951.11 1952.5 Ret BG usacc
Crea R D CPT 16-E 53 Bernard 1949.10 1950.2 usacc
Crescioni C R 44-S-2 102 Ingalls 1984.6 1984.11 mfh
Crichlow R W Jr CPT 44-N-2 108 Ingalls 1932.7 1936.8 Ret MG
Crichlow R W Jr LTC 66-S 38 Ingalls 1940.3 1942.5 Chrichlow
Crim H C 1LT 16-E 53 Bernard 1921.10 1922.8
Crimm P D MAJ 34-S-2 94 Ingalls 1963.1 1964.8 mfh
Crisp F W 1LT 3-N 169 Bernard 1922.8 1924.6 '23cd AN306
Crissy M S 1LT 18-W-1 29-A Bernard 1908.9 1909.9 '09cd

Crocker G MAJ 50 A 125 Bernard 1979.7 1981.8 mfh
Croft N A C COL 45-W-2 110 Ingalls 1952.9 1954.9 usacc
Cronkhite A BG 119 33 Fenwick 1919.9 1920.9 Ret MG w
Cronkhite A CPT 3-S 167 Bernard 1899 1900 Ret MG '00cd
Cronkhite A LT 17-W-1 41-A Bernard 1886.9 1888.6 c-27
Crosby R D COL 70-N 91 Ingalls 1962.7 1966.6 mfh
Crosby R D COL 51-S-1 120 Ingalls 1961.1 1962.7 mfh
Crosby G D COL 35-E-2 8 Reeder 1947.10 1950.8 usacc
Cross COL 128-E 109 Bernard 1976.7 1980.7 mfh
Cross M A LTC 101-S 55 Ingalls 1928.7 1929.8 '29cd
Crowell E R CPT 16-E 53 Bernard 1924.8 1925.5 Ret BG Crowell
Crowell M MG 118 29 Fenwick 1977.9 1981.8 mfh
Crowell E R CPT 67-S 34 Ingalls 1925.5 1926.5 Ret BG Crowell
Crowley J B MAJ 144-S-1 41-A Ingalls 1984.6 1986.6 mfh
Crowley A F Jr MAJ 44-N-2 108 Ingalls 1971.1 1973.2 mfh
Crumley D LTC 16-W 53 Bernard 1980.7 1981.7 mfh
Crump I A MAJ 123-E 4 Ruckman 1932.6 1934.8 JHC '33cd
Cruzan W V COL 143-S-1 35-A Ingalls 1965.11 1967.10 mfh
Cruz-Santiago F SGM 35-E-2 8 Reeder 1982.6 1985.6 mfh
Cullen E J 1LT 143-N-2 35-D Ingalls 1910.9 1911.9 '11cd
Cullen E J MAJ 102-S 59 Ingalls 1924.8 1927.7 '25cd
Cullen E J CPT 124-N 69 Ingalls 1919.6 1920.7 '20cd
Cullis R E COL 33-W-1 59 Fenwick 1965.6 1965.12 mfh
Culp C R MAJ 17-W-2 41-B Bernard 1973.11 1976.6 mfh
Culpepper W S MAJ 128-E 109 Bernard 1930.6 1934.8 Coates '33cd
Culton W H COL 127-W 145 Bernard 1973.8 1975.8 mfh
Cummings E A LTC 43-W-2 1 Reeder 1947.2 1947.8 usacc
Cummings J W MAJ 35-W-2 2 Reeder 1973.10 1976.7 mfh
Cummings S F Jr COL 52-W-2 132 Ingalls 1958.9 1961.9 usacc
Cummings S F Jr LTC 45-E-2 116 Ingalls 1950.10 1951.8 usacc
Cummins A S MAJ 66-S 38 Ingalls 1902.8 1903.8 c-4 b-21
Cummins A S CPT 50-E 129 Bernard 1898.3 1902.7 '02cd
Cummins A S MAJ 1 151 Bernard 1904.1 1904.2 w
Cumpson G J MAJ 17-E-2 47-B Bernard 1979.6 1981.1 mfh
Cunningham W C 1LT 67-S 34 Ingalls 1918 1919 BOQ WWI '19cd
Cunningham F J MAJ 121-W 41 Fenwick 1928.7 1931.6 '29cd
Cunningham J H MAJ 127-W 145 Bernard 1923.9 1924.6 Ret BG Widow
Currier W P 1LT 17-E-1 47-A Bernard 1912.12 1913.12 '13cd
Curtis W J COL 144-S-1 41-A Ingalls 1964.7 1966.6 mfh
Curtis LT 18-W-1 29-A Bernard 1890 1892 d-691
Cuttino P LTC 35-W-1 4 Reeder 1976.9 1979.7 mfh
Cygon J R 1LT 64-N 20 Ruckman 1916.12 1917.12 Ford
Cygon J R 2LT 17-W-1 41-A Bernard 1912.1 1912.4 Ford '12cd
Dabney J A MG 1 151 Bernard 1957.7 1958.7 Ret LTG usacc
Dadd M W CPT 51-N-2 124 Ingalls 1944.8 1945.4 Dadd PhBks
Dahl F J MAJ 144-S-1 41-A Ingalls 1970.9 1972.6 mfh
Dahlquist J E GEN 119 33 Fenwick 1953.7 1956.2 usacc
Dailey B C CPT 43-W-1 3 Reeder 1931.7 1932.7 deCamp
Dailey B C 1LT 67-S 34 Ingalls 1919.2 1919.10 AN306 '19cd
Daknis W R COL 79-N 95 Ingalls 1984.7 1986.7 mfh
Dale J W COL 35-E-2 8 Reeder 1966.7 1968.7 mfh
Dale J W COL 66-N 40 Ingalls 1968.7 1969.5 mfh
Daley J P LTG 142 51 Fenwick 1961.10 1962.6 mfh

Dana N G CPT 18-E-1 37-A Bernard 1826.5 1828.3 '25-28cd rms?
Daniels P B LTC 35-E-2 8 Reeder 1957.3 1960.6 usacc
Dans H C CPT 61-S 43 Ingalls 1902 b-19
Darneille J F 2LT 130-N 24 Tidball 1917.6 1918.3 S&F Arthur
Darnell R J COL 143-N-2 35-D Ingalls 1961.6 1962.7 mfh
Darnell L J MAJ 16-W 53 Bernard 1983.6 1984.6 mfh
Darrah J T 1LT 18-E-1 37-A Bernard 1935.6 1936.9 Darrah
Darrah J T 1LT 35-E-1 6 Reeder 1936.9 1937.6 Darrah
Darrah J T LTC 50 A 125 Bernard 1948.7 1948.10 usacc
Darrah J W Jr COL 146 146 Engr Ln 1957.8 1961.11 usaccc
Dasher C L Jr COL 69-N 87 Ingalls 1950.10 1951.10 usacc
Daugherity R D MAJ 50-W 121 Bernard 1938.7 1938.12 Daugherity
Daugherity R D LTC 127-E 147 Bernard 1938.12 1940.6 PhBk
Daugherty J B COL 14 32 Ruckman 1948.3 1950.3 usacc
Daum G H 1LT 16-E 53 Bernard 1941.1 1942.4 Chapel Records
Davenport LT 17-W-1 41-A Bernard 1885.4 1886.9 c-691
Davenport J D COL 18-E-1 37-A Bernard 1966.1 1967.6 mfh
Davidson C H LTC 54-S-1 136 Ingalls 1953.7 1954.9 usacc
Davies F J COL 44-N-1 106 Ingalls 1967.11 1968.2 mfh
Davies F J COL 15-N 34 Ruckman 1968.2 1968.10 mfh
D'Avignon G C MAJ 18-W-1 29-A Bernard 1972.7 1973.4 mfh
Davis K L LTC 16-E 53 Bernard 1947.6 1948.11 Ret MG usacc
Davis LT 3-S 167 Bernard 1895 b-12
Davis W V 1LT 18-E-2 37-B Bernard 1933.8 1934.7 '34BtryOCs
Davis L L CPT 15-S 36 Ruckman 1930.8 1931.8 Ret BG '31cd
Davis A C SGT 61-S 43 Ingalls 1916 1917 '16-17cd
Davis W V CPT 35-W-2 2 Reeder 1939.7 1940.11 PhBks
Davis P H LTC 51-N-1 122 Ingalls 1969.8 1970.12 Chaplain mfh
Davis W V CPT 144-N-2 41-D Ingalls 1936.8 1937.8 Shepherd
Davis L L CPT 44-N-1 106 Ingalls 1932.8 1936.6 Ret BG Davis
Davis P H LTC 16-E 53 Bernard 1970.12 1972.7 Chaplain mfh
Davis J M K CPT 18-W-2 29-B Bernard 1886.6 1891.1 S&F c-27
Davis H BG 121-W 41 Fenwick 1980.8 1982.5 mfh
Davis R P MAJ 141 53 Fenwick 1910.1 1911.9 Ret MG '11cd
Davis H V CPT 63-N 24 Ruckman 1944 1945 PhBk
Davis J W MAJ 34-S-1 96 Ingalls 1981.6 1984.4 mfh
Davis E CPT 3-N 169 Bernard 1892 d-613
Davis R P COL 119 33 Fenwick 1920.11 1922.12 Ret MG w
Davis W COL 128-W 107 Bernard 1980.8 1893.4 mfh
Davis E LTC 144-S-2 41-C Ingalls 1981.5 1983.6 mfh
Davis J W COL 15-N 34 Ruckman 1946.8 1948.7 usacc
Davis K L LTC 45-E-1 114 Ingalls 1948.11 1949.12 Ret MG usacc
Davis H C CPT 67-S 34 Ingalls 1900.8 1903.9 S&F '03cd
Davis J C CPT 64-S 22 Ruckman 1918 '19cd
Davis J W 2LT 17-W-2 41-B Bernard 1931.9 1932.8 '31cd
Davis C E COL 3-S 167 Bernard 1972.6 1973.10 mfh
Davis W C CPT 121-E 43 Fenwick 1907.6 1909.9 '08cd
Davis H CPT 16-E 53 Bernard 1902 c-46
Davis R P MAJ 93 75 Ingalls 1908 1910 Ret MG '10cd
Davis H C Jr 2LT 16-E 53 Bernard 1912.1 1912.4 '12cd
Davis J W Jr LTC 34-N-2 100 Ingalls 1971.8 1972.6 mfh
Dawe G 1LT 79-S 93 Ingalls 1918 1919 BOQ WWI '19cd
Day J B CPT 17-E-2 47-B Bernard 1922.6 1923.8 Cary '23cd

Day S A COL 62-N 28 Ruckman 1972.6 1973.5 mfh
Day W E LTC 44-S-1 104 Ingalls 1950.11 1954.5 usacc
Day F E MAJ 33-E-2 63 Fenwick 1941.5 1942.3 Day
Day F E LTC 51-S-1 120 Ingalls 1949.9 1950.5 usacc
Day W E LTC 18-E-1 37-A Bernard 1946.10 1947.10 usacc
Day F E CPT 144-N-1 41-B Ingalls 1937.9 1938.6 Day '37cd
Day F L COL 15-N 34 Ruckman 1984.11 1985.9 mfh
Day F E COL 33-E-1 61 Fenwick 1955.8 1957.6 usacc
Day F E LTC 34-N-2 100 Ingalls 1945.10 1946.6 Day
DeBord N D COL 70-S 89 Ingalls 1972.6 1974.8 mfh
DeCamp J G CPT 43-E-1 5 Reeder 1931.8 1936.6 deCamp
DeCarre O MAJ 67-N 36 Ingalls 1921.8 1924.7 '23cd Btry + AdvCs
DeCesare A G MAJ 45-E-1 114 Ingalls 1975.8 1979.6 mfh
Decker S M 2LT 17-W-2 41-B Bernard 1915.9 1916.9 Aurand
DeFaye T LTC 68-N 83 Ingalls 1959.8 1961.7 usacc
DeGavre C B BG 125 73 Ingalls 1961.7 1963.8 mfh Ret BG?
Deichelman M K 1LT 35-W-1 4 Reeder 1937.8 1938.8 Ret MG '37cd
Delamater B F III COL 18-W-2 29-B Bernard 1963.11 1966.7 mfh
Delaney J C 1LT 63-N 24 Ruckman 1928.8 1929.7 '29cd
Delaney M A MAJ 14 32 Ruckman 1902 1902.9 '02cd
Delano F G CPT 103-N 65 Ingalls 1919.9 1921.8 '20cd
DeLong J C CPT 66-N 40 Ingalls 1920.6 1921.8 '20cd
Demerritt R E LTC 51-S-2 118 Ingalls 1940.10 1941.1 Demerritt
Demerritt R E LTC 128-E 109 Bernard 1941.1 1942.5 Demerritt +
DeMilt I F COL 51-N-2 124 Ingalls 1966.11 1967.11 mfh
Dengler F L CPT 102-N 61 Ingalls 1909.9 1910.8 CAS'10
Denholm C J MAJ 68-N 83 Ingalls 1935.2 1938.12 Dentist Denholm
Dennen W L COL 102-S 59 Ingalls 1941.9 1943.1 Dennen AN306
Dennis L C COL 120 37 Fenwick 1943.6 1945.9 PhBk
Dennis L C LTC 128-W 107 Bernard 1938.8 1942.6 PhBk
Dennis E B CPT 1 151 Bernard 1919 1920 '20cd
Dennis L C CPT 54-S-1 136 Ingalls 1932.7 1934.7 '33cd
Dennis L F CPT 102-N 61 Ingalls 1918 1919 BOQ WWI '19cd
Dennis L C COL 121-W 41 Fenwick 1942.6 1943.6 Dennis
DePuy W E GEN 119 33 Fenwick 1973.6 1977.6 mfh Ret GEN
DeRamus T B COL 129-S 101 Ingalls 1972.7 1973.6 mfh
DeRussy R E LTC 1 151 Bernard 1838.11 1841.9 w
DeRussy G A MAJ 18-E-1 37-A Bernard 1871.3 1874.5 S&F c-27
DeSantis J A LTC 16-E 53 Bernard 1966.1 1967.10 mfh
DeSaussure E H Jr MAJ 33-E-1 61 Fenwick 1946.9 1947.6 Ret MG usacc
DeSombre W E CPT 65-S 46 Ingalls 1911.9 1912.9 '12cd
Detrich V COL 103-S 63 Ingalls 1981.3 1982.12 mfh
Detwiler H P CPT 50-W 121 Bernard 1930.4 1930.9 Detwiler
Detwiler H P CPT 16-W 51 Bernard 1921 1923 Detwiler
Detwiler H P CPT 143-S-1 35-A Ingalls 1931.8 1935.7 Detwiler '35cd
DeValin H DR 64 71 Fenwick 1924 1927 Hartel MedC
Devanny W G COL 101-N 57 Ingalls 1973.5 1973.8 Chaplain mfh
Devens W G 1LT 54-S-1 136 Ingalls 1934.7 1935.7 Devens
Devereaux R A LTC 34-N-2 100 Ingalls 1970.1 1971.7 mfh
Devers J L GEN 119 33 Fenwick 1946.9 1949.9 Devers Ret GEN
Devine H BG 43-W-1 3 Reeder 1964.7 1964.8 mfh Ret BG
Devine J G CPT 52-E-1 128 Ingalls 1931.9 1932.9 Ret BG deCamp
Devine J H MG 118 29 Fenwick 1948.1 1949.1 usacc

Devine P H BG 125 73 Ingalls 1964.8 1966.6 mfh Ret BG
DeVoe R G COL 125 73 Ingalls 1939.6 1940.11 Ret BG PhBk
Devolites M C COL 65-N 48 Ingalls 1966.7 1969.7 mfh
Devolites M C COL 54-S-1 136 Ingalls 1965.8 1966.7 mfh
Devore J CW4 144-S-2 41-C Ingalls 1977.4 1981.5 mfh
DeVore J L 2LT 17-W-2 41-B Bernard 1943.6 1944.1 PhBk
Dewitt J L COL 43-E-1 5 Reeder 1949.10 1954.6 usacc
Dice J B F 1LT 43-E-2 7 Reeder 1936.8 1937.7 Taber Roy
DiCillo F Jr COL 158 32 Ingalls 1975.9 1978.6 mfh
Dickens R C BG 146 146 Engr Ln 1963.9 1964.3 Ret BG mfh
Dickens R C COL 15-S 36 Ruckman 1961.8 1963.9 Ret BG mfh
Dickerson G W BG 118 29 Fenwick 1967.9 1968.12 mfh Ret BG
Dickie R L COL 51-N-1 122 Ingalls 1954.8 1956.9 usacc
Dickson R MAJ 17-W-1 41-A Bernard 1976.2 1977.11 mfh
Diehl W MAJ 33-E-2 63 Fenwick 1979.3 1981.7 mfh
Dierauf F Jr COL 129-N 103 Ingalls 1970.12 1972.6 mfh
Dierickx J COL 127-E 147 Bernard 1981.6 1984.5 mfh
Diestel C J LTC 52-E-2 126 Ingalls 1948.8 1950.6 usacc
Diestel C J 1LT 43-W-1 3 Reeder 1939.6 1940.6 Diestel
Diez E S LTC 50-A 125 Bernard 1973.8 1975.7 mfh
Diez E COL 143-N-2 35-D Ingalls 1976.9 1977.8 mfh
Diez E COL 102-N 61 Ingalls 1977.8 1980.6 mfh
DiFronzo A T CWO 147 147 Engr Ln 1959.6 1962.12 mfh
Dillinger Jr COL 33-E-2 63 Fenwick 1956.5 1957.12 usacc
Dillon G M 1LT 16-E 53 Bernard 1944.11 1946.10 PhBk usacc
Dimick J COL 1 151 Bernard 1859.11 1861.10 CO Arthur
Dingeman R E CPT 64-N 20 Ruckman 1937 '37cd
Dingeman G R COL 101-S 55 Ingalls 1968.6 1970.7 mfh
Dingeman R E COL 118 29 Fenwick 1945.7 1946.8 Dingeman
Dingeman R E COL 55 42 Ingalls 1944.12 1945.7 Dingeman
Dingley N III CPT 66-S 38 Ingalls 1922.8 1923.7 Journal Ed.
Dingley N III MAJ 126-N 165 Bernard 1933.1 1934.7 Dingley
Dirska J D MAJ 35-W-1 4 Reeder 1974.10 1976.7 mfh
Dishman S B LTC 33-W-2 57 Fenwick 1950.1 1952.7 usacc
Dishman B LTC 43-W-2 1 Reeder 1978.8 1979.7 mfh
Disney C A COL 17-W-2 41-B Bernard 1947.8 1947.8 usacc
Disney C A COL 52-W-1 130 Ingalls 1947.8 1948.12 usacc
Disney C A COL 67-S 34 Ingalls 1948.12 1950.6 usacc
Dix J A COL 70-S 89 Ingalls 1964.6 1968.12 mfh
Dix J A COL 144-S-1 41-A Ingalls 1962.7 1964.6 mfh
Dix J A MG 1 151 Bernard 1862.6 1863.7 CG w
Dixon O O COL 63-S 26 Ruckman 1960.7 1961.11 usacc
Dixon O H Jr LTC 123-W 2 Ruckman 1940.7 1942.1 Vet PhBks
Doan L L COL 52-E-1 128 Ingalls 1946.7 1948.8 Ret MG usacc
Doan L L MG 120 37 Fenwick 1955.1 1958.5 usacc
Doan L L MG 141 53 Fenwick 1960.11 1961.10 usacc
Dockler C J MAJ 129-S 101 Ingalls 1939.6 1940.9 PhBk
Dodge R T COL 70-S 89 Ingalls 1962.2 1964.6 Ret BG mfh
Dodge R T COL 52-W-2 132 Ingalls 1961.9 1962.2 Ret BG PhBk
Dodson R S 1LT 63-N 24 Ruckman 1914.12 1915.12 '16cd
Dodson M B COL 3-N 169 Bernard 1955.11 1958.1 usacc
Doherty H A COL 66-S 38 Ingalls 1947.6 1947.9 usacc
Doherty H A COL 144-N-2 41-D Ingalls 1946.10 1947.6 usacc

Dolph E A 1LT 65-N 48 Ingalls 1919.5 1920.8 CAS'20
Dolph E A 1LT 43-E-1 5 Reeder 1930.12 1931.8 '31cd
Donaldson W H CPT 17-E-1 47-A Bernard 1926.6 1929.8 Ret BG Bennett
Doney C S MAJ 65-N 48 Ingalls 1930.8 1931.7 '31cd
Donnelly A P COL 43-W-2 1 Reeder 1965.4 1966.7 Chaplain mfh
Donnelly W M MAJ 127-E 147 Bernard 1920.9 1921.9 '20cd
Donnely I W 1LT 70-S 89 Ingalls 1918 1919 BOQ WWI '19cd
Donohue C F 2LT 64-N 20 Ruckman 1903 1904.4 b-23
Donovan R MAJ 103-S 63 Ingalls 1922.6 1925.6 Ret LTG '23cd
Donovan C F MAJ 51-S-2 118 Ingalls 1974.9 1977.5 mfh
Doores W R 1LT 63-N 24 Ruckman 1902 c-46 b-19
Dore B C Mr 61-N 45 Ingalls 1946.8 1955.11 usacc
Dorman J R LTC 51-N-2 124 Ingalls 1955.12 1958.6 usacc
D'Orsa C S LTC 17-W-2 41-B Bernard 1949.10 1950.9 usacc
Dorschler R K LTC 3-S 167 Bernard 1973.12 1976.2 mfh
Dougan R C COL 103-S 63 Ingalls 1962.7 1963.11 mfh
Douglas H A MAJ 34-N-1 98 Ingalls 1972.7 1973.7 mfh
Dovell C E COL 69-N 87 Ingalls 1951.10 1953.9 usacc
Dovell C E CPT 70-S 89 Ingalls 1925.6 1929.6 '25-29cd
Dowd W S 1LT 69-S 85 Ingalls 1913.12 1914.12 CAS'14 PhBk
Dowles M A COL 123-E 4 Ruckman 1947.11 1951.6 Ret BG usacc
Downey W G COL 33-E-2 63 Fenwick 1965.10 1967.8 mfh
Doyal D A LTC 43-E-1 5 Reeder 1967.7 1968.3 mfh
Doyle F C CPT 67-S 34 Ingalls 1906.9 1907.9 CAS'07
Doyle P V 1LT 63-S 26 Ruckman 1938.8 1939.8 Ogden
Dragotta H A COL 62-N 28 Ruckman 1969.8 1972.5 mfh
Dramis G LTC 128-W 107 Bernard 1979.6 1980.8 mfh
Dranis G LTC 54-S-1 136 Ingalls 1977.10 1979.7 mfh
Dressler C B Mr 61-N 45 Ingalls 1912 1943.7 Fire Chief PhBk
Drewery G H 1LT 17-E-2 47-B Bernard 1917.9 1918.1 Ret BG
Drewery G H CPT 158 32 Ingalls 1921.4 1921.9 Ret BG Drewery
Driscoll W COL 123-E 4 Ruckman 1983.4 1986.1 mfh
Driver MAJ 50-A 125 Bernard 1949.4 1949.11 usacc
Drozd W M COL 64 71 Fenwick 1973.7 1975.1 mfh
Drummond J E BG 121-W 41 Fenwick 1982.6 1983.7 mfh
Dubois B S MAJ 102-N 61 Ingalls 1928.6 1931.6 '29cd
Dudley J E 1LT 18-W-2 29-B Bernard 1941.11 1942.8 '40-41 PhBks
Dudley J H COL 34-N-1 98 Ingalls 1946.10 1947.9 Ret BG usacc
Duff C B 1LT 43-W-2 1 Reeder 1939.6 1941.7 Ret LTG PhBks
Duke R W BG 127-W 145 Bernard 1967.1 1967.11 mfh Ret BG
Dukes H BG 121-W 41 Fenwick 1977.8 1979.9 mfh
Duncan G T MG 120 37 Fenwick 1962.6 1964.9 mfh Ret MG
Duncan G T MG 142 51 Fenwick 1964.9 1966.4 mfh Ret MG
Duncan G LTC 54-N-1 138 Ingalls 1977.9 1980.5 mfh
Duncan T 2LT 64-N 20 Ruckman 1906 '06cd
Dunham C E 1LT 35-E-1 6 Reeder 1934.9 1935.6 Ward deCamp
Dunham W H Jr 1LT 3-N 169 Bernard 1933.6 1935.6 Dunham
Dunkerley R P CPT 54-S-2 134 Ingalls 1942.6 1943 '43 PhBk
Dunlop J E Jr MAJ 144-S-2 41-C Ingalls 1971.10 1973.11 mfh
Dunn C G 1LT 17-E-2 47-B Bernard 1934.6 1935.6 Ret BG Dunn
Dunn C G 1LT 43-E-1 5 Reeder 1938.6 1939.6 Ret BG '39cd
Dunn J M LTC 102-N 61 Ingalls 1920.8 1921.6 '21FOcs
Dunne M F 1LT 17-E-2 47-B Bernard 1919 '19cd

Dunning J MAJ 44-S-1 104 Ingalls 1978.7 1981.5 mfh
Dunwoody H 1LT 16-W 51 Bernard 1906.9 1908 '08cd b-26
DuParc J M MAJ 43-W-2 1 Reeder 1943.6 1945.5 DuParc PhBks
Dupuy H H CWO 61-N 45 Ingalls 1956.1 1958.11 usacc
Duquemin G J BG 121-E 43 Fenwick 1971.12 1972.12 Ret MG mfh
Duquemin G J BG 52-E-2 126 Ingalls 1971.9 1971.12 Ret MG mfh
Durham J T COL 143-S-2 35-C Ingalls 1965.12 1967.8 mfh
Dusenbury J S 1LT 63-S 26 Ruckman 1907.9 1908.9 '08cd
Dutton S T CPT 3-S 167 Bernard 1901 1902.7 '02cd
Dutton D L CPT 102-N 61 Ingalls 1918 1919 BOQ WWI '19cd
Dutton D L CPT 69-N 87 Ingalls 1922.7 1927.4 Dutton
Duval D F COL 125 73 Ingalls 1929.6 1935.6 MedC '33cd
Duvall E W COL 35-W-1 4 Reeder 1955.3 1957.6 usacc
Duvall LT 69-N 87 Ingalls 1895 b-12
Dwyer T F CPT 66-N 40 Ingalls 1906.5 1906.9 CAS'06 b-26
Dwyer T F CPT 67-N 36 Ingalls 1908.9 1909.9 '09cd
Dye T A LTC 43-W-1 3 Reeder 1965.11 1968.8 mfh
Dye J C MAJ 70-N 91 Ingalls 1935.9 1937.8 MedC Coates
Dyer H A CPT 102-N 61 Ingalls 1918 1919 BOQ WWI '19cd
Dyment W L Jr COL 68-S 81 Ingalls 1975.8 1979.3 mfh
Earl R W 1LT 70-S 89 Ingalls 1918 1919 BOQ WWI '19cd
Earnest C T LTC 17-W-2 41-B Bernard 1968.12 1970.5 mfh
Earnest H L MG 118 29 Fenwick 1946.9 1947.9 usacc
Eason J F COL 126-N 165 Bernard 1961.3 1965.5 mfh
Easterbrook E P COL 121-E 43 Fenwick 1923.9 1926.10 Ret MG Chaplain
Eastman 1LT 63-S 26 Ruckman 1890 1892 c-26
Eastman W R MAJ 14 32 Ruckman 1923.6 1924.7 MedC Putney
Easton W G COL 45-W-2 110 Ingalls 1963.7 1964.3 mfh
Easton W G COL 127-W 145 Bernard 1964.3 1966.8 mfh
Eastwold O A 1LT 62-N 28 Ruckman 1916.12 1917.12 Ford
Eaves J CPT 43-W-1 3 Reeder 1979.9 1980.3 mfh
Ebel H W 1LT 1 151 Bernard 1939 1940 PhBk
Ebesugawa L I LTC 17-W-2 41-B Bernard 1970.5 1971.1 mfh
Ebey F L 1LT 45-E-2 116 Ingalls 1938.6 1939.6 '39PhBk
Echols L LTC 18-E-1 37-A Bernard 1950.4 1951.10 usacc
Eckert E N COL 65-N 48 Ingalls 1973.6 1974.10 mfh
Eckert E N CPT 35-E-1 6 Reeder 1963.2 1963.2 mfh
Eckert J P COL 127-W 145 Bernard 1948.7 1953.8 usacc
Eddy R C 1LT 144-S-2 41-C Ingalls 1910.8 1911.8 '11cd
Eddy R C 1LT 15-N 34 Ruckman 1907.9 1908.9 '08cd rms
Eddy R C MAJ 123-W 2 Ruckman 1921.9 1922.6 '22FOcs
Eddy R N LTC 144-N-1 41-B Ingalls 1962.9 1964.6 mfh
Edelstein R B CPT 68-N 83 Ingalls 1944.7 1945.1 PhBk
Edelstein R B CPT 45-W-1 112 Ingalls 1945.1 1946.9 '45PhBk
Eder F M MAJ 127-W 145 Bernard 1943.9 1944.9 PhBk
Eder F M MAJ 33-W-2 57 Fenwick 1944.9 1946.6 Eder PhBk
Edgecomb F E MAJ 144-S-1 41-A Ingalls 1935.7 1941.3 '37-41PhBk
Edger B J Jr 1LT 62-N 28 Ruckman 1900 1902 '00cd
Edmonds M MG 158 32 Ingalls 1981.9 1985.6 mfh
Edmunds J M COL 62-N 28 Ruckman 1966.8 1969.7 mfh
Edmunds J D LTC 35-W-2 2 Reeder 1952.8 1955.8 usacc
Edson H D LTC 44-S-1 104 Ingalls 1948.10 1950.9 Ret BG usacc
Edwards N B COL 35-W-2 2 Reeder 1946.8 1948.1 Ret MG usacc

Edwards C V 1LT 17-E-1 47-A Bernard 1916.12 1918.10 Ford CAS'17
Edwards F B CPT 66-N 40 Ingalls 1906.9 1907.9 CAS'07
Edwards C V MAJ 126-N 165 Bernard 1918.10 1919.2 '19cd
Edwards W B COL 128-E 109 Bernard 1965.8 1968.3 mfh
Edwards R O 1LT 55 42 Ingalls 1912.12 1913.12 '13cd
Edwards A 1LT 68-S 81 Ingalls 1916.12 1917.12 Ford
Edwards D L COL 64 71 Fenwick 1964.8 1965.11 mfh
Edwards B E LTC 18-E-1 37-A Bernard 1953.7 1955.10 usacc
Edwards H COL 103-N 65 Ingalls 1946.8 1947.4 usacc
Edwards W B COL 34-N-2 100 Ingalls 1965.7 1965.7 mfh
Edwards J S COL 70-S 89 Ingalls 1976.3 1977.12 mfh
Edwards B E LTC 17-E-2 47-B Bernard 1952.8 1953.7 usacc
Edwards L S LTC 65-N 48 Ingalls 1920.9 1921.8 CAS'21
Egbert G L Jr COL 65-N 48 Ingalls 1974.11 1977.7 mfh
Eglin H W T 1LT 143-S-1 35-A Ingalls 1913.12 1914.12 CAS'14
Ehlen E S 1LT 34-S-2 94 Ingalls 1938.9 1939.9 INF Ehlen PhBk
Ehrgood J CSM 33-E-1 61 Fenwick 1978.7 1981.12 mfh
Ehrlich A COL 15-N 34 Ruckman 1982.7 1984.10 mfh
Ekman W E COL 129-N 103 Ingalls 1960.8 1961.11 Ret BG usacc
Elder S S MAJ 17-W-1 41-A Bernard 1869.8 1885.4 S&F c-27
Elders B C WO 50 A 125 Bernard 1934.7 1939.7 '37cd
Elges C H Jr COL 68-N 83 Ingalls 1962.9 1965.8 mfh
Elges C H Jr COL 51-N-2 124 Ingalls 1962.8 1962.9 mfh
Elias P 1LT 34-S-2 94 Ingalls 1935.9 1936.6 Elias
Eller H B MAJ 52-E-1 128 Ingalls 1944 1945 '44-45PhBk
Ellerson G E COL 19 18 Bernard 1956.4 1959.7 usacc
Ellerson G E COL 35-E-1 6 Reeder 1955.6 1956.4 usacc
Ellerthorpe D S CPT 63-S 26 Ruckman 1936.8 1937.7 Kimmer
Ellicott B R 1LT 14 32 Ruckman 1898 1899 QMC Micro
Ellicott R M 2LT 69-N 87 Ingalls 1900.9 1902.5 S&F Arthur
Elliott R COL 69-N 87 Ingalls 1980.8 1980.12 mfh
Elliott W S LTC 68-N 83 Ingalls 1939.1 1942.8 Lewis PhBk
Elliott E 1LT 3-N 169 Bernard 1930.8 1932.6 '31cd
Elliott E H MAJ 55 42 Ingalls 1940.6 1942.3 PhBk
Elliott C B Jr COL 51-N-1 122 Ingalls 1956.10 1956.12 usacc
Elliott C B Jr COL 14 32 Ruckman 1956.12 1959.3 usacc
Ellis W R 1LT 68-N 83 Ingalls 1928.8 1929.7 '29cd
Ellis R I MAJ 16-W 51 Bernard 1970.8 1971.4 mfh
Ellis W F LTC 35-E-2 8 Reeder 1939.9 1944.2 Ellis PhBks
Ellis H E 1LT 143-N-1 35-B Ingalls 1916.12 1917.6 CAS'17 Ford
Ellis W R CPT 65-N 48 Ingalls 1929.8 1930.7 '31cd
Ellis W H N LTC 52-E-2 126 Ingalls 1969.4 1970.7 mfh
Ellis H P 1LT 16-E 53 Bernard 1923 1924
Ellis R T COL 158 32 Ingalls 1927.6 1929.6 '27-29cd
Ellison B R CW3 43-E-1 5 Reeder 1982.7 1984.9 mfh
Elmore D G MAJ 33-W-2 57 Fenwick 1975.11 1979.1 mfh
Elmore S R Jr LTC 34-N-1 98 Ingalls 1971.6 1972.6 mfh
Ely L B COL 128-E 109 Bernard 1947.1 1949.10 usacc
Ely L B COL 79-N 95 Ingalls 1946.12 1947.1 usacc
Ely E B COL 123-E 4 Ruckman 1946.9 1947.11 usacc
Embick S D 1LT 63-S 26 Ruckman 1902.9 1903.3 Ret LTG CAS'03
Embick S D CPT 66-N 40 Ingalls 1903.3 1906.5 S&F '06cd
Embick S D BG 119 33 Fenwick 1930.9 1932.4 Ret LTG w

Emerson G V MAJ 101-N 57 Ingalls 1922.1 1925.6 MedC '23cd
Emery F E Jr MAJ 65-N 48 Ingalls 1928.7 1929.7 Putnam
Emery F E Jr LTC 102-N 61 Ingalls 1936.6 1938.7 '37cd
Emery F E Jr COL 121-E 43 Fenwick 1942.6 1943.8 PhBk
Emery F E Jr LTC 101-N 57 Ingalls 1938.7 1940.6 PhBk
Emma J A LTC 18-W-1 29-A Bernard 1978.1 1980.5 mfh
Emory S H MAJ 68-S 81 Ingalls 1918.6 1919.5 '19cd
Emrick G W LTC 79-N 95 Ingalls 1949.2 1951.10 usacc
Engel H J COL 144-S-2 41-C Ingalls 1960.11 1963.1 Ret MG mfh
Engelhart E C 1LT 34-N-2 100 Ingalls 1932.8 1934.6 Engelhart
Engelhart E C CPT 44-S-2 102 Ingalls 1934.7 1938.8 '37cd
Engineer Office 147 147 Engr Ln 1910.5 1946.11
England J M 1LT 18-E-1 37-A Bernard 1931.8 1932.6 '31cd
Englehard A F MAJ 68-S 81 Ingalls 1920.6 1923.6 Ret BG JHC
Englehard A F MAJ 129-S 101 Ingalls 1935.7 1937.6 Ret BG Paul +
Engler J E MG 121-E 43 Fenwick 1959.6 1961.4 Ret LTG usacc
Ennis A I MAJ 65-S 46 Ingalls 1940.6 1941.4 PhBk
Ennis R F BG 126-S 163 Bernard 1950.9 1951.6 Ret MG usacc
Epley G G COL 127-E 147 Bernard 1958.7 1962.6 mfh
Epling F G 1LT 14 32 Ruckman 1916 1917 Epling
Epling F G 1LT 3-N 169 Bernard 1925.11 1926.6 Epling
Epling F G CPT 1 151 Bernard 1917 1918 Student Epling
Eppley V M COL 43-E-1 5 Reeder 1968.12 1970.8 mfh
Erickson J L LTC 35-E-2 8 Reeder 1953.11 1955.10 usacc
Ericson R A 2LT 17-E-1 47-A Bernard 1919.6 1920.6 Ericson
Erving J CPT 18-E-2 37-B Bernard 1824.3 1826.3 '25rq rms?
Erving J MAJ 1 151 Bernard 1837.10 1838.11 w
Eschbach E V CPT 45-E-2 116 Ingalls 1943 1944 '43PhBk
Estes H N MAJ 129-N 103 Ingalls 1927.8 1930.6 CAV Bartlett +
Estes E F COL 146 146 Engr Ln 1984.5 1985.5 mfh
Ettershank J P COL 15-S 36 Ruckman 1982.7 1985.1 mfh
Ettridge J B CPT 33-E-2 63 Fenwick 1930.12 1932.8 '31cd
Ettridge J B CPT 79-N 95 Ingalls 1928.8 1929.8 '29cd
Eubanks J COL 66-S 38 Ingalls 1977.6 1979.2 mfh
Eustis A BG 1 151 Bernard 1837.9 1837.10 CG w
Eustis A COL 17-E-1 47-A Bernard 1825.12 1828.11 '26rq
Eustis A COL 1 151 Bernard 1831.10 1834.6 CO w
Eustis A LTC 17-E-2 47-B Bernard 1824.3 1828.11 '25-26rq
Evans W D CPT 126-S 163 Bernard 1929.8 1930.6 Evans son
Evans R B COL 15-S 36 Ruckman 1975.8 1976.11 mfh
Evans J P COL 129-N 103 Ingalls 1952.5 1964.10 usacc
Evans L W COL 126-N 165 Bernard 1956.7 1961.2 usacc
Evans A E 1LT 79-N 95 Ingalls 1919 1919.6 '19cd
Evans R H LTC 54-N-2 140 Ingalls 1963.10 1965.8 mfh
Evans B F Jr BG 34-S-2 94 Ingalls 1961.9 1961.12 usacc Ret MG
Evans B F Jr COL 50-E 129 Bernard 1956.1 1959.4 usacc Ret MG
Evans B F Jr COL 45-W-1 112 Ingalls 1955.8 1956.1 usacc Ret MG
Evans B F Jr BG 146 146 Engr Ln 1961.12 1963.8 mfh Ret MG
Eve R C CPT 62-N 28 Ruckman 1902 1905 '02cd
Everett DR 18-W-1 29-A Bernard 1828 1829 '29rq
Evers R R COL 45-E-1 114 Ingalls 1965.12 1966.6 mfh
Ewalt LT 64-N 20 Ruckman 1890 1892 c-25
Ewbank K COL 123-E 4 Ruckman 1957.11 1960.8 usacc

Ewbank K COL 54-S-1 136 Ingalls 1957.9 1957.11 usacc
Ewell J T Jr COL 51-N-2 124 Ingalls 1962.9 1963.7 mfh
Ewell J T Jr COL 79-N 95 Ingalls 1963.7 1969.2 mfh
Ewing C B COL 44-N-2 108 Ingalls 1954.2 1954.7 usacc
Ewing C B COL 128-E 109 Bernard 1954.7 1957.6 usacc
Exton H M MG 121-E 43 Fenwick 1963.7 1964.10 Ret LTG mfh
Exton H M MG 128-W 107 Bernard 1962.8 1963.7 Ret LTG mfh
Exton H M BG 33-E-1 61 Fenwick 1962.7 1962.8 Ret LTG mfh
Faiks W A COL 66-S 38 Ingalls 1962.1 1963.12 mfh
Fain P 1LT 102-N 61 Ingalls 1918 1919 BOQ WWI '19cd
Fairchild F H 1LT 18-E-2 37-B Bernard 1837.8 1838.5 '37cd
Fairlamb J C COL 3-N 169 Bernard 1971.7 1973.9 mfh
Faith J C BG 121-E 43 Fenwick 1973.5 1973.11 mfh Ret MG?
Faith J C COL 33-E-1 61 Fenwick 1972.12 1973.1 mfh Ret MG?
Faith J C BG 127-E 147 Bernard 1973.1 1973.5 mfh Ret MG?
Fallon W A Rev 7 Frank Lane 1901.8 1908.11 St Mary's Priest PhBk
Fambrough J A LTC 52-E-1 128 Ingalls 1976.3 1978.7 mfh
Fanning A C W COL 1 151 Bernard 1841.8 1841.12 w
Fanning R COL 66-S 38 Ingalls 1980.9 1983.7 mfh
Fanning A C W LTC 1 151 Bernard 1834.6 1834.8 w
Faris J E DR 64 71 Fenwick 1940.5 1952.2 PubH usacc
Farley W P SSG 18-W-2 29-B Bernard 1933.7 1933.11 Farley
Farmer R CPT 153-S 15 Hatch 1917 1920 '17-20cd
Farnsworth E E 1LT 70-N 91 Fenwick 1910.9 1915.6 Farnsworth
Farnsworth C L 1LT 167 A 7 Patch Road 1966.12 1968.10 mfh
Farnsworth E E MAJ 70-S 89 Ingalls 1921.9 1922.7 Son +
Farnsworth E E Jr COL 52-W-2 132 Ingalls 1954.9 1958.6 usacc
Farnsworth E E Jr 1LT 34-N-1 98 Ingalls 1939.9 1940.2 Farnsworth
Farnsworth E E Jr LTC 34-N-2 100 Ingalls 1949.5 1950.9 usacc
Farrar H B 1LT 63-S 26 Ruckman 1900.9 1901.9 '02cd
Farrell F W COL 127-W 145 Bernard 1946.9 1948.6 Ret LTG usacc
Farrell J S MAJ 167 B 9 Patch Road 1963.6 1965.7 mfh
Farren J H COL 101-S 55 Ingalls 1965.1 1967.7 mfh
Farren J H COL 43-E-2 7 Reeder 1964.11 1965.1 mfh
Farris G A LTC 51-N-1 122 Ingalls 1948.8 1950.9 usacc
Faulkner A T 1LT 1 151 Bernard 1940 1941 PhBk
Fauntleroy P C MAJ 125 73 Ingalls 1913.7 1915.6 MedC PhBk
Fawcett H O LTC 3-N 169 Bernard 1946.7 1949.5 usacc
Fay E N MAJ 66-S 38 Ingalls 1935.6 1937.7 QMC Daughter
Fay E N MAJ 67-S 34 Ingalls 1937.8 1940.5 Daughter Huge
Fayard M J MAJ 35-W-2 2 Reeder 1972.2 1973.7 mfh
Featherston J H 1LT 16-W 51 Bernard 1934.11 1936.6 AN306
Featherston J H 1LT 64-S 22 Ruckman 1931.7 1934.11 Featherston
Fedrizzi G J CPT 167 A 7 Patch Road 1966.9 1966.10 mfh
Feeley R F COL 50-W 121 Bernard 1974.8 1975.7 mfh
Feeman W E COL 129-N 103 Ingalls 1966.6 1968.9 mfh
Fellenz L E COL 69-N 87 Ingalls 1953.10 1956.6 Ret MG usacc
Fellows F E LTC 51-N-2 124 Ingalls 1947.11 1948.6 usacc
Fenn H L LTC 60 67 Fenwick 1975.11 1977.1 mfh
Fenn H L MAJ 35-E-2 8 Reeder 1972.9 1974.1 mfh
Fenn A L COL 123-E 4 Ruckman 1956.6 1957.10 usacc
Fenner R H CPT 79-S 93 Ingalls 1906.9 1907.9 CAS'07
Fenner R H CPT 69-S 85 Ingalls 1910.9 1911.8 '11cd

Fenton C L MAJ 118 29 Fenwick 1924.7 1925.5 Hartel
Fenton C L CPT 123-W 2 Ruckman 1914.12 1916.12 Ret BG JHC +
Fenton C L CPT 121-W 41 Fenwick 1917.1 1917.11 Ret BG '17cd
Fenwick J R COL 17-E-1 47-A Bernard 1824.3 1825.12 Ret BG '25rq USMC
Ferenbaugh C B MG 121-W 41 Fenwick 1952.4 1952.8 Ret LTG usacc
Ferguson M M MAJ 18-W-2 29-B Bernard 1983.7 1984.8 mfh
Ferguson J COL 123-W 2 Ruckman 1979.12 1982.7 mfh
Fergusson F K CPT 64-S 22 Ruckman 1902.2 1903.3 Ret BG b-21
Fergusson F K BG 119 33 Fenwick 1918.9 1919.1 Ret BG
Fergusson F K COL 118 29 Fenwick 1918.3 1918.9 Ret BG w
Fernandez C COL 67-S 34 Ingalls 1977.11 1979.3 mfh
Ferner R D MAJ 43-W-1 3 Reeder 1974.8 1976.6 mfh
Fernstrom C H 1LT 45-E-2 116 Ingalls 1939.6 1940.3 '40PhBk
Fickett E M COL 124-S 67 Ingalls 1947.5 1949.11 PhBk usacc
Fields H T BG 157 101 Bernard 1984.11 1986.6 mfh
Finch F R 1LT 102-N 61 Ingalls 1918 1919 BOQ WWI '19cd
Fincham J E COL 66-S 38 Ingalls 1976.7 1977.6 mfh
Fincher H T Jr MAJ 51-S-2 118 Ingalls 1972.9 1974.7 mfh
Fingarson G E COL 43-E-2 7 Reeder 1949.7 1949.8 usacc
Fingarson G E COL 127-E 147 Bernard 1949.8 1952.8 usacc
Fink R A LTC 43-E-2 7 Reeder 1966.3 1966.5 mfh
Finkenaur R G 1LT 33-W-2 57 Fenwick 1939.7 1940.7 Finkenaur
Finkenaur R G 1LT 17-E-1 47-A Bernard 1938.8 1939.7 Finkenaur
Finley C R MAJ 69-S 85 Ingalls 1924.8 1928.6 Finley
Finley C R 2LT 16-E 53 Bernard 1915.8 1915.12 '15cd
Finn R T COL 43-E-2 7 Reeder 1949.9 1949.12 Ret BG usacc
Finn R T COL 65-S 46 Ingalls 1949.12 1952.8 Ret BG usacc
Finney H D COL 126-S 163 Bernard 1972.9 1973.6 mfh
Finnigan LTC 33-E-1 61 Fenwick 1948.11 1950.7 usacc
Finnigan LTC 16-W 51 Bernard 1947.8 1948.11 usacc
Fischer H H LTG 141 53 Fenwick 1965.3 1967.8 mfh Ret LTG
Fischer K P COL 54-S-1 136 Ingalls 1969.6 1969.8 mfh
Fischer H H LTG 15-S 36 Ruckman 1965.2 1965.3 mfh Ret LTG
Fish E LTC 52-W-2 132 Ingalls 1981.7 1985.6 mfh
Fisher J S CPT 50 A 125 Bernard 1940.9 1941.11 Old Point Bank
Fisher J S WO 50 A 125 Bernard 1940.2 1940.9 BOQ PhBk
Fisher LT 70-S 89 Ingalls 1903.11 1905.9 c-52
Fisher H G COL 52-E-1 128 Ingalls 1951.10 1952.6 usaccc
Fisher B 1LT 156-N 181 Bernard 1919 '19cd rms?
Fisher H G COL 129-S 101 Ingalls 1952.6 1954.9 usacc
Fisher M N 1LT 18-E-1 37-A Bernard 1919.3 1919.6 '19cd
Fiskin A D CPT 50-W 121 Bernard 1929.9 1930.4 CAS'30
Fite W C II COL 43-E-1 5 Reeder 1958.2 1959.12 usacc
Fitzgerald E W LTC 143-S-1 35-A Ingalls 1954.10 1957.8 usacc
Fitzhugh H W 1LT 17-W-2 41-B Bernard 1829 1830 '29rq d-684
Flake J LTC 35-W-1 4 Reeder 1962.8 1963.7 mfh
Flake J COL 68-N 83 Ingalls 1968.6 1970.10 mfh
Flanagan R W LTC 33-W-1 59 Fenwick 1972.7 1974.8 mfh
Flanigan B L LTC 65-N 48 Ingalls 1941.11 1942.7 Flanigan
Flanigen B L CPT 70-N 91 Ingalls 1919.3 1919.10 Flanigen
Flannagan T MAJ 17-W-1 41-A Bernard 1977.11 1978.8 mfh
Fleming R J Jr COL 124-N 69 Ingalls 1952.7 1954.2 Ret MG usacc
Fletcher C E COL 102-S 59 Ingalls 1956.3 1958.7 usacc

Fletter R W LTC 144-N-2 41-D Ingalls 1949.5 1952.7 usacc
Flory L D 1LT 34-S-1 96 Ingalls 1930.12 1934.6 Flory + cds
Flournoy J MAJ 33-W-1 59 Fenwick 1980.4 1983.1 mfh
Fogle G C BG 158 32 Ingalls 1969.6 1970.8 mfh
Folda J T Jr MG 142 51 Fenwick 1969.10 1970.12 mfh
Foley P P MAJ 143-N-2 35-D Ingalls 1972.11 1974.8 mfh
Folk F T 1LT 45-W-1 112 Ingalls 1937.8 1938.6 Folk '37cd
Foltz C G CPT 144-N-1 41-B Ingalls 1921.6 1922.6 '21BtryOcs
Foltz C G MAJ 126-S 163 Bernard 1938.6 1941 PhBk Foltz
Fooks N I COL 102-N 61 Ingalls 1953.8 1954.8 usacc
Fooks N I COL 158 32 Ingalls 1954.8 1956.12 usacc
Foote S M COL 119 33 Fenwick 1916.10 1917.8 Ret BG Foote
Foote S W 1LT 1 151 Bernard 1939 1940.2 Ret BG Foote
Foote S W 1LT 43-E-2 7 Reeder 1940.2 1940.6 Foote Ret BG
Foote W C MAJ 143-S-1 35-A Ingalls 1919.11 1920.11 Clark '20cd
Foote W C CPT 144-N-1 41-B Ingalls 1917.8 1919.11 Chapin
Foote S M 1LT 65-N 48 Ingalls 1890 b-6
Foote W C MAJ 144-S-2 41-C Ingalls 1931.3 1934.8 JHC Morton
Ford A W 2LT 16-W 51 Bernard 1912 1913 '12cd BOQ
Ford A W 1LT 67-N 36 Ingalls 1916.12 1917.6 Ford
Forde H M COL 66-S 38 Ingalls 1955.1 1956.6 usacc
Foreman A H LTC 17-W-2 41-B Bernard 1947.2 1947.8 usacc
Forestiere F MAJ 3-N 169 Bernard 1977.2 1978.6 mfh
Forman O T COL 44-N-1 106 Ingalls 1953.5 1953.8 usacc
Forman O T COL 126-N 165 Bernard 1953.8 1954.9 usacc
Forman R H LTG 142 51 Fenwick 1983.7 1987.9 mfh
Forney A C 1LT 70-S 89 Ingalls 1918 1919 BOQ WWI '19cd
Forney Dr 18-W-2 29-B Bernard 1886 c-14 Surgeon
Forney Dr 18-W-1 29-A Bernard 1886 d-691 rms
Forrest F G LTC 35-W-1 4 Reeder 1953.9 1955.2 usacc
Forse W CPT 68-S 81 Ingalls 1910.9 1911.9 '11cd
Forst G H COL 52-W-2 132 Ingalls 1948.1 1948.9 usacc
Fort R MAJ 52-W-2 132 Ingalls 1973.12 1978.6 mfh
Fossum E A LTC 44-S-2 102 Ingalls 1956.3 1958.8 usacc
Foster G B CPT 3-S 167 Bernard 1919.6 1920.1 '20cd
Foster R A LTC 144-S-2 41-C Ingalls 1974.3 1977.3 mfh
Foster V P CPT 44-S-1 104 Ingalls 1930.12 1931.6 deCamp Burnell
Foster V P CPT 15-N 34 Ruckman 1922.9 1923.6 CAS'23 Arthur
Foster E M MAJ 66-N 40 Ingalls 1933.6 1938.8 Ret MG Wolfe +
Fountain C COL 66-N 40 Ingalls 1980.6 1982.10 mfh
Fournier A COL 126-S 165 Bernard 1980.10 1983.5 mfh
Fowler H C 1LT 16-W 51 Bernard 1928 1929 '28cd
Fowler C F COL 35-E-1 6 Reeder 1947.9 1949.8 usacc
Fox L I DR 124-S 67 Ingalls 1956.11 1973.9 mfh
Fox L I DR 79-N 95 Ingalls 1953.12 1956.11 usacc
Fox L I DR 34-S-2 94 Ingalls 1951.3 1953.12 usacc
Frame M-W COL 15-N 34 Ruckman 1955.9 1959.6 usacc
Francis W H 2LT 16-W 51 Bernard 1929 1930 Francis
Francis W H 2LT 1 151 Bernard 1931 1932.8 Francis
Francis W H 2LT 18-W-2 29-B Bernard 1932.8 1933.7 Francis '33cd
Francis W C CPT 52-W-1 130 Ingalls 1943.6 1945 '43-45 PhBks
Frank K C 1LT 18-W-1 29-A Bernard 1929.7 1930.7 Frank
Frank R T MAJ 18-E-1 37-A Bernard 1886.7 1888.11 c-14 c-27

Frank S H 2LT 16-E 53 Bernard 1913.11 1914.4 Ret BG Frank
Frank S H 2LT 18-E-1 37-A Bernard 1914.4 1914.8 Ret BG Frank
Frank R T COL 1 151 Bernard 1888.11 1898.5 CO micro-617 w
Franklin J R LTC 33-W-2 57 Fenwick 1973.9 1975.10 mfh
Franklin E C 1LT 63-N 24 Ruckman 1931.6 1931.8 Franklin
Franklin R B COL 103-S 63 Ingalls 1954.12 1956.3 usacc
Franklin J F Jr COL 51-S-2 118 Ingalls 1958.7 1958.9 Ret MG usacc
Franklin J F Jr COL 121-W 41 Fenwick 1959.7 1961.5 Ret MG usacc
Franklin J F Jr COL 63-N 24 Ruckman 1958.9 1959.7 Ret MG usacc
Franks F COL 70-S 89 Ingalls 1979.7 1982.2 mfh
Frans W D CPT 51-N-2 124 Ingalls 1943.8 1844.8 '43PhBk
Fraser F G CPT 143-N-2 35-D Ingalls 1936.8 1937.7 '37cd
Fraser E S CPT 3-S 167 Bernard 1919.1 1919.6 '19cd
Fraser A G Jr COL 33-W-1 59 Fenwick 1961.1 1963.7 mfh
Frazer W D 1LT 63-S 26 Ruckman 1914.12 1915.12 '16cd
Frederick R T MG 141 53 Fenwick 1945.11 1946.5 Ret MG RLT w
Frederick R T 1LT 34-S-1 96 Ingalls 1937.7 1938.8 Ret MG Stryker
Freeland E H MAJ 79-N 95 Ingalls 1927.8 1928.7 '28AdvCs
Freeland E H MAJ 121-W 41 Fenwick 1919.2 1920.3 S&F Arthur
Freeman R F COL 52-W-1 130 Ingalls 1965.11 1966.2 mfh
Freeman P L Jr LTG 1 151 Bernard 1961.9 1962.4 Ret GEN mfh
Freeman P L Jr LTG 142 51 Fenwick 1960.4 1961.8 Ret GEN usacc
Freeman P L Jr GEN 119 33 Fenwick 1965.4 1967.6 mfh Ret GEN
French F J 1LT 16-W 51 Bernard 1929 1930 KIA '44 Widow
French P H CPT 143-N-1 35-B Ingalls 1925.7 1926.7 '25cd
French A J MAJ 143-S-1 35-A Ingalls 1923.8 1924.8 Ret BG Hartel
French F J CPT 34-N-2 100 Ingalls 1934.8 1936.1 KIA '44 Meyer
French A J MAJ 143-S-2 35-C Ingalls 1925.8 1926.6 Ret BG Hartel
French A J MAJ 101-N 57 Ingalls 1928.6 1929.6 Ret BG '29cd
French F J 1LT 17-W-2 41-B Bernard 1932.8 1933.7 KIA '44 Widow
French P H MAJ 19 18 Bernard 1936.7 1939.7 PhBk
French D MG 141 53 Fenwick 1978.12 1981.6 mfh
Friday W P MAJ 143-S-2 35-C Ingalls 1978.2 1981.8 mfh
Frinak J M MAJ 18-E-2 37-B Bernard 1955.12 1958.4 usacc
Frinak J M MAJ 17-E-2 47-B Bernard 1954.9 1955.12 usacc
Frith R E CPT 45-E-1 114 Ingalls 1940.8 1941.2 Frith + PhBks
Frohwitter C L J Jr 1LT 15-S 36 Ruckman 1900.9 1901.6 Shull
Frolich A J COL 52-W-1 130 Ingalls 1955.10 1956.12 usacc
Frolich A J COL 79-N 95 Ingalls 1956.12 1959.7 usacc
Frowitter C L J Jr 1LT 64-N 20 Ruckman 1907 1909 b-26
Fry E M COL 101-N 57 Ingalls 1969.7 1972.11 mfh
Fry E M COL 45-E-1 114 Ingalls 1968.6 1969.7 mfh
Fry J L MAJ 18-W-2 29-B Bernard 1981.11 1983.6 mfh
Fuller A L CPT 126-N 165 Bernard 1914.12 1915.12 Cochran
Fuller A L CPT 127-E 147 Bernard 1917.6 1918.9 '17cd
Fuller A L CPT 79-S 93 Ingalls 1910.9 1911.9 '11cd
Fulton J M 1LT 18-W-1 29-A Bernard 1909.9 1910.9 CAS'10
Fulton W S CPT 69-N 87 Ingalls 1913.12 1914.12 PhBk
Furnival R CPT 143-N-2 35-D Ingalls 1912.12 1913.12 '13cd
Furnival R CPT 103-N 65 Ingalls 1913.12 1914.12 PhBk
Gage P S 1LT 15-S 36 Ruckman 1913.12 1914.12 Ret BG Gage
Gaither R LTG 142 51 Fenwick 1956.10 1958.4 usacc Ret LTG
Gaither R LTG 34-S-2 94 Ingalls 1956.8 1956.10 usacc Ret LTG

Gall J B COL 50-W 121 Bernard 1961.8 1966.1 mfh
Gallagher C P COL 69-S 85 Ingalls 1973.12 1976.10 mfh
Gallagher F F MAJ 128-W 107 Bernard 1929.1 1929.8 Gallagher
Gallagher F F MAJ 55 42 Ingalls 1923.11 1924.6 Gallagher
Gallahan A III CPT 79-N 95 Ingalls 1943 1944 PhBk
Gallant W M MAJ 167 A 7 Patch Road 1963.2 1966.1 mfh
Galloway J C CPT 35-W-2 2 Reeder 1943.8 1944.8 PhBk
Gallup F H 1LT 70-N 91 Ingalls 1900.9 1903.9 BOQ '02cd CAS'03
Gallup P M 1LT 65-N 48 Ingalls 1912.12 1913.12 '13-14cd
Galt P H CPT 18-E-2 37-B Bernard 1842.7 1846.5 d-686
Galvin J BG 120 37 Fenwick 1980.7 1981.6 mfh
Gantringer CPT 18-W-1 29-A Bernard 1825 1826.3 d-684 rms
Garcia A MAJ 34-N-2 100 Ingalls 1977.2 1981.6 mfh
Gard H P CPT 52-W-2 132 Ingalls 1935.8 1936.6 Gard
Gard H P CPT 16-W 51 Bernard 1936.7 1937.7 Gard
Gardner MAJ 18-W-1 29-A Bernard 1824.7 d-684
Gardner F Q C COL 142 51 Fenwick 1934.6 1937.11 Ret MG Daughter
Gardner F Q C 1LT 79-N 95 Ingalls 1911.7 1912.9 Ret MG S&F '12cd
Gardner J L COL 1 151 Bernard 1856.5 1856.12 CO w
Gardner J L MAJ 18-W-1 29-A Bernard 1834.4 1836.6 '34-36rq
Gardner F Q C MAJ 103-S 63 Ingalls 1925.6 1927.6 Ret MG '25cd
Garfield J CPT 141 53 Fenwick 1919 1919 '19cd
Garigan T P COL 101-N 57 Ingalls 1983.9 1987.7 mfh
Garrett R C CPT 65-N 48 Ingalls 1917 Ret BG '17cd
Garrett R C LTC 128-W 107 Bernard 1935.6 1937.6 Ret BG Garrett
Garrison W C BG 125 73 Ingalls 1960.5 1961.5 Ret MG usacc
Garton G G COL 35-W-2 2 Reeder 1958.1 1958.7 usacc
Gaskins P W COL 63-N 24 Ruckman 1984.8 1986.7 mfh
Gates W G MAJ 17-E-2 47-B Bernard 1832.11 1833.11 Dimmock Letter
Gather L W COL 167 A 7 Patch Road 1951.8 1953.10 usacc
Gatlin J D MAJ 35-W-1 4 Reeder 1970.10 1974.7 mfh
Gavalas L G BG 54-N-1 138 Ingalls 1963.7 1963.8 Ret MG mfh
Gavalas L G BG 157 101 Bernard 1963.10 1968.3 Ret MG mfh
Gavalas L G BG 128-W 107 Bernard 1963.8 1963.10 Ret MG mfh
Gavin J A COL 101-N 57 Ingalls 1959.1 1960.9 usacc
Gavin J A COL 51-S-2 118 Ingalls 1958.9 1959.1 usacc
Gay A C 1LT 34-N-1 98 Ingalls 1936.8 1937.6 Taber Roy
Gay J M Jr COL 51-S-2 118 Ingalls 1968.10 1970.6 mfh
Gearhart G L 1LT 63-N 24 Ruckman 1911.9 1912.9 NAdoc 335547
Gearhart G L 1LT 129-S 101 Ingalls 1912.9 1913.12 '12AdvCs '13cd
Geary J T 1LT 66-S 38 Ingalls 1902.8 1903.8 '02cd
Gee S E COL 65-S 46 Ingalls 1956.8 1957.3 Ret MG usacc
Geere F CPT 143-S-1 35-A Ingalls 1911.9 1912.9 CAS'12 '12cd
Geere F MAJ 143-S-1 35-A Ingalls 1927.7 1929.6 Ellis
Geldreth C CPT 34-N-2 100 Ingalls 1981.7 1984.6 mfh
Gell R COL 128-W 107 Bernard 1977.10 1979.6 mfh
George W R 1LT 15-N 34 Ruckman 1906.9 1907.9 b-25 Surgeon
George M S COL 44-N-2 108 Ingalls 1952.8 1954.2 usacc
George A M SSG 61-S 43 Ingalls 1937 1938 '37cd
George R T 1LT 44-N-1 106 Ingalls 1930.12 1931.8 '31 AdvCs
Gerhard F W 1LT 67-S 34 Ingalls 1918 1919 BOQ WWI '19cd
Gerhardt W R LTC 19 18 Bernard 1940.7 1941.8 Gerhardt
Gerhardt W R MAJ 3-N 169 Bernard 1940.5 1940.7 Gerhardt

Gerhardt H A 1LT 43-W-2 1 Reeder 1938.6 1939.6 Ret MG PhBk
Gerhart G H COL 15-S 36 Ruckman 1954.9 1956.7 usacc
Gerhartz S 1LT 35-W-1 4 Reeder 1979.7 1982.5 mfh
Gershenow L COL 66-N 40 Ingalls 1957.11 1960.11 usacc
Gershenow L COL 35-W-1 4 Reeder 1957.7 1957.11 usacc
Gettings J J Jr COL 65-N 48 Ingalls 1962.8 1966.6 mfh
Gettings J J Jr COL 143-S-1 35-A Ingalls 1962.6 1962.8 mfh
Getty G W MG 1 151 Bernard 1877.3 1883.7 CG w Ret MG
Gettys C W 1LT 17-W-2 41-B Bernard 1928.9 1931.9 Gettys Pohl
Geyer E H CPT 63-S 26 Ruckman 1934.8 1936.7 QMC *Sojourner*
Gibbs D P COL 102-N 61 Ingalls 1955.12 1957.6 Ret MG usacc
Gibbs G G 2LT 17-W-1 41-A Bernard 1925.7 1926.7 '25cd
Gibbs D P COL 35-W-2 2 Reeder 1955.9 1955.12 Ret MG usacc
Gibney R F COL 17-E-1 47-A Bernard 1965.7 1967.11 mfh
Gibney R F COL 16-E 53 Bernard 1967.11 1969.6 mfh
Gibson R T MAJ 65-S 46 Ingalls 1927.8 1928.6 Gibson
Gibson E J MG 93 75 Ingalls 1967.4 1969.1 mfh Ret MG?
Gibson A 1LT 129-S 101 Ingalls 1911.9 1912.9 S&F '12cd
Gibson F S LTC 54-S-1 136 Ingalls 1967.8 1969.5 mfh
Gibson A 1LT 18-E-1 37-A Bernard 1909.9 1911.9 '11cd
Gibson A 1LT 129-S 101 Ingalls 1915.4 1916.12 '16cd
Gibson E J MG 118 29 Fenwick 1969.1 1970.7 mfh Ret MG?
Gibson A CPT 123-W 2 Ruckman 1916.12 1917.12 '17cd
Giddings D W CW4 18-W-1 29-A Bernard 1982.6 1983.6 mfh
Giffin S S MAJ 126-S 163 Bernard 1919.8 1921.9 CAS Secy '20cd
Giffin S S 2LT 16-W 51 Bernard 1913 1914 PhBk BOQ
Giffin S L 1LT 45-W-2 110 Ingalls 1938.6 1939.6 Ret BG '39PhBk
Gifford J H 1LT 63-S 26 Ruckman 1889 1890 Cunningham
Gildart R C COL 16-W 51 Bernard 1956.1 1957.8 Ret BG usacc
Gildart R C COL 33-E-2 63 Fenwick 1954.9 1956.1 Ret BG usacc
Gildart R C 1LT 143-N-2 35-D Ingalls 1915.12 1916.12 Ret BG '16CAS
Gildart R C 1LT 15-S 36 Ruckman 1918 Ret BG '17cd
Gill G G COL 144-N-2 41-D Ingalls 1954.6 1955.3 usacc
Gill W A Rev 7 Frank Lane 1921.4 1933.1 St Mary's Priest
Gillem R D COL 146 146 Engr Ln 1985.5 1987.2 mfh
Gillespie R E LTC 44-S-2 102 Ingalls 1984.12 1986.6 mfh
Gillespie J M CPT 101-N 57 Ingalls 1919.1 1920.1 '19cd
Gillespie A G 1LT 79-N 95 Ingalls 1914.12 1915.7 S&F Arthur
Gillespie J M 1LT 67-S 34 Ingalls 1918 1919 BOQ WWI '19cd
Gillette C A CPT 3-S 167 Bernard 1929.7 1930.8 '30BtryOCs
Gillette C A CPT 14 32 Ruckman 1928.6 1929.6 '29cd
Gillis T D COL 62-S 30 Ruckman 1959.9 1962.6 mfh
Gillis T D COL 33-W-2 57 Fenwick 1952.9 1953.7 usacc
Gillis T D LTC 44-N-1 106 Ingalls 1948.2 1950.9 usacc
Gillispie A G 1LT 15-N 34 Ruckman 1910.9 1911.9 CAS'11 '11cd
Gilman S I 1LT 1 151 Bernard 1937 1938 Gilman
Gilman S I LTC 33-W-2 57 Fenwick 1948.9 1950.1 usacc
Gilmore J C CPT 18-W-2 29-B Bernard 1908.9 1909.4 '09cd
Gilmore J COL 124-S 67 Ingalls 1978.8 1981.6 mfh
Girard C J BG 128-W 107 Bernard 1967.12 1969.2 mfh Ret BG?
Gist E H CPT 19 18 Bernard 1923.7 1926.6 MedC Hartel
Glabus E COL 103-S 63 Ingalls 1982.12 1985.6 mfh
Glafka A R COL 102-N 61 Ingalls 1957.7 1959.3 usacc

Glasgow E L CPT 68-N 83 Ingalls 1905.9 1906.9 '06cd b-26
Glasgow R I 1LT 68-S 81 Ingalls 1931.12 1932.3 Ret BG Glasgow
Glasgow R I 1LT 62-N 28 Ruckman 1931.8 1931.12 Ret BG Glascow
Glass L R Mr 61-N 45 Ingalls 1943.7 1948.7 Fire Chief PhBk
Glass G E LTC 51-N-2 124 Ingalls 1986.6 1987.5 mfh
Glassburn N D 1LT 43-W-1 3 Reeder 1938.10 1939.6 D-POW Ship'45
Glassburn R P LTC 128-W 107 Bernard 1932.6 1935.6 '33cd +
Glassburn R P MAJ 50-E 129 Bernard 1921.9 1922.8 '22FOcs
Glavin E J F COL 123-E 4 Ruckman 1952.11 1954.6 usacc
Glavin E J F COL 33-E-1 61 Fenwick 1952.1 1952.11 usacc
Glover C D 1LT 63-N 24 Ruckman 1919 1919 BOQ ? '19cd
Goeppert L W MAJ 126-N 165 Bernard 1937.9 1941.3 PhBk
Goering J D LTC 33-E-2 63 Fenwick 1972.8 1974.7 mfh
Goers M A BG 127-E 147 Bernard 1968.12 1972.1 mfh Ret BG?
Goff J L 1LT 17-E-2 47-B Bernard 1928.6 1930.5 Goff
Goforth R C COL 43-E-2 7 Reeder 1969.10 1970.8 mfh
Goforth R C COL 63-S 26 Ruckman 1970.8 1973.7 mfh
Goldschmidt M W LTC 16-E 53 Bernard 1969.9 1970.11 mfh
Goodall J R CPT 43-W-1 3 Reeder 1934.7 1935.7 deCamp
Goodall J R 1LT 18-E-2 37-B Bernard 1932.8 1933.8 '33cd
Goode P R COL 124-S 67 Ingalls 1949.12 1952.7 usacc
Goodfellow J C 1LT 66-N 40 Ingalls 1902.9 1903.3 '02cd
Goodman W M MAJ 51-S-1 120 Ingalls 1932.7 1933 Ret MG VanBuskirk
Goodridge J LTC 52-W-1 130 Ingalls 1979.11 1981.6 mfh
Gordner H L COL 14 32 Ruckman 1967.3 1970.8 mfh
Gordon D B COL 45-W-1 112 Ingalls 1965.7 1967.2 mfh
Gordon R L BG 121-E 43 Fenwick 1982.7 1985.7 mfh
Gordon L C CPT 69-S 85 Ingalls 1945.6 1946.5 Gordon
Gordon T L COL 68-S 81 Ingalls 1969.8 1970.7 mfh
Gordon R E 1LT 156-N 181 Bernard 1919 '19cd rms?
Gordon T L COL 144-N-1 41-B Ingalls 1969.7 1969.8 mfh
Gorham G B 1LT 63-S 26 Ruckman 1917.6 1918.4 '17cd
Gorham G B 1LT 65-S 46 Ingalls 1915.12 1916.12 '16CAS
Gorman P F BG 120 37 Fenwick 1973.11 1977.6 Ret GEN mfh
Gorman P F BG 146 146 Engr Ln 1973.10 1973.11 Ret GEN mfh
Gorton G G COL 128-W 107 Bernard 1958.7 1960.8 usacc
Govaert J F Rev 7 Frank Lane 1936.9 1940.7 St Mary's Priest
Gower A W CPT 63-S 26 Ruckman 1928.8 1930.8 Gower
Gower A W CPT 51-S-2 118 Ingalls 1932.8 1933.7 Gower
Grace J J CPT 70-S 89 Ingalls 1915.12 1916.12 '16 CAS
Grace J J CPT 129-S 101 Ingalls 1916.12 1917.6 '17cd
Graham L B COL 45-E-1 114 Ingalls 1946.10 1947.6 KIA usacc
Graham L B CPT 52-E-2 126 Ingalls 1940.9 1941.8 KIA MacAdams
Graham E D LTC 103-S 63 Ingalls 1942 1943 PhBk
Grahan K LTC 3-S 167 Bernard 1979.9 1985.2 mfh
Grandelli C M LTC 144-S-1 41-A Ingalls 1967.3 1969.7 mfh
Graney P MAJ 51-N-2 124 Ingalls 1977.7 1980.6 mfh
Granger R S 1LT 79-N 95 Ingalls 1900.9 1901.6 CAS'01 '00cd
Gransback D H COL 63-S 63 Ruckman 1980.7 1982.9 mfh
Grant M F COL 50-W 121 Bernard 1951.12 1954.9 usacc
Grant E P CPT 30-A 34 Hampton 1983.11 1984.12 mfh
Gratiot C MAJ 1 151 Bernard 1819.0 1831.10 Constr. Engr.
Gray W S LTC 143-S-2 35-C Ingalls 1972.8 1972.9 mfh

Gray M G COL 18-W-1 29-A Bernard 1956.11 1958.8 usacc
Gray Q CPT 1 151 Bernard 1912.9 1916 S&F
Gray Q CPT 158 32 Ingalls 1919.8 1921.4 '20cd Cochran +
Gray F MAJ 45-E-2 116 Ingalls 1978.6 1979.4 mfh
Gray Q CPT 62-N 28 Ruckman 1911.9 1912.9 '12cd
Grayson E H COL 129-S 101 Ingalls 1984.8 1985.8 mfh
Greanery W J Rev 7 Frank Lane 1919.8 1920.4 St Mary's Priest
Greco J F COL 43-W-1 3 Reeder 1953.9 1953.11 usacc
Greco J F COL 70-N 91 Ingalls 1953.11 1956.7 usacc
Green J A MAJ 129-S 101 Ingalls 1923.9 1926.6 Ret MG JHC +
Green F M MAJ 123-E 4 Ruckman 1925.6 1929.6 Hartel '24-29cd
Green J A MAJ 101-N 57 Ingalls 1920.2 1922.1 Ret MG Clark
Green T CPT 1 151 Bernard 1837.1 1837.5 w
Green F M 1LT 67-N 36 Ingalls 1915.12 1916.12 CAS'16
Green C W MAJ 141 53 Fenwick 1919 1919 '19cd rms?
Green T CPT 17-W-2 41-B Bernard 1837.5 1844.10 QMC c-285 w
Green F M LTC 103-N 65 Ingalls 1935.9 1936.3 JHC
Green F M COL 142 51 Fenwick 1937.11 1938.12 PhBk
Green G R CPT 18-W-1 29-A Bernard 1906.9 1907.9 CAS'07
Green C E 1LT 44-S-1 104 Ingalls 1938.7 1939.7 CAS'39
Green T C COL 143-N-2 35-D Ingalls 1948.6 1951.7 usacc
Greene R J COL 102-S 59 Ingalls 1972.7 1976.7 mfh
Greene E H COL 67-N 36 Ingalls 1983.6 1985.4 mfh
Greene H F MAJ 126-S 163 Bernard 1944 1946.8 PhBk
Greene E M LTC 44-S-2 102 Ingalls 1973.3 1975.1 mfh
Greene L V COL 17-W-2 41-B Bernard 1963.8 1964.3 Ret BG mfh
Greene H F MAJ 144-N-2 41-D Ingalls 1942 1943 '43PhBk
Greene L V COL 102-N 61 Ingalls 1964.3 1965.1 Ret BG mfh
Greene R J COL 51-N-1 122 Ingalls 1971.12 1972.7 mfh
Greene F W III MAJ 45-W-1 112 Ingalls 1971.7 1973.7 mfh
Greene J S Jr COL 45-W-2 110 Ingalls 1967.1 1967.3 mfh
Greene J S Jr COL 15-S 36 Ruckman 1967.3 1968.7 mfh
Greening O L LTC 52-E-2 126 Ingalls 1960.9 1961.7 usacc
Greenough E A 1LT 63-S 26 Ruckman 1904.9 1905.9 CAS'05
Greenwood D E CPT 54-S-1 136 Ingalls 1931.8 1932.7 deCamp
Green D Jr COL 54-N-1 138 Ingalls 1959.7 1963.6 usacc
Greer H W COL 124-N 69 Ingalls 1963.7 1966.1 mfh
Greer D L LTC 144-N-1 41-B Ingalls 1983.7 1986.5 mfh
Greer H W COL 45-W-2 110 Ingalls 1962.10 1963.7 mfh
Gregory F G 1LT 17-E-2 47-B Bernard 1940.6 1943.7 '40-43 PhBks
Gregory P T 1LT 17-E-2 47-B Bernard 1924.6 1925.7 '25BtryOCs
Gregory P T 1LT 3-N 169 Bernard 1928.8 1929.8 '29cd
Greig A Jr LTC 62-N 28 Ruckman 1920.7 1921.7 CAS'21
Grier C V CPT 18-W-1 29-A Bernard 1944 1945 PhBks
Grier T F COL 127-W 145 Bernard 1984.10 1987.6 mfh
Griffith E G 1LT 45-E-2 116 Ingalls 1936.8 1937.8 '37cd
Grigg W A CPT 35-W-2 2 Reeder 1944.8 1946.8 '44-45PhBks
Griggs D M COL 158 32 Ingalls 1941.6 1942.6 Kimmel Madison
Griggs D M LTC 50-E 129 Bernard 1938.7 1941.6 PhBk
Grimm H F COL 118 29 Fenwick 1940.12 1942.1 Grimm Son
Grimm H F 1LT 16-E 53 Bernard 1919.6 1920.1 '19cd Clark
Grimm H F MAJ 144-S-2 41-C Ingalls 1934.8 1936.7 Detwiler +
Grimm H F CPT 143-N-2 35-D Ingalls 1932.8 1934.8 Detwiler +

Grimm H F CPT 79-S 93 Ingalls 1920.1 1923.1 Grimm Son
Grimsley R J COL 35-W-1 4 Reeder 1969.7 1969.7 mfh
Griscti W E COL 33-W-1 59 Fenwick 1963.8 1964.7 mfh
Griswald H W 1LT 18-E-1 37-A Bernard 1829 1830 '29rq
Griswald H W ADJ 18-W-1 29-A Bernard 1828 1829 d-684
Gritz S COL 143-N-1 35-B Ingalls 1966.8 1968.3 mfh
Gross J LTC 144-S-2 41-C Ingalls 1983.7 1985.4 mfh
Gross F E MAJ 70-S 89 Ingalls 1922.7 1923.6 '23AdvCs
Gross F E MAJ 101-N 57 Ingalls 1925.8 1926.7 '25-26cd
Growdon J S LTC 34-N-1 98 Ingalls 1953.8 1955.6 usacc
Grummt O C LTC 18-W-1 29-A Bernard 1970.10 1972.7 mfh
Guenther F L COL 1 151 Bernard 1899.5 1902.2 CO w
Guest House 16-E 53 Bernard 1950 1959
Guest House 63-S 26 Ruckman 1946 1950 usacc
Guest House 64-S 22 Ruckman 1935 1940 Martin
Guest House 63-N 24 Ruckman 1945 1950 usacc
Guidera T F COL 126-N 165 Bernard 1965.6 1966.7 mfh
Guidera T F COL 51-N-2 124 Ingalls 1964.8 1965.6 mfh
Guild E R CPT 70-S 89 Ingalls 1936.8 1937.7 '37cd
Guiney P W Jr 2LT 17-W-1 41-A Bernard 1932.3 1933.9 deCamp
Guinn F CPT 43-W-2 1 Reeder 1982.10 1983.4 mfh
Gulick J W BG 119 33 Fenwick 1936.12 1938.10 Ret MG w
Gulick J W CPT 126-N 165 Bernard 1910.6 1911.11 Ret MG '11cd +
Gulick J W CPT 17-E-1 47-A Bernard 1907.9 1908.9 Ret MG '08cd
Gulick J W CPT 1 151 Bernard 1916 1917 Ret MG '17cd
Gulick J W 1LT 16-E 53 Bernard 1905.8 1907.9 Ret MG '08-09cd
Gulick J W CPT 3-S 167 Bernard 1908.9 1910.6 Ret MG '09cd
Gullis R E COL 64 71 Fenwick 1965.12 1968.7 mfh
Gundner F COL 67-N 36 Ingalls 1980.1 1981.7 mfh
Gunn C O COL 158 32 Ingalls 1943.3 1945.9 PhBk
Gunn F L BG 125 73 Ingalls 1966.6 1968.8 mfh Ret BG
Gunn F L BG 33-W-2 57 Fenwick 1966.6 1966.6 mfh Ret BG
Gunn F L BG 121-W 41 Fenwick 1970.4 1971.3 mfh Ret BG
Gurley F K 1LT 17-W-1 41-A Bernard 1931.8 1932.3 Gurley
Gurney A M COL 45-W-1 112 Ingalls 1947.5 1948.9 usacc
Gurney A M COL 121-W 41 Fenwick 1948.9 1950.9 usacc
Gustafson K W COL 45-W-1 112 Ingalls 1959.7 1961.4 Ret MG usacc
Gustafson M E LTC 45-W-2 110 Ingalls 1967.3 1969.6 mfh
Gustafson K W COL 3-N 169 Bernard 1961.4 1962.7 Ret MG mfh
Gutherie R E MAJ 157 101 Bernard 1928.8 1929.6 Gutherie
Gutherie R E MAJ 128-E 109 Bernard 1927.8 1928.8 Gutherie O'Rear
Gutherie R E MAJ 144-S-2 41-C Ingalls 1922.7 1923.6 '23cd
Gutherie R E CPT 143-S-1 35-A Ingalls 1916.12 1917.6 CAS'17 Ford
Gutherie R E MAJ 103-N 65 Ingalls 1925.8 1926.6 JHC '25cd
Guthrie S H 1LT 18-W-2 29-B Bernard 1912.12 1913.12 '13cd
Guthrie S H 1LT 102-N 61 Ingalls 1913.12 1915.8 PhBks
Guthrie S H 1LT 55 42 Ingalls 1915.10 1916.12 '16cd
Guyer L M 1LT 35-E-2 8 Reeder 1935.8 1936.7 Ret BG Guyer
Hackett SGT 61-S 43 Ingalls 1945.4 1946.7 D V Lewis
Hafer J B CPT 54-N-2 140 Ingalls 1934.8 1935.7 deCamp
Haff R A CWO 147 147 Engr Ln 1957.1 1959.5 usacc
Hagan J P Rev 7 Frank Lane 1873.10 1875.5 St Mary's Priest
Hagan C A COL 124-N 69 Ingalls 1985.8 1987.1 mfh

Hagen R P COL 3-S 167 Bernard 1954.11 1957.6 usacc
Hagen R P COL 43-E-2 7 Reeder 1954.7 1954.11 usacc
Hagood J BG 120 37 Fenwick 1919.10 1922.1 Ret MG w
Hagood J BG 119 33 Fenwick 1919.9 1919.9 w
Hahn O S 2LT 111-E 36 Tidball 1917.6 1918.9 '17cd S&F
Haight R LTC 51-S-2 118 Ingalls 1979.9 1981.6 mfh
Hailorn F S CPT 64-N 20 Ruckman 1902 b-19
Haines R E 1LT 62-N 28 Ruckman 1915.12 1916.12 Ret BG Haines
Haines R E MAJ 67-S 34 Ingalls 1919.11 1921.7 Ret BG '20cd
Haines P C 1LT 70-S 89 Ingalls 1902.9 1903.9 c-46
Haines R E MAJ 127-W 145 Bernard 1921.7 1923.8 Ret BG Haines
Haines R E Jr GEN 119 33 Fenwick 1970.12 1973.1 Ret GEN mfh
Haines P B Jr CPT 15-N 34 Ruckman 1965.11 1968.1 USN mfh
Haines R E Jr COL 33-E-1 61 Fenwick 1953.1 1954.8 Ret GEN usacc
Haines P B Jr CPT 51-S-2 118 Ingalls 1965.8 1965.11 USN mfh
Haines R E Jr GEN 127-W 145 Bernard 1970.11 1970.12 Ret GEN mfh
Halada R J LTC 3-S 167 Bernard 1946.6 1948.4 usacc
Haldeman R E MAJ 33-W-2 57 Fenwick 1944.4 1944.9 MedC Haldeman
Haldeman R E MAJ 50-W 121 Bernard 1944.9 1946.11 Haldeman
Hale H R 1LT 51-S-1 120 Ingalls 1939.8 1940.5 CAS'40
Hale H R 2LT 17-E-2 47-A Bernard 1935.9 1936.6 Clark
Hall R M COL 33-W-2 57 Fenwick 1968.8 1968.10 mfh
Hall C R 1LT 93 75 Ingalls 1919 WWI BOQ '19cd
Hall R P 1LT 144-N-1 41-B Ingalls 1915.12 1916.12 CAS'16
Hall D F COL 123-E 4 Ruckman 1951.6 1952.9 usacc
Hall D F COL 51-S-2 118 Ingalls 1948.1 1951.6 usacc
Hall H CPT 18-E-1 37-A Bernard 1905.9 1907.9 CAS'06 S&F
Hall H CPT 103-N 65 Ingalls 1910.9 1911.9 '11cd
Hall D 1LT 67-N 36 Ingalls 1914.12 1915.12 '16cd
Hall R P CPT 62-N 28 Ruckman 1921.8 1922.8 Sojourner
Hall R P 1LT 63-N 24 Ruckman 1917.6 1917.12 '17cd
Hall H CPT 65-N 48 Ingalls 1908.9 1909.9 '09cd
Hall R B MAJ 127-W 145 Bernard 1918.7 1921.6 '19cd
Hall D F COL 34-S-1 96 Ingalls 1946.9 1948.1 usacc
Hall W P G CPT 44-S-2 102 Ingalls 1944 1945 '44-45PhBks
Hall R M COL 129-N 103 Ingalls 1968.10 1969.5 mfh
Hall R P MAJ 129-N 103 Ingalls 1924.7 1926.7 Hartel Higgins
Halper M J BG 35-W-1 4 Reeder 1970.6 1970.7 mfh Ret MG
Halper M J BG 126-S 163 Bernard 1970.7 1971.9 mfh Ret MG
Hamberg W A COL 69-N 87 Ingalls 1959.10 1961.6 usacc
Hamberg W A COL 44-S-2 102 Ingalls 1958.9 1959.10 usacc
Hames W E Jr COL 50-W 121 Bernard 1970.6 1973.9 mfh
Hames W E Jr COL 18-W-2 29-B Bernard 1969.8 1970.6 mfh
Hamilton R M COL 123-E 4 Ruckman 1967.9 1970.1 mfh
Hamilton A CPT 16-W 51 Bernard 1904.8 1906.9 '04-06cds
Hamilton A CPT 103-N 65 Ingalls 1909.9 1910.9 '09cd
Hamilton H E COL 127-E 147 Bernard 1965.11 1968.8 mfh
Hamilton B COL 126-S 165 Bernard 1979.9 1980.9 mfh
Hamilton J A LTC 45-W-2 110 Ingalls 1950.10 1951.3 usacc
Hamilton A CPT 19 18 Bernard 1906.9 1909.9 S&F Shull Son
Hamilton J L COL 124-N 69 Ingalls 1987.1 1987.10
Hamilton R M COL 45-E-2 116 Ingalls 1967.5 1967.9 mfh
Hamilton H E COL 44-S-1 104 Ingalls 1965.8 1965.11 mfh

Hamilton F CPT 70-S 89 Ingalls 1918 1919 BOQ WWI '19cd
Hamilton A MAJ 126-S 163 Bernard 1910.9 1912.6 '11cd
Hamilton S A CPT 144-N-2 41-D Ingalls 1917.6 1919.6 '19cd
Hamm A LTC 45-E-1 114 Ingalls 1979.7 1982.8 mfh
Hammock L A COL 45-E-2 116 Ingalls 1946.8 1947.12 usacc
Hammond D G COL 66-S 38 Ingalls 1963.12 1964.6 mfh
Hammond D G COL 17-W-1 41-A Bernard 1963.8 1963.12 mfh
Hammond J W COL 50-W 121 Bernard 1948.7 1951.12 usacc
Hammond R D BG 121-W 41 Fenwick 1983.7 1984.8 mfh
Hampton W A 1LT 51-N-2 124 Ingalls 1939.6 1940.3 Hampton
Hampton W A COL 158 32 Ingalls 1945.9 1946.7 Hampton
Hampton A G DR 64 71 Fenwick 1956.7 1959.1 PubH usacc
Hanburger C COL 143-S-1 35-A Ingalls 1957.8 1959.12 usacc
Hanburger C COL 63-S 26 Ruckman 1959.12 1960.6 usacc
Hanchin R J COL 123-W 2 Ruckman 1968.2 1970.8 mfh
Hancock F R MAJ 52-E-1 128 Ingalls 1983.7 1984.8 mfh
Hancock W F 1LT 79-S 95 Ingalls 1901.9 1902.9 '02cd
Hancock G R 1LT 69-N 87 Ingalls 1903.9 1904.9 CAS'04
Handley G E Jr COL 69-S 85 Ingalls 1970.6 1973.6 mfh
Handwerk M C MAJ 69-S 85 Ingalls 1936.6 1937.5 Ret BG '37cd
Handwerk M C MAJ 55 42 Ingalls 1937.6 1940.6 Ret BG Daughter
Handwerk M C MAJ 33-E-1 61 Fenwick 1935.9 1936.6 Ret BG JHC +
Handy H F COL 143-S-2 35-C Ingalls 1947.4 1949.2 usacc
Handy H F COL 45-W-1 112 Ingalls 1947.4 1947.4 usacc
Haneke W C COL 67-S 34 Ingalls 1958.9 1961.6 Ret MG usacc
Haneke W C COL 52-W-2 132 Ingalls 1958.7 1958.9 Ret MG usacc
Hankins R BG 1 151 Bernard 1978.8 1980.10 mfh
Hankins G?C?B COL 35-E-2 8 Reeder 1963.8 1966.6 mfh
Hankins W B Jr COL 126-N 165 Bernard 1970.12 1972.6 mfh Ret BG?
Hankins W B Jr COL 33-E-1 61 Fenwick 1969.12 1970.12 mfh Ret BG?
Hanna G B G CPT 65-N 48 Ingalls 1911.9 1912.9 CAS'12 '12cd
Hanna G T COL 52-W-1 130 Ingalls 1963.3 1964.6 mfh
Hanna F 1LT 62-N 28 Ruckman 1913.12 1914.12 PhBk
Hannah R W COL 143-N-1 35-B Ingalls 1961.9 1963.3 mfh
Hannah J MAJ 44-S-2 102 Ingalls 1981.7 1984.6 mfh
Hannum C P BG 121-W 41 Fenwick 1971.10 1973.3 mfh Ret BG?
Hansen W MAJ 17-E-2 47-B Bernard 1977.7 1979.6 mfh
Hansen A M MAJ 51-S-2 118 Ingalls 1982.8 1985.4 mfh
Hansen H D COL 44-N-1 106 Ingalls 1958.1 1958.12 usacc
Hanson C C COL 167 A 7 Patch Road 1953.11 1955.4 usacc
Haralson J LTC 52-E-2 126 Ingalls 1979.5 1981.7 mfh
Hardaway F P MAJ 103-N 65 Ingalls 1926.6 1929.6 Ret BG Hardaway
Hardaway F P MAJ 126-S 163 Bernard 1925.8 1926.5 Ret BG '25cd +
Hardaway F P COL 142 51 Fenwick 1938.12 1940.11 Ret BG
Hardaway F P 1LT 3-N 169 Bernard 1913.12 1914.12 Ret BG
Hardaway F P CPT 127-W 145 Bernard 1917.6 1917.12 Ret BG
Hardaway F P MAJ 126-S 163 Bernard 1923.8 1924.9 Ret BG
Harden R C MAJ 52-W-1 130 Ingalls 1981.6 1981.12 mfh
Harden J H COL 16-W 51 Bernard 1964.8 1967.1 mfh
Hardenberg H COL 54-N-1 138 Ingalls 1953.6 1954.12 usacc
Hardick W L COL 35-E-1 6 Reeder 1954.2 1955.6 usacc Ret BG
Hardie P W CPT 66-S 38 Ingalls 1924.8 1925.7 '25BtryOCs
Hardigg W B MAJ 68-S 81 Ingalls 1923.6 1925.6 '23 cd

Hardin J S CPT 102-N 61 Ingalls 1906.5 1907.9 CAS'07
Harding H J P COL 52-W-2 132 Ingalls 1946.9 1948.1 usacc
Harding H COL 103-S 63 Ingalls 1948.12 1951.1 Ret BG usacc
Harding H J P COL 54-S-2 134 Ingalls 1948.10 1952.11 usacc
Harding E 1LT 18-E-2 37-B Bernard 1826.8 1828 '26rq rms?
Hardy B A 1LT 15-S 36 Ruckman 1919 '19cd
Hardy C W COL 45-E-2 116 Ingalls 1950.8 1950.10 usacc
Harllee R LTC 34-N-2 100 Ingalls 1974.10 1977.1 mfh
Harlow F S LT 18-W-1 29-A Bernard 1887 1890 d-691 room
Harlow F S CPT 67-N 36 Ingalls 1900.7 1904.9 S&F c-46
Harmon C C CW3 43-W-2 1 Reeder 1982.6 1982.10 mfh
Harmon M F LT 55 42 Ingalls 1890 b-6
Harmon M F CPT 18-E-2 37-B Bernard 1902 b-26
Harmon B F CPT 144-N-2 41-D Ingalls 1928.6 1930.6 Killed '34 Case
Harper H F MAJ 54-N-2 140 Ingalls 1984.3 1986.12 mfh
Harrell B MG 157 101 Bernard 1959.11 1960.6 Ret GEN usacc
Harrell B MG 54-S-2 134 Ingalls 1959.8 1959.11 Ret GEN usacc
Harriman J E CPT 144-N-1 41-B Ingalls 1932.7 1934.8 Ret BG
Harriman J E 1LT 1 151 Bernard 1928 1929 Ret BG '29cd Detwiler
Harriman J E 1LT 15-N 34 Ruckman 1923.8 1924.6 '23cd Ret BG
Harriman J E COL 14 32 Ruckman 1946.9 1948.3 Ret BG usacc
Harrington J H CPT 51-N-1 122 Ingalls 1932.8 1933.6 Covington
Harrington R E CPT 15-S 36 Ruckman 1922.9 1923.6 '23CAS Arthur
Harris W H 1LT 35-W-2 2 Reeder 1936.7 1937.7 Ret BG Roy
Harris H P GEN 119 33 Fenwick 1964.4 1965.2 Ret GEN mfh
Harris F V COL 143-S-2 35-C Ingalls 1967.8 1968.2 mfh
Harris G W CWO 167 A 7 Patch Road 1966.10 1966.10 mfh
Harris F V COL 101-N 57 Ingalls 1968.2 1969.6 mfh
Harris W M CPT 3-N 169 Bernard 1943 1945 PhBk
Harris H P MG 125 73 Ingalls 1958.6 1960.4 Ret GEN usacc
Harris L CPT 69-S 85 Ingalls 1919.9 1920.9 '20cd
Harris H P GEN 142 51 Fenwick 1964.4 1964.4 Ret GEN mfh
Harris C S CPT 1 151 Bernard 1923 1924 Ret BG Harris
Harris P J COL 101-N 57 Ingalls 1966.7 1968.2 mfh
Harris F V COL 44-S-2 102 Ingalls 1967.7 1967.8 mfh
Harris C S CPT 144-N-2 41-D Ingalls 1925.6 1927.4 Ret BG Harris
Harris C S CPT 52-E-1 128 Ingalls 1932.9 1935.4 Ret BG Harris
Harris F E CPT 50-W 121 Bernard 1903.3 1906.8 S&F '03cd b-21
Harris O R CPT 45-E-2 116 Ingalls 1944 1945 '44-45PhBks
Harris P A 1LT 102-N 61 Ingalls 1918 1919 BOQ WWI '19cd
Harrison J H LTC 17-W-2 41-B Bernard 1964.3 1967.8 mfh
Harrison F B COL 50-W 121 Bernard 1959.1 1960.9 usacc
Harrison F B COL 144-N-2 41-D Ingalls 1957.7 1959.1 usacc
Harrison E S 1LT 18-E-2 37-B Bernard 1916.8 1917.1 '17cd
Harrison E H 1LT 17-E-2 47-B Bernard 1931.9 1933.6 Harrison
Harrison G F E LTC 119 33 Fenwick 1907.7 1909.1 w
Harrison E S 1LT 16-W 51 Bernard 1911 1912 BOQ? '11cd
Harrison E S 1LT 17-E-2 47-B Bernard 1915.7 1916.8 '16cd
Harrison G F E LTC 1 151 Bernard 1906.10 1907.7 CO w
Harrison E H 1LT 1 151 Bernard 1934 1935 Harrison
Harrison R C 1LT 18-W-2 29-B Bernard 1915.9 1916.9 Small
Hart F A COL 70-N 91 Ingalls 1975.9 1977.8 mfh
Hartman N E MAJ 144-N-2 41-D Ingalls 1937.8 1940.8 '37cd '40PhBk

Hartman A R 1LT 1 151 Bernard 1936 1936.11 Hartman
Hartman J L MAJ 143-S-2 35-C Ingalls 1935.7 1937.3 Ret BG Vet
Hartman L Y 1LT 18-E-1 37-A Bernard 1927.7 1928.7 Goff
Hartman A R 1LT 33-W-1 59 Fenwick 1936.11 1937.3 Hartman
Hartman J L LTC 123-W 2 Ruckman 1937.3 1940.7 Vet PhBk Ret BG
Hartman L Y 1LT 102-N 61 Ingalls 1918 1919 BOQ WWI '19cd
Hartman N E CPT 34-N-1 98 Ingalls 1930.12 1931.6 Jackson
Hartmann J P MAJ 144-N-2 41-D Ingalls 1943 1945 '43-45PhBks
Hartsock F M COL 125 73 Ingalls 1935.7 1939.5 MedC JHC +
Harty W Q LTC 44-S-1 104 Ingalls 1970.3 1973.5 mfh
Hartzog W W COL 102-S 59 Ingalls 1984.7 1985.11 mfh
Harvey R MAJ 52-W-2 132 Ingalls 1978.7 1981.7 mfh
Harvey N C COL 68-S 81 Ingalls 1958.9 1960.8 usacc
Harwell M H 2LT 18-E-2 37-B Bernard 1930.9 1931.8 '31cd
Harwood R D LTC 52-W-2 132 Ingalls 1966.2 1966.9 PhBk
Hasbrouck A COL 121-E 43 Fenwick 1918.5 1919.6 '19cd
Hasbrouck A CPT 1 151 Bernard 1910.9 1911.0 '11cd
Hasbrouck H C LTC 1 151 Bernard 1898.5 1898.6 w
Hasbrouck A CPT 19 18 Bernard 1909.9 1910.9 CAS'10
Hase W F CPT 68-N 83 Ingalls 1908.9 1909.9 Hase
Hase W F CPT 15-N 34 Ruckman 1902.9 c-46
Hase W F CPT 126-N 165 Bernard 1911.11 1912.12 S&F '12cd +
Hase W F CPT 123-E 4 Ruckman 1909.9 1910.9 '11PhBk
Hase W F 1LT 63-S 26 Ruckman 1901.9 1902.9 '03cd
Haskell J B MAJ 68-S 81 Ingalls 1925.6 1928.6 Haskell
Haskell L W COL 66-S 38 Ingalls 1946.9 1947.5 usacc
Haskins G D COL 35-W-2 2 Reeder 1962.8 1965.8 mfh
Hasley M B MG 120 37 Fenwick 1949.5 1951.1 usacc Ret MG?
Hastings F H CPT 3-S 167 Bernard 1928.8 1929.7 '29cd
Hastings F H CPT 15-S 36 Ruckman 1927.8 1928.8 Bennett
Hastings F H CPT 34-N-2 100 Ingalls 1931.8 1932.8 deCamp
Hastings F W CPT 34-S-2 94 Ingalls 1932.8 1934.6 Flory
Hasty P J Rev 7 Frank Lane 1875.5 1877.2 St Mary's Priest
Hatch M A 1LT 45-E-1 114 Ingalls 1930.12 1932.6 '31cd
Hatch H J 1LT 55 42 Ingalls 1900.1 1901.11 Incks '02cd
Hatch H J CPT 50-E 129 Bernard 1907.9 1910.9 RLT
Hatch H J COL 158 32 Ingalls 1923.6 1925.6 '23cd
Hatch M A 1LT 15-S 36 Ruckman 1932.6 1933.7 '33cd
Hause F A CPT 66-N 40 Ingalls 1927.8 1928.8 Bradshaw
Hause F A CPT 62-S 30 Ruckman 1921.8 1923.8 '23cd
Hauser B MAJ 45-E-2 116 Ingalls 1979.5 1981.7 mfh
Havard V LTC 93 75 Ingalls 1903 1904 MedC '03cd
Hawes G P Jr 1LT 17-W-2 41-B Bernard 1909.9 1910.9 CAS'10
Hawes G P Jr 2LT 55 42 Ingalls 1902.8 b-19
Hawes G P Jr CPT 14 32 Ruckman 1913.12 1915.2 PhBk
Hawkin M R 1LT 3-S 167 Bernard 1898 1899 micro 617
Hawkins A C 1LT 1 151 Bernard 1917 1918 Hawkins
Hawkins R L COL 62-S 30 Ruckman 1954.8 1958.8 usacc
Hawkins S F COL 93 75 Ingalls 1940.7 1942 Clark
Hawkins R L COL 44-N-2 108 Ingalls 1954.7 1954.8 usacc
Hawthorne W B LTC 1 151 Bernard 1942.9 1944.3 Hawthorne
Hawthorne W B CPT 143-N-1 35-B Ingalls 1938.6 1940.7 Hawthorne
Hawthorne W B LTC 143-S-1 35-A Ingalls 1940.7 1941.7 Splain

Hayden J L MAJ 1 151 Bernard 1932.8 1934 deCamp
Hayden J L CPT 143-N-1 35-B Ingalls 1921.8 1922.8 JHC
Hayden R COL 158 32 Ingalls 1978.7 1979.11 mfh
Hayduck L E COL 143-S-2 35-C Ingalls 1946.9 1947.4 usacc
Hayduck L E COL 102-S 59 Ingalls 1947.4 1949.11 usacc
Hayes H G COL 101-N 57 Ingalls 1954.7 1955.8 usacc
Hayes T CW3 34-N-1 98 Ingalls 1980.3 1983.1 mfh
Haynes I A COL 119 33 Fenwick 1913.2 1916.8 Ret BG PhBk
Haynes I A CPT 65-N 48 Ingalls 1902.8 1903.8 Ret BG '02cd
Haynes I A CPT 16-W 51 Bernard 1902 1902.8 Ret BG '02cd
Haynes A M Jr MAJ 35-E-2 8 Reeder 1974.4 1976.6 mfh
Hays W MAJ 18-E-1 37-A Bernard 1868.5 1869.4 S&F c-27
Hays W BG 1 151 Bernard 1867.7 1867.11 CG w Ret BG?
Hayward J O COL 103-S 63 Ingalls 1976.1 1979.3 mfh
Hayward B M COL 67-N 36 Ingalls 1976.1 1976.3 mfh
Hayward B M COL 101-N 57 Ingalls 1976.3 1976.8 mfh
Hazeltine C B Jr LTC 52-E-2 126 Ingalls 1954.9 1957.7 usacc
Healy D F Jr COL 34-N-1 98 Ingalls 1947.9 1948.6 usacc
Healy D F Jr COL 65-S 46 Ingalls 1948.6 1949.11 usacc
Hearin J N Jr COL 68-N 83 Ingalls 1971.8 1972.2 mfh
Heath L T COL 51-S-1 120 Ingalls 1946.8 1948.8 Ret MG usacc
Heath L T MG 118 29 Fenwick 1960.7 1962.7 Ret MG mfh
Heathcock J T COL 79-S 93 Ingalls 1975.3 1976.8 mfh
Heckemeyer B W COL 19 18 Bernard 1959.8 1964.10 mfh
Heddleston E W 1LT 54-N-2 140 Ingalls 1935.7 1936.7 Ramsay
Hedge A A CPT 50-W 121 Bernard 1920.6 1922.6 S&F Arthur
Heferstay H K 2LT 16-E 53 Bernard 1944 1945 PhBk
Heffil D L BEOlc 34-S-2 94 Ingalls 1967.3 1969.3 mfh
Heiberg H H COL 102-S 59 Ingalls 1951.5 1953.7 Ret BG usacc
Heidland E F 1LT 34-N-1 98 Ingalls 1935.8 1936.8 Levy CAS'36
Heidner S J 2LT 18-W-2 29-B Bernard 1913.12 1914.12 '14PhBk
Heiker J H LTC 18-W-2 29-B Bernard 1970.6 1972.3 mfh
Heileman J F MAJ 18-E-1 37-A Bernard 1824.4 1826.3 '25rq d-684
Heileman J F MAJ 17-E-2 47-B Bernard 1834.4 1835.2 '34rq
Heileman J F MAJ 17-E-1 47-A Bernard 1834.4 1835.2 '34rq
Heilfron N CPT 43-W-2 1 Reeder 1932.8 1933.6 '33cd
Heimstead M K COL 128-W 107 Bernard 1963.11 1966.1 mfh
Heimstead M K COL 43-E-1 5 Reeder 1963.6 1963.11 mfh
Heinemann W E 1LT 16-E 53 Bernard 1940 1941 PhBk
Heiner G G CPT 61-S 43 Ingalls 1889 1902 micro 617
Heiner G G CPT 101-N 57 Ingalls 1907.7 1908.3 '08cd
Heiner G G MAJ 126-S 163 Bernard 1909.9 1910.9 CAS'10 Arthur
Heinitsh G 1LT 17-W-2 41-B Bernard 1938.6 1940.6 MedC PhBks
Heinitsh G LTC 16-W 51 Bernard 1941.4 1944.9 MedC wife
Heintges J A COL 79-S 93 Ingalls 1953.11 1954.11 Ret LTG usacc
Heintges J A COL 17-E-1 47-A Bernard 1952.9 1953.11 Ret LTG usacc
Helmboldt H E COL 3-S 167 Bernard 1960.7 1961.8 usacc
Helmboldt H E COL 54-S-1 136 Ingalls 1957.12 1960.7 usacc
Helton C LTC 16-E 53 Bernard 1972.8 1976.6 mfh
Hemby R MAJ 17-W-1 41-A Bernard 1981.2 1983.7 mfh
Hemphill J A COL 44-N-2 108 Ingalls 1970.1 1971.1 mfh Ret BG
Hemphill J A COL 70-S 89 Ingalls 1971.1 1972.5 mfh Ret BG
Henderson J C MAJ 50-E 129 Bernard 1920.11 1921.8 '20cd

Henderson J C 1LT 67-N 36 Ingalls 1910.9 1911.9 '11cd
Henderson J C CPT 93 75 Ingalls 1919.12 1920.11 '20cd
Hendrix R R COL 67-S 34 Ingalls 1946.11 1948.12 Ret MG usacc
Henglein R J COL 51-N-2 124 Ingalls 1967.12 1970.10 mfh
Henion J Q MG 125 73 Ingalls 1971.7 1973.6 mfh Ret LTG
Hennig W H COL 18-E-2 37-B Bernard 1952.4 1952.8 Ret MG usacc
Hennig W H 1LT 33-W-2 57 Fenwick 1937.6 1938.6 Ret MG Tarrant
Henry F S COL 123-E 4 Ruckman 1954.7 1956.6 Ret BG usacc
Henry G V CPT 17-E-1 47A Bernard 1868.10 1869.5 S&F c-27
Henry F S COL 144-N-1 41-B Ingalls 1953.7 1954.7 Ret BG usacc
Henry C B LTC 18-W-1 29-A Bernard 1946.10 1953.1 usacc
Hensey W R Jr COL 33-E-2 63 Fenwick 1947.7 1949.8 '47PhBk
Henshel W E LTC 33-W-2 57 Fenwick 1971.10 1973.7 mfh
Herber D COL 54-S-1 136 Ingalls 1966.7 1967.8 mfh
Hergenroeder L A COL 102-S 59 Ingalls 1976.7 1977.9 mfh
Hergenroeger L A LTC 43-E-1 5 Reeder 1975.8 1976.7 mfh
Hering E L MAJ 124-N 69 Ingalls 1924.8 1928.7 '25-28cds
Herman P H 1LT 144-N-1 41-B Ingalls 1913.12 1914.12 CAS'14 PhBk
Herman P H LTC 121-E 43 Fenwick 1930.10 1936.5 RLT JHC
Hero A Jr MAJ 157 101 Bernard 1911.9 1912.9 Ret MG '12cd
Hero A Jr MAJ 14 32 Ruckman 1915.2 1916.7 Ret MG Tilton
Hero A Jr CPT 50-E 129 Bernard 1902.7 1907.9 Ret MG b-19
Herrick J R MAJ 101-N 57 Ingalls 1933.6 1935.6 MedC JHC Ely
Herrick H N CPT 79-N 95 Ingalls 1930.9 1932.8 Ret BG Herrick
Herrick J R MAJ 1 151 Bernard 1929 1930 MedC '29cd
Herrick H S 1LT 17-E-2 47-B Bernard 1905.9 1906.9 CAS'06
Herrick 16-W 51 Bernard 1886 c-14 Chaplain
Herring R E CPT 67-S 34 Ingalls 1911.9 1912.9 CAS'12 '12cd
Herring R E 1LT 68-N 83 Ingalls 1907.9 1908.9 '08cd
Herring R E MAJ 121-W 41 Fenwick 1920.4 1923.9 Killed '25
Herrod J T COL 51-N-2 124 Ingalls 1951.6 1955.2 usacc
Hert P COL 15-S 36 Ruckman 1963.10 1965.2 mfh
Hertzog J M COL 50-E 129 Bernard 1966.8 1967.8 mfh
Hesketh W LTC 123-E 4 Ruckman 1940.6 1941.12 Ret BG Hesketh
Hesketh W CPT 17-W-1 41-A Bernard 1923.8 1925.7 Ret BG Hesketh
Hesketh W CPT 62-S 30 Ruckman 1927.11 1930.3 Ret BG Hesketh
Hesnan T F Rev 7 Frank Lane 1947 '47PhBk Priest
Hess G A COL 17-W-2 41-B Bernard 1960.9 1962.2 mfh
Hess L E LTC 43-E-2 7 Reeder 1968.2 1969.9 mfh
Hess W W Jr 2LT 16-W 51 Bernard 1915 ? Ret BG
Hewes H G 1LT 15-N 34 Ruckman 1943 1944 PhBk
Hewett H CPT 70-S 89 Ingalls 1938.7 1939.6 Ret MG son
Hewett H COL 69-N 87 Ingalls 1946.7 1946.8 Ret MG son
Hewett H COL 68-N 83 Ingalls 1946.8 1949.7 Ret MG usacc
Hewett H COL 125 73 Ingalls 1946.5 1946.7 Ret MG son
Hewett H CPT 79-S 93 Ingalls 1937.7 1938.7 Ret MG son
Hewett H CPT 17-E-2 47-B Bernard 1925.8 1928.6 Ret MG Mitchell
Hewett H CPT 67-N 36 Ingalls 1929.6 1934.6 Ret MG son
Heye J G Rev 7 Frank Lane 1944 1945 '44-45PhBks St Mary's Priest
Heyme D H LTC 35-E-2 8 Reeder 1950.9 1953.8 usacc
Hickey D O BG 158 32 Ingalls 1946.7 1949.3 usacc Ret BG?
Hickey D W Jr CPT 69-S 85 Ingalls 1934.9 1936.6 Ret BG Hickey
Hickey D W Jr CPT 43-E-2 7 Reeder 1931.8 1934.9 Ret BG Hickey

Hickman D R BG 157 101 Bernard 1969.6 1972.7 Ret MG mfh
Hickock M J 1LT 144-N-1 41-B Ingalls 1914.12 1915.12 '15CAS
Hickock M J MAJ 102-N 61 Ingalls 1921.8 1922.6 '22FOcs
Hicks W W MAJ 101-S 55 Ingalls 1925.8 1926.6 Kaufman Daughter
Hicks W W 1LT 18-E-2 37-B Bernard 1911.9 1912.9 CAS'12 '12cd
Hicks W W MAJ 18-E-2 37-B Bernard 1923.8 1925.8 '23cd
Hicks W W CPT 120 37 Fenwick 1918.6 1918.9 Daughter
Hicks M J 1LT 68-N 83 Ingalls 1914.12 1915.12 '16cd
Hicks T A Jr COL 123-E 4 Ruckman 1970.1 1972.1 mfh
Hicks T A Jr COL 144-S-1 41-A Ingalls 1969.8 1970.1 mfh
Hicks G L Jr 1LT 69-N 87 Ingalls 1905.9 1906.9 '06cd
Hiddleston E W 1LT 44-N-2 108 Ingalls 1936.8 1937.8 CAS'37
Hierholzer F H COL 126-N 165 Bernard 1946.2 1948.5 usacc
Higgins C W CPT 3-N 169 Bernard 1924.6 1925.11 Higgins
Higgins C W CPT 70-S 89 Ingalls 1931.6 1933.7 Higgins
Higgins C W CPT 69-N 87 Ingalls 1929.6 1931.6 Higgins
Higgins E R COL 44-N-1 106 Ingalls 1959.3 1960.2 usacc
Higgins H R BG 118 29 Fenwick 1970.9 1971.7 Ret MG mfh
Higgins H R BG 127-W 145 Bernard 1969.6 1970.9 mfh Ret MG
Hightower L V MG 141 53 Fenwick 1963.3 1963.9 mfh Ret MG?
Hightower L V COL 50-E 129 Bernard 1984.7 1986.8 mfh
Hildebrant C W 1LT 18-E-1 37-A Bernard 1939.7 1940.4 Moorman
Hill I B COL 121-E 43 Fenwick 1944.2 1946.3 PhBk
Hill H C 1LT 63-S 26 Ruckman 1918.4 1919.6 AN306
Hill R D COL 44-S-2 102 Ingalls 1963.8 1964.7 mfh
Hill J F P LTC 16-E 53 Bernard 1946.10 1947.2 usacc
Hill C W 1LT 34-N-1 98 Ingalls 1940.2 1941 Hill
Hill E W CPT 143-S-2 35-C Ingalls 1926.7 1927.6 Ret BG AF AdvCs
Hill LT 14 32 Ruckman 1888 1890 c-46
Hill R D COL 69-N 87 Ingalls 1964.7 1969.8 mfh
Hill R E CPT 15-S 36 Ruckman 1920.6 1922.8 Helmboldt
Hill R E COL 127-W 145 Bernard 1944.9 1946.8 PhBk
Hill R E CPT 50-E 129 Bernard 1928.6 1930.7 R T Chaplin
Hill R E CPT 1 151 Bernard 1925 1926 '25cd
Hill G L COL 45-E-2 116 Ingalls 1963.8 1964.1 mfh
Hill I B CPT 67-N 36 Ingalls 1924.8 1928.6 Crowell
Hill R E CPT 1 151 Bernard 1923 1924 Helm Higgins
Hill V C CPT 62-N 28 Ruckman 1932.6 1935.7 Vet '33cd
Hill G L COL 64 71 Fenwick 1964.1 1964.7 mfh
Hill H C 1LT 79-S 93 Ingalls 1917 1918.4 BOQ WWI '19cd
Hill J P COL 33-W-1 59 Fenwick 1967.6 1971.7 mfh
Hill R E MAJ 19 18 Bernard 1934.7 1936.7 Helm
Hill R E CPT 51-N-1 122 Ingalls 1933.7 1934.6 VanBuskirk +
Hillberg L J 2LT 17-E-2 47-B Bernard 1933.9 1934.6 Hillberg
Hilling D CPT 54-S-2 134 Ingalls 1983.1 1984.8 mfh
Hill G P Jr COL 69-N 87 Ingalls 1956.8 1959.7 usacc
Hilton C H 1LT 68-S 81 Ingalls 1902 c-46
Hilton C H CPT 79-N 95 Ingalls 1905.9 1906.9 '06cd
Hincke J I COL 102-S 59 Ingalls 1953.8 1954.9 usacc
Hincke J I COL 16-W 51 Bernard 1953.5 1953.8 usacc
Hindle C D CPT 16-W 51 Bernard 1923 1924 BOQ? '24cd
Hinds J H BG 141 53 Fenwick 1954.9 1956.2 Ret MG usacc
Hines C CPT 69-S 85 Ingalls 1916.12 1917.12 Ret BG Hines

Hines F T CPT 128-E 109 Bernard 1917.1 1918.1 Ret BG JHC +
Hines F T CPT 65-S 46 Ingalls 1910.9 1911.9 Ret BG '11cd
Hines J B R LTC 43-W-2 1 Reeder 1954.9 1957.6 usacc
Hinkle F M 1LT 65-S 46 Ingalls 1909.9 1910.9 CAS'10
Hinman D D MAJ 129-S 101 Ingalls 1929.6 1930.7 Ret BG Blood
Hinman D D MAJ 65-S 46 Ingalls 1930.7 1932.7 Reg BG '31cd
Hinman D D CPT 15-S 36 Ruckman 1925.8 1926.8 Ret BG Chapel
Hinman D D CPT 144-N-2 41-D Ingalls 1923.7 1925.7 Ret BG '23cd
Hinshaw F A CPT 51-N-1 122 Ingalls 1944.4 1945 '44-45PhBks
Hinternhoff W A COL 103-S 63 Ingalls 1968.8 1969.7 mfh
Hinternhoff W A LTC 143-N-2 35-D Ingalls 1960.2 1961.6 usacc
Hinton J COL 101-S 55 Ingalls 1951.8 1953.9 usacc
Hirsch J G Rev 7 Frank Lane 1943 1947 PhBks St Mary's Priest
Hixon R C MG 142 51 Fenwick 1975.8 1979.7 mfh Ret MG
Hoag W M 1LT 44-S-1 104 Ingalls 1944 1945 '44-45PhBk
Hoag R E COL 33-W-1 59 Fenwick 1953.9 1955.5 usacc
Hoar R S 1LT 93 75 Ingalls 1919 WWI BOQ '19cd
Hobbs R H LTC 144-S-1 41-A Ingalls 1941.3 1944.2 Bennett PhBks
Hobson H M COL 18-W-2 29-B Bernard 1951.7 1951.9 Ret BG usacc
Hobson J B LTC 16-W 51 Bernard 1967.2 1967.8 mfh
Hobson H M COL 62-S 30 Ruckman 1951.9 1953.8 Ret BG usacc
Hobson V W Jr BG 127-E 147 Bernard 1964.10 1965.9 mfh Ret BG
Hocker C E MAJ 123-W 2 Ruckman 1930.6 1934.6 '31-33cds
Hoddinott G R LTC 52-E-2 126 Ingalls 1967.7 1969.4 mfh
Hodge J R GEN 119 33 Fenwick 1952.7 1953.7 Ret GEN usacc
Hodges R COL 51-S-2 118 Ingalls 1962.3 1962.7 mfh
Hodges J P CPT 143-N-2 35-D Ingalls 1935.7 1936.5 Ret MG AF JHC
Hodges J P CPT 34-S-1 96 Ingalls 1934.6 1935.7 Ret MG AF +
Hodges W J Jr 1LT 16-E 53 Bernard 1938 1939 Hoffman '39cd
Hoff S S LTC 45-W-1 112 Ingalls 1948.9 1950.9 Ret MG usacc
Hoffman J H COL 17-E-1 47-A Bernard 1967.12 1969.7 mfh
Hoffman T F 1LT 16-E 53 Bernard 1938.9 1939.8 Hoffman
Hoffmeister D E LTC 43-W-1 3 Reeder 1953.11 1957.1 usacc
Hofheinz W J E-4 33 CGH 67 Fenwick 1970.7 1972.3 usacc
Hogan J L 1LT 63-S 26 Ruckman 1923.7 1924.7 '23cd
Hoge D H CPT 14 32 Ruckman 1935.6 1936 Dunham JHC
Hoge D H 1LT 143-N-1 35-B Ingalls 1919.6 1920.9 '20cd
Hoge D H CPT 3-S 167 Bernard 1925.6 1928.7 Hoge
Hoge B F COL 142 51 Fenwick 1944.10 1945.9 PhBk + Tilton
Hoge D H MAJ 19 18 Bernard 1930.7 1933.6 Hoge
Hoge D H 1LT 18-W-1 29-A Bernard 1919.3 1919.6 Hoge
Hohenthal W D CPT 15-N 34 Ruckman 1932.5 1933.8 Hohenthal
Hohenthal W D 2LT 112-W 30 Tidball 1918.4 1919.1 Hennessy '19cd
Hohenthal W D 1LT 16-E 53 Bernard 1927 1928 Hohenthal
Holcomb C W 1LT 33-W-1 59 Fenwick 1934.7 1935.7 Holcomb
Holcomb C W CPT 143-N-1 35-B Ingalls 1937.6 1938.6 '37cd
Holcomb C W CPT 51-N-2 124 Ingalls 1938.7 1939.5 PhBks
Holcombe J L 1LT 67-N 36 Ingalls 1912.12 1914.12 PhBk
Holder W G 1LT 18-W-1 29-A Bernard 1930.7 1931.7 Chitterling
Holland D K COL 50-W 121 Bernard 1975.7 1978.6 mfh
Holland P J MAJ 35-W-2 2 Reeder 1968.8 1970.8 mfh
Holland G D 1LT 143-N-1 35-B Ingalls 1915.12 1916.12 CAS'16
Hollender D W MAJ 52-E-1 128 Ingalls 1964.11 1966.7 KIA-RVN mfh

Holley J L Jr LTC 51-N-2 124 Ingalls 1965.7 1966.1 mfh
Hollinger J C LTC 143-S-2 35-C Ingalls 1960.9 1963.4 mfh
Hollister J B CPT 65-N 48 Ingalls 1919 BOQ? '19cd
Holly J H COL 102-N 61 Ingalls 1950.2 1951.2 usacc
Hollyday T W 1LT 63-N 24 Ruckman 1906.9 1907.9 CAS'07
Holm G P BG 127-W 145 Bernard 1967.12 1968.6 Ret MG mfh
Holmes J W MAJ 44-N-2 108 Ingalls 1985.7 1987.3 mfh
Holmes H B Jr CPT 144-S-1 41-A Ingalls 1923.12 1927.9 Ret BG Holmes
Holmes J L Jr CPT 54-N-2 140 Ingalls 1962.2 1962.12 USN mfh
Holmes H B Jr 1LT 18-W-1 29-A Bernard 1922.7 1923.7 Ret BG Holmes
Holmes H B Jr MAJ 144-S-2 41-C Ingalls 1918.7 1918.11 Ret BG Holmes
Holmquist C A CPT 17-E-1 47-A Bernard 1918.10 1919.6 '19cd
Holst J J 1LT 35-E-1 6 Reeder 1933.9 1934.8 '34BtryOCs
Holterman G H 1LT 35-W-1 4 Reeder 1940.7 1941.9 Holterman
Holtz J G 1LT 144-S-2 41-C Ingalls 1912.12 1913.12 CAS'13 '13cd
Holtzworth B A BG 121-E 43 Fenwick 1954.9 1956.6 usacc Ret BG?
Homer J L MAJ 102-N 61 Ingalls 1923.6 1924.6 Ret MG '24AdvCs
Homer J L 1LT 67-S 34 Ingalls 1916.12 1917.6 Ret MG Ford
Homer W O LT 16-E 53 Bernard 1889.8 1891.6 c-26
Hood J H 1LT 143-N-2 35-D Ingalls 1914.12 1915.12 PhBk
Hood J H MAJ 14 32 Ruckman 1918.11 1918.12 Hood
Hooper L COL 67-N 36 Ingalls 1981.7 1983.5 mfh
Hoops D L E-2 33 CGH 67 Fenwick 1972.3 1973.11 usacc
Hoover P F COL 144-N-1 41-B Ingalls 1954.8 1954.8 usacc
Hoover P F COL 102-N 61 Ingalls 1954.8 1955.6 usacc
Hoover P E COL 62-N 28 Ruckman 1958.7 1960.12 usacc
Hope O 1LT 66-S 38 Ingalls 1909.8 1910.8 S&F '11cd
Hope O CPT 124-S 67 Ingalls 1910.8 1912.7 S&F '12cd
Hopkins J P CPT 101-N 57 Ingalls 1908.3 1912.8 Ret BG S&F '11-12cd
Hopkins A CPT 54-S-1 136 Ingalls 1935.7 1936.7 Hopkins
Hopkins J P CPT 17-E-1 47-A Bernard 1906.9 1907.9 Ret BG CAS'07
Hopkins F E 1LT 17-W-1 41-A Bernard 1905.9 1906.9 '06cd
Hopper R F MAJ 51-S-1 120 Ingalls 1971.6 1972.5 mfh
Hornback R G LTC 143-N-2 35-D Ingalls 1970.6 1972.10 mfh
Hornsey J W LTC 61-N 45 Ingalls 1963.10 1966.10 mfh
Horowitz N CPT 79-S 93 Ingalls 1915.12 1916.12 '17cd
Hort J H LTC 45-E-2 116 Ingalls 1970.9 1974.6 mfh
Horton P J MAJ 127-W 145 Bernard 1927.7 1928.7 Ellis
Hougton F E COL 35-W-1 4 Reeder 1957.11 1959.5 usacc
House J C COL 103-N 65 Ingalls 1982.9 1986.6 mfh
House J CPT 17-E-1 47-A Bernard 1829 1829.11 '29rq d-684
House J CPT 17-E-2 47-B Bernard 1829 1829.11 '29rq d-684
Hovey G W CPT 65-S 46 Ingalls 1932.7 1933.7 '33cd
Howard E B COL 128-E 109 Bernard 1949.10 1951.6 Ret BG usacc
Howard C E N 1LT 64-S 22 Ruckman 1906 '06cd
Howard C E N CPT 103-N 65 Ingalls 1914.12 1915.12 '15cd
Howard T LTC 93 75 Ingalls 1895 1902 b-19
Howe R G COL 3-S 167 Bernard 1948.6 1948.7 usacc
Howe A P CPT 1 151 Bernard 1856.12 1857.1 w
Howe T B CPT 31-B 40 Hampton 1982.8 1986.6 mfh
Howe A P CPT 1 151 Bernard 1857.3 1857.4 w
Howell J F COL 120 37 Fenwick 1922.1 1924.6 Higgins +
Howell J N 1LT 44-S-2 102 Ingalls 1940.10 1941.10 Howell PhBk

Howell R 1LT 34-N-1 98 Ingalls 1983.2 1985.11 mfh
Howell J N 1LT 16-E 53 Bernard 1940.6 1940.10 PhBk
Howell J F CPT 124-N 69 Ingalls 1909.9 1911.9 '11cd
Howell J CPT 126-N 165 Bernard 1909.7 1910.6 Tilton JHC
Howell J F 1LT 69-S 85 Ingalls 1902.9 1903.9 '02cd
Howell J F CPT 121-W 41 Fenwick 1911.9 1912.9 '12cd
Howell J F Jr COL 65-N 48 Ingalls 1950.11 1951.8 usacc
Howell J F Jr 1LT 34-S-2 94 Ingalls 1930.12 1931.6 '31BtryOCs
Howze H H LTG 34-S-2 94 Ingalls 1961.8 1961.9 Ret GEN usacc
Hozier E A Mr 33 CGH 67 Fenwick 1912 1920 '13-20cd
Hubbard F 1LT 17-W-2 41-B Bernard 1917.6 1919.6 Axelson
Hubbard E W CPT 14 32 Ruckman 1902 1902 c-46 b-21 ORD
Hudgins S F LTC 14 32 Ruckman 1944.12 1945.11 PhBk
Huffman B E Jr MG 1 151 Bernard 1973.7 1975.7 Ret MG mfh
Huffman B E Jr MG 127-E 147 Bernard 1973.6 1973.7 Ret MG mfh
Huger B CPT 18-W-2 29-B Bernard 1824 ORD d-684
Huger B CPT 18-W-2 29-B Bernard 1832 1834 '34rq ORD
Huggins J B COL 125 73 Ingalls 1919.6 1922.10 MedC '20cd +
Hughes H L 2LT 18-E-1 37-A Bernard 1930.8 1931.8 '31cd
Hughes J F Jr COL 52-E-2 126 Ingalls 1961.12 1964.6 mfh
Hulse A D COL 51-S-1 120 Ingalls 1953.4 1955.8 Ret BG usacc
Humbert G F 2LT 16-E 53 Barnard 1912.1 1912.4 '12cd
Humbert G F MAJ 70-N 91 Ingalls 1927.6 1928.7 '28AdvCs
Hume W S COL 52-W-1 130 Ingalls 1959.8 1963.1 mfh
Hummell A V LTC 45-W-1 112 Ingalls 1967.3 1968.1 mfh
Humphrey G E CPT 18-W-2 29-B Bernard 1917.5 1917.11 ENGR '17cd
Humphrey M E CW2 54-N-1 138 Ingalls 1984.12 1985.6 mfh
Humphries F M 2LT 17-W-2 41-B Bernard 1934.7 1935.6 Cochran
Humphries T O MAJ 144-S-2 41-C Ingalls 1921.9 1922.6 '22FOcs
Hunt G COL 79-N 95 Ingalls 1979.8 1982.6 mfh
Hunt P E COL 129-S 101 Ingalls 1969.10 1971.6 mfh
Hunt W S 1LT 16-E 53 Bernard 1940.11 1941.1 PhBk
Hunt P E COL 18-E-2 37-B Bernard 1969.7 1969.10 mfh
Hunt W LTC 65-N 48 Ingalls 1982.4 1984.7 mfh
Hunter H W 1LT 44-N-1 106 Ingalls 1937.8 1938.7 Hunter
Hunter W H COL 44-S-2 102 Ingalls 1950.8 1952.8 usacc
Hunter H W 1LT 43-E-1 5 Reeder 1940.6 1941.5 Hunter
Hunter J L LTC 52-W-1 130 Ingalls 1974.11 1977.5 mfh
Hunter C N COL 54-N-1 138 Ingalls 1946.8 1947.1 usacc
Hunter W H COL 34-S-1 96 Ingalls 1954.2 1954.3 usacc
Hunter W H COL 66-N 40 Ingalls 1955.7 1957.8 usacc
Hunter W H COL 143-S-2 35-C Ingalls 1954.4 1955.7 usacc
Hunt I A Jr BG 120 37 Fenwick 1971.9 1973.10 mfh Ret MG
Huppert G H Jr COL 43-W-1 3 Reeder 1964.1 1964.7 mfh
Hurlbut O E MG 93 75 Ingalls 1963.8 1966.6 Ret LTG mfh
Hurlbut O E BG 14 32 Ruckman 1962.6 1963.8 Ret LTG mfh
Huston R M MAJ 68-N 83 Ingalls 1942.10 1944.7 PhBk
Huston M N COL 15-S 36 Ruckman 1958.10 1961.6 Ret BG usacc
Huston M N COL 34-N-2 100 Ingalls 1958.8 1958.10 Ret BG usacc
Hutchinson P A CPT 34-S-1 96 Ingalls 1942 1943 '43PhBk
Hutchinson P A 1LT 18-W-2 29-B Bernard 1941.1 1941.11 Hutchinson
Hutson J C CPT 63-S 26 Ruckman 1923.6 1923.8 Hutson
Hutson J C 1LT 16-W 51 Bernard 1917 1918 Hutson

Hutton P COL 158 32 Ingalls 1979.11 1981.6 mfh
Hutton W M COL 45-E-2 116 Ingalls 1948.1 1949.8 usacc
Hutton P COL 124-S 67 Ingalls 1981.6 1982.6 mfh
Hyde A P S CPT 69-S 85 Ingalls 1906.9 1907.9 CAS'07
Hyde R G COL 62-N 28 Ruckman 1974.7 1980.7 mfh
Hyde E B 2LT 16-E 53 Bernard 1915 '15cd
Hyde R D LTC 35-W-1 4 Reeder 1964.3 1966.9 mfh
Ide C E 1LT 3-S 167 Bernard 1914.12 1915.12 '16cd
Igo C C CPT 167 B 9 Patch Road 1959.3 1961.3 usacc
Igoe J Rev 7 Frank Lane 1940.7 1950.2 St Mary's Priest
Illig J M BG 118 29 Fenwick 1964.8 1965.6 mfh Ret BG
Illig J M BG 127-E 147 Bernard 1962.7 1964.8 mfh Ret BG
Imperatori R J CPT 3-N 169 Bernard 1927.7 1928.8 '28AdvCs
Ingalls J M MAJ 55 42 Ingalls 1884.6 1886.1? '00cd
Ingalls J M CPT 3-N 169 Bernard 1882.12 1891.1? c-14 c-27
Inskeep J L LTC 63-S 26 Ruckman 1951.5 1953.7 usacc
Inskeep J L LTC 51-N-2 124 Ingalls 1950.9 1951.5 usacc
Ippolito R MAJ 43-E-2 7 Reeder 1976.9 1978.6 mfh
Ireland M L 1LT 33 CGH 67 Fenwick 1910 1911.9 Rogers Daughter
Ireland M L 1LT 55 42 Ingalls 1911.9 1912.9 '12cd
Ireland M L 2LT 63-S 26 Ruckman 1905.9 1906.9 '06cd
Irish W E Jr LTC 33-E-2 63 Fenwick 1968.4 1968.7 mfh
Irvine M M COL 15-N 34 Ruckman 1952.9 1955.6 usacc
Irvine M M 1LT 45-E-2 116 Ingalls 1940.6 1943.6 '40-42PhBks
Irvine W W CPT 126-S 163 Bernard 1931.1 1932.1 Ret MG Irvine
Irvine M M 1LT 45-E-1 114 Ingalls 1936.7 1937.7 CAS'37
Irvine W W CPT 62-N 28 Ruckman 1930.12 1931.1 Ret MG Irvine
Irvine W W CPT 66-S 38 Ingalls 1925.8 1926.7 Ret MG Irvine
Irvine W W MAJ 124-N 69 Ingalls 1934.6 1936.6 Ret MG Irving
Irvine W W CPT 143-N-2 35-D Ingalls 1922.7 1925.7 Ret MG Irvine
Irving CPT 18-W-1 29-A Bernard 1825 d-684 room
Irving R K CPT 144-S-1 41-A Ingalls 1955.8 1958.7 USN usacc
Irving G A CPT 1 151 Bernard 1919 1919 '19cd
Irwin J R 2LT 18-W-2 29-B Bernard 1826 1828.4 '26rq rms
Ischinger M MAJ 34-E-1 6 Reeder 1976.12 1980.8 mfh
Israel I S COL 79-N 95 Ingalls 1972.10 1975.2 mfh
Ivey C T BG 157 101 Bernard 1982.7 1983.8 mfh
Jablonsky H J COL 35-W-1 4 Reeder 1955.3 1955.3 Ret MG usacc
Jablonsky H J COL 146 146 Engr Ln 1955.3 1957.6 Ret MG usacc
Jaccard R B LTC 17-E-2 47-B Bernard 1963.4 1964.6 mfh
Jackson R MAJ 17-E-1 47-A Bernard 1976.2 1976.6 mfh
Jackson A H LTC 17-W-2 41-B Bernard 1954.3 1957.9 usacc
Jackson T H 1LT 102-N 61 Ingalls 1918 1919 BOQ WWI '19cd
Jackson H R MAJ 124-S 67 Ingalls 1934.8 1938.6 Ret BG Jackson
Jackson J J COL 14 32 Ruckman 1970.10 1973.2 mfh
Jackson J J COL 43-E-1 5 Reeder 1970.9 1970.10 mfh
Jackson A F 1LT 16-E 53 Bernard 1940 PhBk
Jacobs J P CPT 52-W-2 132 Ingalls 1932.8 1933.6 '33cd
Jacobs E C COL 129-N 103 Ingalls 1956.8 1960.7 usacc
Jacobs J P CPT 3-S 167 Bernard 1930.8 1931.6 '31cd
Jacobs J P CPT 127-E 147 Bernard 1933.7 1935.7 Dunham +
Jacobson C C COL 102-S 59 Ingalls 1970.9 1972.6 mfh
Jacobson C C COL 34-S-1 96 Ingalls 1970.8 1970.9 mfh

196

Jacoby L E COL 66-S 38 Ingalls 1947.9 1948.2 usacc
Jakaitis B L COL 63-S 26 Ruckman 1962.12 1965.7 mfh
James G W LTC 43-W-1 3 Reeder 1957.3 1959.7 usacc
James LT 70-S 89 Ingalls 1903.11 1905.9 c-56
James J H LTC 54-S-1 136 Ingalls 1972.3 1974.5 mfh
James J E LTC 34-S-1 96 Ingalls 1950.4 1952.8 usacc
James C F Jr MAJ 43-W-2 1 Reeder 1942.5 1943.6 MedC '43PhBk
Janowski R A MAJ 67-N 36 Ingalls 1942.10 1943.2 PhBk
Janutolo D M MAJ 54-N-2 140 Ingalls 1971.9 1972.7 mfh
Jarman S MAJ 141 53 Fenwick 1922 1923 Ret BG '20cd
Jarock N COL 33-W-1 59 Fenwick 1977.9 1980.3 mfh
Jarvis G M LTC 50-E 129 Bernard 1942.6 1944.6 PhBk
Jefferson J L MAJ 143-S-2 35-C Ingalls 1938.3 1939.6 '39PhBk
Jefferson L W CPT 3-S 167 Bernard 1922.2 1925.6 Jefferson
Jefferson L W CPT 34-N-1 98 Ingalls 1934.8 1935.8 deCamp JHC
Jeffrey P R COL 103-N 65 Ingalls 1957.8 1961.7 usacc
Jellison C D LTC 143-N-1 35-B Ingalls 1970.11 1973.3 mfh
Jemison J K 1LT 69-N 87 Ingalls 1914.12 1915.12 '16cd
Jenes T G Jr COL 79-S 93 Ingalls 1973.7 1975.2 mfh Ret MG
Jenkins J F COL 44-S-1 104 Ingalls 1965.11 1967.2 mfh
Jenkins C W 1LT 64-S 22 Ruckman 1916.12 1917.12 Ford
Jenkins A G 1LT 62-S 30 Ruckman 1901.9 1902.4 '02cd
Jenkins J F COL 144-N-2 41-D Ingalls 1967.2 1967.12 mfh
Jenkins M SFC 35-E-1 6 Reeder 1980.8 1984.5 mfh
Jenna R W COL 43-E-2 7 Reeder 1956.8 1957.4 usacc
Jenna R W COL 158 32 Ingalls 1957.4 1959.8 usacc
Jennings J E MAJ 34-S-1 96 Ingalls 1940 1942.6 AN360
Jennings J E LTC 128-E 109 Bernard 1942.6 1944.2 PhBk
Jensen D P MAJ 144-S-1 41-A Ingalls 1983.7 1984.6 mfh
Jewell F C CPT 126-S 163 Bernard 1912.6 1914.9 PhBk +
Jewell F C CPT 66-S 38 Ingalls 1903.8 1904.8 CAS'04
Johannsen D F CWO 147 147 Engr Ln 1965.6 1969.6 mfh
Johnson H W COL 93 75 Ingalls 1946.10 1947.5 Ret MG usacc
Johnson W L 1LT 18-W-1 29-A Bernard 1931.8 1932.7 '32BtryOCs
Johnson R H BG 44-S-2 102 Ingalls 1970.6 1970.8 mfh Ret BG
Johnson E A COL 124-S 67 Ingalls 1952.8 1953.4 usacc
Johnson B P MG 142 51 Fenwick 1963.1 1963.12 Ret MG mfh
Johnson W P COL 33-E-2 63 Fenwick 1950.9 1951.4 Ret MG usacc
Johnson J C COL 119 33 Fenwick 1922.12 1923.1 Ret BG w
Johnson C R LTC 144-S-1 41-A Ingalls 1975.2 1977.7 mfh
Johnson W A MAJ 62-N 28 Ruckman 1945 1946 PhBk
Johnson J C COL 142 51 Fenwick 1919.6 1924.3 Ret BG JHC cds
Johnson G G Mr 33 CGH 67 Fenwick 1942.6 1949.10 '43-48PhBks
Johnson D B 1LT 35-E-1 6 Reeder 1937.6 1938.8 Johnson
Johnson D W MAJ 44-N-1 106 Ingalls 1972.9 1976.11 mfh
Johnson E A COL 34-N-1 98 Ingalls 1952.6 1952.8 usacc
Johnson L M COL 70-S 89 Ingalls 1949.3 1953.3 usacc
Johnson J C CPT 18-E-1 37-A Bernard 1908.9 1909.9 Ret BG CAS'09
Johnson R E COL 44-N-1 106 Ingalls 1947.4 1947.7 usacc
Johnson H W MG 120 37 Fenwick 1958.3 1961.1 Ret MG usacc
Johnson H S CPT 65-S 46 Ingalls 1928.6 1929.6 Parsons
Johnson B P MG 55 42 Ingalls 1962.9 1963.1 Ret MG mfh
Johnson W F 1LT 1 151 Bernard 1936 1937 VanOrmer

Johnson J C CPT 68-S 81 Ingalls 1909.9 1910.9 Ret BG CAS'10
Johnson B P LTC 35-W-2 2 Reeder 1948.2 1949.1 Ret MG usacc
Johnson A D COL 68-S 81 Ingalls 1983.5 1984.11 mfh
Johnson J J 1LT 65-N 48 Ingalls 1922.7 1923.7 '23cd
Johnson R H BG 93 75 Ingalls 1970.8 1972.6 mfh Ret BG
Johnston J A COL 127-E 147 Bernard 1941.12 1944.3 PhBk
Johnston N COL 66-N 40 Ingalls 1977.12 1980.5 mfh
Johnston J S 2LT 79-N 95 Ingalls 1905.9 1906.9 '06cd
Johnstone W COL 35-E-2 8 Reeder 1962.8 1963.8 mfh
Jones J B Mr 33 CGH 67 Fenwick 1901 1906 '02-06cd
Jones M D COL 125 73 Ingalls 1955.1 1956.7 usacc
Jones P L 1LT 64-N 20 Ruckman 1904.4 b-23
Jones T A 2LT 18-E-2 37-B Bernard 1905.9 1906.9 '06cd
Jones T A MAJ 50-W 121 Bernard 1924.8 1925.8 Cramer
Jones A W CPT 63-S 26 Ruckman 1925.8 1926.8 '25BtryOCs
Jones F D CPT 62-N 28 Ruckman 1925.6 1928.8 QMC Ely '27cd
Jones H COL 63-N-24 Ruckman 1977.8 1979.6 mfh
Jones L M BG 158 32 Ingalls 1970.9 1973.5 mfh Ret MG?
Jones W I COL 45-E-1 114 Ingalls 1957.11 1960.11 usacc
Jones C 1LT 63-S 26 Ruckman 1906.9 1907.9 CAS'07
Jones M D COL 54-N-1 138 Ingalls 1954.12 1955.1 usacc
Jones C R MAJ 157 101 Bernard 1922.1 1923.8 Jones
Jones R D COL 35-W-2 2 Reeder 1966.1 1966.11 mfh
Jones N A MAJ 14 32 Ruckman 1933.1 1935.6 Bennett
Jones R P CPT 33-W-1 59 Fenwick 1944.1 1945.8 Phillips PhBk
Jones COL 64 71 Fenwick 1976.6 1977.6 mfh
Jones A P COL 45-E-2 116 Ingalls 1956.11 1958.1 usacc
Jones M H LTC 35-E-1 6 Reeder 1951.9 1954.2 usacc
Jones T H LTC 123-W 2 Ruckman 1926.9 1930.6 Ret BG Cramer +
Jones R S LTC 70-S 89 Ingalls 1943 1944 '44 PhBk
Jones R P Jr CPT 17-E-2 47-B Bernard 1943.7 1944.1 Phillips
Jones J P Jr COL 44-N-2 108 Ingalls 1957.9 1959.10 usacc
Jones J L Jr LTC 34-N-1 98 Ingalls 1975.7 1976.6 mfh
Jones J P Jr COL 79-N 95 Ingalls 1959.10 1960.12 usacc
Jordan R H 1LT 17-E-2 47-B Bernard 1909.9 1910.9 Ret BG CAS'10
Jordan R H CPT 126-S 163 Bernard 1916.12 1917.7 JHC Ret BG
Jordan R H 1LT 63-N 24 Ruckman 1910.9 1911.9 Ret BG '11cd
Jouett J H 2LT 17-W-1 41-A Bernard 1915.3 1915.9 Villaret
Jowers G MAJ 33-W-1 59 Fenwick 1983.2 1985.7 mfh
Julian H 2LT 17-W-2 41-B Bernard 1933.9 1934.7 Hain
Junken C A CPT 129-N 103 Ingalls 1909.7 1912.12 '08-12cd
Junken C A 1LT 18-W-2 29-B Bernard 1906.9 1908.9 '08cd
Junken C A MAJ 129-N 103 Ingalls 1916.12 1919.5 '17-19cd
Justis J C LTC 16-W 53 Bernard 1986.8 1987.7 mfh
Kabrick W C 1LT 63-S 26 Ruckman 1924.8 1925.8 Ret BG '25BtryOCs
Kahle J F MAJ 129-N 103 Ingalls 1933.7 1935.7 Kahle
Kaiser F MAJ 51 N-2 124 Ingalls 1980.6 1981.7 mfh
Kaiser G COL 67-S 34 Ingalls 1980.10 1983.8 mfh
Kaiser S LTC 143-N-2 35-D Ingalls 1980.6 1983.8 mfh
Kait H H CPT 52-W-1 130 Ingalls 1953.8 1955.8 USN usacc
Kane F B CPT 52-E-1 128 Ingalls 1937.6 1939.6 '37cd '39PhBk
Kane F B 1LT 33-E-1 61 Fenwick 1934.7 1935.8 Ellsworth
Kane F B COL 129-S 101 Ingalls 1950.8 1952.5 usacc

Karas D S MAJ 45-E-1 114 Ingalls 1982.8 1985.6
Karjala L COL 52-E-2 126 Ingalls 1981.7 1983.10 mfh
Katsarsky S COL 123-W 2 Ruckman 1954.10 1957.1 usacc
Kauffman A D CPT 35-E-1 6 Reeder 1944 1946 PhBk
Keefer F R CPT 63-S 26 Ruckman 1902 1902.9 c-46 b-19 MedC
Keefer F R MAJ 14 32 Ruckman 1902.9 1906.5 MedC '03cd
Keeler J P CPT 65-N 48 Ingalls 1915.12 1916.12 '16CAS
Keeler F R 1LT 33-E-1 61 Fenwick 1930.12 1931.7 deCamp
Keeler M G MAJ 103-N 65 Ingalls 1933.7 1935.9 Ret BG MedC AF
Keeler G E Jr CPT 33-E-2 63 Fenwick 1938.7 1939.6 Ret BG Tarrant
Keen P 1LT 70-S 89 Ingalls 1918 1919 BOQ WWI '19cd
Keenan J MAJ 18-W-1 29-A Bernard 1980.6 1982.6 mfh
Keesling A L 2LT 70-S 89 Ingalls 1905.9 1906.9 '06cd
Keithly T G LTC 35-W-1 4 Reeder 1950.8 1953.7 usacc
Keleher W P COL 67-N 36 Ingalls 1964.4 1968.7 mfh
Kelley S H COL 93 75 Ingalls 1984.8 1987.7
Kelley A P COL 103-N 65 Ingalls 1948.7 1949.9 usacc
Kelley E A Jr COL 68-N 83 Ingalls 1972.3 1974.2 mfh
Kellum G G COL 50-W 121 Bernard 1985.9 1987.5 mfh
Kelly J D MAJ 70-N 91 Ingalls 1924.7 1927.1 CAV JHC Hartel
Kelly T S LTC 45-E-1 114 Ingalls 1966.6 1968.6 mfh
Kelly E COL 69-N 87 Ingalls 1977.6 1980.7 mfh
Kelly P B CPT 15-S 36 Ruckman 1931.8 1932.5 Ret BG JHC +
Kelly P B 1LT 33-W-2 57 Fenwick 1932.6 1934.6 '33cd Ret BG
Kelly E L LTC 17-W-2 41-B Bernard 1919.6 1920.7 Ericson '20cd
Kelton E C CPT 123-W 2 Ruckman 1922.6 1924.8 ENGR '23cd
Kelton R H C CPT 50-W 121 Bernard 1902.9 1903.3 CAS '03
Kemble F LTC 126-S 163 Bernard 1936.11 1937.6 Cochran
Kemble F 1LT 64-N 20 Ruckman 1918 '17cd
Kemble F 1LT 63-S 26 Ruckman 1915.12 1916.12 Cochran
Kendall P W MG 144-S-2 41-C Ingalls 1951.4 1951.6 Ret LTG usacc
Kenerick K R 1LT 34-N-2 100 Ingalls 1938.7 1939.8 39 CAS
Kenna G W COL 43-E-2 7 Reeder 1961.1 1963.5 mfh
Kennedy J C LTC 44-S-2 102 Ingalls 1964.12 1967.6 mfh
Kennedy F J MAJ 50-A 125 Bernard 1982.9 1984.8 mfh
Kennedy M CPT 167-A 7 Patch Road 1947.2 1949.6 usacc
Kent L P 1LT 102-N 61 Ingalls 1918 1919 BOQ WWI '19cd
Keown-Boyd W D COL 68-S 81 Ingalls 1954.9 1956.8 usacc
Keppel J MAJ 54-N-2 140 Ingalls 1977.6 1979.12 mfh
Kern W B LTC 45-E-1 114 Ingalls 1950.1 1951.8 usacc
Kerr C MAJ 127-W 145 Bernard 1932.9 1937.6 Frith +
Kerr C CPT 68-N 83 Ingalls 1930.6 1932.9 Daughter
Kerr C LTC 127-W 145 Bernard 1938.6 1943.7 PhBk
Kerr C CPT 65-S 46 Ingalls 1919.6 1921.12 Daughter
Kerr J W COL 64 71 Fenwick 1928 1936 PubH MedC
Kerrett S LT 17-W-1 41-A Bernard 1895.2 c-12
Kerrigan A L 1LT 17-W-1 41-A Bernard 1921.7 1922.7 '22BtryOCs
Kerscher T E LTC 70-N 91 Ingalls 1977.10 1980.8 mfh
Kerwin W T Jr GEN 119 33 Fenwick 1973.2 1973.6 Ret GEN mfh
Kessler R H 2LT 17-W-1 41-A Bernard 1937.2 1938.6 Kessler
Kessler P M MAJ 157 101 Bernard 1912.9 1915.9 PhBk Kessler
Ketcham E F LTC 144-S-1 41-A Ingalls 1951.3 1955.7 usacc
Ketcham D W LTC 93 75 Ingalls 1917 '17cd

199

Ketchum R COL 102-S 59 Ingalls 1977.9 1981.6 mfh
Keusel G A CPT 18-W-1 29-A Bernard 1873.5 1874.5 S&F c-27
Key M E BG 52 E-2 126 Ingalls 1972.1 1972.3 mfh Ret MG
Key M E BG 127-E 147 Bernard 1972.3 1973.1 mfh Ret MG
Key M E BG 121-E 43 Fenwick 1973.1 1973.4 mfh Ret MG
Kibler E H Jr 2LT 16-E 53 Bernard 1933 1934 Kibler
Kieffer P V 1LT 67-S 34 Ingalls 1912.12 1913.12 CAS'13 '13cd
Kiel A G COL 67-N 36 Ingalls 1957.11 1959.6 usacc
Kiel A G COL 52-E-1 128 Ingalls 1957.3 1957.11 usacc
Kilbourne C E 1LT 79-N 95 Ingalls 1901.6 1902.9 Ret MG '02cd
Kilbourne C E CPT 3-S 167 Bernard 1906.5 1908.9 Ret MG Tracy +
Kilbreth J W Jr 1LT 66-N 40 Ingalls 1902 BOQ c-46 b-19
Kilburn C L MAJ 121-W 41 Fenwick 1917.11 1919.2 Secy CAS '19cd
Kilburn C L 2LT 16-E 53 Bernard 1913.12 1914.12 PhBk
Killingstad C P COL 63-S 26 Ruckman 1982.10 1984.7 mfh
Killough W B CPT 102-N 61 Ingalls 1918 1919 BOQ WWI '19cd
Kilpatrick P E COL 69-S 85 Ingalls 1976.10 1977.5 mfh
Kimball C Y LTC 44-S-1 104 Ingalls 1957.3 1960.7 usacc
Kimball D G LTC 102-N 61 Ingalls 1943 1944 PhBk
Kimberly A MAJ 143-S-1 35-A Ingalls 1924.8 1925.6 Loomis
Kimberly A 1LT 143-N-1 35-B Ingalls 1912.12 1913.12 '13-14cds
Kimbrell G T COL 18-W-2 29-B Bernard 1959.6 1959.7 Ret MG usacc
Kimbrell G T COL 15-N 34 Ruckman 1959.7 1962.8 Ret MG mfh
Kimm V M CPT 63-N 24 Ruckman 1936.11 1937.9 Kimm
Kimm V N CPT 54-S-1 136 Ingalls 1937.9 1938.6 Kimm
Kimmel E F 1LT 69-S 85 Ingalls 1901.9 1902.9 c-46 b-19
Kimmel E COL 142 51 Fenwick 1927.11 1930.9 '29cd JHC +
Kimmel M M Jr CPT 65-S 46 Ingalls 1918.9 1918.10 '19cd
Kimmel M M Jr 2LT 17-E-2 47-B Bernard 1913.12 1914.8 Kimmel
Kimmel M M Jr COL 121-E 43 Fenwick 1940.5 1942.6 PhBk
King K LTC 44-N-1 106 Ingalls 1981.7 1984.6 mfh
King J MAJ 34-S-2 94 Ingalls 1981.9 1983.4 mfh
King R W COL 45-E-2 116 Ingalls 1958.3 1962.5 mfh
King E N MAJ 64-N 20 Ruckman 1940 1941 '40-41PhBk
King E B COL 127-W 145 Bernard 1956.6 1958.7 usacc
King E G COL 103-N 65 Ingalls 1966.6 1967.3 mfh
King J P COL 62-N 28 Ruckman 1973.6 1974.5 mfh
King E W LTC 17-E-1 47-A Bernard 1956.1 1958.8 usacc
King D A COL 44-S-2 102 Ingalls 1961.7 1963.7 mfh
King J M LTC 62-S 30 Ruckman 1948.10 1951.8 usacc
King J MAJ 144-S-1 41-A Ingalls 1983.4 1983.7 mfh
Kingman A F COL 143-S-2 35-C Ingalls 1949.6 1949.9 Ret BG usacc
Kingman F E 1LT 18-E-2 37-B Bernard 1914.12 1915.12 CAS'15
Kingman A F COL 93 75 Ingalls 1949.9 1953.5 Ret BG usacc
King J J Jr COL 52-E-1 128 Ingalls 1967.8 1968.4 mfh
King J J Jr COL 68-S 81 Ingalls 1968.4 1969.7 mfh
Kinman S C 1LT 34-S-2 94 Ingalls 1985.2 1987.3 mfh
Kinnard L D COL 158 32 Ingalls 1968.3 1969.5 Ret BG mfh
Kinnard L D COL 143-S-2 35-C Ingalls 1968.2 1968.3 Ret BG mfh
Kinsella H F COL 43-E-2 7 Reeder 1963.6 1964.11 mfh
Kirby R M CPT 18-W-2 29-B Bernard 1828 1829 '29rq
Kirksey O T COL 51-S-2 118 Ingalls 1947.2 1947.4 usacc
Kirksey O T COL 103-N 65 Ingalls 1947.4 1948.7 usacc

Kirkwood C E CPT 52-E-2 126 Ingalls 1944 1945 Kirkwood PhBk
Kleinman E A 1LT 79-N 95 Ingalls 1932.8 1933.8 '33cd
Klett P E LTC 45 W-1 112 Ingalls 1968.4 1970.7 Chaplain mfh
Knapp V A CW4 147 147 Engr Ln 1969.9 1971.3 mfh
Knerr H J 2LT 17-W-2 41-B Bernard 1912.1 1912.4 Ret BG '12cd
Knight P CPT 14 32 Ruckman 1963.8 1965.6 USN mfh
Knight W C 1LT 66-N 40 Ingalls 1912.9 1913.12 '13cd
Knight W S CPT 143-S-1 35-A Ingalls 1917.6 1917.12 '17cd
Knox O LTC 18-W-2 29-B Bernard 1960.9 1963.10 mfh
Knudsen W H Jr LTC 16-W 51 Bernard 1973.10 1975.10 mfh
Knutson O R MAJ 51-N-1 122 Ingalls 1975.6 1978.9 mfh
Kobbe W A CPT 70-S 89 Ingalls 1895 b-12 Ret MG
Kobbe W A CPT 50-E 129 Bernard 1885.7 1891.1 Ret MG S&F c-27
Koch T H CPT 79-S 93 Ingalls 1911.9 1912.12 '12cd
Koch T H 1LT 18-W-1 29-A Bernard 1902 1902.11 d-691 rms
Koch T H 1LT 68-N 83 Ingalls 1902.11 1905.9 S&F '04cd
Kochevar J H LTC 43-W-2 1 Reeder 1948.8 1950.9 usacc
Koehler B M CPT 18-E-1 29-A Bernard 1907.9 1908.9 '08cd
Koenig W C MAJ 126-S 163 Bernard 1927.8 1928.8 CAS'28
Koenig W C 1LT 66-S 38 Ingalls 1917 BOQ WWI '17cd
Koenig W C 1LT 3-S 167 Bernard 1913.12 1914.12 PhBk
Koerbel F H CPT 51-N-2 124 Ingalls 1931.8 1932.8 Bray Cochran
Koffler C A LTC 17-W-2 41-B Bernard 1971.1 1973.7 mfh
Kohn J P CPT 33-W-2 57 Fenwick 1931.12 1932.6 '31cd
Kohn J P CPT 33-E-1 61 Fenwick 1932.7 1934.6 '33cd
Kolb R L COL 66-S 38 Ingalls 1964.6 1966.12 mfh
Komaniecki R P LTC 51-S-1 120 Ingalls 1970.7 1971.5 mfh
Korschel F M Jr COL 51-N-1 122 Ingalls 1960.6 1963.5 usacc
Koscielniak A A CPT 52-E-2 126 Ingalls 1940.7 1940.8 '40-41PhBk
Koscielniak A A 1LT 44-N-1 106 Ingalls 1936.8 1937.8 Taber +
Kosiba L M COL 66-S 38 Ingalls 1983.7 1986.2 mfh
Koskins F L MAJ 68-N 83 Ingalls 1927.7 1928.7 CAS'28
Kovacs L B COL 18-E-2 37-B Bernard 1961.8 1966.1 mfh
Krahe F X MAJ 51-N-1 122 Ingalls 1974.4 1975.6 mfh
Kramer A 1LT 44-S-2 102 Ingalls 1939.6 1940.9 Kramer
Kratz W G COL 101-S 55 Ingalls 1970.8 1973.3 mfh
Kratz W G COL 144-S-1 41-A Ingalls 1970.4 1970.8 mfh
Krausz G M MG 120 37 Fenwick 1985.7 1987.6 mfh
Krawciw N COL 68-N 83 Ingalls 1977.8 1979.6 mfh
Kretlow S A COL 143-S-2 35-C Ingalls 1955.8 1957.1 usacc
Kreuter R H MAJ 66-N 40 Ingalls 1938.8 1942.5 Kreuter
Kreuter R H COL 144-S-2 41-C Ingalls 1949.8 1950.8 usacc
Krise E F LTC 45-E-2 116 Ingalls 1967.10 1969.8 mfh
Kroeker S P CPT 51-N-2 124 Ingalls 1945.6 1946.8 '45PhBk
Krohn C MAJ 16-W 51 Bernard 1975.11 1978.6 mfh
Krueger R H 1LT 34-N-1 98 Ingalls 1931.6 1932.7 '31cd
Krueger R H 1LT 18-W-1 29-A Bernard 1932.7 1933.7 '33cd
Kruger H W 1LT 102-N 61 Ingalls 1918 1919 BOQ WWI '19cd
Kruger H W COL 65-N 48 Ingalls 1946.9 1947.8 usacc
Krupp O 1LT 127-E 147 Bernard 1916.12 1917.6 Krupp
Krupp O MAJ 143-S-2 35-C Ingalls 1917.6 1918.4 AN306
Krupp O MAJ 69-N 87 Ingalls 1918.4 1918.6 Krupp
Kuhl C W CPT 18-W-2 29-B Bernard 1942.8 1943 '43PhBk

Kuhn J E MAJ 14 32 Ruckman 1907.9 1909.9 ENGR Ret MG '09cd
Kuhn G W S Jr COL 144-N-2 41-D Ingalls 1968.1 1971.6 mfh
Kuhn G W S Jr COL 34-S-1 96 Ingalls 1967.8 1968.1 mfh
Kulik F M COL 101-N 57 Ingalls 1973.9 1976.1 mfh
Kunzig H B LTC 43-E-2 7 Reeder 1948.3 1949.5 usacc
Kunzig H B LTC 45-W-2 110 Ingalls 1949.9 1950.8 usacc
Kunzmann H CPT 68-S 81 Ingalls 1919.6 1920.6 '20cd
Kwasigroch J F COL 70-N 91 Ingalls 1973.9 1975.8 mfh
Kyster O H Jr 1LT 34-N-2 100 Ingalls 1930.12 1931.8 Ret MG Tarrant
Kyster O H Jr 1LT 15-S 36 Ruckman 1936.6 1938.5 Ret MG '37cd
Lackey C L 1LT 154-N 54 Murray 1918 1919 '19cd
Ladd R V CPT 3-N 169 Bernard 1919.6 1920.8 '20cd
Ladson R N COL 144-S-1 41-A Ingalls 1966.7 1967.3 mfh
Ladson R N COL 63-N 24 Ruckman 1967.3 1968.5 mfh
Lahti E H COL 50-E 129 Bernard 1959.5 1962.6 mfh
Laiche W E COL 15-S 36 Ruckman 1968.8 1971.7 mfh
Lambdin W M 1LT 65-S 48 Ingalls 1905.9 1906.5 '06cd
LaMendola C CPT 43-E-2 7 Reeder 1981.6 1986.12 mfh
Lancaster J M MAJ 14 32 Ruckman 1899 1901 '00cd
Landers H L CPT 79-N 95 Ingalls 1908.9 1909.9 '09cd
Landon E CPT 66 N-40 Ingalls 1908.8 1909.8 S&F '09cd
Landon E CPT 65 N-48 Ingalls 1903.8 1905.9 b-26
Lane T A COL 125 73 Ingalls 1954.8 1955.1 Ret MG usacc
Lane S B 1LT 143-N-2 35-D Ingalls 1916.12 1917.6 CAS'17 Ford
Lane W P COL 1 151 Bernard 1898.6 1898.9 micro-617 w
Lane W T LTC 45-W-2 110 Ingalls 1959.8 1961.8 usacc
Lane J J COL 15-S 36 Ruc..man 1956.8 1958.9 Ret MG usacc
Lang P R CPT 51-S-1 120 Ingalls 1942 1943 '43PhBk
Lang F E COL 35-E-1 6 Reeder 1968.1 1972.2 mfh
Langdon W H COL 54-S-2 134 Ingalls 1946.9 1948.7 usacc
Langdon W H COL 15-S 36 Ruckman 1948.7 1949.9 usacc
Langhorst A 1LT 70-N 91 Ingalls 1906.9 1907.9 CAS'07
Langman F W MAJ 54-S-1 136 Ingalls 1974.7 1975.6 mfh
Lanham C L 1LT 70-N 91 Ingalls 1905 BOQ c-46
Lanham C L 1LT 18-W-2 29-B Bernard 1902 b-21
Lansing C C 1LT 15-N 34 Ruckman 1905.9 1906.9 b-25
Lapp E COL 65-N 48 Ingalls 1977.7 1979.6 mfh
Larrabee W F 1LT 34-S-1 96 Ingalls 1935.8 1936.6 AN306
Larsen S R LTG 141 53 Fenwick 1967.8 1968.7 mfh Ret LTG?
Larson S A MAJ 54-N-1 138 Ingalls 1972.2 1974.8 mfh
Latimer D B 1LT 3-S 167 Bernard 1931.6 1935.8 '32cd
Latimer D B CPT 65-N 48 Ingalls 1935.9 1937.8 Wolfe
Laubscher W R LTC 33-E-1 61 Fenwick 1974.3 1976.6 Chaplain mfh
Laughlin G T COL 52-E-2 126 Ingalls 1957.8 1960.8 usacc
Laughlin G T COL 54-N-1 138 Ingalls 1956.1 1956.7 usacc
Laughon W R CPT 93 75 Ingalls 1960.2 1963.6 USN mfh
Lavin G S MAJ 3-N 169 Bernard 1937.6 1938.8 ORD '37cd
Lavin R N Jr MAJ 65-N 48 Ingalls 1933.8 1935.8 Wolfe +
Lawler H J CPT 34-S-1 96 Ingalls 1944 1946 '44-45PhBks
Lawless R B COL 68-S 81 Ingalls 1974.11 1975.7 mfh
Lawley F COL 65-S 46 Ingalls 1979.6 1980.11 mfh
Lawrason G B 1LT 144-N-2 41-D Ingalls 1913.12 1914.12 CAS'14 PhBk
Lawrence W J COL 129-S 101 Ingalls 1973.10 1975.12 mfh

Lawson J L 1LT 167-B 9 Patch Road 1961.3 1962.12 mfh
Lawson J E LTC 54-S-1 136 Ingalls 1984.7 1986.8 mfh
Lawson W F Jr COL 17-W-1 41-A Bernard 1967.6 1970.9 mfh
Lawson W F Jr COL 68-S 81 Ingalls 1970.9 1971.8 mfh
Lawson H B Jr COL 18-E-2 37-B Bernard 1970.5 1971.2 Chaplain mfh
Lawton W S 1LT 18-E-1 37-A Bernard 1929.8 1930.8 Ret LTG '30BtryOCs
Lawton W S BG 142 51 Fenwick 1950.1 1952.11 Ret LTG usacc
Lawton W O COL 129-N 103 Ingalls 1974.9 1977.8 mfh
Lay J R COL 66-N 40 Ingalls 1972.6 1974.7 mfh
Lazar A M 1LT 18-W-1 29-A Bernard 1936.6 1937.8 Whipple
Lazar A M 1LT 45-E-1 114 Ingalls 1939.6 1940.8 '40PhBk
Leach J H COL 126-N 165 Bernard 1975.10 1978.9 mfh
Leary J E COL 52-W-1 130 Ingalls 1946.9 1947.8 Ret BG usacc
Leathers B J COL 50-W 121 Bernard 1973.9 1974.6 mfh
Leavenworth J P 1LT 63-S 26 Ruckman 1916.12 1917.6 Ford
Leavitt T P COL 128-W 107 Bernard 1983.8 1986.7 mfh
LeCocq F MAJ 79-N 95 Ingalls 1920.8 1921.8 '21FOcs
LeCocq F LTC 141 53 Fenwick 1930 1934 Huger
Ledebuhr A F COL 93 75 Ingalls 1975.10 1979.7 mfh
Lee E O COL 70-S 89 Ingalls 1953.7 1954.9 usacc
Lee R E 2LT 17-W-2 41-B Bernard 1832 1834.8 Ret GEN '34rq
Lee R E 1LT 17-W-1 41-A Bernard 1831.5 1834.8 Ret GEN Polaski
Lee Robt 2LT 17-W-2 41-B Bernard 1824.7 d-684
Lee E O COL 79-S 93 Ingalls 1952.8 1953.7 usacc
Lee J H COL 64 71 Fenwick 1968.8 1969.7 mfh
Leech H E COL 126-S 163 Bernard 1964.9 1965.7 mfh
Leek C B CPT 45-W-2 110 Ingalls 1942.4 1943.2 AN306
Leer J B COL 52-E-1 128 Ingalls 1960.4 1960.7 usacc
Lee R V Jr COL 70-S 89 Ingalls 1974.8 1978.2 mfh
Lee R V Jr COL 118 29 Fenwick 1974.7 1974.8 mfh
Lehrfeld I COL 43-E-2 7 Reeder 1950.1 1951.8 usacc
Leight W J COL 35-W-2 2 Reeder 1958.9 1961.12 usacc
Leist G F 1LT 34-N-2 100 Ingalls 1940 1941 '40-41PhBk
Leister J WO1 34-S-2 94 Ingalls 1980.8 1981.9 mfh
Lemaster T A CPT 110-W 38 Tidball 1917.11 1920.8 '20cd
Lemley K M COL 35-W-1 4 Reeder 1969.7 1969.8 mfh
Lemley K M COL 65-N 48 Ingalls 1969.8 1970.4 mfh
Lemmon K B 1LT 66-N 40 Ingalls 1913.12 1914.12 PhBk
Lemnitzer L L CPT 144-S-2 41-C Ingalls 1936.7 1939.7 Ret GEN
Lennon C COL 124-N 69 Ingalls 1975.10 1979.10 mfh
Lennon J J COL 15-N 34 Ruckman 1973.8 1977.7 mfh
Lentin J LTC 15-S 36 Ruckman 1980.6 1982.7 mfh
Lentz J M MG 120 37 Fenwick 1952.5 1954.12 usacc Ret MG
Lenzner D S COL 157 101 Bernard 1939.7 1946.5 PhBk
Lenzner D S MAJ 68-N 83 Ingalls 1929.7 1930.6 CAS'30
Lenzner D S COL 123-W 2 Ruckman 1946.5 1948.9 usacc Tilton
Lenzner D S MAJ 128-W 107 Bernard 1930.6 1932.6 Cochran +
Leonard R J MAJ 44-S-1 104 Ingalls 1941.7 1943 AN306
Leonard D S COL 67-N 36 Ingalls 1976.3 1978.6 mfh
Leonard R LTC 65-S 46 Ingalls 1984.7 1987.7 mfh
Leonard M C CPT 17-W-2 41-B Bernard 1921.7 1922.6 '22BtryOcs
Lepping A J 1LT 15-N 34 Ruckman 1934.6 1935.6 Lepping
Lesley S J MAJ 16-W 51 Bernard 1971.5 1973.7 mfh

Levine S LTC 144-N-2 41-D Ingalls 1973.8 1974.6 mfh
LeVine L H COL 33-W-2 57 Fenwick 1966.8 1967.3 mfh
Levy R M 2LT 17-W-1 41-A Bernard 1916.9 1916.12 Levy
Lew J LTC 63-S 26 Ruckman 1978.7 1980.7 mfh
Lewane L L COL 64 71 Fenwick 1975.8 1976.6 mfh
Lewis P W LTC 69-S 85 Ingalls 1937.5 1941.5 PhBk
Lewis W N COL 45-W-1 112 Ingalls 1952.3 1954.8 usacc
Lewis I N MAJ 103-S 63 Ingalls 1906.9 1909.9 '06-19cd
Lewis I N CPT 19 18 Bernard 1904.8 1906.9 S&F Shull Son
Lewis H duB CPT 52-E-1 128 Ingalls 1940.6 1940.7 Lewis
Lewis J T CPT 66-S 38 Ingalls 1929.9 1933.9 Ret LTG Lewis
Lewis J T CPT 16-W 51 Bernard 1923 1924 Ret LTG Lewis
Lewis D V Mr 61-S 43 Ingalls 1946.7 1973.10 usacc Post electrician Lewis
Lewis L L COL 129-S 101 Ingalls 1961.6 1963.7 mfh
Lewis A N 2LT 127-E 147 Bernard 1918.9 1918.12 Lewis
Lewis V B Jr BG 121-E 43 Fenwick 1973.11 1974.7 mfh Ret MG
Lieber A C Jr COL 128-W 107 Bernard 1946.8 1948.8 usacc
Liepert G C COL 79-N 85 Ingalls 1982.7 1984.6 mfh
Liesman J COL 123-E 4 Ruckman 1981.7 1983.3 mfh
Ligon W B COL 52-E-1 128 Ingalls 1961.11 1962.7 mfh
Lincoln F H CPT 101-N 57 Ingalls 1914.4 1917.11 PhBk + cds
Lincoln F H CPT 68-N 83 Ingalls 1909.9 1910.9 CAS'10
Lincoln F H LTC 141 53 Fenwick 1928 1929 Tilton
Linderman J C MAJ 143-N-2 35-D Ingalls 1941.8 1942.6 Tolley
Lindner C B MAJ 62-N 28 Ruckman 1918.12 1919.8 S&F Arthur
Lindquist R E COL 66-S 38 Ingalls 1951.8 1953.4 Ret MG usacc
Lindsey W CPT 43-E-1 5 Reeder 1978.6 1979.8 mfh
Lindstrom H M LTC 51-S-1 120 Ingalls 1950.6 1953.4 usacc
Lippitt W F CPT 65-S 46 Ingalls 1902.9 1903.9 MedC '03cd
Lipscomb L Jr LTC 62-N 28 Ruckman 1943.5 1943.11 PhBk
Lipscomb L Jr LTC 93 75 Ingalls 1943.12 1945.10 PhBk
Lipscomb L Jr 1LT 18-W-2 29-B Bernard 1937.6 1937.7 Lipscomb
Lising D LTC 3-N 169 Bernard 1983.3 1985.2 mfh
Little W L MAJ 157 101 Bernard 1915.9 1917.9 MedC
Little R E LTC 52-E-1 128 Ingalls 1984.8 1985.6 mfh
Little MAJ 66-S 38 Ingalls 189? 1898.8 c-41
Litz W P COL 50-A 125 Bernard 1957.11 1961.3 usacc
Livingston L R MAJ 14 32 Ruckman 1881.4 1885.7 S&F c-27
Ljungstedt P M 1LT 127-E 147 Bernard 1914.12 1915.12 CAS'15 Arthur
Lluesma-Parez E A CPT 167-B 9 Patch Road 1969.1 1969.9 mfh
Lodor R MAJ 50-W 121 Bernard 1871.1 1886.7 c-27 ORD
Loewus J D COL 52-E-2 126 Ingalls 1965.5 1967.7 mfh
Lofquist F CPT 43-E-2 7 Reeder 1930.12 1931.7 '31cd
Lofquist F CPT 66-S 38 Ingalls 1921.8 1922.8 '22BtryOcs
Loftin J R COL 144-S-2 41-C Ingalls 1964.2 1966.2 mfh
Lohmann L H MAJ 101-S 55 Ingalls 1939.12 1940.9 Died 9/40
Lohr C A CPT 144-S-1 41-A Ingalls 1915.10 1916.12 '17cd
Lohr C A CPT 55 42 Ingalls 1913.12 1915.10 PhBk
Lomax M P CPT 18-W-1 29A Bernard 1823.7 1824.6 d-684
Lomax F H 1LT 68-S 81 Ingalls 1903.9 1904.9 CAS'04
Lomax M P CPT 18-W-2 29-B Bernard 1823.7 1824.6 d-684
Lombard R T LTC 43-E-1 5 Reeder 1967.1 1967.6 mfh
Long F W 1LT 18-W-1 29-A Bernard 1905.9 1906.9 '06cd

Long F S CPT 128-E 109 Bernard 1914.12 1915.12 Cochran
Long H E LTC 17-W-1 41-A Bernard 1955.3 1955.12 usacc
Long E A CPT 103-N 65 Ingalls 1916.12 1918.12 '17cd
Long J L CPT 14 32 Ruckman 1909.9 1910.9 CAS'10
Long E C CPT 129-N 103 Ingalls 1915.12 1916.12 CAS'16
Long H E LTC 35-W-2 2 Reeder 1955.12 1958.1 usacc
Long 1LT 18 W-2 29-B Bernard 1826 1828 '26rq rooms
Longino O H MAJ 102-S 59 Ingalls 1922.8 1924.8 Ret BG JHC cd
Longino O H 1LT 143-N-1 35-B Ingalls 1913.12 1914.12 Ret BG PhBk
Lonning S N COL 54-N-1 138 Ingalls 1956.7 1959.6 usac
Lonning S N COL 33-E-1 61 Fenwick 1954.9 1955.8 usacc
Loomis H F MAJ 123-E 4 Ruckman 1929.6 1932.6 Ret BG Loomis
Loomis H F MAJ 144-S-1 41-A Ingalls 1918.6 1921.8 Ret BG Villaret
Loop C H 1LT 62-S 30 Ruckman 1919.6 1920.6 '20cd
Lorain L CPT 18-W-2 29-B Bernard 1875.5 1881.5 S&F c-27
Lott G B Jr MAJ 45-W-1 112 Ingalls 1970.7 1971.7 mfh
Loud R A 1LT 61-N 45 Ingalls 1955.11 1956.1 usacc
Loughry H K MAJ 124-S 67 Ingalls 1923.6 1926.6 Ret MG '25cd
Loughry H K 1LT 70-S 89 Ingalls 1910.9 1911.9 Ret MG '09cd
Loustalot A L MAJ 1 151 Bernard 1923 1924 Putney
Loustalot A L CPT 69-N 87 Ingalls 1915.12 1916.12 CAS'16
Love J W LTC 17-E-2 47-B Bernard 1959.11 1960.8 usacc
Love R V CPT 63-S 26 Ruckman 1919.6 1921.8 '20cd
Love H CPT 63-N 24 Ruckman 1919 1919 BOQ ? '19cd
Lovell J R 1LT 43-W-2 1 Reeder 1936.6 1937.6 AF KIA Korea
Lovell J R 2LT 17-E-1 47-A Bernard 1931.7 1932.8 AF KIA Korea
Lowe H A COL 51-S-2 118 Ingalls 1968.9 1968.10 mfh
Lowe R G COL 15-N 34 Ruckman 1948.7 1951.5 usacc
Lowe P S CPT 18-E-2 37-B Bernard 1927.8 1930.9 Lowe '29cd
Lowe E L 1LT 71-W 17 Harrison 1942 1943 '43PhBk AN306
Lowe H A COL 3-S 167 Bernard 1968.10 1969.12 mfh
Lowry T M COL 102-S 59 Ingalls 1944.10 1946.9 PhBks
Lowry P P LTC 103-N 65 Ingalls 1936.3 1941.5 PhBk
Lowry P P MAJ 127-E 147 Bernard 1935.8 1936.3 Lowry
Luce D COL 129-N 103 Ingalls 1942.1 1942.8 Luce
Luce D MAJ 63-N 24 Ruckman 1940.6 1941.1 PhBk
Lucy D H MAJ 43-E-1 5 Reeder 1973.2 1975.8 mfh
Luczak B R 2LT 43-E-2 7 Reeder 1939.7 1940.1 Ret BG Luczak
Ludwigs J R CPT 15-N 34 Ruckman 1928.8 1929.8 '29cd
Lull C E T 1LT 62-N 28 Ruckman 1910.9 1911.9 '11cd
Lull C E T 1LT 67-N 36 Ingalls 1909.9 1910.9 CAS'10
Lundeen J A COL 119 33 Fenwick 1917.8 1918.3 w
Lundeen J A COL 120 37 Fenwick 1918.9 1918.12 '19cd
Lundeen J A COL 142 51 Fenwick 1917.6 1917.8 Arthur
Lundgren D COL 63-N 24 Ruckman 1979.7 1984.8 mfh
Lundquist C E COL 62-N 28 Ruckman 1946.8 1948.8 usacc
Lunn W Y 1LT 18-E-2 37-B Bernard 1920.8 1921.8 CAS'21
Lutes L CPT 62-S 30 Ruckman 1925.6 1926.7 Ret LTG Lutes
Lutes L CPT 126-N 165 Bernard 1925.7 1927.6 Ret LTG Lutes
Lyle R T MAJ 52-W-2 132 Ingalls 1985.6 1987.8 mfh
Lynch W F COL 18-E-2 37-B Bernard 1960.8 1961.6 usacc
Lynch C E COL 144-S-2 41-C Ingalls 1946.9 1949.8 usacc
Lynch G COL 127-E 147 Bernard 1977.10 1978.9 mfh

Lynch G P COL 66-N 40 Ingalls 1974.8 1977.11 mfh Ret BG
Lynch J H BG 158 32 Ingalls 1966.7 1968.1 mfh Ret BG
Lynde N M Jr COL 55 42 Ingalls 1948.10 1952.2 Ret MG usacc
Lynn W M Jr MG 118 29 Fenwick 1966.7 1967.7 Ret MG mfh
Lynn W M Jr BG 33-W-2 57 Fenwick 1966.7 1966.7 Ret MG mfh
Lyon R R 1LT 143-N-1 35-B Ingalls 1914.12 1915.12 '16cd
Lyon J W 1LT 16-E 53 Bernard 1912.12 1913.12 '12cd
Lyster T C MAJ 141 53 Fenwick 1912.9 1914.12 Ret BG PhBk
Mabbott H C CPT 144-N-2 41-D Ingalls 1921.3 1923.6 Mabbott
Mabbott H C MAJ 44-N-2 108 Ingalls 1930.12 1932.7 Mabbott
Mabbott H C MAJ 69-S 85 Ingalls 1932.7 1934.9 Mabbott
Mabry G L LTC 45-E-2 116 Ingalls 1954.1 1955.10 Ret MG MOH
MacAdam L R CPT 52-E-1 128 Ingalls 1940.7 1941.8 MacAdam PhBks
MacArthur R A LTC 79-S 93 Ingalls 1942.12 1946.10 PhBks
Mace R R COL 15-S 36 Ruckman 1953.9 1954.8 usacc
Mace J S COL 101-S 55 Ingalls 1973.5 1975.8 mfh
Mace R R COL 16-W 51 Bernard 1953.8 1953.9 usacc
Macey R MAJ 44-N-2 108 Ingalls 1979.6 1982.6 mfh
Macherey E J COL 34-N-2 100 Ingalls 1951.7 1953.7 usacc
Machle J B Mr 61-S 43 Ingalls 1911 1914 '12-14cd Electrician
Macia T E MAJ 51-S-1 120 Ingalls 1984.5 1986.12 mfh
Mack J A 1LT 3-S 167 Bernard 1910.6 1912.9 '11-12cd
MacKenzie S CPT 1 151 Bernard 1841.12 1842.7 w
Mackey R J COL 52-W-1 130 Ingalls 1985.7 1987.6 mfh
Mackin R E COL 93 75 Ingalls 1982.7 1984.8 mfh
Mackin R N Jr MAJ 65-S 46 Ingalls 1934.8 1937.6 Son Wolfe
MacKirdy H S CPT 66-N 40 Ingalls 1931.7 1933.6 '33cd
MacKirdy H S CPT 63-S 26 Ruckman 1933.7 1934.8 Bennett
MacMullen J D MAJ 70-N 91 Ingalls 1929.7 1930.6 '30CAS
MacMullen J D CPT 69-S 85 Ingalls 1922.6 1923.7 '23cd
MacNair T K 1LT 18-W-1 29-A Bernard 1937.8 1938.7 '37cd
MacNair T K 1LT 45-W-1 112 Ingalls 1938.7 1939.6 '39PhBk
Macon R C MG 141 53 Fenwick 1949.3 1952.7 usacc Ret MG
MacPherson W J LTC 18-W-2 29-B Bernard 1959.9 1960.8 usacc
MacRae C 1LT 44-S-1 104 Ingalls 1943 1944 '43PhBk
Madden J P LTC 67-N 36 Ingalls 1972.10 1973.8 mfh
Maddox H G MG 142 51 Fenwick 1952.11 1953.7 usacc Ret MG?
Maddox H G MG 123-E 4 Ruckman 1952.10 1952.11 usacc Ret MG?
Maddox B BG 121-E 43 Fenwick 1980.8 1982.6 mfh
Maddux R F 1LT 129-N 103 Ingalls 1914.12 1915.12 CAS'15 cd
Maddux H C 1LT 16-E 53 Bernard 1911 1912 '11cd
Madigan E COL 70-N 91 Ingalls 1980.8 1984.7 mfh
Madison J H LTC 67-S 34 Ingalls 1940.5 1943.10 Madison
Madison J H COL 103-S 63 Ingalls 1952.12 1954.7 usacc
Madison J H CPT 3-S 167 Bernard 1935.9 1936.6 Madison Son
Magadieu W J LTC 35-E-1 6 Reeder 1956.5 1957.2 usacc
Maggart L MAJ 144-N-1 41-B Ingalls 1977.8 1980.7 mfh
Maginson H E 1LT 45-E-1 114 Ingalls 1935.9 1936.6 Jaccard
Magruder L B MAJ 50-E 129 Bernard 1925.7 1928.5 Putney
Magruder L W Jr COL 17-W-1 41-A Bernard 1964.10 1966.9 mfh
Maguire C F MAJ 124-N 69 Ingalls 1933.8 1934.6 Phillips
Maguire C F CPT 18-E-1 37-A Bernard 1920.8 1921.7 Phillips
Maher J J CPT 18-W-2 29-B Bernard 1921.7 1922.7 CAS'22

Mahoney W C MAJ 14 32 Ruckman 1937 1941 PhBk
Majauskas R CPT 35-E-2 8 Reeder 1979.4 1982.6 mfh
Malison J H COL 67-S 34 Ingalls 1952.9 1952.12 usacc
Mallonee R C COL 124-S 67 Ingalls 1953.4 1954.9 usacc
Mallonee R C COL 54-S-1 136 Ingalls 1953.1 1953.4 usacc
Mallory H S 1LT 18-W-2 29-B Bernard 1826 1828.4 '26rq rooms
Malone D COL 62-S 30 Ruckman 1977.8 1980.6 mfh
Maloney J P CPT 18-E-2 37-B Bernard 1940.2 1940.10 PhBk
Manganaro S COL 62-N 28 Ruckman 1980.8 1984.7 mfh
Manlove A W COL 14 32 Ruckman 1959.4 1962.2 mfh
Manlove A W COL 51-S-2 118 Ingalls 1959.1 1959.4 usacc
Mann N CPT 34-S-2 94 Ingalls 1978.6 1979.5 mfh
Mansfield H W 1LT 43-E-1 5 Reeder 1939.6 1940.6 Diestel
Mansfield H W COL 69-S 85 Ingalls 1942.4 1945.6 PhBk
Mansur R W LTC 52-E-2 126 Ingalls 1970.8 1971.8 Chaplain mfh
Mansur R COL 102-N 61 Ingalls 1980.7 1983.4 mfh
Maret R COL 103-S 64 Ingalls 1963.11 1965.6 usacc
Markle N K Jr LTC 50-A 125 Bernard 1951.9 1954.11 usacc
Marks A E 1LT 67-S 34 Ingalls 1918 1919 BOQ WWI '19cd
Marnane T J COL 66-S 38 Ingalls 1956.7 1961.7 usacc
Marocchi J L CPT 52-E-1 128 Ingalls 1962.7 1963.6 USN mfh
Marquat W F CPT 1 151 Bernard 1926 1927 Ret MG '26cd
Marquat W F CPT 64-N 20 Ruckman 1928.6 1930.6 Ret MG '29cd
Marsh A H COL 67-N 36 Ingalls 1968.7 1969.6 mfh
Marsh C T 1LT 65-N 48 Ingalls 1914.12 1915.12 CAS'15 '16cd
Marsh C T CPT 124-S 67 Ingalls 1915.12 1917.6 Bennett
Marshall O K LTC 102-N 61 Ingalls 1944.7 1946.8 Marshall
Marshall S LTC 144-S-2 41-C Ingalls 1942.1 1946.6 Tolley PhBks
Marshall G MAJ 19 18 Bernard 1922.7 1923.6 CAS'23
Marshall O K 1LT 17-W-2 41-B Bernard 1925.9 1926.6 Higgins
Marshall R C Jr CPT 50-E 129 Bernard 1912.12 1914.12 PhBk
Marshall R C Jr 1LT 18-E-2 37-B Bernard 1907.9 1908.9 '08cd
Marshall R C Jr 1LT 67-N 36 Ingalls 1905.9 1907.9 S&F Arthur
Martin E G CPT 79-N 95 Ingalls 1935.9 1936.6 Martin
Martin K A MAJ 18-W-2 29-B Bernard 1954.3 1954.5 usacc
Martin H L 1LT 63-N 24 Ruckman 1909.9 1910.9 CAS'10
Martin E G COL 62-S 30 Ruckman 1946.10 1947.7 usacc
Martin A L 2LT 79-N 95 Ingalls 1902 c-46
Martin N E COL 3-S 167 Bernard 1962.8 1966.11 mfh
Martin H L 1LT 17-W-1 41-A Bernard 1912.12 1913.12 '13-14cd
Martin P M COL 101-N 57 Ingalls 1953.7 1954.7 usacc
Martin W L COL 65-S 46 Ingalls 1961.6 1962.6 mfh
Martin P M COL 54-S-1 136 Ingalls 1953.4 1953.7 usacc
Martin M J LTC 147 147 Engr Ln 1946.11 1947.10 usacc
Martin D T MAJ 35-W-1 4 Reeder 1942.9 1945.9 PhBks
Martin J B MAJ 127-W 145 Bernard 1929.8 1931.2 CAS'30
Martin E G CPT 62-S 30 Ruckman 1939.5 1940.5 Martin
Martingale E B 1LT 79-S 93 Ingalls 1902.9 1903.9 '03cd
Marvine W A CPT 64-N 20 Ruckman 1919.6r 1921 '20cd Chaplain
Marvine W A CPT 128-E 109 Bernard 1918.1 1919.6 '19cd Chaplain
Marye W A LTC 93 75 Ingalls 1902 1903 ORD '02cd
Maslowski L C COL 143-S-1 35-A Ingalls 1962.9 1963.1 mfh
Maslowski L C COL 65-S 46 Ingalls 1963.1 1967.5 mfh

Masoero A R COL 50-W 121 Bernard 1982.6 1985.9 mfh
Mason C F COL 121-E 43 Fenwick 1919.6 1921.7 MedC '29cd
Massello W Jr 1LT 54-S-2 134 Ingalls 1939.10 1940.2 Massello
Massoglia M F COL 52-W-2 132 Ingalls 1966.9 1968.3 PhBks
Masteller K C CPT 121-E 43 Fenwick 1911.9 1915.9 PhBk
Matassarin L C MAJ 33-E-1 61 Fenwick 1970.12 1972.6 mfh
Mather J CPT 15-S 36 Ruckman 1916.12 1917.12 Ret BG Ford
Matheson S H BG 127-W 145 Bernard 1971.10 1973.3 mfh Ret MG
Matheson A D M Jr LTC 67-S 34 Ingalls 1970.8 1973.5 Canadian mfh
Mathews P CPT 3-S 167 Bernard 1916.12 1917.12 CAS'17 Ford
Mathews W R Jr COL 43-W-1 3 Reeder 1968.8 1969.6 mfh
Mathews W R Jr COL 67-N 36 Ingalls 1969.6 1972.8 mfh
Matson J CPT 79-S 93 Ingalls 1907.9 1909.9 cds
Matsuda R LTC 44-S-1 104 Ingalls 1982.2 1982.12 mfh
Mattern R H 1LT 34-N-1 98 Ingalls 1941 1942 Died Saipan '45 LTC
Matthews H T CPT 128-E 109 Bernard 1909.7 1912.12 '12cd
Matthews H T 1LT 67-N 36 Ingalls 1904.9 1905.9 CAS'05
Maxey H C LTC 34-S-2 94 Ingalls 1960.10 1961.8 usacc
Maxfield H A LTC 33-W-2 57 Fenwick 1942.3 1944.4 Maxfield
Maxwell W P LTC 144-S-1 41-A Ingalls 1949.5 1951.2 usacc
May R M LTC 54-N-1 138 Ingalls 1974.11 1977.8 mfh
May E W MAJ 143-N-2 35-D Ingalls 1942.6 1943.5 '43 PhBk
Maybach A A CPT 144-N-1 41-B Ingalls 1919.11 1920.9 '20cd
Maybach A A CPT 66-S 38 Ingalls 1911.7 1912.8 '12cd
Maybach A A LTC 118 29 Fenwick 1922.8 1924.5 '23cd
Mayfield T M LTC 51-N-1 122 Ingalls 1984.8 1985.5 mfh
Mayfield T M LTC 67-N 36 Ingalls 1985.5 1986.12 mfh
Maynard J B 1LT 79-N 95 Ingalls 1912.12 1913.12 Ret BG PhBk
Maynard J B MAJ 63-N 24 Ruckman 1922.6 1924.9 Ret BG '23cd
Mayo W CSM 60 67 Fenwick 1981.1 1984.8 mfh
Mays S E COL 50-W 121 Bernard 1947.9 1948.7 usacc
McAdams M COL 124-N 69 Ingalls 1979.11 1982.5 mfh
McAlister R C MG 142 51 Fenwick 1973.7 1975.7 mfh Ret LTG
McAlister R C MG 127-W 145 Bernard 1973.6 1973.7 mfh Ret LTG
McArthur C L MAJ 18-W-2 29-B Bernard 1978.2 1981.6 mfh
McBride H M MAJ 33-E-2 63 Fenwick 1970.9 1972.7 mfh
McBride R B CPT 68-N 83 Ingalls 1906.9 1907.9 QMC Crowell
McBride R B CPT 123-W 2 Ruckman 1911.5 1912.12 Crowell '12cd QMC
McBride J L CPT 14 32 Ruckman 1929.6 1930.6 Chaplain Eli
McBride R B LTC 65-S 46 Ingalls 1921.12 1923.5 QMC Hartel
McBride D G COL 70-N 91 Ingalls 1948.7 1953.8 usacc
McBride J Jr CPT 17-E-2 47-B Bernard 1912.12 1913.12 CAS'13 '13cd
McCabe R E COL 34-N-2 100 Ingalls 1953.8 1955.7 usacc
McCaffrey W J BG 146 146 Engr Ln 1964.8 1965.7 Ret LTG mfh
McCaffrey W B DR 64 71 Fenwick 1917 1920 PubH '17cd
McCaffrey W J BG 158 32 Ingalls 1965.7 1966.5 Ret LTG mfh
McCain J D CPT 66-S 38 Ingalls 1920.8 1921.8 S&F Arthur
McCain P B COL 19 18 Bernard 1971.4 1973.1 mfh
McCammon F E 1LT 15-N 34 Ruckman 1913.12 1914.12 PhBk
McCann J D Jr CPT 19 18 Bernard 1944 1945 PhBk
McCann J D Jr 1LT 16-E 53 Bernard 1943 1944 PhBk
McCarey A A 2LT 17-E-1 47-A Bernard 1934.7 1935.6 McCarey
McCarthy E B CPT 55 42 Ingalls 1918.11 1919.7 S&F Chapin

McCarthy E B CPT 65-S 46 Ingalls 1929.6 1930.7 Pope Heaney
McCaskey J P Jr 1LT 15-N 34 Ruckman 1914.12 1915.12 '15cd
McCaskey J P Jr MAJ 143-S-2 35-C Ingalls 1921.7 1922.7 '22FOcs
McCatty K CPT 65-S 46 Ingalls 1925.8 1926.7 '25cd
McCatty K MAJ 143-S-1 35-A Ingalls 1929.8 1930.8 Heaney '30AdvC
McCatty K CPT 66-S 38 Ingalls 1923.8 1924.8 Higgins +
McCauley H W CPT 70-N 91 Ingalls 1909.9 1910.9 CAS'10
McCleary W R MAJ 128-W 107 Bernard 1924.8 1925.8 JHC
McCleary W R 1LT 143-N-1 35-B Ingalls 1910.9 1911.9 CAS'11 '11cd
McClellan S L MG 157 101 Bernard 1974.1 1977.1 Ret MG
McClellan J LT 16-E 53 Bernard 1886 d-687
McClintic B S LTC 93 75 Ingalls 1939.6 1940.7 MedC PhBk
McClintock W L CPT 18-W-1 29-A Bernard 1825 1826 '25-26rq
McClure R LTC 52-W-1 130 Ingalls 1964.7 1965.10 mfh
McCoach D 1LT 79-S 93 Ingalls 1902.9 c-46
McCoach D 1LT 66-S 38 Ingalls 1901.8 1902.8 '02cd
McConnell J K COL 123-W 2 Ruckman 1967.3 1968.2 mfh
McConnell W M COL 79-S 93 Ingalls 1954.11 1957.8 usacc
McCormick R A 34-S-2 94 Ingalls 1983.4 1985.2 mfh
McCoy G W 1LT 1 151 Bernard 1935 1936 MedC McCoy
McCrary B N MAJ 17-E-2 47-B Bernard 1981.1 1983.5 mfh
McCrea J H MG 1 151 Bernard 1985.6 1987.3 mfh
McCroskey S L COL 101-N 57 Ingalls 1947.3 1950.9 Ret BG usacc
McCroskey S L CPT 68-N 83 Ingalls 1924.8 1927.6 Ret BG '25cd
McCroskey S L CPT 52-W-1 130 Ingalls 1932.6 1935.7 Ret BG '33-34cd
McCuen J J COL 50-E 129 Bernard 1974.2 1976.7 mfh
McCune H A 1LT 143-S-1 35-A Ingalls 1914.12 1915.12 '16cd
McCutchen G COL 45-E-1 114 Ingalls 1956.8 1957.11 usacc
McDaniel J E LTC 52-E-2 126 Ingalls 1986.6 1987.5 mfh
McDaniel P B COL 69-S 85 Ingalls 1973.8 1973.11 mfh
McDaniel J LTC 34-S-1 96 Ingalls 1976.8 1978.3 mfh
McDevitt J J MAJ 51-N-2 124 Ingalls 1974.7 1977.6 mfh
McDonald A M MAJ 44-S-1 104 Ingalls 1974.5 1977.5 mfh
McDonald H S Jr LTC 16-E 53 Bernard 1947.3 1947.5 usacc
McElmore E N COL 146 146 Engr Ln 1951.9 1955.2 usacc
McElroy R L COL 68-N 83 Ingalls 1986.9 1987.10 mfh
McEnery J W COL 35-W-1 4 Reeder 1969.8 1970.6 mfh Ret LTG
McFadden W G 1LT 16-E 53 Bernard 1923 1925 '23cd
McFarland G C CPT 65-N 48 Ingalls 1932.8 1933.8 '33cd
McFerren C D COL 144-N-2 41-D Ingalls 1966.9 1967.2 mfh
McFerren C D COL 55 42 Ingalls 1967.2 1969.8 mfh
McGarraugh R E CPT 50-W 121 Bernard 1933.6 1938.7 Dunham JHC +
McGarry O A 1LT 114-E 24 Harrison 1918 1920 '19-20cd
McGarry O A SGT 61-S 43 Ingalls 1917 1918 '17cd
McGiffert J R MG 121-W 41 Fenwick 1973.4 1975.5 Ret LTG mfh
McGinn F W LTC 51-S-2 118 Ingalls 1952.9 1953.8 usacc
McGovern D H MG 125 73 Ingalls 1968.9 1971.6 mfh Ret MG
McGrady L W MAJ 18-E-1 37-A Bernard 1982.7 1984.7 mfh
McGurl P COL 129-N 103 Ingalls 1977.9 1981.6 mfh
McIntyre A CPT 15-N 34 Ruckman 1907.9 1908.9 Ret MG CAS'07
McIntyre A 1LT 18 W-2 29-B Bernard 1824 1826 '25rq +
McKay W G CPT 50-W 121 Bernard 1918.4 1920.6 '19cd AN306
McKeeman M W MAJ 44-S-1 104 Ingalls 1984.6 1986.7 mfh

McKell D Mc 1LT 18-E-2 37-B Bernard 1909.9 1910.9 CAS'10
McKell D Mc 1LT 63-N 24 Ruckman 1907.9 1908.9 '08cd
McKenney R I 1LT 70-N 91 Ingalls 1907.9 1908.9 '08cd
McKenney R I CPT 121-W 41 Fenwick 1912.12 1916.12 '13PhBk
McKenney R I CPT 1 151 Bernard 1911 1912.12 '12cd
McKinney M J 1LT 143-N-2 35-D Ingalls 1934.8 1935.7 Shunk
McKnight J T COL 18-E-1 37-A Bernard 1964.8 1965.12 mfh
McKnight J T COL 69-S 85 Ingalls 1965.12 1968.10 mfh
McKnight J T COL 17-W-1 41-A Bernard 1961.4 1963.8 mfh
McLarty W T LTC 33-E-1 61 Fenwick 1981.12 1984.6 mfh
McLaughtlin J C COL 55 42 Ingalls 1946.10 1947.4 usacc
McLean J R COL 52-W-2 132 Ingalls 1953.9 1954.8 usacc
McLean D COL 102-N 61 Ingalls 1951.2 1953.7 usacc
McLeary S H MAJ 128-E 109 Bernard 1919.6 1921.9 '19-21cd
McLeary S H 1LT 143-N-2 35-D Ingalls 1913.12 1914.12 '14PhBk
McLendon L J MAJ 54-S-1 136 Ingalls 1975.6 1977.10 mfh
McLennan D G COL 52-E-2 126 Ingalls 1961.8 1961.12 usacc
McLennan D G COL 129-N 103 Ingalls 1961.12 1964.7 mfh
McMains J R LTC 52-E-2 126 Ingalls 1984.3 1986.6 mfh
McManus H F COL 54-N-2 140 Ingalls 1946.10 1949.7 usacc
McMillan D L LTC 51-S-2 118 Ingalls 1953.10 1956.5 usacc
McMillen J A LTC 18-E-2 37-B Bernard 1971.2 1973.3 mfh
McMinn T L Jr LTC 43-E-1 5 Reeder 1968.4 1968.11 Chaplain mfh
McMorrow H A CPT 33-W-1 59 Fenwick 1933.8 1934.7 '34AdvCs
McNair C H MG 141 53 Fenwick 1983.6 1987.9 mfh
McNally E J COL 33-E-2 63 Fenwick 1946.9 1947.7 usacc
McNamee W L 1LT 43-W-1 3 Reeder 1937.7 1936.8 deCamp
McNamee W L COL 69-S 85 Ingalls 1946.8 1947.11 usacc
McNamee W L CPT 144-N-2 41-D Ingalls 1940.8 1941 '40-41PhBks
McNeely O D MAJ 50-W 121 Bernard 1939 1941 PhBk
McNeil C H CPT 66-S 38 Ingalls 1908.8 1909.8 S&F '09cd
McNeil C H MAJ 141 53 Fenwick 1911.9 1912.9 '12cd
McNeil C H CPT 102-S 59 Ingalls 1909.9 1911.9 '11cd
McNeill T L 1LT 66-S 38 Ingalls 1912.8 1916.12 PhBk
McPheron D A COL 67-N 36 Ingalls 1954.6 1957.7 usacc
McPherson W L 1LT 62-S 30 Ruckman 1933.9 1934.6 McPherson
McPherson W L CPT 143-N-1 35-B Ingalls 1935.9 1937.6 McPherson
McQuinn A D COL 43-E-1 5 Reeder 1965.4 1966.12 mfh
McRae R B LTC 45-E-1 114 Ingalls 1954.4 1956.6 usacc
McReynolds S M Jr 1LT 35-W-1 4 Reeder 1938.8 1939.7 CAS'38
McSherry F J CPT 67-N 36 Ingalls 1928.6 1929.6 Ret BG '29cd
McSherry E D LTC 18-W-1 29-A Bernard 1953.2 1953.11 usacc
McSlarrow J MAJ 143-S-2 35-C Ingalls 1974.6 1977.11 mfh
McSweeney D MAJ 17-E-1 47-A Bernard 1977.9 1980.6 mfh
McWhorter T CPT 67-N 36 Ingalls 1920.1 1921.8 '20cd
Mead E C MAJ 68-N 83 Ingalls 1934.8 1935.2 '35FOcs
Mead A D MG 66-N 40 Ingalls 1955.1 1955.6 usacc Ret MG
Mead A D MG 1 151 Bernard 1955.6 1957.4 CG usacc Ret MG
Meade D C LTC 126-S 165 Bernard 1983.6 1984.7 mfh
Meads J A Jr COL 35-E-1 6 Reeder 1965.9 1968.1 mfh
Medaris J B COL 19 18 Bernard 1946.9 1948.10 Ret MG usacc
Medley R H BEOlc 34-S-2 94 Ingalls 1965.3 1967.3 mfh
Meeks R C MAJ 35-E-2 8 Reeder 1970.9 1972.7 mfh

Meeks W D LTC 33-W-2 57 Fenwick 1964.1 1966.6 mfh
Meermans L H MAJ 143-S-1 35-A Ingalls 1944 1945 '44-45PhBks
Melberg R MAJ 55 42 Ingalls 1929.8 1931.6 '29FOcs
Mellnik S M 1LT 35-E-1 6 Reeder 1938.9 1939.8 Ret BG Mellnik
Mellon C CPT 17-E-2 47-B Bernard 1833.11 1834.4 d-686
Mellon C CPT 17-E-1 47-A Bernard 1832 1833.11 '34rq
Mellon C CPT 1 151 Bernard 1836.11 1837.1 w
Mendenhall J H LTC 34-S-1 96 Ingalls 1973.1 1973.6 mfh
Mendenhall C M Jr LTC 33-E-1 61 Fenwick 1940.9 1943.7 Mendenhall
Mendenhall C M Jr 1LT 16-E 53 Bernard 1926.9 1930.2 Mendenhall
Meneely J K MAJ 126-N 165 Bernard 1919.2 1920.3 Meneely
Meneely J K 2LT 18-W-1 29-A Bernard 1915.9 1916.12 Meneely
Mercer T J Rev 7 Frank Lane 1886.4 1901.1 St Mary's Priest
Merchant C S 1LT 18-E-2 37-B Bernard 1826.8 1828.3 '26-27rq rooms
Merriam W G COL 33-W-1 59 Fenwick 1958.12 1960.12 Ret BG usacc
Merriam H C CPT 70-N 91 Ingalls 1908.9 1909.9 '09cd
Merriam H M CPT 19 18 Bernard 1903.9 1904.8 CAS'04
Merriam L W COL 44-N-1 106 Ingalls 1954.11 1957.12 usacc
Merrill J O CPT 64-S 22 Ruckman 1919 '19cd
Merrill W W MAJ 70-S 89 Ingalls 1920.9 1921.8 Daughter +
Merritt W E MAJ 33-E-2 63 Fenwick 1939.6 1941.5 PhBks Shepherd
Merritt A G COL 144-N-2 41-D Ingalls 1960.10 1961.9 usacc
Merritt W B 1LT 18-W-1 29-A Bernard 1928.8 1929.7 '29cd
Merryman J MG 141 53 Fenwick 1977.9 1978.12 mfh
Merryman J MG 157 101 Bernard 1977.2 1977.9 mfh
Messinger E J LTG 141 53 Fenwick 1964.3 1965.2 mfh Ret LTG?
Meszar F BG 146 146 Engr Ln 1965.8 1967.3 mfh Ret BG
Meszar F COL 51-S-2 118 Ingalls 1965.7 1965.8 mfh Ret BG
Metcalf G T COL 18-E-1 37-A Bernard 1959.9 1961.7 usacc
Metz T M LTC 33-W-1 59 Fenwick 1948.9 1950.5 usacc
Metzger E H CPT 144-S-1 41 A Ingalls 1916.12 1917.6 Ret BG Metzger
Metzger E H LTC 121-W 41 Fenwick 1931.6 1935.12 Ret BG JHC +
Metzger E H MAJ 123-W 2 Ruckman 1924.8 1925.9 Ret BG Gage +
Metzler J E 1LT 54-N-1 138 Ingalls 1937.7 1938.6 '37cd
Meyer G R MAJ 126-S 163 Bernard 1918.10 1919.5 Ret MG Heaney
Meyer C R COL 45-W-1 112 Ingalls 1954.10 1955.7 Ret BG usacc
Meyer G R MAJ 55 42 Ingalls 1924.8 1929.7 Ret MG Heaney
Meyer G R MAJ 123-E 4 Ruckman 1923.9 1924.8 Ret MG Meyer
Meyer R D MG 158 32 Ingalls 1961.7 1963.8 Ret LTG mfh
Meyer R J MG 1 151 Bernard 1962.12 1964.6 mfh Ret MG
Meyer R J MG 142 51 Fenwick 1962.6 1962.12 mfh Ret MG
Meyer C B MAJ 123-E 4 Ruckman 1920.7 1923.8 Meyer Burgess
Meyers F L LTC 44-N-2 108 Ingalls 1985.7 1987.3 mfh
Meyers H F COL 123-W 2 Ruckman 1942.1 1942.6 Ret BG Meyers
Meyers H F COL 121-E 43 Fenwick 1943.8 1944.2 Ret BG Meyers
Michael W N 1LT 79-N 95 Ingalls 1905.9 1906.9 '06cd
Michelet H E MAJ 45-W-1 112 Ingalls 1941.6 1944.11 Ret BG '44PhBk
Mickelsen S R 2LT 1 151 Bernard 1918 1918 Ret LTG Huger
Mickelsen S R CPT 79-S 93 Ingalls 1931.1 1933.6 Ret LTG cds
Mickelsen S R MAJ 67-S 34 Ingalls 1936.8 1937.7 Ret LTG Huger
Mickelson A E 1LT 18-E-2 37-B Bernard 1919.6 1920.6 '20BtryOCs
Middlebrooks R R LTC 66-N 40 Ingalls 1946.11 1948.1 usacc
Middleworth H V COL 34-S-1 96 Ingalls 1956.11 1959.8 usacc

Midgett C F Jr COL 65-S 46 Ingalls 1959.11 1961.4 Ret BG usacc
Milani J COL 129-S 101 Ingalls 1980.7 1984.7 mfh
Milburn B L CPT 44-S-1 104 Ingalls 1931.6 1933.8 Ret MG Milburn
Milburn F W LTG 121-W 41 Fenwick 1951.9 1952.3 Ret GEN usacc
Milburn E MAJ 124-S 67 Ingalls 1919.6 1920.8 '20cd
Mildren F T LTG 118 29 Fenwick 1970.7 1970.9 Ret GEN mfh
Mildren F T LTG 141 53 Fenwick 1970.10 1971.3 Ret GEN mfh
Miles R CPT 54-S-1 136 Ingalls 1943 1944 '43 PhBk
Miles N A MG 1 151 Bernard 1865.5 1866.9 CG w
Miles S MAJ 128-W 107 Bernard 1926.8 1928.12 Ely +
Miley W W MG 118 29 Fenwick 1954.7 1955.7 usacc Ret MG?
Millard V MAJ 54-S-2 134 Ingalls 1980.5 1983.1 mfh
Miller N C COL 34-N-1 98 Ingalls 1962.10 1962.11 mfh
Miller F C COL 55 42 Ingalls 1958.12 1961.9 Ret MG usacc
Miller R O COL 143-S-1 35-A Ingalls 1968.2 1969.6 Ret BG mfh
Miller LTC 93 75 Ingalls 1892 1895 b-12
Miller R O COL 129-S 101 Ingalls 1969.6 1969.10 Ret BG mfh
Miller F J CPT 65-N 48 Ingalls 1906.9 1907.9 '08cd
Miller N C COL 65-S 46 Ingalls 1962.11 1963.1 mfh
Miller M P MAJ 3-N 169 Bernard 1879.10 1881.8 c-27
Miller D B LTC 52-E-1 128 Ingalls 1953.1 1957.2 usacc
Miller R L CPT 144-N-1 41-B Ingalls 1934.9 1936.8 Morton
Miller S T MAJ 167-A 7 Patch Road 1950.5 1951.8 usacc
Miller F W CPT 17-W-2 41-B Bernard 1908.9 1909.9 '09cd
Miller F R CPT 50-A 125 Bernard 1946.9 1947.3 USN usacc
Miller R G MAJ 18-W-2 29-B Bernard 1975.7 1978.1 mfh
Miller D LTC 51-N-1 122 Ingalls 1981.7 1984.7 mfh
Miller C M 1LT 167-A 7 Patch Road 1949.6 1950.5 usacc
Miller A D 1LT 18-E-1 37-A Bernard 1932.8 1933.8 33BtryOCs
Miller M G COL 102-S 59 Ingalls 1962.9 1966.6 mfh
Miller D L COL 101-S 55 Ingalls 1983.7 1985.8 mfh
Miller C P 1LT 50-E 129 Bernard 1885 c-14 d-691
Miller J COL 129-S 101 Ingalls 1978.6 1980.7 mfh
Miller W R 1LT 102-N 61 Ingalls 1918 1919 BOQ WWI '19cd
Miller B B COL 143-N-2 35-D Ingalls 1962.8 1964.9 mfh
Millerlile W COL 70-S 89 Ingalls 1984.7 1986.5 mfh
Milling J S LTC 18-E-2 37-B Bernard 1986.6 1986.8 mfh
Mills S M MAJ 1 151 Bernard 1899.3 1899.4 w
Mills G A LT 131-W 20 Tidball 1918.4 1919 '19cd
Mills S MAJ 79-N 95 Ingalls 1925.6 1927.6 '25cd
Mills S M CPT 50-E 129 Bernard 1885.9 1889.8 b-3 c-27
Mills J LTC 44-N-2 108 Ingalls 1979.6 1982.6 mfh
Mills G A 2LT 130-S 22 Tidball 1917.6 1918.4 S&F Arthur
Milmore C W LTC 34-S-1 96 Ingalls 1966.10 1967.6 mfh
Milton W E COL 33-E-2 63 Fenwick 1968.7 1969.11 mfh
Mims R L CPT 43-W-2 1 Reeder 1983.4 1984.1 mfh
Miner R M 1LT 17-E-1 47-A Bernard 1939.8 1940.1 Moore
Minson R T LTC 44-N-2 108 Ingalls 1966.7 1970.1 mfh
Mise E N MAJ 16-E 53 Bernard 1947.3 1947.11 Chaplain usacc
Mitchell J B COL 141 53 Fenwick 1919 1922 Ret BG JHC
Mitchell R M LTC 158 32 Ingalls 1921.9 1922.7 Ret BG '22FOcs
Mitchell L C CPT 126-N 165 Bernard 1929.11 1930.11 Mitchell
Mitchell E O 1LT 54-N-1 138 Ingalls 1938.6 1939.6 '39cd

Mitchell J D 1LT 18-E-2 37-B Bernard 1925.9 1927.8 Mitchell '25cd
Mitchell L C CPT 51-S-2 118 Ingalls 1931.7 1932.6 Mitchell
Mitchell R M CPT 68-S 81 Ingalls 1907.9 1909.9 Ret BG '08-09cd
Mix G A 1LT 3-N 169 Bernard 1912.12 1913.12 CAS'13 '13cd
Mix G A 1LT 17-W-2 41-B Barnard 1910.9 1911.12 '11cd
Mize P H COL 143-S-2 35-C Ingalls 1963.5 1965.9 mfh
Mojecki J COL 50-W 121 Bernard 1978.6 1982.5 mfh
Mollen I R COL 52-W-2 132 Ingalls 1964.4 1964.8 PhBks
Mollen I R COL 55 42 Ingalls 1964.8 1966.11 mfh
Momfron ADJ 17-W-2 41-B Bernard 1825 d-684
Monroe W H 1LT 70-N 91 Ingalls 1904 BOQ c-46
Monroe H M COL 45-W-2 110 Ingalls 1949.6 1949.9 Ret BG usacc
Monroe K L COL 102-N 61 Ingalls 1972.6 1973.9 mfh
Monroe W H CPT 103-S 63 Ingalls 1911.9 1913.12 '12cd
Monroe H M COL 126-N 165 Bernard 1949.9 1951.1 Ret BG usacc
Montague R M MG 121-W 41 Fenwick 1952.9 1955.6 usacc Ret MG?
Montgomery J E MAJ 144-S-1 41-A Ingalls 1922.7 1923.10 RetBG CAS'23
Montrone A J COL 43-E-1 5 Reeder 1962.5 1963.6 mfh
Moody R L MAJ 45-E-1 114 Ingalls 1973.4 1975.7 mfh
Moon G A II COL 143-S-1 35-A Ingalls 1960.1 1960.8 usacc
Moore G F COL 121-W 41 Fenwick 1935.12 1938.? Ret MG Cox +
Moore L R LTC 51-N-1 122 Ingalls 1946.9 1948.7 usacc
Moore M N MAJ 143-S-2 35-C Ingalls 1972.9 1974.1 mfh
Moore J R LTC 51-N-1 122 Ingalls 1985.5 1986.4 mfh
Moore A J COL 50-A 125 Bernard 1966.8 1968.8 mfh
Moore E W 1LT 43-E-2 7 Reeder 1938.6 1939.7 '39CAS
Moore L R COL 18-E-1 37-A Bernard 1961.10 1964.8 mfh
Moore R F 1LT 1 151 Bernard 1937 1938 Gilman
Moore J C COL 51-S-1 120 Ingalls 1955.8 1956.4 usacc
Moore G F 1LT 16-E 53 Bernard 1914.12 1915.12 Ret MG CAS'15
Moore R CW2 43-W-2 1 Reeder 1984.4 1986.10 mfh
Moore W W CPT 79-S 93 Ingalls 1933.6 1934.6 JHC Bartlett
Moore R W 1LT 35-E-2 8 Reeder 1938.8 1939.9 Moore
Moore J O LTC 34-S-2 94 Ingalls 1948.7 1951.2 usacc
Moore J C 2LT 17-E-1 47-A Bernard 1935.10 1936.6 Clark
Moore J C 1LT 17-E-2 47-B Bernard 1936.6 1937.5 Moore
Moore H C COL 127-E 147 Bernard 1956.4 1958.7 usacc
Moore C D CPT 66-N 40 Ingalls 1942.6 1946.9 PhBk
Moore G F MAJ 103-N 65 Ingalls 1921.8 1923.8 Ret MG S&F '23cd
Moorman R R CPT 18-E-1 37-A Bernard 1938.8 1939.7 Moorman
Moorman R R LTC 127-E 147 Bernard 1945.10 1946.5 Moorman
Moran R D LTC 3-N 169 Bernard 1949.8 1952.8 usacc
Morelli D R BG 68-S 81 Ingalls 1982.8 1983.5 mfh
Morelli D BG 157 101 Bernard 1980.1 1982.7 mfh
Morelli D MG 125 73 Ingalls 1983.5 1984.3 mfh
Morgan A S CPT 69-S 85 Infalls 1905.9 1906.9 CAS'06
Morgan J B MAJ 67-N 36 Ingalls 1942.7 1942.10 Morgan
Morgan A S 1LT 18-W-2 29-B Bernard 1902 b-19 rms
Morgan J B CPT 54-S-1 136 Ingalls 1941.12 1942.3 Morgan
Morgan J B 2LT 18-W-2 29-B Bernard 1936.8 1937.6 Morgan
Morgan M MAJ 68-N 83 Ingalls 1933.8 1934.8 '34AdvCs
Morgan J B 1LT 50-A 125 Bernard 1939.8 1940.2 Morgan
Morgan J S COL 52-W-2 132 Ingalls 1950.5 1953.7 usacc

Morgan C H MAJ 18-E-1 37-A Bernard 1869.8 1871.1 S&F c-27
Morrill L S CPT 141 53 Fenwick 1919 1919 '19cd rms?
Morris C CPT 50-E 129 Bernard 1883.1 1885.7 S&F c-27
Morris H A LTC 17-W-2 41-B Bernard 1947.9 1948.1 usacc
Morris W W MAJ 18-E-1 37-A Bernard 1842.7 1845.9 '44rq d-686
Morris G W 1LT 143-N-1 35-B Ingalls 1922.8 1923.8 '23cd
Morris R H CPT 68-N 83 Ingalls 1917.6 1919.6 QMC Morris
Morris R 1LT 16-E 53 Bernardd 1939 1940 Morris
Morris S J COL 125 73 Ingalls 1927.6 1929.6 MedC Ely +
Morrison J B MAJ 45-W-2 110 Ingalls 1971.3 1973.3 mfh
Morrison R L COL 103-N 65 Ingalls 1977.8 1979.7 mfh
Morrison D E LTC 70-S 89 Ingalls 1939.6 1941.9 Ph Bks
Morrissey J LTC 143-N-1 35-B Ingalls 1981.8 1984.6 mfh
Morrow C Jr COL 63-S 26 Ruckman 1973.9 1978.6 mfh
Morrow J L Jr COL 54-N-1 138 Ingalls 1969.8 1969.11 mfh
Morrow J L Jr COL 103-N 65 Ingalls 1969.11 1972.9 mfh
Morsch P A LTC 45-E-1 114 Ingalls 1969.7 1971.3 mfh
Morse H L CPT 103-N 65 Ingalls 1912.12 1913.12 CAS'12 '13cd
Morse H L 1LT 64-N 20 Ruckman 1911.9 1912.9 '12cd
Mortimer J E CPT 51-N-1 122 Ingalls 1938.8 1939.8 '39PhBk
Morton K R COL 65-N 48 Ingalls 1970.5 1972.7 mfh
Morton L M CPT 144-N-2 41-D Ingalls 1932.9 1935.6 Morton '33cd
Moseley DR 68-N 83 Ingalls 1895 b-12 MedC
Moseley L L LTC 143-N-1 35-B Ingalls 1968.4 1969.6 mfh
Moss R E LTC 35-W-2 2 Reeder 1970.8 1972.1 mfh
Moss J D CPT 33-E-2 63 Fenwick 1936.12 1937.7 Shepherd JHC
Mossman A P COL 43-E-2 7 Reeder 1951.8 1954.6 usacc
Mosteller J W Jr 1LT 17-W-1 41-A Bernard 1930.12 1931.7 '31cd
Motes P M COL 63-N 24 Ruckman 1959.8 1961.8 usacc
Motley A COL 101-N 57 Ingalls 1978.6 1981.6 mfh
Mott L E COL 64 71 Fenwick 1969.8 1971.6 mfh
Mott L E COL 18-W-1 29-A Bernard 1969.7 1969.8 mfh
Mountford F A 1LT 63-S 26 Ruckman 1913.9 1914.12 PhBk
Mountford F A MAJ 123-E 4 Ruckman 1924.9 1925.6 Daughter Ely
Mountford F A MAJ 124-S 67 Ingalls 1927.8 1930.6 Ely '29cd
Mountfort J CPT 18-E-2 37-B Bernard 1824.3 1826.3 '25rq rooms?
Moya M E MAJ 33-W-1 59 Fenwick 1974.10 1975.6 mfh
Mudgett C F Jr COL 43-W-1 3 Reeder 1959.8 1959.11 Ret BG usacc
Mueller E L P COL 51-N-2 124 Ingalls 1961.4 1962.6 mfh
Muir J Jr CPT 54-N-1 138 Ingalls 1931.6 1932.6 VanBuskirk
Muller W J BG 103-S 63 Ingalls 1947.12 1948.11 usacc Ret BG?
Muller A L MAJ 127-W 145 Bernard 1928.8 1929.8 '29cd
Muller M T COL 34-N-2 100 Ingalls 1966.8 1967.1 mfh
Mulligan B MAJ 45-E-2 116 Ingalls 1981.7 1984.8 mfh
Munford T W 1LT 18-E-1 37-A Bernard 1919.6 1920.7 '20cd Ericson
Munford T W 1LT 16-W 51 Bernard 1925 1927 BOQ '27cd
Munroe J E 1LT 68-N 83 Ingalls 1910.9 1912.12 '11-12cd
Murphy C A COL 129-S 101 Ingalls 1964.3 1966.6 mfh
Murphy A COL 129-N 103 Ingalls 1981.7 1984.4 mfh
Murphy P J C COL 143-S-1 35-A Ingalls 1949.4 1950.11 usacc
Murphy J B MG 125 73 Ingalls 1956.7 1958.6 usacc Ret MG?
Murphy C A COL 35-W-1 4 Reeder 1963.7 1964.3 mfh
Murphy J G 2LT 18-E-2 37-B Bernard 1917.6 1917.11 Murphy

Murray C R COL 124-N 69 Ingalls 1957.9 1960.10 usacc
Murray M 1LT 143-N-1 35-B Ingalls 1911.9 1912.12 CAS'12 '12cd
Murray W E 1LT 17-W-2 41-B Bernard 1906.9 1907.9 CAS'07
Murray T J Rev 7 Frank Lane 1877.2 1886.4 St Mary's Priest
Murray H L Jr COL 103-N 65 Ingalls 1963.4 1965.3 mfh
Murrin W R LTC 55 42 Ingalls 1945.8 1946.6 Murrin
Musgrave J R 2LT 69-N 87 Ingalls 1902.5 1902.9 BOQ? c-46
Musgrave J R 2LT 16-E 53 Bernard 1905 1906.5 c-46 b-26
Mussil J J 1LT 67-S 34 Ingalls 1918 1919 BOQ WWI '19cd
Muth R W COL 51-S-2 118 Ingalls 1956.6 1958.6 usacc
Myers H M COL 44-N-2 108 Ingalls 1959.12 1963.2 mfh
Myers C M 1LT 18-E-1 37-A Bernard 1928.7 1929.7 '29cd
Myers B LTC 51-S-2 118 Ingalls 1978.8 1979.9 mfh
Myers H M COL 129-S 101 Ingalls 1966.6 1969.4 mfh
Myers H F LTC 144-S-2 41-C Ingalls 1941.8 1942.1 Ret BG Meyers
Myrah H H 1LT 18-W-2 29-B Bernard 1926.8 1927.8 '27BtryOCs
Myrick J R CPT 18-W-2 29-B Bernard 1874.5 1875.5 S&F c-27
Narel J L LTC 143-S-2 35-C Ingalls 1986.6 1987.7 mfh
Nash A M COL 43-E-2 7 Reeder 1966.6 1968.1 mfh
Nason S B MG 157 101 Bernard 1957.2 1958.7 usacc Ret MG?
Naylor R H COL 101-S 55 Ingalls 1950.2 1951.8 usacc
Naylor R H COL 143-S-2 35-C Ingalls 1949.9 1950.2 usacc
Naylor R H COL 43-E-1 5 Reeder 1949.8 1949.9 usacc
Neal P L COL 123-W 2 Ruckman 1952.9 1954.8 Ret BG usacc
Neal P L COL 66-N 40 Ingalls 1952.7 1952.9 Ret BG usacc
Neale C L CPT 44-S-2 102 Ingalls 1931.6 1932.6 Coates
Needels E V R COL 45-W-2 110 Ingalls 1961.8 1962.10 mfh
Needels E V R COL 15-N 34 Ruckman 1962.10 1965.10 mfh
Neely R A MAJ 17-W-1 41-A Bernard 1983.8 1986.9 mfh
Neide W B CPT 66-S 38 Ingalls 1944 1945 PhBk
Nelson O A 1LT 45-W-1 112 Ingalls 1930.12 1931.6 Nelson
Nelson R M 1LT 44-S-1 104 Ingalls 1939.7 1941.1 PhBks
Nelson R T LTC 35-W-2 2 Reeder 1949.10 1950.8 Ret MG usacc
Nelson R L 1LT 79-S 93 Ingalls 1918 1919 BOQ WWI '19cd
Nelson R T COL 67-S 34 Ingalls 1950.8 1952.7 Ret MG usacc
Nelson O A 2LT 63-N 24 Ruckman 1918 Nelson
Nelson G R 1LT 18-E-1 37-A Bernard 1940.8 '41 PhBk
Nelson P B 1LT 15-N 34 Ruckman 1933.8 1934.6 Nelson
Nerdahl C B COL 144-N-1 41-B Ingalls 1969.8 1970.4 mfh
Nerdahl C B COL 102-N 61 Ingalls 1970.4 1972.5 mfh
Nesbitt T E LTC 14 32 Ruckman 1973.2 1975.6 Fire June '75 mfh
Nesbitt T E COL 126-S 163 Bernard 1975.7 1976.8 mfh
Nettles J S Jr MAJ 51-N-1 122 Ingalls 1972.8 1974.1 mfh
Newark H G CWO 167-A 7 Patch Road 1955.12 1958.9 usacc
Newby G U COL 144-S-2 41-C Ingalls 1966.2 1967.8 mfh
Newell R C LTC 54-S-2 134 Ingalls 1969.6 1972.9 mfh
Newell R C LTC 44-N-1 106 Ingalls 1965.8 1967.11 mfh
Newgord J G CPT 68-N 83 Ingalls 1919.6 1922.10 MedC Clark
Newman H H CPT 62-S 30 Ruckman 1935.8 1937.6 Newman
Newman H H 1LT 18-W-1 29-A Bernard 1918.6 1918.12 Newman
Newman H H 1LT 67-S 34 Ingalls 1919 1919.11 BOQ WWI '19cd
Newman O P MG 118 29 Fenwick 1956.9 1958.6 usacc Ret MG?
Newman A S MG 118 29 Fenwick 1958.6 1960.6 usacc Ret MG?

Newsome F C 1LT 63-S 26 Ruckman 1945 1946 PhBk
Newton A COL 63-N 24 Ruckman 1969.7 1971.6 mfh
Niblo BG 101-N 57 Ingalls 1952.2 1952.5 Ret BG usacc
Niblo U BG 1 151 Bernard 1952.5 1954.11 Ret BG usacc
Nicholls J C 1LT 70-S 89 Ingalls 1902.9 1903.11 CAS'03 '03cd
Nichols H F MAJ 66-S 38 Ingalls 1919.3 1920.7 Ret BG Nichols
Nichols H F MAJ 66-S 38 Ingalls 1926.7 1928.7 Ret BG Nichols
Nichols W R 1LT 65-S 46 Ingalls 1913.12 1915.12 Ret BG PhBk +
Nichols G P LTC 17-E-2 47-B Bernard 1950.11 1952.7 usacc
Nichols W R MAJ 70-N 91 Ingalls 1922.8 1923.7 Ret BG CAS'23
Nichols W R COL 141 53 Fenwick 1936.6 1939.7 Ret BG Shedd +
Nichols H F 2LT 16-W 51 Bernard 1912 1912 Ret BG Nichols
Nichols H F LTC 124-S 67 Ingalls 1938.8 1940.11 Ret BG PhBk
Nicholson J W LTC 18-W-1 29-A Bernard 1975.10 1976.7 mfh
Nicholson A B 1LT 45-E-2 116 Ingalls 1930.12 1931.7 Goeppert
Nicholson A B MAJ 3-N 169 Bernard 1938.8 1940.5 Goeppert
Niethamer W F CPT 54-N-1 138 Ingalls 1932.6 1935.7 '34BtryOCs AN306
Nisley H A BG 121-E 43 Fenwick 1946.9 1948.8 usacc Ret BG?
Noah M BG 125 73 Ingalls 1977.8 1979.9 mfh
Noah M W COL 63-N 24 Ruckman 1976.5 1977.8 mfh
Nock C COL 101-N 57 Ingalls 1981.6 1983.9 mfh
Nones E P CPT 123-E 4 Ruckman 1913.12 1914.12 PhBk '14cd
Norling R L LTC 17-E-1 47-A Bernard 1953.12 1955.11 usacc
Norling R L LTC 18-E-1 37-A Bernard 1955.11 1956.11 usacc
Norman N LTC 44-S-2 102 Ingalls 1977.10 1981.7 mfh
Norris J I COL 43-W-2 1 Reeder 1962.3 1963.5 mfh
Norris S R MAJ 126-N 165 Bernard 1927.7 1929.11 MedC '29cd
Norris J K COL 43-W-2 1 Reeder 1957.7 1959.8 usacc
Norris D R CPT 143-S-2 35-C Ingalls 1927.7 1928.7 '27cd
Norris J K COL 79-S 93 Ingalls 1959.8 1960.6 usacc
Norton A CPT 50-E 129 Bernard 1914.12 1916.12 Norton
Norton J COL 33-E-2 63 Fenwick 1960.9 1961.1 Ret LTG usacc
Norton J COL 124-N 69 Ingalls 1961.1 1963.6 Ret LTG mfh
Norton A MAJ 144-N-2 41-D Ingalls 1920.3 1921.3 '20cd
Norton A 1LT 17-E-1 47-A Bernard 1913.12 1914.12 PhBk '14cd
Norton M C Jr CPT 146 146 Engr Ln 1968.9 1971.7 USN mfh
Noyes E P Jr 1LT 62-N 28 Ruckman 1914.12 1915.12 CAS'15 '15cd
Nugent G A COL 119 33 Fenwick 1929.6 1929.8 w Ret BG
Nugent G A MAJ 118 29 Fenwick 1913.7 1916.7 Ret BG PhBk
Nugent G A COL 120 37 Fenwick 1929.8 1932.8 Ret BG '29cd
Nugent G A CPT 69-S 85 Ingalls 1908.9 1909.9 Ret BG '09cd
Nye CPT 55 42 Ingalls 1886 1888 c-14 d-691
Oakes J C COL 15-S 36 Ruckman 1946.9 1948.7 Ret LTG usacc
Oblinger J B MG 141 53 Fenwick 1982.7 1983.6 mfh
O'Brien M J MAJ 143-S-1 35-A Ingalls 1930.8 1931.8 '30AdvCs
O'Brien E S LTC 17-E-1 47-A Bernard 1974.10 1976.1 mfh
O'Brien R A Jr COL 43-E-2 7 Reeder 1958.10 1960.12 usacc
O'Brien R A Jr COL 50-W 121 Bernard 1960.12 1961.8 usacc
O'Connell J G COL 126-S 165 Bernard 1985.6 1987.12 mfh
O'Connell G M CPT 66-N 40 Ingalls 1928.8 1931.7 '29-31cd
O'Connell J J Rev 7 Frank Lane 1947 '47 PhBk Priest
O'Conner G G MG 1 151 Bernard 1968.3 1969.9 Ret LTG mfh
O'Daniel J W MG 120 37 Fenwick 1951.3 1951.7 Ret LTG usacc

O'Daniel J W MG 125 73 Ingalls 1950.10 1951.3 Ret LTG usacc
Odegard D COL 101-S 55 Ingalls 1980.6 1983.7 mfh
Oden'hal E P MAJ 143-S-2 35-C Ingalls 1919.9 1920.9 '20cd
Odenwaller C J 1LT 44-N-2 108 Ingalls 1937.8 1938.8 CAS'38
O'Donnell R F LTC 43-E-2 7 Reeder 1957.6 1958.10 usacc
Offutt H D Jr COL 16-W 51 Bernard 1963.7 1964.7 mfh
Offutt H D Jr COL 17-W-2 41-B Bernard 1962.7 1963.7 mfh
Ogden M L 1LT 63-N 24 Ruckman 1938.6 1939.8 '39cd
Oglesby C J CPT 79-S 93 Ingalls 1918 1919 BOQ WWI '19cd
O'Hara W A Rev 7 Frank Lane 1901.1 1901.8 St Mary's Priest
Ohnstad J C CPT 127-W 145 Bernard 1913.12 1915.6 PhBk
Ohnstad J C LT 70-N 91 Ingalls 1904.3 1905.9 BOQ c-53
Ohnstad J C CPT 102-N 61 Ingalls 1910.8 1913.12 S&F '10-12cd
Ohnstad J C LTC 93 75 Ingalls 1921.8 1923.6 S&F Arthur
Ohnstad J C CPT 65-N 48 Ingalls 1909.9 1910.8 CAS'10
Ohnstad J C COL 118 29 Fenwick 1930.8 1933.7 Cochran
Okarski G M LTC 34-S-2 94 Ingalls 1970.6 1974.8 mfh
O'Kelley G W MAJ 35-E-1 6 Reeder 1972.3 1974.6 mfh
Oldfield H R CPT 3-N 169 Bernard 1916.12 1917.6 Ret MG Ford
Oldfield H R LTC 102-S 59 Ingalls 1919.2 1921.8 Ret MG Oldfield
Olliver L E COL 143-S-1 35-A Ingalls 1963.5 1965.10 mfh
Olliver L E COL 68-N 83 Ingalls 1965.10 1966.8 mfh
Olsen H L LTC 34-N-2 100 Ingalls 1948.4 1949.2 usacc
Olsen E J COL 124-S 67 Ingalls 1974.1 1975.7 mfh
Olson J MAJ 52-E-2 126 Ingalls 1975.7 1979.5 mfh
Olson H C COL 34-N-1 98 Ingalls 1960.4 1961.5 usacc
Olson R E LTC 17-W-1 41-A Bernard 1973.8 1974.9 mfh
Olson H COL 15-S 36 Ruckman 1977.7 1978.6 mfh
O'Neill D W CPT 167-B 9 Patch Road 1967.6 1968.12 mfh
O'Neill J T COL 43-E-2 7 Reeder 1946.9 1948.3 usacc
Ono A K MG 1 151 Bernard 1983.9 1985.6 mfh
Ordway G LTC 55 42 Ingalls 1920.9 1921.6 CAS'21
Ordway G 1LT 68-S 81 Ingalls 1902.9 1903.9 '02cd
O'Rear J T H MAJ 126-N 165 Bernard 1917.12 1918.10 '19cd
O'Rear J T H 2LT 16-E 53 Bernard 1911 1912 '11cd
O'Rear J T H CPT 79-N 95 Ingalls 1915.8 1916.12 O'Rear CAS'16
O'Rourke P W MAJ 33-W-2 57 Fenwick 1984.6 1986.6 mfh
Orsini LTC 51-N-1 122 Ingalls 1978.9 1981.7 mfh
Orth E C Jr COL 69-S 85 Ingalls 1955.5 1957.2 usacc
Orth E C Jr COL 167-B 9 Patch Road 1954.8 1955.5 usacc
Ortiz C MAJ 51-S-1 120 Ingalls 1977.10 1980.12 mfh
Osborne R M MG 141 53 Fenwick 1956.3 1958.1 usacc Ret MG?
Osgard J L COL 102-N 61 Ingalls 1965.2 1966.6 mfh
Osgard J L COL 34-S-2 94 Ingalls 1964.8 1965.2 mfh
Osgood CPT 55 42 Ingalls 1888 1890 b-6
Osterhouse B CPT 143-S-1 35-A Ingalls 1919 '19cd rms?
Ostrander H W 1LT 16-E 53 Bernard 1922 1923 CAS'23
Ostrom C D Y CPT 67-S 34 Ingalls 1921.7 1922.7 Ret BG Ostrom
Ostrom C D Y MAJ 126-N 165 Bernard 1930.11 1931.7 Ret BG Irvine
Otis G GEN 119 33 Fenwick 1981.8 1983.3 mfh
Ottosen P H MAJ 143-N-1 35-B Ingalls 1923.8 1924.8 Irvine
Ottosen P H CPT 102-N 61 Ingalls 1919.6 1920.6 '20cd
Overdahl N L COL 101-S 55 Ingalls 1975.8 1980.5 mfh

Owen T E COL 146 146 Engr Ln 1948.1 1951.8 usacc
Owens G R CPT 64-S 22 Ruckman 1925 '25cd
Owen M B Jr CPT 35-E-2 8 Reeder 1944.2 1946.6 PhBks
Oxx F H COL 54-N-2 140 Ingalls 1950.3 1950.8 Ret BG usacc
Oxx F H BG 19 18 Bernard 1950.8 1951.11 Ret BG usacc
Packard D F COL 146 146 Engr Ln 1973.11 1974.8 mfh Ret BG
Page H 1LT 17-E-2 47-B Bernard 1902 b-19 c-46 MedC
Painter B R 2LT 18-E-2 37-B Bernard 1940.10 1941.11 PhBk
Palizza M J MAJ 65-N 48 Ingalls 1944.7 1946.8 PhBk
Palmer R S LTC 147 147 Engr Ln 1947.11 1948.8 usacc
Palmer C D MG 157 101 Bernard 1951.9 1953.6 Ret GEN usacc
Palmer G W CPT 51-S-1 120 Ingalls 1935.8 1936.6 Palmer
Palmer C D MG 118 29 Fenwick 1953.6 1954.4 Ret GEN usacc
Palmieri G J LTC 45-E-1 114 Ingalls 1971.4 1973.1 mfh
Pamplin D G MAJ 79-N 95 Ingalls 1938.6 1941 PhBk
Pamplin D G 1LT 45-W-2 110 Ingalls 1930.12 1931.8 HWC
Papenfoth W H 1LT 18-W-2 29-B Benard 1922.8 1923.8 '23BtryOCs
Parker J M COL 34-N-1 98 Ingalls 1962.11 1963.7 mfh
Parker S F MAJ 101-N 57 Ingalls 1935.6 1938.6 MedC Parker
Parker C G MAJ 50-A 125 Bernard 1972.9 1973.7 mfh
Parker J M COL 67-N 36 Ingalls 1963.7 1964.4 mfh
Parker T R CPT 63-S 26 Ruckman 1927.8 1928.8 '28BtryOCs
Parker F H MAJ 50-E 129 Bernard 1876.6 1879.6 ORD
Parker H C COL 50-W 121 Bernard 1946.11 1947.8 usacc
Parker F O MAJ 18-W-2 29-B Bernard 1972.4 1975.6 mfh
Parker R W MAJ 33-E-2 63 Fenwick 1974.9 1978.8 mfh
Parkhurst LT 14 32 Ruckman 1890 1892 c-46
Parks H C 1LT 17-W-1 41-A Bernard 1935.9 1936.6 Ret MG Parks
Parks H C CPT 16-W 51 Bernard 1939.6 1940.6 Ret MG PhBk
Parks G SSG 35-W-1 4 Reeder 1982.5 1983.3 mfh
Parks H C CPT 44-S-2 102 Ingalls 1938.9 1939.6 Ret MG Parks
Parr D CPT 44-S-1 104 Ingalls 1982.12 1984.6 mfh
Parsons N W LTC 52-E-2 126 Ingalls 1953.8 1954.9 usacc
Parsons M A CPT 129-S 101 Ingalls 1919 BOQ WWI '19cd
Parsons M H CPT 65-S 46 Ingalls 1924.6 1924.11 Parsons' Widow
Partin C L LTC 33-W-1 59 Ingalls 1946.11 1948.8 usacc
Partridge R B COL 3-S 167 Bernard 1957.8 1960.5 usacc
Paterson R D 1LT 16-W 51 Bernard 1924 1925 Levy
Paterson J A 2LT 16-E 53 Bernard 1917 1919 Paterson
Paterson W CPT 67-N 36 Ingalls 1911.9 1912.9 CAS'12 '12cd
Patrick G A CPT 63-S 26 Ruckman 1933.8 1934.8 Wilson +
Patrick G A CPT 64-S 22 Ruckman 1928 1930 Evans
Patrick T MAJ 44-N-1 106 Ingalls 1976.12 1980.6 mfh
Patten H T CPT 62-N 28 Ruckman 1905 1906 '06cd
Patten H T CPT 66-N 40 Ingalls 1908.9 1909.9 '08cd
Patten H T CPT 121-E 43 Fenwick 1909.9 1911.9 '11cd
Patterson C G COL 102-S 59 Ingalls 1955.12 1956.3 usacc
Patterson R H CPT 50-E 129 Bernard 1896.10 1898.3 S&F Arthur
Patterson C G 1LT 16-E 53 Bernard 1937.5 1938.7 Patterson
Patterson C G COL 51 N-2 124 Ingalls 1955.3 1955.12 usacc
Patterson W H COL 51 S-1 120 Ingalls 1957.11 1960.6 usacc
Paul F C LTC 35-E-2 8 Reeder 1946.8 1947.9 usacc
Paul F M MAJ 143-S-1 35-A Ingalls 1935.8 1940.6 Paul '37cd

Payne B CPT 62-S 30 Ruckman 1903.9 1905.9 S&F b-26
Payne L MAJ 33-W-2 57 Fenwick 1980.11 1981.11 mfh
Payne H N MAJ 16-E 53 Bernard 1948.11 1949.10 usacc
Payne A MAJ 124-N 69 Ingalls 1918.9 1919.6 '19cd
Payne A 1LT 68-N 83 Ingalls 1913.12 1914.12 PhBk
Payne H N MAJ 16-E 53 Bernardd 1948.7 1948.11 usacc
Payne G M LTC 51-S-1 120 Ingalls 1956.5 1956.12 usacc
Peace W G CPT 126-S 163 Bernard 1915.12 1916.12 '17cd
Pearson R W MAJ 124-N 69 Ingalls 1921.7 1924.8 Dentist JHC
Peatfield N E COL 126-S 163 Bernard 1963.8 1964.9 Ret BG mfh
Peca P S COL 51-N-1 122 Ingalls 1953.6 1954.8 usacc
Peck T M CPT 43-W-2 1 Reeder 1984.2 1984.4 mfh
Peddicord E D COL 146 146 Engr Ln 1946.9 1948.1 usacc
Peddicord E D LTC 124-S 67 Ingalls 1944.2 1944.6 Peddicord
Peddicord E D CPT 16-W 51 Bernard 1937.7 1939.6 Peddicord
Peed G P COL 125 73 Ingalls 1922.10 1925.6 MedC '23cd +
Peed G P CPT 18-W-1 29-A Bernard 1910.9 1911.0 '11cd MedC
Peek G M 1LT 144-S-1 41-A Ingalls 1912.12 1913.12 CAS'13 '13cd
Peirce G F COL 68-N 83 Ingalls 1953.7 1954.4 usacc
Pence W P CPT 68-N 83 Ingalls 1900.9 1901.6 '02cd
Pence W P MAJ 120 37 Fenwick 1911.9 1912.7 '12cd
Pence W P MAJ 93 75 Ingalls 1912.7 1913.7 '13cd
Pence W P CPT 102-N 61 Ingalls 1907.9 1909.9 '08-09cd
Pence W P CPT 55 42 Ingalls 1906.5 1907.9 S&F Arthur
Pendleton R T LTC 158 32 Ingalls 1936.8 1940.8 Ret BG Daughter
Pendleton R T 1LT 68-N 83 Ingalls 1916.12 1917.6 Ret BG Ford
Pendleton R T MAJ 65-S 46 Ingalls 1924.11 1925.8 Ret BG Hartel
Pendleton R T MAJ 143-S-1 35-A Ingalls 1926.7 1927.7 Ret BG Huger
Pendleton H E CPT 3-N 169 Bernard 1929.8 1930.8 Pope '30AdvC
Pendleton R T MAJ 143-S-2 35-C Ingalls 1928.7 1930.7 Ret BG Huger +
Pendleton A G 1LT 65-N 48 Ingalls 1910.9 1911.9 '11cd
Pendleton A L 1LT 17-W-2 41-B Bernard 1916.12 1917.6 Ford CAS'17
Pennington A C M MAJ 50-W 121 Bernard 1886.8 1891.1 c-27 b-3 d-691
Penn W S Jr LTC 44-S-2 102 Ingalls 1954.8 1956.3 usacc
Penzler H D MG 121-W 41 Fenwick 1984.10 1986.7 mfh
Pepke D R MG 1 151 Bernard 1969.12 1973.6 Ret LTG mfh
Pepper G W 1LT 65-N 48 Ingalls 1919 BOQ? '19cd
Perkins G R COL 127-E 147 Bernard 1984.5 1985.7 mfh
Perkins R M MAJ 128-W 107 Bernard 1919.6 1921.1 Ret BG '29cd
Perkins J CPT 61-S 43 Ingalls 1918 1919 '19cd
Perkins R M MAJ 129-N 103 Ingalls 1926.8 1927.7 Ret BG Huger
Perkins A COL 101-N 57 Ingalls 1976.9 1978.6 mfh
Perkins R M MAJ 79-S 93 Ingalls 1927.7 1929.6 Ret BG '29cd
Perkins G T CPT 103-N 65 Ingalls 1906.9 1907.9 CAS'07
Perley R N 2LT 16-E 53 Bernard 1912.1 1912.4 '12cd
Perrigo J G LTC 45-W-2 110 Ingalls 1964.6 1965.6 mfh
Perry H E COL 17-E-2 47-B Bernard 1968.11 1969.3 mfh
Perry F L CPT 50-E 129 Bernard 1910.9 1912.12 '11-12cd
Perry W A MAJ 103-N 65 Ingalls 1941.10 1943.8 Ret BG Perry
Perry W A 1LT 43-W-1 3 Reeder 1936.8 1937.6 Ret BG Perry
Perry N A CPT 54-N-1 138 Ingalls 1940.6 1941.10 Weld
Perry H E COL 70-S 89 Ingalls 1969.3 1970.11 mfh
Persons H P Jr 1LT 52-W-1 130 Ingalls 1940.7 1941.8 Ret BG Person

Pervier G W COL 43-E-1 5 Reeder 1964.8 1965.4 mfh
Pervier G W COL 15-S 36 Ruckman 1965.4 1967.2 mfh
Pervier G W LTC 45-W-2 110 Ingalls 1957.2 1959.7 usacc
Peters W J H CSM 64 71 Fenwick 1983.8 1987.7 mfh
Peters B COL 123-E 4 Ruckman 1977.6 1979.7 mfh
Peterson S R LTC 18-W-2 29-B Bernard 1954.5 1956.1 usacc
Peterson P L COL 17-W-1 41-A Bernard 1966.9 1967.6 mfh
Peterson A C 1LT 35-E-2 8 Reeder 1937.8 1938.7 '37cd
Peterson J C 1LT 79-N 95 Ingalls 1909.9 1910.9 CAS'10
Peterson A C 1LT 33-W-2 57 Fenwick 1938.7 1939.7 Whipple
Peterson S L LTC 17-W-2 41-B Bernard 1948.2 1949.8 usacc
Petrig D L CW3 167-A 7 Patch Road 1970.9 1972.8 mfh
Pettus H L MAJ 142 51 Fenwick 1912.7 1914.12 QMC PhBk
Pfeffer C A LTC 101-N 57 Ingalls 1940.6 1941.7 MedC PhBk
Pflanz J MAJ 52-E-1 128 Ingalls 1978.7 1980.10 mfh
Phelan D A COL 101-S 55 Ingalls 1955.1 1958.6 usacc
Phifer C J LTC 144-N-1 41-B Ingalls 1970.4 1971.8 mfh
Philips R H COL 158 32 Ingalls 1973.8 1975.9 mfh
Phillips W S 2LT 18-E-2 37-B Bernard 1917.1 1917.5 Phillips
Phillips R E 2LT 50-W 121 Bernard 1917.1 1917.4 WWI BOQ Purdie
Phillips R E CPT 127-W 145 Bernard 1925.6 1926.8 '25cd
Phillips C L CPT 65-N 48 Ingalls 1900.8 1901.8 '00cd
Phillips W N COL 54-S-2 134 Ingalls 1965.9 1966.7 mfh
Phillips W S MAJ 143-S-2 35-C Ingalls 1930.7 1935.7 Phillips '31cd
Phillips R E CPT 67-S 34 Ingalls 1922.7 1925.5 Crowell Clark
Phillips W S COL 118 29 Fenwick 1942.1 1945.7 Phillips
Phillips P D CPT 35-E-1 6 Reeder 1943 1944 '43PhBk
Philpot W C C 1LT 18-E-1 37-A Bernard 1944.10 1946.10 '44-45PhBks
Phipps F H Jr 1LT 79-N 95 Ingalls 1910.9 1911.7 '11cd
Phisterer F W 1LT 18-W-2 29-B Bernard 1902 c-14
Pichel J F 1LT 67-S 34 Ingalls 1918 1919 BOQ WWI '19cd
Pickett J K MAJ 52-E-1 128 Ingalls 1936.6 1937.7 Cochran Diary
Pickett G E LTC 17-E-2 47-B Bernard 1946.10 1947.8 Ret LTG usacc
Pickett G E LTC 17-E-1 47-A Bernard 1946.11 1949.6 Ret LTG usacc
Pierce G F LTC 52-E-2 126 Ingalls 1950.6 1953.7 usacc
Pierce C D 1LT 3-N 169 Bernard 1913.12 1914.12 CAS'15 '15cd
Pierce B K MAJ 18-E-1 37-A Bernard 1824.2 1826.3 '25rq rooms?
Pierce H R MAJ 54-N-2 140 Ingalls 1931.8 1932.7 HWC
Pierce W H LTC 43-W-1 3 Reeder 1970.2 1972.8 mfh
Pierre G H COL 67-S 34 Ingalls 1962.7 1963.4 mfh
Pierre G H Jr COL 35-E-2 8 Reeder 1960.7 1962.7 mfh
Pillsbury R D COL 55 42 Ingalls 1969.9 1973.6 mfh
Pillsbury R D COL 69-S 85 Ingalls 1969.6 1969.9 mfh
Pinney H D COL 79-N 95 Ingalls 1971.5 1972.9 mfh
Pipe S T 1LT 63-N 24 Ruckman 1919 1919 BOQ ? '19cd
Piper J W CPT 18-E-2 37-B Bernard 1869.8 1876.5 S&F c-27
Pipia F P 1LT 51-S-1 120 Ingalls 1940.5 1941 MedC '40-41PhBk
Pipia F P 1LT 18-W-2 29-B Bernard 1938.8 1940.5 MedC Simms
Piram J S 1LT 1 151 Bernard 1938 1939 Piram
Pirchon J R 1LT 18-W-1 29-A Bernard 1902 b-19 rms
Pirie J H MAJ 123-W 2 Ruckman 1919.9 1920.6 JHC '20cd
Pirie J H 1LT 65-S 46 Ingalls 1912.12 1913.12 '13cd CAS'13
Pitt L A COL 143-S-2 35-C Ingalls 1968.8 1969.8 mfh

Pittman G L MAJ 18-E-2 37-B Bernard 1982.9 1984.6 mfh
Pitts R B MAJ 143-N-2 35-D Ingalls 1944.5 1944.11 '44PhBk
Pitts R B MAJ 127-E 147 Bernard 1944.11 1945.10 PhBk
Pitts R W COL 55 42 Ingalls 1974.6 mfh
Pittsburg H C CPT 124-N 69 Ingalls 1914.12 1915.12 '16cd
Pitz H E 1LT 79-S 93 Ingalls 1913.12 1914.12 PhBk CAS'14
Platt W 1LT 33-E-1 61 Fenwick 1944 1945 PhBks
Plum J B COL 17-E-2 47-B Bernard 1960.8 1963.4 mfh
Plummer H L 1LT 17-E-2 47-B Bernard 1944.1 1946.10 '44-45PhBks
Podufaly E T LTC 143-N-1 35-B Ingalls 1954.10 1957.5 Ret BG usacc
Poel D COL 128-E 109 Bernard 1980.8 1984.7
Pohl M G 1LT 45-E-1 114 Ingalls 1934.8 1935.8 Pohl
Pohl M G 2LT 16-E 53 Bernard 1928 Pohl
Pohly G COL 103-N 65 Ingalls 1979.8 1982.9 mfh
Poindexter F S 2LT 68-N 83 Ingalls 1902 c-46
Poinier N E COL 67-N 36 Ingalls 1952.5 1954.5 usacc
Pokorny A G LTC 50-A 125 Bernard 1975.8 1079.6 mfh
Poland E L LTC 102-S 59 Ingalls 1933.8 1940.8 Poland
Polhemus A S CPT 62-N 28 Ruckman 1889 1890 MedC Gifford
Polonsky S I COL 16-W 51 Bernard 1967.9 1970.7 mfh
Polonsky S I COL 18-E-2 37-B Bernard 1967.2 1967.9 mfh
Pond L O LTC 45-E-1 114 Ingalls 1952.9 1954.4 usacc
Pool R V CWO 61-N 45 Ingalls 1961.10 1963.8 mfh
Poor B W COL 144-N-1 41-B Ingalls 1951.12 1953.6 usacc
Poor B W LTC 17-W-1 41-A Bernard 1950.7 1951.12 usac
Pope W P LTC 44-N-1 106 Ingalls 1953.10 1954.11 usacc
Pope W P LTC 50-A 125 Bernard 1954.11 1957.7 usacc
Porteous C E COL 70-N 91 Ingalls 1966.7 1970.8 mfh
Porteous C E COL 54-N-2 140 Ingalls 1965.8 1966.7 mfh
Porter G U COL 51-S-2 118 Ingalls 1951.7 1952.8 usacc
Porter W N MAJ 123-E 4 Ruckman 1917.7 1919.7 '19cd
Porter W N 1LT 17-E-1 47-A Bernard 1910.12 1911.12 '11cd
Porter F B COL 68-S 81 Ingalls 1949.5 1950.6 usacc
Porter F B COL 143-S-2 35-C Ingalls 1949.5 1949.5 usacc
Post A G MG 118 29 Fenwick 1974.9 1975.9 mfh Ret MG
Post E D BG 121-E 43 Fenwick 1952.8 1954.8 usacc
Post E D BG 126-S 163 Bernard 1952.7 1952.8 usacc
Potts A E COL 120 37 Fenwick 1945.9 1946.6 Wife
Potts A E MAJ 127-W 145 Bernard 1931.3 1932.9 Elliott
Potts R D COL 1 151 Bernard 1904.2 1906.8 Ret BG CO w
Potts R D 1LT 15-N 34 Ruckman 1890 Ret BG Gifford
Pourie J R 1LT 68-S 81 Ingalls 1904.9 1905.9 '05cd
Powell C W 1LT 44-N-1 106 Ingalls 1938.8 1939.8 PhBk
Powell B E MG 101-N 57 Ingalls 1966.4 1966.5 Ret GEN mfh
Powell B E MG 142 51 Fenwick 1966.5 1967.8 Ret GEN mfh
Powell H B LTG 142 51 Fenwick 1958.5 1960.3 Ret GEN usacc
Powell C W LTC 35-W-1 4 Reeder 1948.8 1950.6 usacc
Powell J S COL 129-N 103 Ingalls 1986.2 1986.9 mfh
Powell H B GEN 141 53 Fenwick 1960.8 1960.11 Ret GEN usacc
Powell H B GEN 119 33 Fenwick 1960.11 1963.1 Ret GEN mfh
Powell W B LTC 33-W-2 57 Fenwick 1959.8 1961,1 usacc
Powell M L Jr COL 124-N 69 Ingalls 1968.1 1972.1 mfh
Powell J S Jr LTC 144-S-1 41-A Ingalls 1980.1 1981.6 mfh

Powell M L Jr COL 144-S-2 41-C Ingalls 1967.9 1968.1 mfh
Power C CPT 70-S 89 Ingalls 1911.9 1912.12 '12cd
Powers E D LT 64-N 20 Ruckman 1906 '06cd
Powers J D CPT 15-N 34 Ruckman 1931.6 1932.3 '31cd
Powers J D MAJ 126-S 163 Bernard 1932.3 1935.8 JHC '33cd
Powers R E 1LT 102-N 61 Ingalls 1918 1919 BOQ WWI '19cd
Powers J W COL 52-W-1 130 Ingalls 1968.6 1970.7 mfh
Powers J W COL 79-N 95 Ingalls 1970.7 1971.5 mfh
Powers J D CPT 63-S 26 Ruckman 1926.8 1927.8 '27BtryOcs
Prather R G COL 65-N 48 Ingalls 1947.9 1948.10 Ret MG usacc
Prather E R COL 65-S 46 Ingalls 1972.6 1973.6 mfh
Prather R G COL 123-W 2 Ruckman 1948.10 1950.9 Ret MG usacc
Pratt J S MAJ 102-N 61 Ingalls 1922.6 1923.6 Oldfield
Pratt J S 1LT 144-N-1 41-B Ingalls 1910.8 1911.9 CAS'11 '11cd
Preer C Jr COL 123-W 2 Ruckman 1967.2 1967.3 Ret BG usacc
Preer C Jr BG 146 146 Engr Ln 1967.3 1968.6 Ret BG mfh
Prentice J CPT 70-S 89 Ingalls 1909.9 1910.9 CAS '10
Preston M CPT 167-B 9 Patch Road 1970.3 1971.2 mfh
Price R SFC 61-N 45 Ingalls 1970.5 1971.8 mfh
Price J F COL 35-E-2 8 Reeder 1968.7 1970.8 mfh
Price F A MAJ 144-S-2 41-C Ingalls 1923.6 1924.6 '24AdvCs
Price F A 2LT 17-E-2 47-B Bernard 1910.9 1911.9 '11cd
Price F A LTC 128-W 107 Bernard 1937.6 1938.8 Spann '37cd
Price J F COL 70-N 91 Ingalls 1970.8 1973.5 mfh
Price F A MAJ 143-S-2 35-C Ingalls 1918.4 1918.12 '19cd
Pride H E 1LT 153-N 13 Hatch 1918 1919 '19cd
Pridgen R B COL 123-W 2 Ruckman 1964.11 1967.1 mfh
Pridgen R B COL 52-E-1 128 Ingalls 1963.7 1964.11 mfh
Prillaman J MG 118 29 Fenwick 1983.1 1986.3 mfh
Privett G P COL 33-E-1 61 Fenwick 1947.7 1948.11 usacc
Privett G P COL 129-N 103 Ingalls 1948.11 1949.8 usacc
Procissi F P MAJ 167-B 9 Patch Road 1963.2 1963.6 mfh
Proctor J R CPT 63-S 26 Ruckman 1908.9 1909.9 CAS'09
Proctor J R 1LT 66-N 40 Ingalls 1902 BOQ? c-46
Prost L J LTC 143-N-2 35-D Ingalls 1967.8 1968.7 Ret BG mfh
Pruden A A MAJ 158 32 Ingalls 1913.7 1918.6 Chaplain PhBk
Pruitt D LTC 144-N-1 41-B Ingalls 1980.7 1981.12 mfh
Prusaitis J J Jr COL 143-N-1 35-B Ingalls 1963.3 1966.5 mfh
Pryke W K COL 34-N-1 98 Ingalls 1962.8 1962.10 mfh
Pulsipher W CPT 35-E-2 8 Reeder 1976.6 1977.6 mfh
Pumpelly J W LTC 33-W-1 59 Fenwick 1952.9 1953.9 usacc
Pumpelly J W LTC 3-S 167 Bernard 1953.9 1954.3 usacc
Pumphrey L C MAJ 123-E 4 Ruckman 1942.7 1943.10 Bennett PhBk
Punsalan L F LTC 34-N-2 100 Ingalls 1960.7 1963.9 mfh
Purdie K S 2LT 50-W 121 Bernard 1917.1 1917.4 WWI BOQ Purdie
Purdue B P COL 125 73 Ingalls 1948.10 1949.6 Ret BG usacc
Purdue B P COL 62-S 30 Ruckman 1947.7 1948.10 Ret BG usacc
Purnell V S 1LT 18-W-1 29-A Bernard 1917.1 1917.6 CAS'17 Ford
Purnell E K LTC 45-W-2 110 Ingalls 1948.8 1949.6 usacc
Purvis J LTC 35-E-2 8 Reeder 1977.6 1979.4 mfh
Putnam C W CPT 14 32 Ruckman 1919.6 1921.7 '20cd
Putney E W MAJ 124-N 69 Ingalls 1931.8 1933.6 Putney
Putney E W MAJ 128-W 107 Bernard 1925.9 1926.8 Putney

Putney E W MAJ 127-E 147 Bernard 1923.9 1924.6 Putney
Pyatt M D CPT 30-B 36 Hampton 1984.6 1985.5 mfh
Pyrke W K COL 68-S 81 Ingalls 1962.10 1964.9 mfh
Quarstein V A COL 126-N 165 Bernard 1972.7 1975.9 mfh
Quattlebaum C LTC 33-E-1 61 Fenwick 1976.6 1978.7 mfh
Quinn L LTC 45-E-2 116 Ingalls 1977.1 1978.6 mfh
Quinn J B MAJ 19 18 Bernard 1899 1901 '00cd
Rabin R J MAJ 35-W-2 2 Reeder 1967.8 1968.7 mfh
Radford L C LTC 17-E-2 47-B Bernard 1956.1 1959.10 usacc
Radnor J CPT 35-E-1 6 Reeder 1941 1942 Ellis
Rafferty T A COL 52-W-2 132 Ingalls 1962.2 1963.10 usacc
Rafferty W C MAJ 66-S 38 Ingalls 1904.8 1905.8 '06cd
Rafferty O MAJ 93 75 Ingalls 1905 1906 MedC '06cd
Ragan C A CPT 17-W-1 41-A Bernard 1908.9 1910.3 MedC '09cd
Ragan C A CPT 16-E 53 Bernard 1907.9 1908.9 MedC '08cd
Raiche A L CPT 43-E-1 5 Reeder 1944.6 1946.9 '44-45PhBks
Rainbolt M T LTC 143-S-1 35-A Ingalls 1984.4 1986.6 mfh
Rainey E C LTC 3-N 169 Bernard 1974.1 1977.1 mfh
Raleigh J M COL 33-E-1 61 Fenwick 1962.10 1964.6 mfh
Ralston F W 1LT 17-E-1 47-A Bernard 1905.9 1906.9 CAS'06
Ramage C K LTC 147 147 Engr Ln 1948.9 1950.6 Dentist usacc
Ramsay A B CPT 45-W-1 112 Ingalls 1934.9 1935.9 MedC Ramsay
Ranchin R J COL 34-N-1 98 Ingalls 1961.11 1962.7 mfh
Randolph W F CPT 18-E-2 37-B Bernard 1876.6 1883.1 S&F c-27
Raney J D LTC 17-E-1 47-A Bernard 1950.9 1951.8 usacc
Ransom P L COL 65-S 46 Ingalls 1946.10 1948.6 Ret MG usacc
Ransone A L COL 68-S 81 Ingalls 1964.10 1966.2 mfh
Rasbach J B COL 68-S 81 Ingalls 1950.6 1952.9 usacc
Rasbach J B COL 45-E-2 116 Ingalls 1949.8 1950.6 usacc
Ratcliffe J P LTC 144-S-1 41-A Ingalls 1977.8 1980.1 mfh
Rateau M A COL 67-S 34 Ingalls 1966.8 1967.4 mfh
Rateau M A COL 45-W-2 110 Ingalls 1965.6 1966.8 mfh
Rauscher R C COL 103-S 63 Ingalls 1965.7 1966.6 mfh
Rawie V E R COL 3-S 167 Bernard 1961.8 1962.8 mfh
Rawlins C H COL 128-E 109 Bernard 1971.1 1971.8 mfh
Rawlins C H COL 143-S-2 35-C Ingalls 1969.8 1971.1 mfh
Rawls W O 1LT 62-N 28 Ruckman 1918.9 1918.11 Ford
Rawls L T COL 69-N 87 Ingalls 1970.7 1974.2 mfh
Rawls L T COL 51-S-1 120 Ingalls 1970.4 1970.7 mfh
Ray J F Mr 61-S 43 Ingalls 1943.11 1945.4 '43-45PhBk Electrician
Ray J COL 45-W-1 112 Ingalls 1956.2 1959.6 usacc
Raymond A D 1LT 69-N 87 Ingalls 1904.9 1905.9 Raymond Son
Raymond C W LTC 62-N 28 Ruckman 1948.9 1952.1 usacc
Raymond W H CPT 62-S 30 Ruckman 1906.9 1907.9 CAS'07
Raymond A D LTC 1 151 Bernard 1921 1922 Raymond
Raymond M B LTC 52-E-2 126 Ingalls 1946.12 1948.8 usacc
Razantzinger R A CPT 18-E-2 37-B Bernard 1824.4 1826.3 '25rq rms?
Read A J COL 54-N-1 138 Ingalls 1963.8 1964.3 mfh
Read D A LTC 52-W-2 132 Ingalls 1972.1 1973.8 mfh
Read M M CPT 43-W-1 3 Reeder 1932.7 1933.7 '33cd
Read A J MAJ 123-E 4 Ruckman 1942.1 1942.7 Facility ENGR
Read A J COL 66-N 40 Ingalls 1964.3 1965.9 mfh
Read G W Jr MG 142 51 Fenwick 1953.9 1954.7 Ret LTG usacc

Reaugh V W COL 68-N 83 Ingalls 1966.8 1968.5 mfh
Reaugh V W COL 144-S-2 41-C Ingalls 1963.2 1964.1 mfh
Reaugh V W COL 34-N-2 100 Ingalls 1965.8 1966.8 mfh
Reaves K L MG 1 151 Bernard 1966.10 1967.12 mfh Ret MG
Reed W B COL 127-W 145 Bernard 1961.8 1964.1 mfh
Reed C H COL 70-S 89 Ingalls 1947.11 1949.2 usacc
Reeder B F LTC 51-S-2 118 Ingalls 1967.2 1968.9 mfh
Reeder R P COL 158 32 Ingalls 1925.6 1927.6 Nichols Harte
Reeder R P COL 120 37 Fenwick 1935.7 1936.5 Broudy +
Reeves J W Jr COL 3-N 169 Bernard 1958.1 1961.1 usacc
Reginier F W 1LT 43-E-2 7 Reeder 1940.6 1942.5 MedC '40-41PhBk
Register E C CPT 124-S 67 Ingalls 1917.6 1918.9 '17cd
Rehm H W MAJ 69-S 85 Ingalls 1928.7 1931.7 ORD Higgins
Rehn W F COL 101-N 57 Ingalls 1950.10 1952.2 usacc
Rehn W F COL 129-N 103 Ingalls 1949.9 1950.10 usacc
Reichelderfer H COL 44 S-1 104 Ingalls 1946.10 1948.9 usacc
Reid R COL 65-N 48 Ingalls 1979.8 1981.6 mfh
Reierson J E CPT 65-S 46 Ingalls 1939.8 1940.6 PhBk
Reinken L A CPT 129-S 101 Ingalls 1949.7 1950.7 USN usacc
Reinken L A CPT 17-E-1 47-A Bernard 1949.6 1949.7 USN usacc
Reiss W J COL 128-E 109 Bernard 1961.2 1965.7 Chaplain mfh
Remus J A LTC 143-N-1 35-B Ingalls 1950.12 1952.8 usacc
Reno W H MG 121-E 43 Fenwick 1985.8 1987.7 mfh
Renshaw C CPT 70-N 91 Ingalls 1937.9 1941.1 Ret BG QMC
Rerebeck C G 2LT 79-N 95 Ingalls 1902 c-46
Reuter H C COL 50-E 129 Bernard 1946.8 1946.10 Reuter
Reuter H C COL 55 42 Ingalls 1947.4 1948.10 usacc
Reuter H C LTC 65-N 48 Ingalls 1938.6 1941.8 Reuter
Reuter H C COL 101-N 57 Ingalls 1942.8 1946.8 PhBk Reuter
Reuter H C COL 101-S 55 Ingalls 1948.10 1950.2 usacc
Reuter H C CPT 15-N 34 Ruckman 1937.9 1938.5 Reuter
Revels J W LTC 144-N-1 41-B Ingalls 1975.11 1977.8 mfh
Reybold E MAJ 103-S 63 Ingalls 1918.4 1920.6 Ret LTG '19cd
Reybold E COL 118 29 Fenwick 1919.1 1920.6 CO CAS Ret LTG
Reybold E CPT 19 18 Bernard 1915.12 1916.12 Ret LTG Ford
Reybold E CPT 69-N 87 Ingalls 1917.12 1918.4 Ret LTG '17cd
Reymonds N G COL 34-S-1 96 Ingalls 1959.9 1961.11 usacc
Reynold F P MAJ 125 73 Ingalls 1911.8 1913.7 MedC '12cd
Reynolds J N 1LT 68-N 83 Ingalls 1912.12 1913.12 '13cd
Reynolds J G Rank Unk 34-N-2 100 Ingalls 1939.8 1940 '39PhBk
Reynolds J F CPT 1 151 Bernard 1857.2 1857.3 w
Rhein W W CPT 69-N 87 Ingalls 1921.8 1922.7 Payne
Rhoades A L CPT 19 18 Bernard 1911.9 1914.12 PhBk
Rhoades A L CPT 126-N 165 Bernard 1915.12 1917.12 CAS'16
Rhoades A L CPT 64-S 22 Ruckman 1910.8 1911.9 '11cd AN306
Rice M F CSM 79-N 95 Ingalls 1986.7 1987.3 mfh
Rice J F CSM 60 67 Fenwick 1986.9 1988 mfh
Rich C W G LTG 141 53 Fenwick 1968.9 1970.7 mfh Ret LTG
Rich T C COL 103-N 65 Ingalls 1961.8 1963.4 mfh
Richards W K 1LT 102-S 59 Ingalls 1915.12 1916.12 '16cd
Richards W L MAJ 93 75 Ingalls 1930.7 1931.8 MedC deCamp
Richards W K MAJ 102-S 59 Ingalls 1927.7 1928.7 Ruddell
Richards W K MAJ 19 18 Bernard 1929.7 1930.7 S&F '30cd

Richards W L COL 51-S-2 118 Ingalls 1946.8 1947.2 MedC usacc
Richards R E 1LT 129-S 101 Ingalls 1919 BOQ WWI '19cd
Richardson W L 1LT 63-N 24 Ruckman 1932.4 1936.11 Ret BG Dunham
Richardson W GEN 119 33 Fenwick 1983.4 1986.6 mfh
Richardson W F CPT 35-W-2 2 Reeder 1940.11 1942.9 Richardson
Richardson J A LTC 33-W-2 57 Fenwick 1953.12 1956.8 usacc
Richardson J B LTC 43-W-1 3 Reeder 1950.10 1953.8 usacc
Richardson J T 1LT 43-E-2 7 Reeder 1935.7 1936.7 AN306
Richardson R E COL 51-N-2 124 Ingalls 1962.7 1962.7 mfh
Richardson W F LTC 124-S 67 Ingalls 1942.9 1944.2 Richardson
Richardson R E COL 3-N 169 Bernard 1962.8 1965.4 mfh
Richardson P S Jr COL 62-S 30 Ruckman 1972.8 1974.9 mfh
Richey T G LTC 54-S-1 136 Ingalls 1948.10 1953.1 usacc
Richey T G LTC 54-N-1 138 Ingalls 1947.2 1948.10 usacc
Richmond H W 1LT 17-E-1 47-A Bernard 1920.6 1922.6 '20cd AN306
Ricker G W CPT 144-N-1 41-B Ingalls 1930.6 1932.6 Killed '42
Ricker G W COL 129-S 101 Ingalls 1941.10 1942.2 PhBk KIA WWII
Riddlehoover L P Jr BG 121-E 43 Fenwick 1975.8 1977.7 mfh Ret BG?
Riddlehoover L P Jr BG 121-W 41 Fenwick 1979.8 1980.8 mfh Ret BG?
Riddlehoover L P Jr BG 79-N 95 Ingalls 1975.3 1975.8 mfh Ret BG?
Rider J COL 68-N 83 Ingalls 1976.6 1977.7 mfh
Rider J D LTC 34-S-1 96 Ingalls 1973.8 1976.6 mfh
Ridgway T MAJ 120 37 Fenwick 1908.6 1909.9 Ridgway Son
Ridgway T 1LT 79-S 93 Ingalls 1894 1896 Ridgway Son
Ridgway T MAJ 102-S 59 Ingalls 1907.6 1908.6 '06-08cd
Ridings E W MG 142 51 Fenwick 1954.7 1956.9 usacc Ret MG?
Riefkohl R W 1LT 65-N 48 Ingalls 1916.12 1917.6 Ford
Rigers A LTC 3-N 169 Bernard 1981.2 1983.3 mfh
Riley E A COL 33-E-1 61 Fenwick 1960.2 1960.10 usaccc
Ring T C COL 65-N 48 Ingalls 1981.7 1982.3 mfh
Ringler E L COL 144-N-1 41-B Ingalls 1946.9 1949.9 usacc
Ringold S 1LT 18-W-2 29-B Bernard 1824 1826 '25rq d-684 rms
Ripley J W 1LT 18-W-2 29-B Bernard 1824 1826 '25rq d-684 rms
Ripple L M COL 64 71 Fenwick 1977.6 1978.2 mfh
Ripple L COL 62-S 30 Ruckman 1980.7 1984.7 mfh
Ritchie S B CPT 70-S 89 Ingalls 1919.6 1920.8 '20cd
Ritchie P J COL 62-S 30 Ruckman 1962.8 1965.7 mfh
Ritter J W MAJ 17-E-2 47-B Bernard 1983.6 1985.7 mfh
Robbins O O MAJ 14 32 Ruckman 1944 1944.11 PhBk
Roberts H B LTC 52-E-2 126 Ingalls 1964.6 1965.5 mfh
Roberts C SFC 25-W-1 4 Reeder 1985.8 1987.10 mfh
Roberts J L LTC 17-W-2 41-B Bernard 1868.5 1877.2 S&F c-27
Roberts T E CPT 44-S-2 102 Ingalls 1986.11 1987.7 mfh
Roberts F W LTC 18-E-1 37-A Bernard 1948.10 1950.3 usacc
Roberts J BG 1 151 Bernard 1877 1880 w Ret BG
Roberts D L COL 143-N-1 35-B Ingalls 1969.6 1970.10 mfh
Roberts C R CPT 50-E 129 Bernard 1930.7 1932.8 '31cd
Robertson E COL 18-E-2 37-B Bernard 1981.6 1982.8 mfh
Robertson E H COL 69-S 85 Ingalls 1982.8 1984.6 mfh
Roberts C L Jr COL 19 18 Bernard 1975.3 1980.7 mfh
Roberts J L Jr CPT 70-S 89 Ingalls 1906.9 1907.9 CAS '07
Robeson D L MAJ 33-W-1 59 Fenwick 1932.6 1933.8 MedC Tarrant
Robey R 60 67 Fenwick 1977.1 1979.2 mfh

Robins R R COL 158 32 Ingalls 1953.1 1954.7 usacc
Robins R R COL 143-S-1 35-A Ingalls 1950.12 1951.2 usacc
Robins R R COL 103-S 63 Ingalls 1951.2 1952.11 usacc
Robinson J S CPT 14 32 Ruckman 1936 1937 Ret BG Robins
Robinson G 1LT 17-W-1 41-A Bernard 1906.9 1907.9 CAS'07
Robison G B LTC 103-S 63 Ingalls 1938.6 1940.5 Huger PhBk
Robison G B LTC 129-S 101 Ingalls 1937.6 1938.6 '37-38cds
Robitaille F 54-S-2 134 Ingalls 1979.9 1980.5 mfh
Rodgers G B LTG 1 151 Bernard 1958.12 1961.08 usacc Ret LTG
Rodgers R A LTC 33-W-2 57 Fenwick 1956.8 1959.7 usacc
Rodgers C T COL 68-S 81 Ingalls 1956.9 1958.8 usacc
Roe W W COL 43-W-1 3 Reeder 1946.9 1947.8 usacc
Rogers J E CPT 54-N-1 138 Ingalls 1944 1945 '45PhBk
Rogers G R COL 63-S 26 Ruckman 1956.8 1959.12 usacc
Rogers W T COL 102-S 59 Ingalls 1966.7 1970.7 mfh
Rogers J H MAJ 143-N-2 35-D Ingalls 1974.8 1976.7 mfh
Rogers W T COL 143-N-1 35-B Ingalls 1966.6 1966.7 mfh
Rogers W D LTC 51-N-1 122 Ingalls 1957.2 1960.6 usacc
Rolfe O S COL 1 151 Bernard 1948.5 1952.3 Ret BG usacc
Rolfe O S COL 143-N-1 35-B Ingalls 1947.4 1948.4 Ret BG usacc
Romero R A CPT 34-S-1 96 Ingalls 1984.5 1986.4 mfh
Romlein J W 1LT 17-E-2 47-B Bernard 1938.6 1940.6 '40PhBk
Rooney T O COL 45-E-1 114 Ingalls 1960.12 1962.7 mfh
Root W G 1LT 17-E-1 47-A Bernard 1940.3 1940.9 Weld
Roper D N LTC 18-E-2 37-B Bernard 1958.10 1959.7 usacc
Roquemore F U Jr COL 62-S 30 Ruckman 1969.8 1972.6 mfh
Rorebeck C G 1LT 17-E-2 47-B Bernard 1908.9 1909.9 '09cd
Rorebeck C G CPT 121-W 41 Fenwick 1909.9 1911.9 '11cd
Rose W W 1LT 50 W 121 Bernard 1912.12 1914.12 PhBk
Rose F D LTC 17-E-2 47-B Bernard 1974.10 1975.9 mfh
Rose W W 1LT 70-S 89 Ingalls 1914.12 1915.12 '16cd
Rose K CPT 43-E-2 7 Reeder 1980.9 1981.7 mfh
Roseborough M G COL 34-S-2 94 Ingalls 1958.9 1960.6 usacc Ret MG
Rosell T G COL 52-W-2 132 Ingalls 1968.11 1970.11 usacc
Rosell T G COL 68-N 83 Ingalls 1970.11 1971.8 mfh
Rosenblum D MG 120 37 Fenwick 1979.9 1980.7 mfh
Rosoff M LTC 51-S-2 118 Ingalls 1964.7 1965.7 mfh
Ross T P COL 43-W-1 3 Reeder 1959.11 1962.2 mfh
Ross L G CPT 45-W-1 112 Ingalls 1939.6 1940.6 PhBk Died POW ship '44
Ross C B 1LT 66-N 40 Ingalls 1910.9 1911.9 '11cd
Ross W A COL 19 18 Bernard 1973.3 1975.2 mfh
Ross M R 1LT 69-S 85 Ingalls 1903.9 1904.9 CAS'04
Ross L G CPT 54-S-2 134 Ingalls 1940.6 1942.6 PhBks Died '44
Ross L G 1LT 35-W-1 4 Reeder 1935.6 1936.6 CAS'36 Died POW '44
Roth A MAJ 69-S 85 Ingalls 1941.5 1942.4 Roth
Roth I D 1LT 35-W-2 2 Reeder 1937.7 1938.7 Roth
Roth A COL 17-W-1 41-A Bernard 1946.10 1947.8 Roth usacc
Rothgeb C E 1LT 144-S-1 41-A Ingalls 1934.8 1935.7 Shunk
Roubeck LT 18-W-1 29-A Bernard 1902 d-691 rooms
Rousley P COL 143-S-2 35-C Ingalls 1968.4 1968.8 mfh
Rousseau J H CPT 63-S 26 Ruckman 1937.7 1938.8 '37cd
Routh D B COL 35-E-1 6 Reeder 1946.8 1947.9 usacc
Routh D B COL 33-E-1 61 Fenwick 1957.7 1957.9 usacc

Routh D B COL 79-S 93 Ingalls 1957.9 1959.7 usacc
Rowe J T 1LT 70-S 89 Ingalls 1912.12 1914.12 PhBk
Rowe J T 1LT 64-N 20 Ruckman 1914.12 1916.12 Cochran
Rowe J T CPT 14 32 Ruckman 1916 1917 '17cd
Rowland A E MAJ 62-N 28 Ruckman 1924.8 1925.7 Biehl
Rowls W O CPT 14 32 Ruckman 1918.12 1919.6 '19cd
Roy P A 1LT 34-N-2 100 Ingalls 1936.8 1937.6 Roy Taber
Rozamus W J COL 34-S-2 94 Ingalls 1960.6 1960.9 usacc
Rozamus W J LTC 34-S-1 96 Ingalls 1952.9 1954.2 usacc
Rozamus W J COL 123-E 4 Ruckman 1960.9 1964.6 mfh
Rubin S 1LT 18-E-1 37-A Bernard 1926.7 1927.7 '17BtryOCs
Rucker S L LTC 52-W-1 130 Ingalls 1970.7 1974.9 mfh
Ruckman LT 69-S 85 Ingalls 1895 b-12
Ruddell J C CPT 143-S-2 35-C Ingalls 1923.12 1925.6 Daughter
Ruddell J C MAJ 68-S 81 Ingalls 1928.6 1929.6 '29cd
Rude W A LTC 103-S 63 Ingalls 1944 1945 Rude PhBk
Ruggles J A LTC 63-N 24 Ruckman 1920.6 1921.6 CAS'21
Ruggles J A 1LT 79-S 93 Ingalls 1904.9 1905.9 CAS'05
Ruggles J G LTC 34-S-2 94 Ingalls 1946.8 1948.6 Ret MG usacc
Ruhlen G 1LT 69-S 85 Ingalls 1912.8 1913.12 CAS'13
Ruine M M COL 17-E-1 47-A Bernard 1951.8 1952.9 usacc
Rumaggi L J COL 124-N 69 Ingalls 1954.2 1954.6 Ret MG usacc
Rumer G F COL 35-W-2 2 Reeder 1965.8 1965.12 mfh
Rumer G F COL 33-W-1 59 Fenwick 1965.12 1967.5 mfh
Rushton R T LTC 43-E-2 7 Reeder 1970.9 1973.6 mfh
Russell S C 1LT 43-E-2 7 Reeder 1937.7 1938.6 Ret MG '37cd
Russell O A 1LT 144-S-1 41-A Ingalls 1910.8 1911.9 CAS'11 '11cd
Russell S C 1LT 54-S-1 136 Ingalls 1940.6 1941.12 Ret MG Weld
Russell O A MAJ 144-S-1 41-A Ingalls 1921.8 1922.7 '22FOcs
Rust D LTC 16-W 51 Bernard 1978.6 1985.1 mfh
Ruth H S COL 68-N 83 Ingalls 1950.5 1953.6 usacc
Rutledge P W CPT 52-E-2 126 Ingalls 1932.8 1934.8 Ret MG Harris
Rutledge P W MG 141 53 Fenwick 1952.9 1954.9 usacc Ret MG
Rutter W C CPT 79-S 93 Ingalls 1941.8 1942.12 PhBk
Rutter W C 1LT 18-W-1 29-A Bernard 1934.7 1935.7 CAS'35
Ryan W S LTC 44-N-1 106 Ingalls 1950.9 1953.5 Ret MG usacc
Ryan L S CPT 69-S 85 Ingalls 1907.9 1908.9 '08cd
Ryan E A COL 33-E-2 63 Fenwick 1965.7 1965.9 mfh
Ryan J L Jr COL 129-S 101 Ingalls 1946.9 1947.9 Ret LTG usacc
Ryder D J MAJ 18-W-2 29-B Bernard 1984.8 1987.7 mfh
Sack F R CPT 52-W-1 130 Ingalls 1941.8 1943.6 Bushyaeger
Sackville W COL 128-W 107 Bernard 1942.6 1944.2 PhBk
Sage J M COL 143-S-1 35-A Ingalls 1967.10 1968.1 mfh
Sahms R E MSG 35-W-2 2 Reeder 1981.6 1982.5 mfh
Salada R N LTC 45-E-2 116 Ingalls 1966.2 1967.5 mfh
Salamone R CPT 16-E 53 Bernard 1954.1 1954.3 Guest House
Salomon L LTC 15-N 34 Ruckman 1982.1 1982.7 mfh
Samuels A Jr 2LT 16-W 51 Bernard 1932 1934.3 Hillberg BOQ
Samuels A Jr 1LT 18-E-2 37-B Bernard 1934.9 1936.9 Samuels
Samuels A Jr 1LT 45-W-1 112 Ingalls 1934.3 1934.9 Samuels
Sanduce W A COL 69-S 85 Ingalls 1948.1 1949.12 usacc
Sanford J L CPT 54-S-1 136 Ingalls 1944 1945 '44-45PhBks
Sanford T H BG 121-E 43 Fenwick 1956.8 1959.6 Ret MG usacc

Sanford J L 1LT 62-N 24 Ruckman 1944 1945 PhBk
Santerre F MAJ 35-W-2 2 Reeder 1942.9 1943.8 Ellis
Santerre F MAJ 35-W-1 4 Reeder 1941.9 1942.9 AN306
Satterwhite S B COL 43-E-2 7 Reeder 1954.12 1956.8 usacc
Sauls M N J COL 50-A 125 Bernard 1969.12 1970.7 mfh
Sauls M N J COL 18-E-1 37-A Bernard 1969.8 1969.12 mfh
Saunders C W MAJ 16-W 51 Bernard 1946.10 1947.8 usacc
Saunders J MAJ 18-W-2 29-B Bernard 1981.6 1981.11 mfh
Saunders H CPT 18 -E-2 37-B Bernard 1828 1829 '29rq
Saunders W S COL 51-S-2 118 Ingalls 1962.9 1964.6 mfh
Saunders H CPT 18-W-1 29-A Bernard 1825 d-684 room
Saunders W A MAJ 45-E-2 116 Ingalls 1984.9 1986.2 mfh
Savard R S COL 102-S 59 Ingalls 1981.6 1984.7 mfh
Sawicki S COL 103-S 63 Ingalls 1959.2 1962.6 mfh
Sawyer K T MG 33-E-1 61 Fenwick 1972.10 1972.11 mfh Ret MG
Sawyer J A COL 45-W-1 112 Ingalls 1946.9 1947.3 usacc
Sawyer K T MG 118 29 Fenwick 1972.11 1974.7 mfh Ret MG
Sawyer J A COL 65-S 46 Ingalls 1952.8 1955.1 usacc
Scandrett W COL 129-N 103 Ingalls 1964.8 1965.10 mfh
Scarborough L M COL 45-W-1 112 Ingalls 1951.8 1952.2 usacc
Scarborough L M COL 55 42 Ingalls 1952.2 1954.5 usacc
Schabacker C H COL 129-N 103 Ingalls 1946.9 1947.6 Ret BG usacc
Scheg L J LTC 18-E-2 37-B Bernard 1973.6 1977.8 mfh
Schell J M MAJ 70-N 91 Ingalls 1919.10 1920.8 '20cd
Schellman R H MG 120 37 Fenwick 1969.12 1971.8 mfh Ret MG
Schellman R H MG 54-S-1 136 Ingalls 1969.8 1969.12 mfh Ret MG
Scherer J B LTC 144-N-1 41-B Ingalls 1966.10 1969.6 mfh
Scherrer E C D COL 33-W-2 57 Fenwick 1953.8 1953.12 Ret MG usacc
Scheurlein F W COL 68-S 81 Ingalls 1966.3 1968.2 mfh
Schiele R J COL 123-W 2 Ruckman 1974.10 1975.8 mfh
Schmick P 1LT 43-E-1 5 Reeder 1936.8 1937.6 Ret BG Perry
Schmidhauser J O Rev 7 Frank Lane 1950.2 1969 usacc Priest
Schmidt V 1LT 17-E-1 47-A Bernard 1925.6 1926.6 '25cd
Schmidt H A COL 67-S 34 Ingalls 1963.5 1966.6 mfh
Schmidt H A COL 143-S-1 35-A Ingalls 1963.1 1963.5 mfh
Schmidt C O CPT 68-N 83 Ingalls 1915.12 1916.12 '17cd
Schmidtman M C COL 123-W 2 Ruckman 1982.8 1986.3 mfh
Schmierer E COL 16-W 51 Bernard 1962.7 1963.7 mfh
Schmierer E COL 123-E 4 Ruckman 1964.7 1967.8 mfh
Schoonmaker L E COL 101-S 55 Ingalls 1940.9 1943.12 PhBk
Schoonmaker L E CPT 63-N 24 Ruckman 1926.7 1928.8 Shoonmaker
Schowman H C CPT 45-W-2 110 Ingalls 1939.8 1941.10 '40-41PhBks
Schrader O H MAJ 55 42 Ingalls 1921.7 1922.7 CAS'22
Schrader O H 1LT 69-N 87 Ingalls 1912.12 1913.12 PhBk
Schroeder N M COL 34-S-1 96 Ingalls 1961.12 1963.6 mfh
Schroedl O H CPT 51-S-1 120 Ingalls 1944 1945 '44-45PhBks
Schuber R P COL 128-E 109 Bernard 1975.10 1976.6 mfh
Schudt C O CPT 143-S-1 35-A Ingalls 1915.12 1916.12 CAS'16
Schulz M H COL 16-W 51 Bernard 1953.9 1955.11 usacc
Schulz M H COL 144-S-2 41-C Ingalls 1953.2 1953.9 usacc
Schulz M H COL 127-E 147 Bernard 1955.11 1956.4 usacc
Schumann H G COL 144-N-1 41-B Ingalls 1957.11 1958.7 usacc
Schuyler C V R 2LT 16-W 51 Bernard 1924 1925 Ret GEN Schuyler

Schuyler C V R CPT 15-S 36 Ruckman 1933.7 1936.6 Ret GEN Schuyler
Schuyler C V R MAJ 66-S 38 Ingalls 1937.8 1940.3 Ret GEN Daughter
Schwartz L S 1LT 16-E 53 Bernard 1939.8 1940.6 Morris '40cd
Schwartzman J COL 45-E-1 114 Ingalls 1964.2 1965.11 mfh
Scofield F C COL 103-N 65 Ingalls 1944.8 1946.8 PhBk
Scoggins O CPT 66-N 40 Ingalls 1953.10 1953.7 USN usacc
Scott W 1LT 17-E-2 47-B Bernard 1916.12 1917.6 CAS'17 Ford
Scott J B CPT 17-W-1 41-A Bernard 1842.7 1845.8 '44rq d-686
Scott W W CPT 44-S-1 104 Ingalls 1933.8 1934.6 deCamp
Scott F W COL 17-E-2 47-B Bernard 1964.6 1966.11 mfh
Scott H H 1LT 67-N 36 Ingalls 1907.9 1908.9 '08cd
Scott J L CPT 62-N 28 Ruckman 1922.8 1923.8 '23cd
Scott W R Rev 15-S 36 Ruckman 1909.5 1913.10 Chaplain
Scott J A Jr 1LT 51-S-2 118 Ingalls 1940.8 1941.10 '40-41PhBks
Scoville J N COL 65-N 48 Ingalls 1958.8 1961.3 usacc
Scoville J N COL 33-E-2 63 Fenwick 1958.3 1958.8 usacc
Scribner E COL 15-N 34 Ruckman 1977.7 1981.1 mfh
Scribner G H 1LT 18-W-2 29-B Bernard 1919.1 1919.6 '19cd
Scriven R L 1LT 113-W 26 Tidball 1918 1919 '19cd
Scruggs Jr LTC LTC 17-E-2 47-B Bernard 1969.3 1970.2 mfh
Scully M CPT 43-W-2 1 Reeder 1981.6 1982.6 mfh
Seaman C M CPT 18-W-2 29-B Bernard 1909.4 1911.9 S&F '11cd
Seaman C M CPT 126-S 163 Bernard 1914.12 1915.9 '16cd
Seaman C M CPT 121-E 43 Fenwick 1915.9 1917.6 '17cd Cochran
Seaman E C CPT 1 151 Bernard 1926 1927 '25cd
Sears R COL 68-S 81 Ingalls 1946.9 1949.5 usacc
Seaward G W COL 128-W 107 Bernard 1960.8 1962.7 mfh
Sebree E B MG 121-W 41 Fenwick 1955.8 1957.6 usacc Ret MG?
Sedberry G R Jr COL 55 42 Ingalls 1963.1 1964.6 mfh
Segal R COL 68-N 83 Ingalls 1974.8 1976.5 mfh
Seigle J W BG 121-W 41 Fenwick 1977.6 1977.8 mfh
Seigle J BG 120 37 Fenwick 1977.8 1979.9 mfh
Seland C MAJ 43-E-2 7 Reeder 1978.6 1980.9 mfh
Selegman T H LTC 51-S-1 120 Ingalls 1967.8 1969.8 mfh
Selkirk W O 1LT 66-S 38 Ingalls 1910.8 1911.7 CAS'11
Sevier G LTC 102-S 59 Ingalls 1921.8 1922.6 '22FOcs
Sevigny R LTC 33-E-1 61 Fenwick 1972.7 1972.10 mfh
Seydel F MAJ 101-S 55 Ingalls 1926.7 1927.7 '27AdvCs
Seydel F 1LT 144-N-2 41-D Ingalls 1915.12 1916.12 '17cd
Sgalitzer G W COL 34-N-1 98 Ingalls 1965.9 1971.6 mfh
Shaler M LTC 16-W 53 Bernard 1981.7 1983.6 mfh
Shank V C CPT 18-W-1 29-A Bernard 1919.6 1920.7 '20cd
Shanley T J LTC 34-N-1 98 Ingalls 1952.8 1953.7 usacc
Shannon D MAJ 45-W-1 112 Ingalls 1973.11 1976.3 mfh
Sharp J B MAJ 43-E-1 5 Reeder 1970.10 1972.12 mfh
Sharp W R LTC 16-W 53 Bernard 1984.6 1986.8 mfh
Sharpton A J MAJ 43-W-1 3 Reeder 1972.9 1974.7 mfh
Shartle S G CPT 65-N 48 Ingalls 1907.9 1908.9 '08cd
Shartle S G CPT 70-S 89 Ingalls 1908.9 1909.9 '09cd
Shartle S G CPT 128-W 107 Bernard 1915.12 1917.5 '17cd
Shaver I CW3 34-S-1 96 Ingalls 1978.4 1981.6 mfh
Shawn F D LTC 124-S 67 Ingalls 1944.6 1946.4 PhBks
Shea G D GEN 121-W 41 Fenwick 1950.9 1951.8 usacc Ret GEN

Shearer D N MAJ 18-W-1 29-A Bernard 1976.7 1977.12 mfh
Shedd W E MAJ 127-E 147 Bernard 1924.6 1926.6 Ret MG Son
Shedd W E COL 141 53 Fenwick 1935 1936.6 Ret MG Son
Shedd W E CPT 69-N 87 Ingalls 1916.12 1917.12 Ret MG CAS'17
Shedd W E MAJ 157 101 Bernard 1923.8 1924.6 Ret MG Son
Shedd W E BG 118 29 Fenwick 1936.6 1938.12 Ret MG Shedd
Sheetz K SGM 35-W-1 4 Reeder 1983.3 1985.8 mfh
Sheffield T M COL 70-N 91 Ingalls 1957.10 1961.8 usacc
Sheffield T M COL 51-S-1 120 Ingalls 1957.1 1957.10 usacc
Shellabarger H L LTC 44-N-2 108 Ingalls 1973.8 1977.7 mfh
Shelton C Q 1LT 16-E 53 Bernard 1922.8 1923.6 Shelton
Shepard J C MAJ 143-S-2 35-C Ingalls 1971.2 1972.8 mfh
Shepherd W L MSG 35-E-2 8 Reeder 1985.6 1986.11 mfh
Shepherd C E CPT 33-W-1 59 Fenwick 1937.8 1941.8 Shepherd PhBk
Shepherd C E CPT 144-N-1 41-B Ingalls 1936.9 1937.8 Shepherd
Sheppard P R E COL 125 73 Ingalls 1944.1 1946.5 MedC PhBk
Sheppard L C SP-5 61-N 45 Ingalls 1972.4 1974.5 mfh
Shettle C G COL 50-A 125 Bernard 1962.7 1966.7 mfh
Shinkle E G COL 102-S 59 Ingalls 1958.8 1962.7 mfh
Shinn J B CPT 18-E-2 37-B Bernard 1868.10 1869.8 S&F c-27
Shipp G V LTC 33-W-2 57 Fenwick 1970.8 1971.8 mfh
Shippam W 1LT 18-E-1 37-A Bernard 1913.12 1914.4 '14cd '14PhBk
Shoemaker P S LTC 51-N-1 122 Ingalls 1950.9 1952.6 usacc
Shoffner W A MG 121-W 41 Fenwick 1986.8 1987.4 mfh
Shugart C Z COL 124-S 67 Ingalls 1954.10 1956.9 usacc
Shugart C H MAJ 61-N 45 Ingalls 1959.2 1961.10 usacc
Shull H W CPT 3-N 169 Bernard 1906.5 1907 Ret BG Son
Shumate J P 1LT 43-E-2 7 Reeder 1934.9 1935.6 Shumate
Shunk P W CPT 65-N 48 Ingalls 1937.8 1938.5 Shunk
Shunk P W 1LT 143-N-1 35-B Ingalls 1934.8 1935.7 Shunk
Siekman R MAJ 3-N 169 Bernard 1978.6 1981.2 mfh
Sigerfoos E LTC 52-W-1 130 Ingalls 1948.12 1950.8 usacc
Simenson C G COL 65-N 48 Ingalls 1955.8 1958.6 usacc
Simmonds N B 1LT 16-E 53 Bernard 1930.6 1931.7 Strickland
Simmons F R LTC 17-E-2 47-B Bernard 1970.2 1972.6 mfh
Simmons J F 1LT 1 151 Bernard 1930 1931 Simmons
Simmons J F CPT 3-N 169 Bernard 1935.6 1935.6 Simmons
Simmons M W CPT 167-A 7 Patch Road 1968.10 1970.7 mfh
Simms W B 1LT 43-W-1 3 Reeder 1940.6 1940.12 Dentist Simms
Simms W B 1LT 18-W-1 29-A Bernard 1938.7 1940.6 Simms PhBk
Simpson L L CPT 144-N-1 41-B Ingalls 1922.6 1924.6 '23cd QMC
Simpson B L CPT 65-S 46 Ingalls 1944.10 1946.10 PhBk Simpson
Simpson B L CPT 30-S 34 Hampton 1942.1 1943.10 '43PhBk AN306
Simpson B L 2LT 17-W-2 41-B Bernard 1935.7 1936.9 '36Sojourner
Simpson E E 54-S-1 136 Ingalls 1979.7 1980.5 mfh
Simpson F W 1LT 16-E 53 Bernard 1921 1922 CAS'22
Sinclair J L MAJ 7-S 89 Ingalls 1919.3 1919.9 BOQ WWI '19cd
Sinclair J L MAJ 18-E-1 37-A Bernard 1918.6 1919.3 '19cd
Sinclair J L MAJ 143-N-2 35-D Ingalls 1919.9 1920.9 '20cd
Singles W 1LT 66-N 40 Ingalls 1907.9 1908.9 CAS'08 '08cd
Sizemore C 2LT 43-W-1 3 Reeder 1982.11 1984.6 mfh
Skaggs R N COL 68-N 83 Ingalls 1954.4 1956.10 usacc
Skaggs R N COL 143-S-2 35-C Ingalls 1953.8 1954.4 usacc

Skeath E J LTC 17-W-1 41-A Bernard 1964.1 1964.7 mfh
Skelton W G LTC 101-S 55 Ingalls 1933.1 1933.7 Ret PhBk
Skene C M S MAJ 124-S 67 Ingalls 1930.6 1934.7 Skene '33-34cd
Skene C M S CPT 143-S-1 35-A Ingalls 1919 '19cd rms?
Skene C M S MAJ 1 151 Bernard 1924 1925 Skene
Skidmore W M 1LT 51-S-1 120 Ingalls 1938.7 1939.7 Ret BG
Skidmore W M 1LT 45-E-2 116 Ingalls 1937.9 1938.6 Ret BG
Skidmore W M 2LT 16-W 51 Bernard 1931 1932 Ret BG Skidmore
Skiffington E H LTC 45-E-2 116 Ingalls 1964.1 1966.1 mfh
Skinner D L LTC 54-N-2 140 Ingalls 1968.8 1971.8 mfh
Skinner M L CPT 52-E-1 128 Ingalls 1935.8 1936.6 Pohl Palmer
Slade A R COL 15-S 36 Ruckman 1971.8 1975.7 mfh
Sladen W M COL 44-S-1 104 Ingalls 1954.9 1957.2 usacc
Sladen F W Jr LTC 51-N-2 124 Ingalls 1948.7 1948.11 Ret BG usacc
Sladen F W Jr LTC 19 18 Bernard 1948.11 1950.7 Ret BG
Slaker A CPT 66-S 38 Ingalls 1898.8 c-41
Slaker A CPT 67-S 34 Ingalls 1902 c-46
Slifer B W 1LT 16 W 51 Bernard 1925 1927 Mitchell BOQ
Slocum J M Jr COL 68-S 81 Ingalls 1971.9 1974.9 mfh
Small H E 2LT 18-E-1 37-A Bernard 1915.12 1916.12 Small
Smart W M CPT 102-S 59 Ingalls 1914.12 1915.12 '15cd
Smart W E MAJ 144-N-2 41-D Ingalls 1971.7 1973.6 mfh
Smart Dr 18-W-2 29-B Bernard 1902 c-14 rms MedC
Smart D L COL 69-S 85 Ingalls 1984.7 1986.6 mfh
Smart W M CPT 126-N 165 Bernard 1912.12 1914.12 PhBk
Smee J C COL 51-S-2 118 Ingalls 1961.8 1962.2 mfh
Smee J C COL 79-S 93 Ingalls 1962.2 1965.6 mfh
Smiley L D 1LT 16-W 51 Bernard 1919 '19cd BOQ
Smith H F DR 64 71 Fenwick 1920 1924 PubH '20cd
Smith N E COL 69-N 87 Ingalls 1946.8 1947.6 usacc
Smith H A 1LT 18-E-1 37-A Bernard 1917.12 1918.6 S&F
Smith W COL 68-S 81 Ingalls 1979.3 1982.8 mfh
Smith S MG 121-E 43 Fenwick 1961.5 1963.7 AF mfh Ret MG?
Smith W R CPT 62-N 28 Ruckman 1908.9 1909.9 Ret MG '09cd
Smith F H MAJ 101-S 55 Ingalls 1920.8 1922.8 Ret MG Smith
Smith K C MAJ 143-N-1 35-B Ingalls 1940.8 1942.4 Smith
Smith V R COL 143-N-1 35-B Ingalls 1948.4 1950.11 usacc
Smith H T LTC 45-W-1 112 Ingalls 1968.2 1968.4 mfh
Smith W R MAJ 141 53 Fenwick 1914.12 1917.6 Ret MG Arthur
Smith W 1LT 62-N 28 Ruckman 1902 c-46
Smith W S COL 17-E-1 47-A Bernard 1960.7 1964.2 mfh
Smith W S COL 129-N 103 Ingalls 1965.11 1966.6 mfh
Smith E K MAJ 68-N 83 Ingalls 1923.8 1924.7 '24AdvCs
Smith H W 1LT 16-W 51 Bernard 1925 1927 BOQ Hartel
Smith R M 64 71 Fenwick 1908 '08PhBk
Smith R H MAJ 102-N 61 Ingalls 1924.6 1928.6 Ret BG JHC Ely
Smith R 43-E-1 5 Reeder 1976.8 1978.6 mfh
Smith J A MAJ 43-W-1 3 Reeder 1974.8 1976.6 mfh
Smith F H MAJ 103-N 65 Ingalls 1923.8 1925.8 Ret MG son
Smith P Mc CPT 3-S 167 Bernard 1937.6 1938.8 Smith
Smith D H CPT 33-E-1 61 Fenwick 1940.1 1940.7 PhBk
Smith W K G BG 63-N 24 Ruckman 1973.5 1973.8 mfh Ret BG
Smith W R MAJ 101-S 55 Ingalls 1909.9 1910.9 '11cd Ret MG

Smith P T COL 143-N-2 35-D Ingalls 1968.7 1970.5 Ret BG mfh
Smith F H 1LT 17-W-1 41-A Bernard 1907.9 1908.9 Ret MG son AF
Smith L S 1LT 69-N 87 Ingalls 1932.9 1933.8 '33cd
Smith D H MAJ 33-W-2 57 Fenwick 1940.7 1942.1 Smith
Smith W K G BG 93 75 Ingalls 1973.8 1975.8 mfh Ret BG
Smith S J LTC 128-W 107 Bernard 1921.1 1923.8 Chaplain '23cd
Smith R H MAJ 64-S 22 Ruckman 1923.8 1924.6 Ret BG '23cd
Smith R I MAJ 18-W-2 29-B Bernard 1956.2 1959.6 usacc
Smith H V COL 43-E-1 5 Reeder 1963.12 1964.8 mfh
Smith W D COL 66-S 38 Ingalls 1948.8 1951.7 usacc
Smith J P 1LT 144-S-2 41-C Ingalls 1913.12 1914.12 Ret MG '14PhBk
Smith W R BG 119 33 Fenwick 1923.1 1924.12 Ret MG Hartel w
Smith D H COL 129-S 101 Ingalls 1942.2 1945.4 '42-44PhBk
Smith B L CW4 147 147 Engr Ln 1971.4 1976.11 mfh
Smith P M CPT 3-N 169 Bernard 1936.5 1937.6 Smith
Smith H H 1LT 152-W 12 Patch Rd 1918 1919 '19cd rms?
Smith W D COL 43-W-2 1 Reeder 1947.8 1948.8 usacc
Smith F H MG 119 33 Fenwick 1938.11 1941.1 Ret MG AF Son
Smith T L COL 33-E-2 63 Fenwick 1951.4 1954.8 usacc
Smith W 2LT 64-S 22 Ruckman 1912.1 1912.4 '12cd
Smith L G COL 93 75 Ingalls 1947.6 1948.11 usacc
Smith J D BG 125 73 Ingalls 1984.4 1985.6 mfh
Smith G W CPT 45-W-1 112 Ingalls 1976.4 1977.8 mfh
Smithley J O CPT 18-E-2 37-B Bernard 1921.9 1923.8 '23AdvCs
Smith J A Jr COL 79-S 93 Ingalls 1947.5 1949.3 usacc
Smith C C Jr COL 17-E-1 47-A Bernard 1949.9 1950.9 Ret BG usacc
Smith A H Jr MG 157 101 Bernard 1972.9 1973.12 mfh Ret MG
Smith H D Jr MG 118 29 Fenwick 1975.9 1977.8 mfh Ret MG
Smythe G W BG 103-S 63 Ingalls 1946.10 1947.10 usacc Ret BG?
Snedeker D MAJ 45-W-1 112 Ingalls 1980.7 1982.9 mfh
Snidow R C CPT 68-N 83 Ingalls 1932.9 1933.8 '33cd
Snidow R C CPT 144-N-2 41-D Ingalls 1930.6 1932.8 '31cd
Snow J R COL 102-N 61 Ingalls 1966.6 1969.6 mfh
Snow J R COL 34-S-2 94 Ingalls 1962.1 1963.1 mfh
Snyder H COL 103-S 63 Ingalls 1979.3 1981.2 mfh
Solmiren S SP-6 61-N 45 Ingalls 1968.8 1970.4 mfh
Somerville E C 1LT 35-E-1 6 Reeder 1939.9 1940.2 Died POW MAJ
Southerland N K 2LT 167-B 9 Patch Road 1971.3 1972.8 mfh
Southward C L COL 33-W-2 57 Fenwick 1961.3 1963.12 Ret BG mfh
Sowell H E MAJ 16 W-51 Bernard 1940.6 1941.4 PhBk
Spalding O L 1LT 19 18 Bernard 1902.9 1903.9 Ret BG '03cd
Spangler R S 1LT 44-N-1 106 Ingalls 1939.8 1940.2 Spangler
Spangler R S LTC 15-S 36 Ruckman 1943.8 1945.9 PhBk
Sparrow H G COL 103-S 63 Ingalls 1956.3 1959.1 Ret MG usacc
Speaks R J COL 14 32 Ruckman 1965.7 1967.2 mfh
Speaks R J COL 17-E-1 47-A Bernard 1965.6 1965.7 mfh
Speck T MAJ 144-S-1 41-A Ingalls 1981.6 1983.3 mfh
Speiser R G LTC 45-W-1 112 Ingalls 1950.10 1951.8 usacc
Spencer J J MAJ 3 S 167 Bernard 1976.3 1978.6 mfh
Spencer L E CPT 18-W-1 29-A Bernard 1921.7 1922.7 CAS'22
Spera F P COL 124-N 69 Ingalls 1983.8 1985.8 mfh
Sperry S W 1LT 15-S 36 Ruckman 1914.12 1915.12 '16cd
Spicer J R MAJ 54-S-1 136 Ingalls 1942.3 1943 AN306

Spiller O L MAJ 70-N 91 Ingalls 1923.7 1924.7 Ret BG
Spiller O L MAJ 129-S 101 Ingalls 1919.6 1923.7 Ret BG '20-23cd
Spiller J MAJ 18-E-1 37-A Bernard 1976.9 1979.6 mfh
Spinks M G COL 118 29 Fenwick 1920.7 1922.8 Ret BG Cochran
Spitzer R N LTC 18-W-1 29-A Bernard 1969.8 1970.10 mfh
Splain F 1LT 50-W 121 Bernard 1943 Haldeman
Splain J F MAJ 16-E 53 Bernard 1943.2 1944.11 Splain
Spragins R B LTC 18-E-1 37-A Bernard 1951.11 1953.7 Ret BG usacc
Sprague W R CPT 62-N 28 Ruckman 1919.8 1920.6 '20cd
Sprankle D O COL 18-W-1 29-A Bernard 1958.9 1960.8 usacc
Sprigg W H COL 18-W-1 29-A Bernard 1964.7 1967.8 mfh
Spruill C B FE-5 33 CGH 67 Fenwick 1967.7 1970.7 usacc
Spurgin H F 1LT 17-W-1 41-A Bernard 1910.9 1911.12 '11cd
Spurgin H G COL 120 37 Fenwick 1936.7 1939.6 '37cd
Spurgin H F MAJ 127-E 147 Bernard 1922.8 1923.8 '23cd
Spurgin W F 1LT 17-E-1 47-A Bernard 1936.7 1938.3 '37-39cd Moore
Spurgin H G COL 157 101 Bernard 1933.6 1936.7 JHC
Spurr J P 1LT 18-W-2 29-B Bernard 1905.9 1906.9 '06cd
Squier G O LT 69-N 87 Ingalls 1897 c-38
Stadler G P COL 79-S 93 Ingalls 1983.7 1983.12 mfh
Stahelski A F COL 54-S-2 134 Ingalls 1966.8 1968.6 mfh
Stallings G W LTC 34-S-2 94 Ingalls 1953.12 1956.8 usacc
Standish M E COL 144-S-1 41-A Ingalls 1970.2 1970.4 mfh
Standish M E COL 17-W-2 41-B Bernard 1967.9 1968.11 mfh
Standish M E COL 50-E 129 Bernard 1970.4 1973.11 mfh
Standlee E BG 126-S 163 Bernard 1951.9 1952.7 Ret MG usacc
Standlee E BG 118 29 Fenwick 1952.7 1953.6 Ret MG usacc
Stanford W A COL 144-N-2 41-D Ingalls 1961.9 1963.9 mfh
Stanford L H 2LT 18-W-1 29-A Bernard 1914.9 1915.9 Brooks PhBk
Stanley C M T/Sgt 61-S 43 Ingalls 1939 1940 '40cd '40-41PhBk
Stanley F COL 50-E 129 Bernard 1982.2 1984.6 mfh
Stanton R G COL 127-E 147 Bernard 1953.8 1955.5 usacc
Stanton J D MAJ 52-E-1 128 Ingalls 1966.8 1967.7 mfh
Stapleford F H CPT 17-W-2 41-B Bernard 1940.6 1943.6 PhBks
Staples E E MAJ 70-N 91 Ingalls 1942.8 1945.6 PhBk
Starbird A LT 62-S 30 Ruckman 1902.4 1902.9 b-19
Stark H W MAJ 102-N 61 Ingalls 1931.6 1934.6 Starr Perley
Stark H W MAJ 101-N 57 Ingalls 1930.6 1931.6 '31cd
Stark J MAJ 144-N-2 41-D Ingalls 1980.8 1982.8 mfh
Stark J A MAJ 3-N 169 Bernard 1985.3 1987.6 mfh
Stark A N LTC 120 37 Fenwick 1915.7 1918.6 MedC '17cd
Starkey P L COL 124-N 69 Ingalls 1972.2 1973.11 mfh
Starr R E 1LT 18-W-1 29-A Bernard 1923.9 1927.6 Ret BG Starr
Starr R E CPT 51-S-1 120 Ingalls 1936.7 1938.8 Ret BG Starr
Starry D A GEN 119 33 Fenwick 1977.7 1981.7 Ret GEN mfh
Stayton T V 1LT 52-W-1 130 Ingalls 1937.9 1939.8 Ret MG '37-39cd
Stayton T V COL 144-S-2 41-C Ingalls 1952.7 1953.2 Ret MG usaccc
Stearns C H 1LT 63-N 24 Ruckman 1905.9 1906.9 MedC '06cd
Steckla P R COL 50-E 129 Bernard 1967.9 1969.9 mfh
Steele P LTC 34-N-2 100 Ingalls 1950.9 1951.6 usacc
Steele H L COL 141 53 Fenwick 1934 1935 Ret MG JHC +
Steele P 1LT 34-N-2 100 Ingalls 1937.7 1938.8 Steele
Steele J C 1LT 35-W-1 4 Reeder 1939.7 1940.6 Steele

Steele W M MAJ 144-S-1 41-A Ingalls 1944.2 1946.9 '44-45PhBks
Steere T J 1LT 19 18 Bernard 1914.12 1915.12 '16cd
Stegeman A M LTC 126-S 163 Bernard 1941 1943 PhBk
Steger J O MAJ 127-W 145 Bernard 1917.12 1918.6 S&F Arthur
Steger J O CPT 67-S 34 Ingalls 1907.9 1911.8 S&F'08-11cd
Steger J O CPT 102-S 59 Ingalls 1911.9 1912.9 CAS'11 '11cd
Steinback R COL 126-N 165 Bernard 1954.9 1956.6 Ret MG usacc
Steinback R COL 3-S 167 Bernard 1954.3 1954.9 Ret MG usacc
Stein H J Jr COL 69-N 87 Ingalls 1974.5 1977.6 mfh
Stein H J Jr LTC 44-S-1 104 Ingalls 1973.8 1974.5 mfh
Stephens J C CPT 43-W-2 1 Reeder 1930.12 1931.7 deCamp
Stephenson H W MAJ 70-N 91 Ingalls 1921.9 1922.6 Stephenson
Stern H I LTC 17-E-2 47-B Bernard 1948.2 1950.11 usacc
Sternberg B COL 144-N-2 41-D Ingalls 1955.4 1957.7 Ret MG usacc
Stevens R D MSG 35-E-1 6 Reeder 1986.3 1986.7 mfh
Stevens V C COL 79-S 93 Ingalls 1949.5 1952.8 usacc
Stevens K T COL 18-W-2 29-B Bernard 1966.7 1968.6 mfh
Stevens V C CPT 52-W-2 132 Ingalls 1936.7 1941.6 Stevens
Stevens J D 1LT 35-W-2 2 Reeder 1938.8 1939.7 Ret BG Stevens
Stevens K T COL 45-E-2 116 Ingalls 1969.8 1970.8 mfh
Stevens C L CPT 102-N 61 Ingalls 1918 1919 BOQ WWI '19cd
Stevens J D 1LT 18-W-2 29-B Bernard 1937.12 1938.8 Ret BG Stevens
Stevens V C COL 143-S-2 35-C Ingalls 1949.3 1949.5 usacc
Stevenson H W COL 67-N 36 Ingalls 1946.8 1950.11 usacc
Stevenson DR 18-E-1 37-A Bernard 1826.5 1828.3 '26-28rq rms?
Stevens P M III COL 45-W-1 112 Ingalls 1964.2 1964.9 mfh
Stevens P M III COL 16-E 53 Bernard 1959.3 1961.8 Guest House
Stevens P M III COL 35-E-1 6 Reeder 1957.10 1959.3 usacc
Stevens E L Jr 1LT 67-S 34 Ingalls 1918 1919 BOQ WWI '19cd
Stevers W E COL 67-S 34 Ingalls 1961.8 1962.7 mfh
Stewart C W LTC 18-E-2 37-B Bernard 1977.9 1980.8 mfh
Stewart J C LTC 45-W-2 110 Ingalls 1954.9 1957.1 usacc
Stewart S T MAJ 101-S 55 Ingalls 1927.7 1928.7 '28AdvCs
Stewart W F CPT 1 151 Bernard 1899.4 1899.5 w
Stewart A J CPT 34-N-2 100 Ingalls 1943 1945 '43-45PhBk
Stewart W R 2LT 16-W 51 Bernard 1917 1918 Stewart BOQ
Stewart W F CPT 14 32 Ruckman 1892 1895 b-12
Stewart A Jr LTC 51-S-2 118 Ingalls 1970.6 1972.7 mfh
Stiley J F CPT 52-E-2 126 Ingalls 1931.8 1932.8 deCamp
Stiley J F 1LT 65-S 46 Ingalls 1923.6 1924.6 '23cd
Stillman E H CPT 62-S 30 Ruckman 1930.6 1931.7 Maris
Stilson A H COL 79-S 93 Ingalls 1965.6 1969.2 mfh
Stiness P B 1LT 34-S-2 94 Ingalls 1939.9 1940.9 '40CAS
Stockton E A Jr MAJ 127-W 145 Bernard 1926.9 1927.6 Ret BG Putney
Stockton E A Jr 1LT 17-W-1 41-A Bernard 1915.9 1916.9 Ret BG son
Stockton E A Jr CPT 70-N 91 Ingalls 1916.9 Ret BG '17cd
Stofford F W 1LT 63-S 26 Ruckman 1903.9 1904.9 '04cd
Stone G P CPT 62-N 28 Ruckman 1917.12 1918.9 S&F Arthur
Stoner A F 1LT 54-N-2 140 Ingalls 1942 1943 '43 PhBk
Stone R Jr 1LT 17-E-1 47-A Bernard 1929.9 1930.7 Stone
Stone R Jr LTC 144-N-1 41-B Ingalls 1949.9 1951.12 usacc
Storm H W LTC 18-E-2 37-B Bernard 1948.7 1952.4 usacc
Storrs J N MAJ 70-N 91 Ingalls 1941.1 1942.8 Bennett

Story J P COL 1 151 Bernard 1902.3 1904.1 CO w
Story J P CPT 17-W-1 41-A Bernard 1888.6 1891.1 c-27
Stovall H W 1LT 144-N-2 41-D Ingalls 1914.12 1915.12 CAS'15 '16cd
Stovall H W 2LT 16-W 51 Bernard 1911 1912 BOQ? '11cd
Stovall A S Jr COL 15-S 36 Ruckman 1949.10 1950.2 usacc
Stovall A S Jr COL 124-N 69 Ingalls 1950.2 1952.6 usacc
Stover C W COL 62-S 30 Ruckman 1984.8 1987.6 mfh
Strait L J Jr MAJ 16-E 53 Bernard 1947.1 1948.6 usacc
Strickland H E 2LT 16-E 53 Bernard 1930 Mendenhall
Stromfors R E LTC 33-W-1 59 Fenwick 1971.8 1972.6 mfh
Strong A G MAJ 157 101 Bernard 1924.6 1928.8 Ret BG Hartel
Strong F S LTC 118 29 Fenwick 1907.6 1909.7 Ret MG Son
Strong F S COL 119 33 Fenwick 1911.9 1913.2 Ret MG Son
Strong J E CPT 64-S 22 Ruckman 1940 1941 PhBk
Strong J R CPT 62-N 28 Ruckman 1937 1938.6 Martin
Strong F S CPT 15-N 34 Ruckman 1900.9 1902.1 Ret MG son
Strong F S MAJ 66-S 38 Ingalls 1905.8 1907.6 S&F b-26
Strother K C COL 125 73 Ingalls 1953.6 1954.6 usacc
Struthers D G LTC 43-W-2 1 Reeder 1966.8 1967.5 mfh
Struthers D G LTC 67-S 34 Ingalls 1967.5 1970.7 mfh
Stryker W B 1LT 34-S-2 94 Ingalls 1936.8 1938.9 MedC Taber +
Stryker W B 1LT 18-W-2 29-B Bernard 1935.6 1936.8 MedC Stryker
Stuart A J 1LT 124-N 69 Ingalls 1911.9 1914.12 CAS'12 PhBk
Stuart L L MAJ 124-N 69 Ingalls 1928,7 1931.7 Ret BG DC '28-30cds
Stuart C E COL 126-S 163 Bernard 1966.9 1970.5 mfh
Stuart L L MAJ 55 42 Ingalls 1922.7 1923.7 Ret BG CAS'22
Stuart L L 2LT 17-E-2 47-B Bernard 1914.8 1915.7 Ret BG Daughter
Sturman J F CPT 68-S 81 Ingalls 1938.8 1939.6 Hain
Sucher J G 1LT 67-S 34 Ingalls 1918 1919 BOQ WWI '19cd
Sullivan R A MG 118 29 Fenwick 1981.9 1982.9 mfh
Sullivan R E COL 3-N 169 Bernard 1965.5 1968.1 mfh
Sullivan J B COL 124-N 69 Ingalls 1956.10 1957.7 Ret BG usacc
Sullivan J B LTC 16-E 53 Bernard 1946.10 1947.1 Ret BG usacc
Sullivan J P MG 118 29 Fenwick 1950.6 1952.6 usacc Ret MG
Sullivan J P BG 125 73 Ingalls 1949.11 1950.6 Ret MG usacc
Sullivan C H MAJ 143-S-1 35-A Ingalls 1973.1 1977.1 mfh
Sullivan J B COL 121-W 41 Fenwick 1957.7 1959.6 Ret BG usacc
Sunderland A H MAJ 101-S 55 Ingalls 1916.12 1918.4 Ret MG Broudy
Sunderland A H COL 103-N 65 Ingalls 1932.7 1933.7 Ret MG '33cd
Sunderland A H LTC 141 53 Fenwick 1925 1927 Ret MG Broudy
Sunderland A H LTC 143-N-2 35-D Ingalls 1918.4 1918.11 Broudy
Sunderland A H CPT 69-S 85 Ingalls 1911.8 1912.8 Ret MG Daughter
Sunderland A H COL 118 29 Fenwick 1933.7 1936.6 Ret MG Cochran
Sunderland A H CPT 3-S 167 Bernard 1915.12 1916.12 Ret MG Broudy
Sunderland A H CPT 101-N 57 Ingalls 1912.8 1914.3 Ret MG PhBk
Sundin A B COL 101-N 57 Ingalls 1960.9 1966.3 mfh
Sundt H L COL 62-N 28 Ruckman 1954.7 1958.6 usacc
Supple E L CPT 45-W-1 112 Ingalls 1932.8 1933.7 '33cd
Surles A D Jr MG 121-E 43 Fenwick 1968.5 1968.9 Ret LTG mfh
Surles A D Jr MG 120 37 Fenwick 1968.9 1969.12 Ret LTG mfh
Surratt J F COL 17-W-1 41-A Bernard 1953.7 1953.9 usacc
Surratt J F COL 63-N 24 Ruckman 1954.9 1956.6 usacc
Surratt J F COL 144-S-2 41-C Ingalls 1953.9 1954.9 usacc

Sussmann W A COL 54-S-2 134 Ingalls 1952.11 1953.2 usacc
Sutherland A J 1LT 144-N-1 41-B Ingalls 1938.6 1939.6 '39PhBk
Sutherland J W Jr LTC 54-N-1 138 Ingalls 1949.2 1950.7 usacc
Sutton E E COL 144-N-2 41-D Ingalls 1959.1 1960.9 usacc
Sutton T G MAJ 44-N-1 106 Ingalls 1986.6 1987.12 mfh
Sutton A J COL 35-E-1 6 Reeder 1963.3 1965.5 mfh
Swan D W MAJ 79-N 95 Ingalls 1921.8 1923.6 '22FOcs
Swan D W MAJ 55 42 Ingalls 1923.7 1923.11 Broudy Higgins
Swan D W MAJ 124-S 67 Ingalls 1926.6 1927.8 Broudy Higgins
Swann R A Jr MAJ 54-S-1 136 Ingalls 1970.9 1972.1 mfh
Sweat J E MAJ 144-N-1 41-B Ingalls 1971.9 1974.7 mfh
Sweek J G COL 35-W-2 2 Reeder 1961.12 1962.7 mfh
Sweeney W B MAJ 66-S 38 Ingalls 1986.3 1986.5 mfh
Sweeney W B MAJ 144-S-2 41-C Ingalls 1985.5 1986.3 mfh
Sweet W H CPT 69-S 85 Ingalls 1923.7 1924.8 Higgins
Sweet J B COL 50-E 129 Bernard 1946.11 1948.6 usacc
Sweet E A DR 64 71 Fenwick 1937 1940 PubH '37cd
Sweeting H W Jr COL 45-E-2 116 Ingalls 1951.8 1954.1 usacc
Swoger F R LTC 43-W-2 1 Reeder 1950.9 1951.4 usacc
Sydnor W P CPT 33-E-2 63 Fenwick 1944.6 1946.9 PhBks
Symroski C A BG 121-W 41 Fenwick 1966.9 1970.1 mfh Ret BG
Taber A P 1LT 34-S-1 96 Ingalls 1936.8 1937.6 Ret BG Taber +
Tabor J COL 55 42 Ingalls 1961.9 1962.7 USMC mfh
Talbot B COL 146 146 Engr Ln 1978.6 1982.5 mfh
Talbott O C BG 121-E 43 Fenwick 1967.3 1968.3 Ret LTG mfh
Talbott O C LTG 141 53 Fenwick 1973.3 1975.9 Ret LTG mfh
Talbott C Y Sr COL 17-W-2 41-B Bernard 1957.9 1960.8 usacc
Talcott A CPT 17-W-1 41-A Bernard 1834 '34rq Brother-in-law to REL
Talcott A CPT 17-W-1 41A Bernard 1824 d-684
Taliaferro P B CPT 3-S 167 Bernard 1921.7 1922.1 Taliaferro
Taliaferro P B 1LT 16-E 53 Bernard 1920.7 1921.7 '21cd
Taliaferro E H Jr CPT 62-S 30 Ruckman 1925.6 1926.7 Bailey rms
Taliaferro E H Jr COL 142 51 Fenwick 1943.10 1944.9 PhBk + Tilton
Talley W CSM 60 67 Fenwick 1979.1 1980.10 mfh
Tambling R F LTC 33 CGH 67 Fenwick 1974.1 1975.10 mfh
Tank C P BG 54-N-1 138 Ingalls 1964.5 1964.8 mfh Ret BG
Tannehill I R 1LT 18-W-2 29-B Bernard 1919.6 1920.6 '20cd
Tarkenton J C Jr COL 79-S 93 Ingalls 1960.6 1961.12 usacc
Tarkenton J C Jr COL 17-E-1 47-A Bernard 1958.8 1960.6 usacc
Tarrant L K 1LT 16-E 53 Bernard 1931.9 1932.8 Ret BG Vickers
Tarrant L K 1LT 33-E-2 63 Fenwick 1932.8 1936.12 Ret BG Tarrant
Tasker H P 2LT 16-E 53 Bernard 1927 Tasker
Tasker H P 1LT 1 151 Bernard 1929 1930 Tasker
Tate R A COL 144-N-1 41-B Ingalls 1954.9 1956.8 usacc
Tauer M G COL 16-W 51 Bernard 1950.9 1952.11 usacc
Taulbee J F COL 158 32 Ingalls 1934.6 1936.7 deCamp JHC
Taylor H C LTC 143-N-1 35-B Ingalls 1973.5 1977.7 mfh
Taylor J B 1LT 143-S-1 35-A Ingalls 1910.6 1911.7 '11cd
Taylor F LTC 1 151 Bernard 1855.12 1856.5 w
Taylor C J MAJ 143-S-2 35-C Ingalls 1920.9 1921.7 Ret MG ENGR JHC
Taylor T H COL 51-N-2 124 Ingalls 1958.9 1961.4 usacc
Taylor J G LTC 121-W 41 Fenwick 1923.9 1926.6 '25cd
Taylor E O 1LT 54-S-1 136 Ingalls 1938.7 1939.7 RLT

Taylor J B CPT 124-S 67 Ingalls 1912.7 1914.12 '12-14cd PhBk
Taylor J C COL 45-E-2 116 Ingalls 1955.11 1956.10 usacc
Taylor J 1LT 43-W-1 3 Reeder 1980.4 1982.11 mfh
Taylor H K 1LT 17-W-2 41-B Bernard 1905.9 1906.9 '06cd
Taylor J MAJ 143-N-2 35-D Ingalls 1977.8 1980.6 mfh
Taylor J B CPT 63-S 30 Ruckman 1916 1917 '16-17cd
Taylor J M Jr MAJ 43-W-2 1 Reeder 1973.9 1976.7 mfh
Taylor B G Jr COL 51-S-1 120 Ingalls 1962.9 1964.5 mfh
Teich F C Jr COL 45-W-1 112 Ingalls 1961.5 1964.2 mfh
Teich F C Jr COL 16-E 53 Bernard 1964.2 1965.12 mfh
Tello R C LTC 43-E-2 7 Reeder 1974.7 1975.8 mfh
Terrell J P 1LT 144-N-2 41-D Ingalls 1910.8 1911.9 '11cd
Terrell J P 1LT 62-S 30 Ruckman 1909.10 1910.8 CAS'10
Terry T A MAJ 126-S 163 Bernard 1926.5 1927.7 Arthur
Thayer H J COL 79-S 93 Ingalls 1976.8 1979.7 mfh
Thayer E E MAJ 14 32 Ruckman 1942 1943 PhBk
Theophilus R H MAJ 67-S 34 Ingalls 1943.11 1945.12 Theophilus
Thiele C M MAJ 143-S-1 35-A Ingalls 1925.6 1926.7 Ret BG '25cd
Thiele C M MAJ 79-N 95 Ingalls 1923.7 1924.6 Ret BG Ely
Thiele C M MAJ 129-S 101 Ingalls 1927.6 1929.6 Ret BG Ely
Thomas J A LTC 123-W 2 Ruckman 1920.9 1921.8 '21FOcs
Thomas H G COL 54-N-2 140 Ingalls 1953.9 1956.4 usacc
Thomas E COL 79-S 93 Ingalls 1970.7 1973.7 mfh
Thomas H S 2LT 18-W-2 29-B Bernard 1917.1 1917.5 Underwood rms
Thomas A R 1LT 79-N 95 Ingalls 1934.8 1935.6 Thomas
Thomas J J 2LT 17-E-2 47-B Bernard 1910.9 1911.9 '11cd
Thomas-Stahle C MAJ 128-E 109 Bernard 1922.8 1924.8 S&F Arthur +
Thompson D L COL 44-N-1 106 Ingalls 1946.8 1947.3 usacc
Thompson J H W CPT 33-E-1 61 Fenwick 1943.7 1944 PhBk
Thompson R P COL 44-N-1 106 Ingalls 1958.12 1959.3 usacc
Thompson E B CPT 45-W-2 110 Ingalls 1937.7 1938.6 '37cd
Thompson J W CPT 67-N 36 Ingalls 1918 1919.4 '19cd
Thompson W L CPT 1 151 Bernard 1928 1929 '28cd
Thompson E G 1LT 35-W-1 4 Reeder 1932.8 1933.8 Ellsworth
Thompson M R COL 51-N-2 124 Ingalls 1946.10 1947.10 usacc Ret BG
Thompson E H MAJ 50-W 121 Bernard 1923.9 1924.6 Putney
Thompson A C LTC 103-S 63 Ingalls 1920.8 1921.8 '21FOcs
Thompson H A 1LT 17-W-2 41-B Bernard 1824.7 1825 '25rq
Thompson E B 1LT 45-W-1 112 Ingalls 1931.8 1932.7 deCamp
Thompson P W COL 69-N 87 Ingalls 1947.6 1950.9 usacc Ret BG
Thompson L E COL 103-N 65 Ingalls 1967.3 1969.10 mfh
Thompson R P COL 102 N 61 Ingalls 1959.3 1960.12 usacc
Thompson M R 1LT 35-E-2 8 Reeder 1936.7 1937.8 Darrah Ret BG
Thompson H J Jr LTC 52-E-2 126 Ingalls 1972.4 1975.7 mfh
Thoms H LTC 143-S-2 35-C Ingalls 1981.8 1983.4 mfh
Thomte H D COL 62-N 28 Ruckman 1960.12 1961.8 usacc
Thomte H D COL 51-S-1 120 Ingalls 1960.7 1960.12 usacc
Thornburg M W CPT 15-N 34 Ruckman 1919 '19cd
Thornton F T 2LT 79-N 95 Ingalls 1902 c-46
Throckmorton J L COL 45-W-2 110 Ingalls 1964.3 1964.4 Ret GEN mfh
Thurman M R BG 121-W 41 Fenwick 1975.6 1977.5 Ret GEN mfh
Thurman M GEN 119 33 Fenwick 1987.8 mfh
Tichenor J R COL 79-S 93 Ingalls 1983.12 1986.4 mfh

Tidball J C COL 18-W-1 29-A Bernard 1874.5 1883.11 Ret MG Museum
Tidball J C MAJ 18-E-1 37-A Bernard 1867 1868.5 S&F c-27 Ret MG
Tidball J C COL 1 151 Bernard 1883.11 1888.11 Ret MG c-10 w
Tidball W LTC 157 101 Bernard 1921.8 1922.1 '22FOcs
Tiernon J L CPT 50-W 121 Bernard 1891.2 1898.11 Ret BG c-47
Tiernon J L MAJ 1 151 Bernard 1898.9 1899.9 w Ret BG
Tiery J H LTC 52-W-1 130 Ingalls 1958.1 1959.7 usacc
Tignor E P 1LT 64-N 20 Ruckman 1912.12 1914.12 PhBk
Tignor E P 1LT 50-W 121 Bernard 1915.12 1916.12 Dentist '17cd
Tilton R L BG 118 29 Fenwick 1940.11 1940.12 Ret BG Tilton
Tilton R L BG 142 51 Fenwick 1940.12 1941.1 Ret BG Tilton
Tilton R L 2LT 17-W-1 41-A Bernard 1910.3 1910.7 Ret BG Tilton
Tilton R L BG 119 33 Fenwick 1941.1 1946.7 Ret BG Tilton
Tilton E R CPT 50-W 121 Bernard 1906.8 1906.6 ENGR Tilton
Tilton R L MAJ 103-S 63 Ingalls 1929.9 1933.7 Ret BG Tilton
Tilton R L LTC 125 73 Ingalls 1919.2 1919.6 Ret BG Tilton
Tilton E R 1LT 17-W-1 41-A Bernard 1902 c-12
Tilton R L BG 1 151 Bernard 1946.7 1948.5 Ret BG CG
Timberlake E N CPT 44-N-1 106 Ingalls 1931.9 1932.8 Ret BG deCamp +
Timmerberg P M BG 128-W 107 Bernard 1972.8 1973.8 mfh Ret MG?
Timmerberg P M BG 63-N 24 Ruckman 1972.6 1972.8 mfh Ret MG?
Timmerman A C CPT 43-E-2 7 Reeder 1984.6 1986.12 mfh
Timothy J S BG 128-W 107 Bernard 1970.4 1972.6 mfh Ret BG
Tinder W F COL 126-N 165 Bernard 1983.7 1986.6 mfh
Tinder E P E-7 61-N 45 Ingalls 1967.3 1968.7 mfh
Tinsley P COL 127-W 145 Bernard 1975.10 1980.1 mfh
Tischbein C F CPT 51-S-2 118 Ingalls 1935.8 1936.6 Widow
Tischbein C F CPT 3-S 167 Bernard 1938.8 1940.9 Widow + PhBk
Tito W J Jr LTC 54-N-2 140 Ingalls 1974.6 1977.6 mfh
Todd M H LTC 68-N 83 Ingalls 1945.3 1946.8 PhBk
Todd W B COL 52-W-2 132 Ingalls 1964.8 1966.2 PhBks
Todd W B COL 63-N 24 Ruckman 1966.2 1967.2 mfh
Todd H D Jr LTC 119 33 Fenwick 1916.8 1916.10 Ret MG Cochran
Todd H D Jr MAJ 102-S 59 Ingalls 1908.6 1909.9 Ret MG '09cd
Todd H D Jr LTC 142 51 Fenwick 1916.10 1917.6 Ret MG JHC +
Todd H D Jr MG 119 33 Fenwick 1929.8 1930.8 Ret MG JHC w
Toftoy H N CPT 69-N 87 Ingalls 1938.9 1941.9 Ret MG PhBk
Toftoy H N COL 70-S 89 Ingalls 1941.9 1943 Ret MG PhBk
Toftoy H N 1LT 35-E-1 6 Reeder 1935.8 1936.7 Ret MG deCamp
Toler D A H COL 68-S 81 Ingalls 1960.8 1962.8 British LNO mfh
Tolley R F CPT 143-S-2 35-C Ingalls 1943.3 1946.2 Tolley PhBks
Tolley R F CPT 18-E-2 37-B Bernard 1941.11 1943.3 Tolley Splain
Tolson J J III LTG 141 53 Fenwick 1971.3 1973.2 mfh Ret LTG
Tolstoi G MAJ 52-E-1 128 Ingalls 1942 1943 '43PhBk
Toth N 2LT 43-E-1 5 Reeder 1979.8 1982.7 mfh
Totten J CPT 1 151 Bernard 1857.1 1857.2 w
Totten J CPT 62-N 28 Ruckman 1912.12 1913.12 '13cd
Totten J 1LT 65-S 46 Ingalls 1906.5 1908.5 S&F b-26
Totten J CPT 128-W 107 Bernard 1913.12 1915.12 '15cd
Totten J CPT 103-N 65 Ingalls 1911.10 1912.12 S&F '12cd
Townsend J R MAJ 67-N 36 Ingalls 1934.8 1938.6 Ret BG PhBk
Townsley C P LTC 119 33 Fenwick 1909.2 1911.9 Ret MG w
Townsley C P CPT 50-W 121 Bernard 1900.7 1902.8 Ret MG c-46

Tracy M W CPT 3-S 167 Bernard 1940.9 1941.3 Tracy
Tracy M W CPT 33-W-2 57 Fenwick 1934.6 1937.6 Tarrant +
Tracy J P BG 119 33 Fenwick 1932.8 1936.11 Ret BG JHC w
Tracy J P 1LT 3-N 169 Bernard 1902 1906.5 Ret BG Tracy
Traeger G L LTC 18-W-2 29-B Bernard 1951.11 1953.2 usacc
Traver P C COL 144-S-2 41-C Ingalls 1968.1 1971.7 mfh
Traylor J P MAJ 63-S 26 Ruckman 1944 1945 ORD Ret BG PhBk
Treadway T F Jr CPT 34-N-1 98 Ingalls 1943 1945 PhBks
Tredennick D C LTC 67-N 36 Ingalls 1940.8 1942.6 Tredennick
Tredennick J C MAJ 44-S-2 102 Ingalls 1942 1943 '43PhBk
Tredennick D C 1LT 17-E-1 47-A Bernard 1930.7 1931.7 Tredennick
Tredennick D C LTC 158 32 Ingalls 1942.6 1943.3 Tredennick
Trent F CPT 143-N-2 35-D Ingalls 1918.11 1919.9 '20cd
Trew F G COL 44-N-1 106 Ingalls 1947.7 1948.2 usacc
Trew F G COL 66-N 40 Ingalls 1948.2 1952.6 usacc
Trichel G W 1LT 35-E-2 8 Reeder 1931.6 1934.6 deCamp '31-33cd
Trigg O B MAJ 124-N 69 Ingalls 1936.6 1940.2 '37-39cd Jackson
Trigg C B MAJ 35-W-2 2 Reeder 1935.7 1936.6 deCamp JHC
Trimble R S 1LT 143-N-1 35-B Ingalls 1920.9 1921.8 CAS'21
Trobaugh E L COL 126-S 163 Bernard 1974.6 1975.7 mfh Ret BG?
Trobaugh E L LTC 51-N-2 124 Ingalls 1973.6 1974.6 mfh Ret BG?
Troland T E 1LT 18-E-2 37-B Bernard 1917.11 1919.6 '19cd
Trost R W COL 79-N 95 Ingalls 1975.9 1987.8 mfh
Trost F COL 79-N 95 Ingalls 1975.9 1978.8 mfh
Trotter A 1LT 64-S 22 Ruckman 1906 1908 '06cd b-26
Trotter J J LTC 44-S-1 104 Ingalls 1967.3 1970.2 mfh
Trout R J COL 143-N-1 35-B Ingalls 1957.9 1961.9 usacc
Troutman L A LTC 17-W-1 41-A Bernard 1948.6 1950.6 usacc
Truman L W LTG 157 101 Bernard 1960.7 1963.8 mfh Ret LTG
Tubbs H S 1LT 44-N-2 108 Ingalls 1938.9 1939.6 Tubbs
Tubbs H S LTC 35-W-2 2 Reeder 1950.9 1951.7 usacc
Tubbs H S LTC 63-N 24 Ruckman 1951.7 1953.9 usacc
Tubbs H S 2LT 1 151 Bernard 1935 1936 Tubbs
Tucker R H LTC 45-W-2 110 Ingalls 1951.4 1952.7 usacc
Tucker E LTC 3-S 167 Bernard 1978.6 1979.8 mfh
Tuebner H R COL 43-E-1 5 Reeder 1959.12 1962.4 mfh
Turley R E CPT 129-S 101 Ingalls 1919 BOQ WWI '19cd
Turnage B O Jr COL 54-S-2 134 Ingalls 1953.10 1956.12 Ret MG usacc
Turnage B O Jr LTC 45-W-2 110 Ingalls 1946.9 1948.7 RetMG usacc
Turner N T MAJ 45-E-1 114 Ingalls 1943.12 1946.10 '44-45PhBks
Turner G F CPT 15-N 34 Ruckman 1916.12 1917.6 Ford
Turtle L CPT 144-S-2 41-C Ingalls 1911.8 1912.8 '12cd Turtle
Tussing J T COL 124-S 67 Ingalls 1982.6 1986.9 mfh
Tutin B J COL 50-W 121 Bernard 1967.7 1969.7 mfh
Twyman J H Jr 1LT 79-S 93 Ingalls 1936.6 1937.6 Twyman
Tyndall J B LTC 34-N-2 100 Ingalls 1969.5 1969.12 mfh
Ulmet O MAJ 44 S-1 104 Ingalls 1982.2 1982.12 mfh
Underwood E H 2LT 18-W-2 29-B Bernard 1917.1 1917.5 Underwood rms
Underwood E H CPT 35-W-2 2 Reeder 1930.12 1931.6 Underwood
Unger F T MG 1 151 Bernard 1965.9 1966.10 Ret LTG mfh
Usis F M 1LT 16-W 51 Bernard 1919 1920 Usis
Vallandingham J COL 33-W-2 57 Fenwick 1981.11 1984.5 mfh
Vallery J K COL 35-E-1 6 Reeder 1965.8 1965.9 mfh

Vallery J K COL 66-N 40 Ingalls 1965.9 1968.6 mfh
Valliant C LTC 17-W-2 41-B Bernard 1976.7 1981.4 mfh
Valverde C A COL 93 75 Ingalls 1942 1943 PhBk
VanBuskirk R J CPT 65-N 48 Ingalls 1932.1 1932.8 VanBuskirk
VanBuskirk R J CPT 51-N-2 124 Ingalls 1932.8 1933.6 VanBuskirk
Vance W R CPT 68-S 81 Ingalls 1906.9 1907.9 CAS'07
Vance Z B MAJ 101-S 55 Ingalls 1918 1919 '19cd
VanCourt L P COL 16-W 51 Bernard 1961.8 1962.6 mfh
VanDendriesch CPT 1 151 Bernard 1918 1918 Roundtree
Vandersluis H J COL 68-S 81 Ingalls 1952.10 1954.7 Ret BG usacc
Vandersluis H J LTC 63-S 26 Ruckman 1939.9 1941.1 Ret BG Self
Vann W M MG 118 29 Fenwick 1971.7 1972.10 mfh Ret MG
VanNatta T F COL 65-N 48 Ingalls 1953.6 1954.11 usacc Ret MG
Van Natta T F MG 33-E-2 63 Fenwick 1961.1 1961.3 Ret MG usacc
VanNatta T F MG 120 37 Fenwick 1961.3 1962.2 mfh Ret MG
VanNess D 1LT 18-W-2 29-B Bernard 1826 1828 '25rq rooms
VanOrmer H P 2LT 1 151 Bernard 1935 1937 VanOrmer
VanOrmer H P 1LT 50-A 125 Bernard 1940.2 1940.9 BOQ VanOrmer
VanOrmer H P 1LT 44-S-1 104 Ingalls 1941.1 1941.6 VanOrmer
Vanover J SSG 61-N 45 Ingalls 1971.9 1972.1 mfh
VanValzah S L MAJ 64-S 22 Ruckman 1919.4 1921.1 MedC
VanVolkenburgh R H 2LT 16-W 51 Bernard 1913 1914 PhBk BOQ
VanVolkenburgh R H MAJ 103-N 65 Ingalls 1929.6 1932.6 Tilton
Varela J B CPT 50-W 121 Bernard 1925.8 1928.6 '25cd
Varela J B CPT 69-N 87 Ingalls 1919.6 1920.8 '20cd
Vaughan C N COL 143-S-1 35-A Ingalls 1960.9 1962.6 mfh
Vaughn M F COL 65-S 46 Ingalls 1962.7 1962.10 mfh
Vaughn M F COL 35-W-1 4 Reeder 1959.9 1962.7 mfh
Vaught W CW3 54-S-2 134 Ingalls 1987.1 1979.9 mfh
Vautsmeier W N 1LT 17-W-1 41-A Bernard 1916.12 1917.6 Ford CAS'17
Vavrek F MAJ 54-N-1 138 Ingalls 1980.5 1981.10 mfh
Venable C P COL 17-E-1 47-A Bernard 1964.3 1965.6 mfh
Vennes D D MAJ 50-A 125 Bernard 1970.8 1972.8 mfh
Verona E CPT 15-N 34 Ruckman 1926.6 1927.6 '17BtryOCs
Vestal W M 1LT 143-N-2 35-D Ingalls 1938.9 1939.8 Vestal
Vestal S C MAJ 142 51 Fenwick 1914.12 1915.8 '16cd son
Vestal W M LTC 143-N-2 35-D Ingalls 1943.5 1944.5 Vestal
Vestal S C COL 142 51 Fenwick 1927.7 1927.11 '27cd son
Vestal S C MAJ 125 73 Ingalls 1915.8 1917.8 Vestal son
Vickers L T 2LT 16-E 53 Bernard 1931 1932 Vickers
Vickers L T 1LT 1 151 Bernard 1932 1934 Vickers
Vidlak F J COL 54-S-1 136 Ingalls 1962.10 1963.8 mfh
Vidlak F J COL 65-S 46 Ingalls 1967.7 1972.3 mfh
Villada M 1LT 17-W-1 41-A Bernard 1926.7 1927.6 '27BtryOCs
Vinson W H MG 1 151 Bernard 1975.7 1977.12 mfh Ret MG?
Voehl W E H 1LT 33-E-1 61 Fenwick 1938.7 1939.12 Tarrant
Vogel G H 1LT 17-W-2 41-B Bernard 1920.7 1921.7 Ret BG CAS'21
Vogel G H BG 126-S 163 Bernard 1952.9 1954.6 Ret BG usacc
Volk K W COL 126-N 165 Bernard 1967.6 1970.11 mfh
Vose R E 1LT 144-N-1 41-B Ingalls 1912.8 1913.12 '13-14cds
Vose W P CPT 17-W-2 41-B Bernard 1888.9 1891.1 b-26 c-27
Vowell F C MAJ 127-E 147 Bernard 1944.3 1944.11 PhBk
Vuono C MG 125 73 Ingalls 1979.9 1981.8 mfh

Vuono C E GEN 119 33 Fenwick 1986.7 1987.7 mfh
Waggener R COL 68-N 83 Ingalls 1979.6 1980.8 mfh
Wagner MSG 35-W-2 2 Reeder 1980.6 1981.6 mfh
Wahl L CPT 101-S 55 Ingalls 1910.12 1912.12 '12cd
Wahle C B 1LT 18-W-2 29-B Bernard 1927.8 1928.8 '28BtryOCs
Wahle C B CPT 19 18 Bernard 1939.7 1940.7 PhBk
Waits W B LTC 147 147 Engr Ln 1952.10 1954.11 usacc
Walbach J D COL 17-W-1 41A Bernard 1830 1832 d-684 all rms
Walbach J D COL 17-E-2 47B Bernard 1830 1832 d-684 all rms
Walbach J D COL 17-E-1 47A Bernard 1830 1832 d-684 all rms
Walbach J D 1LT 16-E 53 Bernard 1917 '17cd Ret BG?
Walbach J D BG 1 151 Bernard 1842.8 1848.10 CG w Ret BG
Walbach J D COL 17-W-2 41-B Bernard 1830 1832 d-684 all rms
Walbridge V 1LT 18-E-1 37-A Bernard 1933.8 1934.12 '33cd
Walbridge V 1LT 33-E-1 61 Fenwick 1931.7 1932.7 '31cd
Waldeck J COL 146 146 Engr Ln 1982.5 1984.5 mfh
Waldman F J Jr COL 67-S 34 Ingalls 1973.7 1977.10 mfh
Waldo G E 1LT 17-W-2 41-B Bernard 1924.7 1925.7 Gibbs '25cd
Waldron L T CPT 64-S 22 Ruckman 1908 '08cd
Waldron N E COL 51-S-2 118 Ingalls 1947.4 1948.1 usacc
Waldron E E II COL 127-W 145 Bernard 1975.8 1975.8 mfh
Waligora D L CPT 54-N-2 140 Ingalls 1937.8 1939.12 '37-39cds
Walke 2Lt W 65-S 48 Ingalls 1890 b-6
Walke W CPT 65-N 48 Ingalls 1901.9 1902.8 c-46
Walker ?LT 15-S 36 Ruckman 1886 c-14
Walker G D COL 50-E 129 Bernard 1967.8 1967.9 mfh Ret LTG
Walker J F MAJ 79-N 95 Ingalls 1924.6 1925.6 Hartel
Walker G H COL 64 71 Fenwick 1959.2 1961.9 usacc
Walker G D MG 142 51 Fenwick 1967.9 1969.9 mfh Ret LTG
Walker W H MAJ 144-S-2 41-C Ingalls 1926.7 1927.7 GEN KIA '50
Walker E D LTC 157 101 Bernard 1936.7 1939.7 Phillips
Walker E B MAJ 157 101 Bernard 1929.6 1931.6 Dunham '31cd
Walker G H COL 33-E-2 63 Fenwick 1958.8 1959.2 usacc
Walker E B 1LT 18-E-1 37-A Bernard 1914.12 1915.12 CAS'15
Walkley C S Rev 15-S 36 Ruckman 1905.9 1909.5 Chaplain
Wallace E C 1LT 43-W-1 3 Reeder 1930.12 1931.7 CAS'30 CAS'31
Wallace E J 1LT 18-W-1 29-A Bernard 1902 b-19 rms
Wallace R A LTC 143-N-2 35-D Ingalls 1983.8 1986.6 mfh
Wallace J MAJ 93 75 Ingalls 1936.4 1939.6 MedC Cochran
Wallace W C LTC 18-E-1 37-A Bernard 1974.10 1976.8 mfh
Wallace W E LTC 44-N-2 108 Ingalls 1963.3 1966.6 mfh
Waller C W 1LT 69-N 87 Ingalls 1907.9 1908.9 '08cd
Wallis J W 1LT 66-N 40 Ingalls 1915.12 1916.12 '17cd
Walls J W LTC 35-E-1 6 Reeder 1961.11 1963.1 mfh
Walsh J V 1LT 18-W-2 29-B Bernard 1920.7 1921.7 CAS'21
Walsh R 1LT 68-S 81 Ingalls 1915.12 1916.12 CAS'16
Walsh L A Jr COL 143-N-1 35-B Ingalls 1957.6 1957.8 Ret MG usacc
Walsh L A Jr COL 16-W 51 Bernard 1957.8 1958.5 Ret MG usacc
Walter E H COL 143-N-1 35-B Ingalls 1953.9 1954.10 usacc
Walter E H 2LT 17-W-2 41-B Bernard 1936.10 1937.4 Walter
Walter E H COL 129-N 103 Ingalls 1954.10 1956.8 usacc
Walter E H COL 51-S-2 118 Ingalls 1953.8 1953.9 usacc
Walter E H LTC 52-E-1 128 Ingalls 1948.9 1951.9 usacc

Walter E H LTC 33-W-1 59 Fenwick 1943.9 1944.1 Walter PhBk
Walter E H MAJ 44-N-1 106 Ingalls 1940.2 1943.6 Walter PhBks
Walter E H 1LT 18-E-2 37-B Bernard 1939.9 1940.2 Walter
Walters P R LTC 34-N-1 98 Ingalls 1949.1 1952.6 usacc
Walters T L LTC 18-W-2 29-B Bernard 1946.9 1950.5 usacc
Walters F J Jr MAJ 51-N-2 124 Ingalls 1972.6 1973.6 mfh
Walton D R MAJ 44-S-2 102 Ingalls 1975.2 1977.10 mfh
Walton A H COL 52-W-2 132 Ingalls 1963.10 1964.4 usacc
Walton C A CPT 143-N-1 35-B Ingalls 1919.1 1919.6 '19cd
Ward D R BG 121-W 41 Fenwick 1970.3 1971.9 mfh Ret BG
Ward P O COL 65-N 48 Ingalls 1948.10 1950.9 usacc
Ward E R G CPT 15-S 36 Ruckman 1938.5 1943.8 PhBk
Ward P R CPT 65-S 46 Ingalls 1905.9 1906.5 '06cd b-26
Ward D R BG 128-W 107 Bernard 1969.4 1970.3 mfh Ret BG
Ward S C R 1LT 35-W-1 4 Reeder 1934.9 1935.6 Ward
Ward E C R CPT 17-E-1 47-A Bernard 1938.3 1938.5 Ward
Ware J Mr 146 146 Engr Ln 1911.6 1946.6 Post Engineer
Ware H L MAJ 43-E-1 5 Reeder 1984.9 1987.7 mfh
Warfel C COL 102-N 61 Ingalls 1983.4 1985.3 mfh
Warner L V COL 126-N 165 Bernard 1948.5 1949.8 Ret BG usacc
Warner E R CPT 17-E-1 47A Bernard 1869.8 1874.5 c-27
Warner O C CPT 144-S-2 41-C Ingalls 1915.12 1916.12 '17cd
Warner W W CPT 19 18 Bernard 1920.8 1921.8 S&F Arthur
Warner O C CPT 19 18 Bernard 1916.12 1917.12 S&F Arthur
Warren W H CPT 70-N 91 Ingalls 1930.6 1933.6 Warren
Warren R B BG 118 29 Fenwick 1962.8 1964.8 mfh Ret BG?
Warren W S MAJ 54-S-2 134 Ingalls 1972.11 1976.12 mfh
Warren A H 2LT 16-W 51 Bernard 1915 1916 Levy '16cd BOQ
Washington J M CPT 18-E-2 37-B Bernard 1834.4 1836.5 '34rq
Washington W C CPT 144-N-1 41-B Ingalls 1917.1 1917.6 Washington
Washington R B Rev 7 Frank Lane 1933.1 1936.9 St Mary's Priest
Washington L MAJ 52-E-2 126 Ingalls 1983.10 1984.3 mfh
Washington D LTC 16-W 51 Bernard 1948.12 1950.8 usacc
Washington J M CPT 18-E-2 37-B Bernard 1824.7 d-684
Waters J K GEN 119 33 Fenwick 1963.3 1964.3 Ret GEN mfh
Waters J K MG 141 53 Fenwick 1958.2 1960.3 Ret GEN usacc
Waters J K GEN 141 53 Fenwick 1963.2 1963.3 Ret GEN mfh
Waters J K MG 33-E-2 63 Ingalls 1958.1 1958.2 Ret GEN usacc
Waters T L 1LT 18-E-2 37-B Bernard 1931.8 1932.8 '32BtryOCs
Waters W E MG 93 75 Ingalls 1955.7 1956.7 Ret GEN usacc
Waters W E MG 65-N 48 Ingalls 1955.2 1955.7 Ret GEN usacc
Watson H J CPT 101-S 55 Ingalls 1906.9 1907.9 CAS'07
Watson J E LTC 54-N-1 138 Ingalls 1981.11 1984.12 mfh
Watson H J 1LT 70-N 91 Ingalls 1904.3 1905.9 c-53
Watson H J LTC 69-S 85 Ingalls 1920.9 1922.6 Payne Daughter
Watt J COL 102-N 61 Ingalls 1961.3 1964.2 mfh
Watts L MAJ 126-S 163 Bernard 1919.5 1919.8 '19cd
Watts C MAJ 50-A 125 Bernard 1981.8 1982.9 mfh
Watts H L Jr COL 128-W 107 Bernard 1950.10 1953.8 usacc
Watts H L Jr COL 44-S-1 104 Ingalls 1950.9 1950.10 usacc
Weaner C COL 3-S 167 Bernard 1954.10 1954.11 usacc
Weathers C T LTC 18-E-1 37-A Bernard 1970.10 1974.7 Chaplain mfh
Weaver E M CPT 16-W 51 Bernard 1903 1904 b-19

Weaver E M CPT 62-S 30 Ruckman 1902.4 1902.9 c-46
Weaver C A LTC 144-S-2 41-C Ingalls 1954.10 1957.9 usacc
Weaver E M LT 17-W-2 41-B Bernard 1887 1888.9 c-14
Webber D B CPT 43-W-2 1 Reeder 1941.8 1942.5 Webber
Weber M G 1LT 33-E-1 61 Fenwick 1936.6 1937.6 '37cd Gilman +
Webster G B LTC 143-S-2 35-C Ingalls 1953.4 1953.8 Ret BG usacc
Weed O D 1LT 18-E-2 37-B Bernard 1903 1904 b-21
Weeks J A 2LT 16-E 53 Bernard 1918.7 1919.2 '19cd
Weeks L B LTC 127-E 147 Bernard 1936.5 1938.10 Ret BG '37cd
Weeks L B COL 121-W 41 Fenwick 1939.8 1942.1 Ret BG Weeks
Weeks L B BG 141 53 Fenwick 1942.1 1945.11 Ret BG Weeks
Weeks C R COL 129-S 101 Ingalls 1976.1 1978.1 mfh
Wehle P C COL 68-N 83 Ingalls 1949.8 1950.4 Ret MG usacc
Wehle P C COL 43-E-1 5 Reeder 1946.10 1949.8 Ret MG usacc
Weible W L MG 120 37 Fenwick 1948.4 1949.2 usacc Ret LTG
Weible W L BG 121-W 41 Fenwick 1947.12 1948.4 Ret LTG usacc
Weihl W COL 127-W 145 Bernard 1980.2 1984.9 mfh
Weinchec R H LTC 35-W-2 2 Reeder 1949.2 1949.7 usacc
Weitzel G J 1LT 1 151 Bernard 1936 1936 McCoy
Welborn J C COL 44-N-2 108 Ingalls 1946.9 1950.6 usacc
Welch G B LTC 123-E 4 Ruckman 1936.6 1940.6 Cotter '37cd
Welch G B CPT 144-N-1 41-B Ingalls 1924.6 1930.6 Harris '25-29cd
Welch P B Jr COL 129-S 101 Ingalls 1971.7 1972.6 mfh
Weld S L Jr 1LT 54 N-2 140 Ingalls 1940.2 1941.12 Ret BG
Wells W 1LT 17-W-2 41-B Bernard 1844.10 '44rq d-686
Wells W L COL 43-W-2 1 Reeder 1961.7 1962.2 mfh
Wells W L COL 70-N 91 Ingalls 1962.2 1962.6 mfh
Welsh A B COL 103-N 65 Ingalls 1951.9 1954.11 usacc
Welshimer R R COL 118 29 Fenwick 1918.9 1919.1 '19cd
Welshimer R R 1LT 144-S-2 41-C Ingalls 1914.12 1915.12 CAS'15 '16cd
Welshimer R R MAJ 158 32 Ingalls 1922.7 1923.6 '23cd
Welshimer R R MAJ 103-N 65 Ingalls 1919.2 1919.9 Clark
Werder V C LTC 51-N-1 122 Ingalls 1970.12 1971.12 mfh
Werner G COL 124-N 69 Ingalls 1982.5 1983.8 mfh
Wertenbaker G L COL 157 101 Bernard 1931.6 1933.6 JHC '33cd
Wertenbaker G L LTC 124-S 67 Ingalls 1920.8 1921.7 '21FOcs
Wertenbaker G L LTC 141 53 Fenwick 1924 1925 Hartel
Wertz W W CPT 143-N-1 35-B Ingalls 1932.8 1933.6 deCamp
Wesner C COL 103-N 65 Ingalls 1954.11 1957.8 usacc
Wesner L E CPT 65-S 46 Ingalls 1942.6 1944.9 Ret BG PhBk
West R L BG 93 75 Ingalls 1972.9 1973.8 mfh Ret LTG?
West W W COL 142 51 Fenwick 1941.2 1943.9 Tilton
West R L BG 126-S 163 Bernard 1971.10 1972.8 mfh Ret LTG?
West R L BG 43-W-2 1 Reeder 1971.8 1971.10 mfh Ret LTG?
Weyant W W COL 34-S-1 96 Ingalls 1968.1 1970.7 mfh
Whalen H K COL 67-S 34 Ingalls 1953.6 1957.8 usacc
Whalen T B LTC 51-S-1 120 Ingalls 1969.9 1970.4 mfh
Whaley A M CPT 3-N 169 Bernard 1911.12 1912.12 MedC '12cd rms
Whaley A M CPT 102-S 59 Ingalls 1912.12 1914.12 PhBk
Whaley A M LTC 125 73 Ingalls 1925.6 1927.6 MedC Hartel
Wharton E B CPT 18-E-1 37-A Bernard 1921.8 1922.7 '22BtryOCs
Wharton J H CPT 62-S 30 Ruckman 1926.7 1927.9 INF '20BtryOCs
Whearty W F Rev 7 Frank Lane 1920.4 1921.4 St Mary's Priest

Wheatley C E Jr 2LT 16-E 53 Bernard 1932 1933 Hillberg '33cd
Wheatley C E Jr MAJ 101-S 55 Ingalls 1922.8 1925.8 '23cd
Wheaton J R COL 127-E 147 Bernard 1946.9 1949.7 usacc
Wheeler J M 1LT 65-S 46 Ingalls 1904.9 1905.9 CAS'05
Wheeler LT 16-E 53 Bernard 1891.6 1892 c-26
Wheeler J F LTC 43-E-1 5 Reeder 1954.11 1958.1 usacc
Wheeler M D LTC 54-S-2 134 Ingalls 1936.6 1939.2 '37cd '39PhBk
Whelchel J L 1LT 69-N 87 Ingalls 1927.6 1929.6 Higgins
Whelchel J L 2LT 16-W 51 Bernard 1919 1920 '19cd BOQ
Whelchel W H LTC 18-E-1 37-A Bernard 1947.10 1948.9 usacc
Whelchel W H LTC 54-S-2 134 Ingalls 1948.9 1948.9 usacc
Whichard W K MAJ 62-S 30 Ruckman 1943.1 1945.6 '43-45cd
Whipple H B 1LT 43-W-1 3 Reeder 1940.12 1941.8 Whipple
Whipple H B 2LT 18-E-1 37-A Bernard 1936.9 1938.2 Whipple
Whipple H B 1LT 33-W-1 59 Fenwick 1941.8 1941.12 Whipple
Whistler J M LTC 43-W-2 1 Reeder 1951.4 1952.6 usacc
Whitaker E J COL 34-N-2 100 Ingalls 1963.10 1965.6 mfh
Whitaker W C 1LT 63-N 24 Ruckman 1913.12 1914.12 Widow PhBk
White B B COL 34-N-2 100 Ingalls 1958.10 1960.7 usacc
White W H LTC 43-E-2 7 Reeder 1942.5 1946.6 '43-45PhBks
White L J LTC 43-W-2 7 Reeder 1968.2 1971.7 mfh
Whitham J C 1LT 3-N 169 Bernard 1911.12 1912.12 MedC '12cd rms
Whiting F MAJ 18-E-1 37-A Bernard 1824.7 d-684
Whiting F CPT 17-W-1 41-A Bernard 1824.5 d-684
Whiting F MAJ 18-E-1 37-A Bernard 1832 1834 '32-34rq
Whitman G S CPT 55 42 Ingalls 1919.7 1920.7 '20cd
Whitt H CPT 54-N-2 140 Ingalls 1932.7 1933.7 '33cd
Whittaker L A 1LT 16-E 53 Bernard 1925 1927 '25 cd
Whitted T B CPT 143-N-2 35-D Ingalls 1939.8 1940.8 '40-44PhBk QMC
Whybark G W CPT 62-N 28 Ruckman 1929.6 1930.12 '30AdvCs
Whybark G W CPT 65-N 48 Ingalls 1925.6 1926.6 '25cd
Wickham K G LTC 14 32 Ruckman 1945.11 1946.8 Ret MG usacc
Wicks R M BG 118 29 Fenwick 1949.2 1950.5 usacc Ret BG?
Wieczorek G A CPT 79-S 93 Ingalls 1912.12 1913.12 CAS'13 '13cd
Wikan W W LTC 34-N-2 100 Ingalls 1967.2 1969.5 mfh
Wilbert H E COL 33-W-1 59 Fenwick 1955.6 1958.11 usacc
Wilbur H P COL 157 101 Bernard 1920.8 1921.7 '21FOcs
Wilbur H P CPT 123-W 2 Ruckman 1912.12 1913.12 CAS'13 '13cd
Wilbur H P 1LT 55 42 Ingalls 1901.11 1902.8 '02cd
Wilcox L R COL 18-W-1 29-A Bernard 1960.9 1964.6 mfh
Wilcox C D CPT 62-N 28 Ruckman 1906 b-26
Wild E W COL 35-W-1 4 Reeder 1966.10 1969.2 mfh
Wilder S D MAJ 45-W-2 110 Ingalls 1973.6 1977.5 mfh
Wilder C J COL 101-S 55 Ingalls 1944.1 1947.10 PhBk
Wilderman J J COL 51-S-1 120 Ingalls 1964.6 1967.7 mfh
Wilderson N LTC 144-N-2 41-D Ingalls 1977.10 1980.8 mfh
Wildrick G A CPT 67-S 34 Ingalls 1915.12 1916.12 '16-17cd
Wildrick G A 1LT 62-S 30 Ruckman 1913.12 1915.12 PhBk
Wildrick G A 1LT 143-S-1 35-A Ingalls 1912.12 1913.12 CAS'13 '13cd
Wildrick M CPT 128-W 107 Bernard 1917.5 1919.6 Widow Mansfield
Wildrick M 1LT 143-S-2 35-C Ingalls 1916.12 1917.5 Widow
Wilds H COL 43-W-1 3 Reeder 1962.3 1964.1 mfh
Wiley W J COL 79-S 93 Ingalls 1946.10 1947.4 usacc

Wiley C F LTC 44-N-2 108 Ingalls 1942.5 1945.9 Wiley PhBks
Wiley N J Jr COL 79-N 95 Ingalls 1951.11 1952.6 usacc
Wiley N J Jr COL 33-E-1 61 Fenwick 1957.10 1958.7 usacc
Wiley N J Jr COL 101-N 57 Ingalls 1952.6 1953.6 usacc
Wilkins G S 1LT 18-W-2 29-B Bernard 1824 1826 '25rq d-684 rms
Wilkins F F COL 69-S 85 Ingalls 1952.7 1955.4 usacc
Wilkinson H F CPT 66-N 40 Ingalls 1919 '19cd
Willett M B MAJ 123-W 2 Ruckman 1919.1 '19cd
Willett M B 2LT 16-W 51 Bernard 1911 1912 BOQ? '11cd
Willett M B 1LT 143-N-1 35-B Ingalls 1917.6 1917.12 '17cd
Willett M B CPT 101-N 57 Ingalls 1917.12 1919.1 S&F '17-19cds
Williams E T LTG 118 29 Fenwick 1956.4 1956.7 usacc Ret LTG
Williams R P BG 121-E 43 Fenwick 1951.4 1951.9 usacc Ret BG?
Williams J B COL 102-N 61 Ingalls 1985.4 1986.1 mfh
Williams J C CPT 147 147 Engr Ln 1983.9 1984.7 mfh
Williams S T COL 123-W 2 Ruckman 1950.9 1952.7 Ret LTG usacc
Williams B H L MAJ 121-E 43 Fenwick 1921.7 1923.9 '23cd
Williams R H CPT 70-S 89 Ingalls 1907.9 1908.9 '08-cd
Williams R P BG 102-S 59 Ingalls 1949.12 1951.4 usacc Ret BG?
Williams K T LTC 45-W-2 110 Ingalls 1969.6 1971.2 mfh
Williams C L 1LT 64-S 22 Ruckman 1912.4 1913.12 CAS'13
Williams H C 1LT 62-N 28 Ruckman 1905 1906 '06cd
Williams J M MAJ 120 37 Fenwick 1912.7 1915.7 PhBk '14cd
Williams W D COL 44-S-1 104 Ingalls 1954.6 1954.9 usacc
Williams S F 1LT 149-S 9 Moat Walk 1916 1919 '17-19cd
Williams E T LTG 93 75 Ingalls 1956.8 1959.9 usacc Ret LTG
Williams J S 1LT 79-N 95 Ingalls 1913.12 1914.12 PhBk
Williams U P COL 35-W-2 2 Reeder 1951.7 1952.8 usacc
Williams E W COL 54-S-1 136 Ingalls 1963.8 1964.1 mfh
Williams E W COL 121-W 41 Fenwick 1964.1 1966.7 mfh
Williams R J 1LT 1 151 Bernard 1938 1939 Piram
Williams S T COL 52-W-1 130 Ingalls 1950.9 1950.9 Ret LTG usacc
Williams R H CPT 127-W 145 Bernard 1909.7 1912.7 '12cd
Williamson C E COL 144-S-2 41-C Ingalls 1957.9 1960.10 usacc
Williams D H Jr COL 18-W-2 29-B Bernard 1968.7 1969.7 mfh
Williford F E MAJ 128-E 109 Bernard 1924.9 1925.6 Ret BG '25cd
Williford F E 1LT 69-S 85 Ingalls 1914.12 1916.12 Ret BG CAS'15
Willis P CPT 69-N 87 Ingalls 1905.9 1906.9 06cd
Willis A H MAJ 127-E 147 Bernard 1926.7 1931.7 '27-31cds
Willis W G COL 69-S 85 Ingalls 1981.6 1982.8 mfh
Willis W COL 44-N-1 106 Ingalls 1980.6 1981.7 mfh
Williston E B CPT 17-W-1 41-A Bernard 1868.10 1869.5 c-27
Willoughby K MAJ 51-S-2 118 Ingalls 1977.6 1978.8 mfh
Willoughby W H COL 50-A 125 Bernard 1961.6 1962.6 mfh
Willoughby W H COL 35-E-1 6 Reeder 1959.6 1961.6 usacc
Wills E A CPT 16-E 53 Bernard 1919.2 1920.7 '20cd
Wilson R J COL 126-N 165 Bernard 1966.8 1967.4 mfh
Wilson W K 1LT 62-N 28 Ruckman 1909.8 1910.9 Ret MG Son
Wilson P C CPT 167-B 9 Patch Road 1965.8 1967.6 mfh
Wilson A H COL 129-S 101 Ingalls 1954.10 1957.8 usacc
Wilson J E 1LT 17-E-2 47-B Bernard 1907.9 1908.9 CAS'08
Wilson D M CPT 33-E-1 61 Fenwick 1937.6 1938.7 PhBk
Wilson W P 1LT 68-S 81 Ingalls 1912.12 1915.12 PhBk

Wilson L C CPT 144-S-2 41-C Ingalls 1927.7 1930.7 '27cd
Wilson W D CPT 143-S-2 35-C Ingalls 1919.1 1920.9 '19cd
Wilson W K 1LT 3-N 169 Bernard 1910.9 1911.12 Ret MG '11cd
Wilson W H LTC 142 51 Fenwick 1924.3 1927.7 Ret MG '25cd
Wilson C V COL 52-E-1 128 Ingalls 1957.11 1960.3 Ret MG usacc
Wilson L F COL 44-N-1 106 Ingalls 1953.8 1953.9 usacc
Wilson W H 1LT 63-N 24 Ruckman 1903.8 1905.9 Ret MG Hartel
Wilson C N 1LT 103-N 65 Ingalls 1915.12 1916.12 CAS'16
Wilson G F COL 55 42 Ingalls 1973.7 1974.5 mfh
Wilson J H CPT 64-N 20 Ruckman 1923 Ret BG '23cd
Wilson L F COL 127-W 145 Bernard 1953.9 1956.6 usacc
Wilson J P COL 143-S-1 35-A Ingalls 1951.3 1952.2 usacc
Wilson J H CPT 126-S 163 Bernard 1928.8 1929.8 Ret BG '29cd
Wilson J LTC 70-S 89 Ingalls 1977.12 1979.6 mfh
Wilson N B LTC 50-A 125 Bernard 1947.3 1948.6 usacc
Wilson T J Rev 7 Frank Lane 1908.11 1919.8 St Mary's Priest PhBk
Wilson A M Jr CPT 50-E 129 Bernard 1936.8 1937.6 Wilson
Wilson A M Jr CPT 143-N-2 35-D Ingalls 1936.5 1936.8 Wilson
Wilson A M Jr CPT 52-E-2 126 Ingalls 1935.5 1936.5 Wilson
Wilson A M Jr 1LT 79-N 95 Ingalls 1933.10 1934.5 Wilson
Wilson A M Jr MAJ 129-S 101 Ingalls 1940.10 1941.10 Wilson
Wilson A M Jr 1LT 35-W-2 2 Reeder 1934.5 1935.5 Wilson
Wiltamuth R H LTC 51-N-2 124 Ingalls 1948.12 1950.9 usacc
Winder W J COL 54-S-2 134 Ingalls 1964.8 1965.6 mfh
Wing C K MAJ 65-S 46 Ingalls 1926.7 1927.7 '27AdvCs
Wingate H A CPT 144-N-2 41-D Ingalls 1916.12 1917.6 Ford Washington
Wingfield W L 1LT 17-W-1 41-A Bernard 1939.7 1940.6 MedC PhBk rms
Winn J R BG 158 32 Ingalls 1959.8 1961.5 Ret MG usacc
Winn J J LTC 15-N 34 Ruckman 1951.6 1952.9 usacc
Winn J R COL 54-S-2 134 Ingalls 1959.7 1959.8 Ret MG usacc
Winn J J LTC 18-W-2 29-B Bernard 1950.5 1951.6 usacc
Winslow S S MAJ 93 75 Ingalls 1923.6 1926.6 '23cd
Winslow S S MAJ 126-S 163 Bernard 1930.6 1931.1 S&F '30CAS
Winslow S S CPT 157 101 Bernard 1919.6 1920.7 '20cd
Winslow R P CPT 15-N 34 Ruckman 1911.9 1912.9 '12cd CAS'12
Winston T W MAJ 142 51 Fenwick 1910.7 1912.7 CAS Librarian
Winston T W MAJ 124-S 67 Ingalls 1909.7 1910.7 S&F '11cd
Winton A V CPT 143-N-1 35-B Ingalls 1926.8 1930.6 Winton
Wirt H G BM2 33 CGH 67 Fenwick 1964.6 1967.7 usacc
Wiser R COL 66-N 40 Ingalls 1982.10 1986.9 mfh
Wisser J P CPT 70-S 89 Ingalls 1897.6 1902.6 S&F '00cd
Witherell C H MAJ 123-E 4 Ruckman 1919.7 1920.7 '20cd
Witt W LTC 18-E-1 37-A Bernard 1979.6 1980.6 mfh
Woelfer C P COL 50-A 125 Bernard 1968.9 1969.11 mfh
Woelfer C P COL 50-E 129 Bernard 1969.11 1970.3 mfh
Woerner L G COL 62-N 28 Ruckman 1961.10 1964.8 mfh
Woerner L G COL 35-E-1 6 Reeder 1961.8 1961.10 usacc
Wohner J H COL 16-E 53 Bernard 1961.8 1963.12 mfh
Wolf W P 1LT 15-N 34 Ruckman 1944 1945 PhBk
Wolfe W J CPT 55 42 Ingalls 1934.10 1937.5 Wolfe
Wolfe W J 1LT 45-E-2 116 Ingalls 1933.6 1934.9 Wolfe
Wolfe S E CPT 15-N 34 Ruckman 1927.6 1928.8 '28BtryOCs
Wolfe Y H 1LT 18-E-2 37-B Bernard 1938.5 1939.6 Wolfe

Wolfe S E MAJ 128-E 109 Bernard 1928.8 1929.8 Gallagher
Wollenberg W F COL 129-N 103 Ingalls 1984.4 1986.1 mfh
Wood LT 15-N 34 Ruckman 1886 c-14
Wood C M 1LT 65-S 46 Ingalls 1916.12 1917.6 Ford
Wood W L LTC 124-N 69 Ingalls 1942.9 1946.8 DC Wood PhBk
Wood E C COL 19 18 Bernard 1966.7 1971.2 mfh
Wood R J CPT 51 N-1 122 Ingalls 1939.9 1940.8 Ret GEN Wood +
Wood J E COL 43 W-1 3 Reeder 1947.8 1949.7 Ret BG usacc
Wood E C COL 43 W-2 1 Reeder 1959.8 1961.6 usacc
Wood B A LTC 54 S-1 136 Ingalls 1954.9 1957.9 usacc
Wood J LTC 35 W-2 2 Reeder 1976.8 1978.5 mfh
Wood J H CPT 147 147 Engr Ln 1954.11 1955.8 usacc
Wood L D 1LT 93 75 Ingalls 1919 WWI BOQ '19cd
Wood W L MAJ 143-N-1 35-B Ingalls 1944.2 1945.12 '44-45 PhBk
Wood R J 2LT 18 E-1 37-A Bernard 1934.12 1935.6 Ret GEN Wood
Woodbury E N 1LT 50-W 121 Bernard 1914.12 1915.12 '16cd
Woodbury E N CPT 128-E 109 Bernard 1915.12 1916.12 '16CAS Arthur
Woodbury E N MAJ 144-S-2 41-C Ingalls 1918.11 1921.7 JHC '19cd
Woodmansee J W GEN 15-S 36 Ruckman 1976.11 1977.7 mfh
Woodmansee J W COL 50-E 129 Bernard 1974.4 1975.2 mfh Ret GEN
Woodmansee J BG 121-E-43 Fenwick 1977.7 1980.7 mfh
Woodruff H C MAJ 45-E-2 116 Ingalls 1974.9 1977.1 mfh
Woods J R COL 33-E-1 61 Fenwick 1964.7 1967.6 mfh
Woodward W F COL 143-N-2 35-D Ingalls 1957.9 1959.12 usacc
Wood J E Jr COL 62-S 30 Ruckman 1965.8 1969.7 mfh
Wood J E Jr COL 35-E-1 6 Reeder 1965.6 1965.8 mfh
Wood J E Jr 2LT 50-A 125 Bernard 1940.2 1940.9 BOQ PhBk
Wool J E MG 1 151 Bernard 1861.8 1862.6 CG w Ret MG?
Woolnough J K GEN 119 33 Fenwick 1967.8 1970.10 Ret GEN mfh
Woolnough J K GEN 123-E 4 Ruckman 1967.7 1967.8 Ret GEN mfh
Wooten R J MAJ 34-S-1 96 Ingalls 1971.4 1972.8 mfh
Worcester P H 1LT 17-W-2 41-B Bernard 1907.9 1908.9 '08cd
Worcester W J 2LT 18-E-1 37-A Bernard 1940.4 1940.8 Worcester PhBk
Worfred J H CPT 154-S 13 Murray 1917.6 1920.9 S&F Arthur '19cd
Workizer J G CPT 123-W 2 Ruckman 1913.12 1914.12 CAS'14 PhBk
Worrell E P 1LT 152-W 12 Patch Rd 1918 1919 '19cd rooms?
Worthington R C 1LT 15-S 36 Ruckman 1923.7 1925.7 '23cd
Wortman V W LTC 127-E 147 Bernard 1940.6 1941.12 PhBk
Wortman V W MAJ 79-S 93 Ingalls 1939.6 1940.6 Duff
Wren H CSM 64 71 Fenwick 1987.3 1980.8 mfh
Wren E S MAJ 68-S 81 Ingalls 1932.3 1936.6 Dentist Coates
Wright E P 2LT 112-W 30 Tidball 1918.4 1919.1 Hennessy '19cd
Wright E M COL 51-N-1 122 Ingalls 1963.6 1964.6 mfh
Wright C J COL 124-S 67 Ingalls 1975.8 1976.11 mfh Ret BG
Wright B R COL 102-N 61 Ingalls 1973.10 1977.8 mfh
Wright J W MAJ 54-S-2 134 Ingalls 1984.8 1987.6 mfh
Wright L COL 127-E 147 Bernard 1978.10 1981.6 mfh
Wright R J COL 54-N-1 138 Ingalls 1967.6 1968.7 mfh
Wright G COL 1 151 Bernard 1855.7 1855.12 CO Arthur
Wright D E Jr COL 51-N-2 124 Ingalls 1966.1 1966.11 mfh
Wright F S Jr COL 143-N-2 35-D Ingalls 1954.6 1957.9 usacc
Wruble E G MAJ 52-E-1 128 Ingalls 1981.8 1983.6 mfh
Wuest W J CPT 144-N-1 41-B Ingalls 1940.8 1942.2 K C Smith

Wurz W G MAJ 69-N 87 Ingalls 1943.6 1946.6 PhBk
Wyks E E MAJ 52-W-1 130 Ingalls 1981.12 1984.12 mfh
Wyless E R COL 34-N-1 98 Ingalls 1963.8 1965.7 mfh
Wyman W G GEN 119 33 Fenwick 1956.4 1958.7 Ret GEN usacc
Wyman W G LTG 118 29 Fenwick 1955.9 1956.4 Ret GEN usacc
Wyman W G MG 120 37 Fenwick 1946.9 1947.10 Ret GEN usacc
Yancey T R COL 51-N-1 122 Ingalls 1952.7 1953.5 Ret MG usacc
Yancey T R COL 66-S 38 Ingalls 1953.5 1954.12 Ret MG usacc
Yarbrough J E COL 45-W-1 112 Ingalls 1954.8 1954.9 usacc
Yarbrough J E COL 102-S 59 Ingalls 1954.9 1955.7 usacc
Yelverton R COL 67-S 34 Ingalls 1983.8 1986.7 mfh
York C A MAJ 129-N 103 Ingalls 1943 1944 '43-44PhBks
York C A MAJ 79-N 95 Ingalls 1942 1943 PhBk AN306
Yost P 1LT 67-S 34 Ingalls 1905.10 1906.9 '06cd
Yost J B 1LT 35-E-1 6 Reeder 1940.5 1941.3 Yost PhBks
Young F R 2LT 16-W 51 Bernard 1932 1933 Hillberg
Young H F COL 45-E-2 116 Ingalls 1962.6 1963.6 mfh
Young L A LTC 144-N-1 41-B Ingalls 1974.9 1975.11 mfh
Young E MAJ 52-E-1 128 Ingalls 1980.10 1981.7 mfh
Young G E 1LT 65-S 46 Ingalls 1933.7 1934.8 deCamp
Young E MAJ 63-N 24 Ruckman 1941 PhBk
Young E LTC 50-E 129 Bernard 1941.6 1942.6 Wilson
Young C P 1LT 16-W 51 Bernard 1922 1924 West
Young M CPT 101-N 57 Ingalls 1906 1907.7 b-26
Youngclaus R D MAJ 44-S-2 102 Ingalls 1986.6 1986.11 mfh
Youngs E R COL 3-S 167 Bernard 1971.8 1972.6 mfh
Young M J Jr COL 126-S 163 Bernard 1946.9 1947.9 Ret BG usacc
Yung N D 1LT 67-S 34 Ingalls 1918 1919 BOQ WWI '19cd
Zahrobsky R E COL 44-S-2 102 Ingalls 1964.8 1964.12 mfh
Zahrobsky R E COL 19 18 Bernard 1964.12 1966.6 mfh
Zargan R COL 69-S 85 Ingalls 1977.5 1981.6 mfh
Zeger H Rev 7 Frank Lane 1940 1941 '40-41PhBk Priest
Zeller F J 1LT 17-W-2 41-B Bernard 1937.8 1938.6 Chapman '37cd
Zerlett A 1LT 132-E 15 Tidball 1918 1919 '19cd
Ziegler C S LTC 17-E-1 47-A Bernard 1972.2 1973.6 mfh
Zimmer L A 1LT 50-A 125 Bernard 1933.8 1934.6 '33cd Zimmer
Zimmerman W C BG 121-E 43 Fenwick 1949.8 1951.4 Ret MG usacc
Zimmerman W M COL 45-E-1 114 Ingalls 1962.8 1963.12 mfh
Zimov E LTC 43-W-1 3 Reeder 1969.6 1970.1 mfh
Zinser R F COL 123-W 2 Ruckman 1960.10 1964.9 mfh
Zollars C O CPT 69-N 87 Ingalls 1906.9 1907.9 CAS'07
Zwicker M H 2LT 18-E-1 37-A Bernard 1922.7 1926.7 '23cd Mitchell

GLOSSARY

Amah An oriental nurse
Artificer Skilled ordnance worker
Bastion A projecting point of a fortification
Battery A company of soldiers armed with artillery
Caisson A wheeled vehicle for artillery ammuniton
Cantonment Quarters for troops
Casemate A projecting enclosure from which guns are fired
Commutation Extra pay in lieu of room and board
Embrasure An opening through which to fire artillery
Field Grade Any army officer with rank of major or above
Fosse Ditch
Lavandera Washerwoman
Magazine A room where gunpowder or ammunition is stored
Mess Meals served in a central dining area
Ordnance Military weapons, ammunition, vehicles, equipment etc.
Parapet An elevation of earth or stone to protect soldiers
Postern A back door or private entrance
Rampart A wall or protective barrier
Retreat A military flag-lowering ceremony
Scarp The inner side of the ditch below the parapet of a fort
Sinks Military lavatories and washrooms
Sutler A civilian provisioner to a military installation
Taps Call signaling lights out
Tattoo Call to quarters before Taps
Terreplein The level space behind the parapet of a fortification

BIBLIOGRAPHY

Army Navy Chronicle, v.5, No. 1, 1837.

Army Posts & Towns. War Department Leaflet: 1926, pp 119-21. Contributed by Colonel L T Vickers to McClellan Report, 1975.

Arthur, Robert. *The Coast Artillery School, 1824-1927*. The Artillery School, Fort Monroe, VA: 1928.

"Artillery School of Practice, General Order No. 15," 14 February 1827. Contributed by Lieutenant Colonel V M Kimm to McClellan Report, 1974.

"Army and Navy Lodge, No. 306, Fort Monroe, VA." Contributed by Captain L.C. Baird to McClellan Report, 1975.

Birkhimer, W E. *Historical Sketch of the Organization, Administration, Materiel and Tactics of the Artillery, USA*. Thomas McGill & Co: 1884.

Bradley, C D. *Harrison Phoebus: From Farm to Fortune*. Fort Monroe, VA, Casemate Museum, n.d.

Bradley, C D. Letter to Colonel B Big dated 11 June 1971, re: explosion of the Fort Monroe Arsenal, 22 June 1855.

Bureau of Public Relations. Press Branch: 1941, pp 100-103.

"By-Laws of Army & Navy Lodge No. 306, and Sketch of a Forgotten Lodge." Contributed by W E Hricinak to McClellan Report, 1974.

"Casemates Formerly Used as Living Quarters." The Casemate: 22 June 1984, p 20.

"Chamberlin Hotel Fire." *Daily News*, Newport News, VA: 4 May 1965, p 1.

Christmas greeting sent by Captain and Mrs R E McGarraugh from Quarters #50-W, c1932. Contributed by Colonel H W Cochran, Jr to McClellan Report, 1975.

Clark, F S. *Life with Aunt Lena*. Charlotte: Heritage Printers, Inc, 1962.

Department of the Interior. *The Architectural Heritage of Fort Monroe*. National Park Service: Historic American Buildings Survey/Historic American Engineering Record, v 1 and v 2, 1987.

Dictionary of American Biography, v 8. Scribners & Sons: 1962.

Ennis, D. "Roma Made '22 History." *Times-Herald*, 21 Feb 1976.

"Fort Built to Protect Entrance to Chesapeake Bay." The Casemate: 21 May 1982, p 12.

"Fort Monroe Solid as a Rock." The Casemate: 25 January 1985, p 8.

Fry, J B. *Military Miscellanies*. Brentano's, NY: 1889.

Gaddy, W G. Chief, Military Family Housing Branch, Fort Monroe, VA. "Report of Officers and Noncommissioned Officers Occupying Historic Quarters at Fort Monroe, 1975-1987." Contributed to McClellan Report 10 March 1987.

Getty, M N. *George Washington Getty*. Privately published booklet: 1950.

Ganoe, W A. *History of the U.S. Army*. Appleton Co: 1924.

"Greetings, The Coast Artillery School, Fort Monroe, VA, 1942." Letter from Commandant Brigadier General L B Weeks, Xmas 1942. Contributed by Colonel D C Tredennick to McClellan Report, 1974.

Huidekiper, F L. *Military Unpreparedness of US.* Macmillan: 1915.

Haskins, W L. *History of the 1st Regiment of Artillery from Its Organization in 1821 to January 1st, 1876.* Thurston: 1879.

Heitman, F B. *Historical Register and Dictionary of the United States Army.* US GPO: 1903.

Letter dated 1 June 1987 contributed to McClellan Report with a copy of Chapter 73 from the original Deed (12 December 1838): "Act of Cession by the State of Virginia to the Government of the United States of the Land at Old Point Comfort, Virginia."

Lewis, E R. *Seacoast Fortifications of the US.* Smithsonian Press: 1970.

McClellan, P. "Fort Monroe Historic Quarters Research Report, 1973-1976." Unpublished.

McManus, G H. *Duty, Honor, Country. The Biography of George H McManus, Brig Gen, USA.* Library of Congress Loc Card #74-31125.

"Monroe Railroads Held Role in Coast Defense." The Casemate: 20 May 1983, p 12.

National Archives. Record Group 77, Drawer 57; Microfilm Call No. M-617, Rolls 792-802; Quartermaster "Report of Quarters," (various).

National Archives. Record Group 393, Part V, Entries: 3, 8-Box 24, 9-Box 48; 4123 Div. Art. 1890. "Extract from the report of an inspection of the garrison and post of Fort Monroe made by Colonel R P Hughes, April 3d, 1890." "Table showing new buildings recommended, when they should be built, and their estimated cost," 22 July 1901.

National Archives. Record Group 92, Entry 226.

National Archives. Record Group 89.

"Old Point." *Army Navy Chronicle,* V5, no 1, 1837, p 90.

Polonski, K J and Drum, J M. *The Ghosts of Fort Monroe.* Polyndrum Publications: 1972.

Robinson, W E. *American Forts.* Univ. of Illinois Press: 1977.

Sprock, P. "Famous Guests Sheltered in Quarters One." The Casemate: 5 February 1982, p 5.

Weinert, R P Jr and Arthur, Colonel R. *Defenders of the Chesapeake. The Story of Fort Monroe.* Leward Publications: 1978; White Mane Pub Co, Inc: 1989.

Weinert, R P Jr. "Memo for Mrs McClellan. Subj: Saratoga Gun." 17 March 1975.

This index lists all people mentioned in the main text.

253

TRACY, Gen 9 Mrs 9
TREDENNICK, D C 91 92
TRIGG, Maj 23
TUDOR, R A 92
TURNBULL, H T 91
TYLER, H E 91
UPJOHN, Richard 17
UPTON, Emory 17
VANBUREN, 90
VANBUSKIRK, Lt 10
VANDERSLUIS, H 92
VICKER, Mrs L T 9
VICKERS, L T 28
VILLARET, E 91
VIZEY, Mr 45
VONSCHILLING, Franz 16
WALBACH, Col 74 J D 91
WALDO, G E 92
WARE, James 89
WATKINS, Mr 77
WELD, Seth L Jr 58
WERTENBAKER, Col 18 G L 54
　Werty 54

WERTY, 54
WEST, J M 84
WESTERVELT, Gen 49
WESTOVER, O 91
WHIPPLE, Col 35 H 35
WHITE, S L 93
WHITING, H 90
WILLARD, 85 C C 84
WILLIAM, Black 54
WILLIAMS, J G 91 Mrs R L 29 R L
　29
WILSON, A M Jr 23 C F 91 N B 26
WINNIE, 67
WISSER, J P 59 John 40
WOODS, F J 91
WOOL, Gen 15 66
WOOLDRIDGE, W D 50
WORTH, Lt Col 74
ZANTZINER, R H 90
ZIMMER, L A 24

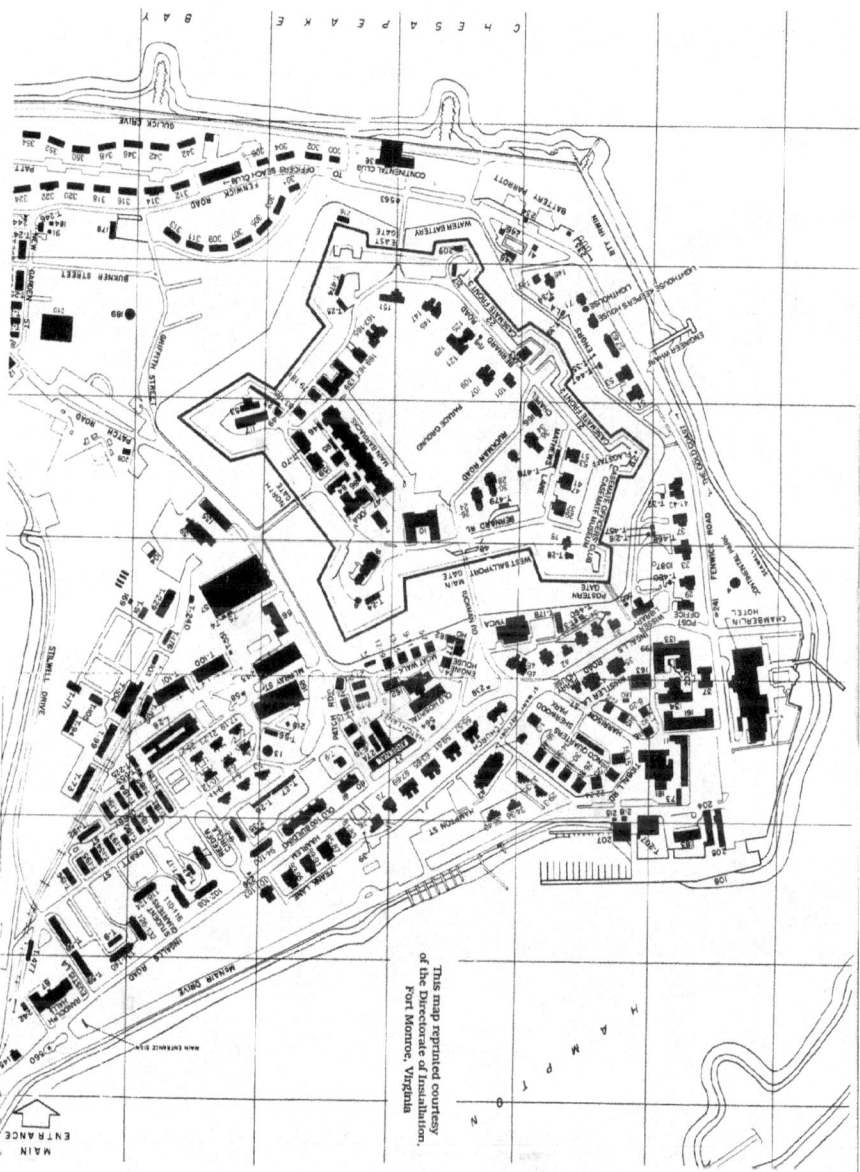

This map reprinted courtesy of the Directorate of Installation, Fort Monroe, Virginia.

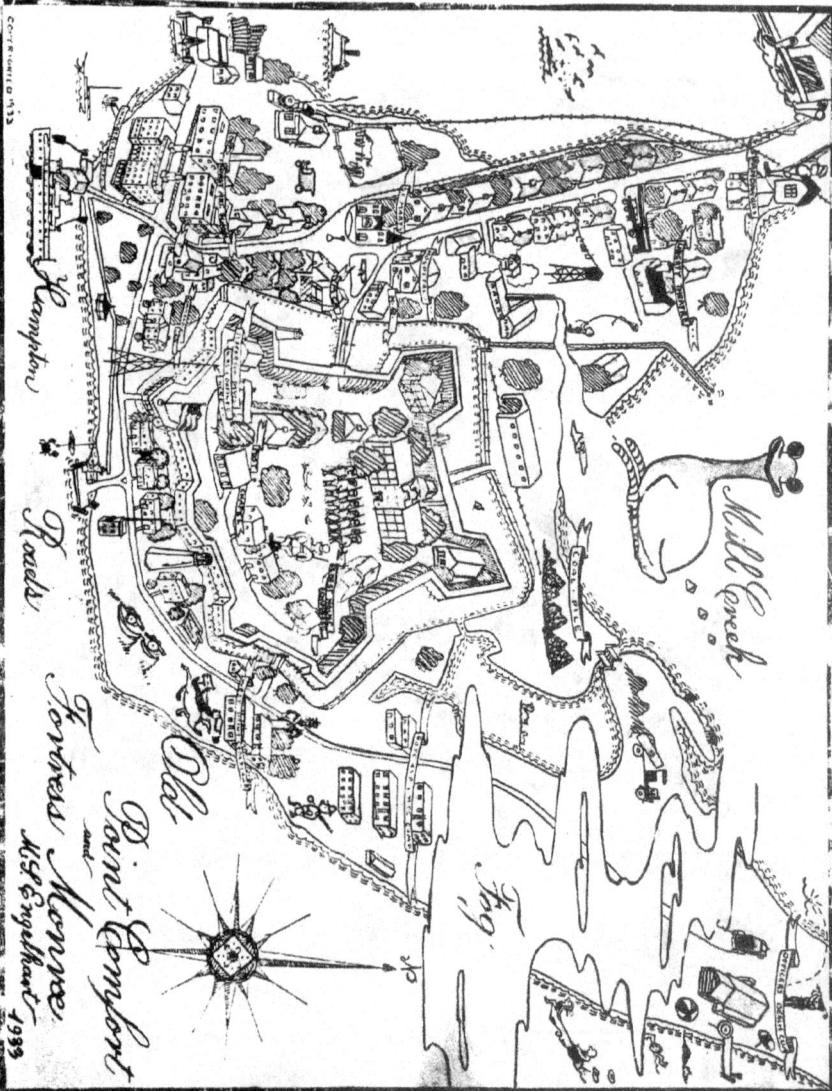

Old Point Comfort
Fortress Monroe and

Mill Creek

Hampton Roads

fig. 9.

COPYRIGHT © 1933

K.S. Engelhart 1933